I0798851

Llewellyn Brown

Beckett, Lacan and the Voice

Samuel Beckett in Company

Edited by Paul Stewart

ISSN 2365-3809

1 *Llewellyn Brown*
Beckett, Lacan and the Voice
With a foreword by Jean-Michel Rabaté
ISBN 978-3-8382-0869-5 (Paperback edition)
ISBN 978-3-8382-0889-3 (Hardcover edition)

Llewellyn Brown

BECKETT, LACAN AND THE VOICE

ibidem-Verlag
Stuttgart

Bibliographic information published by the Deutsche Nationalbibliothek
Die Deutsche Nationalbibliothek lists this publication in the Deutsche Nationalbibliografie; detailed bibliographic data are available in the Internet at http://dnb.d-nb.de.

Bibliografische Information der Deutschen Nationalbibliothek
Die Deutsche Nationalbibliothek verzeichnet diese Publikation in der Deutschen Nationalbibliografie; detaillierte bibliografische Daten sind im Internet über http://dnb.d-nb.de abrufbar.

Cover photograph: Papeterie de la Seine (Nanterre), 1 March 2014. © LB.

ISSN: 2365-3809

ISBN Paperback edition: 978-3-8382-0869-5

ISBN Hardcover edition: 978-3-8382-0889-3

Printed in the United States of America

To Corinne

Samuel Beckett in Company

Beckett and Relation: A Preface to the Series

'Suicides jump from the bridge, not from the bank' (Beckett 1992, 27). In the somewhat confusing world of *Dream of Fair to Middling Women,* the figure of Nemo is at least reliable. Despite the narrator's claim that Nemo is not the sort of character to do his 'dope' – or stick to his role – precisely, here in fact is one character who is knowable and who behaves in what appears to be a coherent, if enigmatic, manner (11). He is always to be found on the middle of a bridge, gazing into the dark, swirling waters below. It comes as no surprise when he is found washed up on the bank after apparently jumping form one such bridge. Like the 'disappointed bridge' of Joyce's *Ulysses* (29), Nemo's bridges do not function as they should. Rather than allowing Nemo a point of crossing, or of connection from one point to another, for Nemo the bridge stops midway, as if the matter of connection from A to B were itself an impossibility, or as if the two banks of the river or canal could not be brought into a simple relation. Indeed, rather than follow the road of relation, Nemo ultimately jumps to his death and thereby into a realm beyond any relation at all.

The figure of Nemo, as if suspended between two points, is a synecdoche for the troubling matter of relation in Beckett's works and of those works. The Samuel Beckett in Company Series that this book inaugurates is dependent on a notion of relation. In order to be in company, one would have thought that some form of relation between discrete subjects is a fundamental assumption, a basic necessity. From a critical perspective, if one were to entertain the idea of Beckett and Contemporary Performance Art, for example, then the assumption must be that these two disparate points can be brought together, that there is a successful rather than a disappointed bridge along which one can travel.

Of course, the question of relating Beckett to any form of company is shadowed by the nature of Beckett's own aesthetics. If the *Three Dialogues with Georges Duthuit* is the most fulsome explication of those aesthetics, it can be no accident that the dialogues repeatedly focus on the problem of relation. In the dialogue concerning van Velde, B argues that the 'analysis of the relation between the artist and his occasion' has produced little because the occasion 'appears as an unstable term of relation' whilst the 'artist, who is the other term, is hardly less so' (124). This instability in the terms of relation – as if the two banks that a bridge joins were in constant flux – itself occasions an 'acute and increasing anxiety of the relation itself, as though shadowed more and more darkly by a sense of invalidity, of inadequacy'. As Beckett and Duthuit corresponded with a view to the publication of *The Three Dialogues*, Beckett's thinking on the question of relation in art became both clearer and more radical. Writing on the 9 March 1949, he defined aesthetic relation:

> By relation we understand, not only the primary form, that between the artist and the outside world, but also and above all those which, within him, ensure that he has lines of flight and retreat, and changes of tension, and make available to him, among other benefits, that of feeling plural (to put it no higher), while remaining (of course) unique. (2011, 138)

There are, then, two problems of relation: between the artist and the world he perceives (the painter with a sitter in front of him, for example), and the relations within the artist him or herself, as the artist is already a multiple rather than a singular entity. In both cases, the paradigm of artistic apprehension basically remains the same: the artist is 'he-who-is-always-*in-front-of*' (139), whether he is in front of an external subject, or one aspect of self in front of another aspect of self. In this regard, the value of van Velde's work for Beckett is that it 'is not the relation with this or that order of opposite that it refuses, but the state of being in relation as such, the state of being in front of' (140).

However, the pull of relation is a strong one. In the same letter, Beckett worries that no matter how he might try he 'shall seem to be locking [van Velde] back into a relation' (140) as the absence of relation could become the very subject which the artist once again places himself in front of. This would mean returning the art of van Velde to the 'bosom of Saint Luke' (1987, 122) and increasing art's scope, mastery and competency.

Much of this can already be seen in the figure of Nemo, and the relations between the narrator of *Dream of Fair to Middling Women* and his characters. The narrator declares himself unable to keep track of what one might have thought were his own creations. In the chapter entitled 'Und' – an overt and therefore perhaps unsuccessful assertion of continuity and relation – the narrator worries over the 'refractory' nature of his characters:

> Their movement is based on a principle of repulsion, their property not to combine but, like heavenly bodies, to scatter and stampede, astral straws on a time-strom, grit in the mistral. And not only to shrink from all that is not they, from all that is without and in its turn shrinks from them, but also to strain away from themselves [...] they will not suffer their systems to be absorbed in the cluster of a greater system [...] because they themselves tend to disappear as systems. (118-9)

The characters of *Dream* therefore behave in a manner similar to that which Beckett theorised in his letter to Duthuit in 1949. They refuse to come into relation with what is external to them, and also refuse to relate to themselves to create a coherent system of personality on which the narrator can rely. This means, of course, that the relation between narrator and character is also far from certain. Nemo appears to not be exempt from this general lack of relation. He is a 'symphonic' rather than a 'melodic unit' (11) and so multiple rather than singular. Yet he is always to be found on one bridge or another, until his act of 'Felo-de-se' (183). Paradoxically, then, Nemo can be brought into relation precisely on the grounds of his inability to achieve relation; he can be fixed and relied upon due to his non-relational position.

In similar vein, Belacqua extolls the virtues not of the terms that are related, but of the site of relation as such:

> For me, he prattles on, he means no harm, for me the only real thing is to be found in the relation: the dumb-bell's bar, the silence between my eyes, between you and me, all the silences between you and me. [...] On the crown of the passional relation I live, dead to oneness, non-entity and unalone [...]. (27-8)

To locate the real thing on the 'dumb-bell bar' of relation is to oscillate between terms, or to rest upon the hyphen that separates and links two terms, the 'hyphen of passion between Shilly and Shally, the old bridge over the river' (27). However, the danger for the artist is in making this 'hyphen of passion' a new occasion for art, and thus absorbing it into the 'greater system' of artistic competence.

By focusing on *Dream of Fair to Middling Women* it becomes apparent that the question of relation – as a human and as an aesthetic issue – was foregrounded from the start of Beckett's writing career. Delineating and questioning this issue of relation will hopefully be one of the tasks of this series.

A further aim of the series, as the name implies, is to place Beckett in company: in company with the social and political milieu he encountered; with the artists and theatre practitioners he knew and worked alongside; with the institutions that facilitated his career; with writers and artists that he influenced, or that influenced him; and, beyond his death, in the company of new contexts, technologies and ideologies. All these attributes hinge on a notion of relation. This might mean a reappraisal of who one thinks Beckett is. Writing of the tendency to think of Beckett as a 'writer hermetically sealed from the world', Anna McMullan and Everett Frost have noted that Beckett

> seems to have genuinely been torn between the competing demands of the need for solitude as the necessary conditions for writing, on the one hand, and, on the other, to be fully engaged in in the lasting personal friendships and professional collegiality that sustained his work. (139)

We might hear in this description an echo of the letter of 1949, in a tension between 'that of feeling plural (to put it no higher), while remaining (of course) unique' (2011, 138); a tension between the social and the solitary. The world of dramatic production – be it on stage, radio, television or film – is inherently a *peopled* one, a social site in which Beckett spent a great deal of his professional life, however unwillingly or however much he might have wished to minimise the input, or interference, of others. If one broadens this out into the wider social and cultural world(s) through which Beckett lived a startling array of possible relations opens up. As Peter Boxall has noted, whilst we might think of Beckett as a contemporary of Bowen and Woolf, he was no less a contemporary of Iris Murdoch and Angela Carter. Boxall goes on to offer an important reminder of the company that Beckett might be seen to keep:

> It is difficult [...] to accustom oneself to the fact that Beckett's *Ghost Trio* was first televised in the year that *Star Wars* was released, that *Mal vu mal dit* was published in the same year that Salman Rushdie published *Midnight's Children*, or that *Quad* was first published in the year that Martin Amis published *Money*. (3)

The title of Boxall's book, *Since Beckett: Contemporary Writing in the Wake of Modernism*, itself displays some reservation concerning the relation between Beckett and those that followed. 'Since' is a decidedly neutral term, somewhat shorn of notions of authority and priority contained in the more common 'after' that might instate a default form of Bloomian Anxiety of Influence. 'Since' also avoids the most simple of conjunctions: the 'and'. One of the problems of this simple conjunction is well illustrated by the current volume. Llewellyn Brown brings together Beckett and Lacan to great effect, but rightly worries about what has previously been understood under the umbrella of the name Lacan, as 'critics have essentially limited their readings of Lacan to his early structuralist developments' and thus created a Beckett by means of this connection. By shifting the focus onto Lacan's later works the simple conjunction of 'Beckett and Lacan' takes on new and insightful possibilities. Similarly, in his introduction to *Beckett and Poststructuralism*, Anthony Uhlmann is concerned with how to relate Beckett to major Poststructuralist thinkers. Rather than asserting an 'and', he suggests that Beckett and the philosophers and theoreticians the book concerns itself with lived through the 'same problem-field' which therefore accounts for the 'numerous and striking points of intersection' which have arisen 'because they have encountered the same non-discursive milieu' (34).[1]

Uhlmann provides a further method of linkage through Deleuze and Guatarri's notion of 'counterpoint' whereby 'new concepts, should the resonance be strong, might shed light on the sensations of existing works of art and enter into counterpoint with them, helping us to recognize aspects of the work we might previously have passed over' (37). This re-contextualization as time passes and new concepts, art forms and media appear, is the final notion of relation Samuel Beckett in Company seeks to explore. Beckett's influence on contemporary performance, live or installation art is one such area in which a relation is *felt* to be at work but has yet to be fully explored. Derval Tubridy, for example, has suggested that 'Beckett's later theatre – particularly *Not I*, which recapitulates the intensity and urgency of *The Unnamable* – exists between theatre and performance art' (47), and that

> [t]hinking about Beckett in the context of Performance Art enables us to reconsider elements vital to his theatre: the experience of the body in space in terms of duration and endurance; the role of repetition, reiteration and rehearsal; and the visceral interplay between language and the body. (49-50)

But resonances, echoes and influences need not be restricted to the gallery, the stage, television or book: Beckett's life after death also involves a virtual presence as the internet disperses his works, adapts them for its own ends, and thereby brings them into a new

1 For a fuller account of the problems of critical conjunctions see Stewart, *Zone of Evaporation* 157-164.

relation. If one were just to take *Waiting for Godot*, we have immediate and virtual access to such delights as a Sesame Street parody, and the Guinea Pig Theater's animated take on the play with all parts, of course, played by guinea pigs. We can also watch a short film of Joyce and Beckett playing pitch and putt. More seriously, perhaps, the materials that are available on the internet might be conditioning a differently nuanced reception of Beckett's works amongst those who might never see a stage version of *Play* but can readily watch Anthony Minghella's film of the work which was part of the 'Beckett on Film' project.

Beckett's virtual presence on the internet is also indicative of how popular culture comes into relation with his works. It is a challenge to a notion of relation and to what 'Beckett' might be when, in episode 7 of season 4, renowned Beckett actor Barry McGovern appeared as the 'dying merchant' in *Game of Thrones*. The dialogue between the merchant, Arya Stark and The Hound was replete with Beckettian resonances – and McGovern himself was one of those resonances – that focused on nothing, worsening and habit. Yet all this was happening in the same hugely popular HBO series that is replete with dragons and swords and the walking dead. To suddenly see and hear clear Beckettian resonances in such a context is at once a surprise, but also a challenge to how one sees Beckett in the mediated world of the 21st century. This is just one of the worlds to which this series hopes to act as a bridge.

Paul Stewart
General Series Editor
The University of Nicosia

Bibliography

Beckett, Samuel. 1992. *Dream of Fair to Middling Women.* Dublin: Black Cat Press.

--. 2011. *The Letters of Samuel Beckett 1941-1956.* Edited by George Craig, Martha Dow Fehsenfeld, Dann Gunn and Lois More Overbeck. Cambridge: Cambridge University Press.

--. 1987. *Proust and Three Dialogues with Georges Duthuit.* London: Calder.

Boxall, Peter. 2009. *Since Beckett: Contemporary Writing in the Wake of Modernism.* London: Continuum Press.

Game of Thrones. 'Mockingbird' (Series 4 episode 7), directed by Alik Sakharov. Home Box Office. 18 May 2014.

Guinea Pig Theater – Waiting for Godot. Musearts Cartoon. www.youtube.com/watch?v=2WzYgFA1mkg (accessed 26 May 2015).

Joyce, James. 1992. *Ulysses.* Harmondsworth: Penguin.

McMullan, Anna and Everett Frost. 2015. 'Samuel Beckett and Artistic Collaboration.' In *On In Their Company; Essays on Beckett with Tributes and Sketches, Presented to Jim Knowlson on his 80th Birthday*, edited by John Pilling and Mark Nixon, 139-162. Reading: the Beckett International Foundation.

Pitch 'n' Putt with Joyce and Beckett. Directed by Donald Clarke. Bórd Scannán na hEireann, Dublin 2006. https://www.youtube.com/watch?v=p856CfM64w8. Accessed 26 May 2015

Play, directed by Anthony Minghella, in *Beckett on Film.* 2001. Dublin: Blue Angel Films, 2001. DVD. Also https://vimeo.com/28766126 (Accessed 26 May 2015).

Sesame Street – Waiting for Elmo. https://www.youtube.com/watch?v=ksL_7WrhWOc (Accessed 26 May 2015).

Stewart, Paul. 2006. *Zone of Evaporation: Samuel Beckett's Disjunctions.* Amsterdam: Rodopi.

Turbidy, Derval. 2014. 'Samuel Beckett and Performance Art.' *The Journal of Beckett Studies* 23: 34-53.

Uhlmann, Anthony. 1999. *Beckett and Postructuralism.* Cambridge: Cambridge University Press.

Table of contents

Abbreviations and editions used for works by Beckett

Abbreviations appear, followed by the page number, upon the reference's first occurrence in the paragraph.

Abbreviations for works in English

AF	*All That Fall* in *CDW*.
AW	*Act Without Words* (I & II) in *CDW*.
Cas	*Cascando* in *CDW*.
CDW	*The Complete Dramatic Works* (London: Faber & Faber, 2006).
Co	*Company in Company, Ill Seen Ill Said, Worstward Ho, Stirring Still* (London: Faber & Faber, 2009).
CPo	*Collected Poems of Samuel Beckett*, Seán Lawlor and John Pilling (eds.) (London: Faber & Faber, 2012).
CSPr	*The Complete Short Prose: 1929-1989* (New York: Grove Press, 1995).
DF	*Dream of Fair to middling Women* (Dublin: The Black Cat Press, 1992).
Dsj	*Disjecta: Miscellaneous Writings and a Dramatic Fragment* (London: John Calder, 1983).
E	*Embers* in *CDW*.
Eg	*Endgame* in *CDW*.
EJ	*Eh Joe* in *CDW*.
F	*Film* in *CDW*.
Ff	*Footfalls* in *CDW*.
FL	*First Love* in *CSPr*.
G	*Waiting for Godot* in *CDW*.
HD	*Happy Days* in *CDW*.
HI	*How It Is* (New York: Grove Press, 1964).
Im	'The Image' in *CSPr*.
IS	*Ill Seen Ill Said* in *Company, Ill Seen Ill Said, Worstward Ho, Stirring Still* (London: Faber & Faber, 2009).

K	*Krapp's Last Tape* in *CDW*.
L1	*The Letters of Samuel Beckett*, t. 1, *'1929–1940'*, Martha Dow Fehsenfeld, Lois More Overbeck (eds.). (Cambridge UP, 2009).
L2	*The Letters of Samuel Beckett*, t. 2, *'1941–1956'*, George Craig, Martha Dow Fehsenfeld, Dan Gunn, Lois More Overbeck (eds.). (Cambridge UP, 2011).
L3	*The Letters of Samuel Beckett*, t. 3, *'1957–1965'*, George Craig, Martha Dow Fehsenfeld, Dan Gunn, Lois More Overbeck (eds.). (Cambridge UP, 2014).
LO	*The Lost Ones* in *CSPr*.
MC	*Mercier and Camier* (New York: Grove Press, 1974).
MD	*Malone Dies* in *TN*.
Mo	*Molloy* in *TN*.
Mu	*Murphy* (London: Faber & Faber, 2009).
NI	*Not I* in *CDW*.
OI	*Ohio Impromptu* in *CDW*.
Pl.	*Play* in *CDW*.
PM	*A Piece of Monologue* in *CDW*.
Pr.	*Proust and Three Dialogues with Georges Duthuit* (London: John Calder, 1999).
Q	*Quad* in *CDW*.
R	*Rockaby* in *CDW*.
RR	*Rough for Radio* (I & II) in *CDW*.
RT	*Rough for Theatre* in *CDW*.
TFN	*Texts for Nothing* in *CSPr*.
TN	*Three Novels* (New York: Grove Press, 1965).
TT	*That Time* in *CDW*.
U	*The Unnamable* in *TN*.
W	*Watt* (New York: Grove Press, 1953).
WH	*Worstward Ho*, in *Company, Ill Seen Ill Said, Worstward Ho, Stirring Still* (London: Faber & Faber, 2009).
WM	*Words and Music* in *CDW*.
WW	*What Where* in *CDW*.

Abbreviations for works in French

Ber	*Berceuse* in *C.*
C	*Catastrophe et autres dramaticules* (Paris: Minuit, 2006).
Cas	*Cascando* in *Com.*
CC	*Comment c'est* (Paris: Minuit, 1992).
Cie	*Compagnie* (Paris: Minuit, 1995).
Com.	*Comédie et actes divers* (Paris: Minuit, 2009).
DB	*La Dernière bande* suivi de *Cendres* (Paris: Minuit, 2007).
ER	*Esquisse radiophonique* in *Pas.*
FP	*Fin de partie* (Paris: Minuit, 1998).
G	*En attendant Godot* (Paris: Minuit, 2004).
I	*L'Innommable* (Paris: Minuit, 1992).
MC	*Mercier et Camier* (Paris: Minuit, 1998).
MP	*Le Monde et le pantalon* suivi de *Peintres de l'empêchement* (Paris: Minuit, 1990).
PA	*Premier amour* (Paris: Minuit, 1995).
Pas	*Pas* suivi de *Quatre esquisses* (Paris: Minuit, 2009).
PR	*Pochade radiophonique* in *Pas.*
TPR	*Nouvelles et Textes pour rien* (Paris: Minuit, 1991).

Nota

Translations from French sources are our own, unless a specific bibliographic reference indicates otherwise.

Acknowledgements

In publishing this work, I am deeply indebted to a number of eminent specialists. Matthew Feldman's generous guidance made this publication possible. I am also infinitely obliged to Jean-Michel Rabaté, who has honoured these pages with his singularly enlightening foreword. Paul Stewart has my heartfelt thanks for accepting the manuscript, and including it in his newly created series. Chris Ackerley and Luke Thurston both generously read the text closely and contributed their endorsement.

Valerie Lange and Christian Schoen, of Ibidem, have been most kind and cooperative, accepting to publish this work, and being constantly available for advice, throughout the publication process.

This work would never have been envisaged without the confidence shown me by publisher Michel Minard (1928–2013) and his wife Danièle (1939–2014), in entrusting me with founding the 'Samuel Beckett' series. This research has also benefited from enriching exchanges with contributing authors: I have learned a lot from Nicolas Doutey, Bruno Geneste, Matthieu Protin and Éric Wessler. Some aspects of this book were presented at the Samuel Beckett Working Group at Southampton in September 2012, organised by the late Julie Campbell, whose memory I warmly recall here.

I wish to thank my mother, Mavis Brown, and Anna Pivovarchuk for having undertaken the proof-reading of this work during its earlier stages.

Thanks are due to Jean-Luc Baffet, who authorised the project of extensively photographing the historic Papeterie de la Seine (Nanterre), from which the cover picture is taken.

This study would have been inconceivable without my decisive encounter with Marie-Hélène Aimé (1946–2007), who introduced me to Lacanian psychoanalysis, and to life as such.

Lacan with Beckett: Departures

Let me begin by quoting two sonnets written in French and dated from 1929/1930. The first one goes like this:

> Tristesse Janale
>
> C'est toi, o beauté blême des subtiles concierges,
> La Chose kantienne, l'icone bilitique;
> C'est toi, muette énigme des aphasiques vierges,
> Qui centres mes désirs d'un trait antithétique.
>
> O mystique carquois! O flèches de Télèphe!
> Correlatif de toi! Abîme et dure sonde!
> Sois éternellement le greffé et la greffe,
> Ma superfétatoire et frêle furibonde!
>
> Ultime coquillage et palais de la bouche
> Mallarméenne et emblème de Michel-Ange,
> Consume-toi, o neutre, en extases farouches,
> Barbouille-toi, bigène, de crispations de fange.
>
> Et co-ordonne enfin, lacustre conifère,
> Tes tensions ambigues de crête et de cratère. (*CPo*, 44)
>
> (Janal Sadness
>
> It is you, o wan beauty of crafty concierges,
> The Kantian Thing, the icon of Bilitis;
> It is you, mute enigma of aphasic virgins,
> Who gathers my desires with a contrarian shaft.
>
> O mystical quiver! Arrows of Telephus!
> Of you the correlative! Abyss and hard fathom!

For ever be the grafted and the graft,
My superfluous and slim fury!

Ultimate shell and mouth palate,
Mallarmean palace, emblem of Michel-Angelo,
Burn, o neuter, in fierce ecstasies,
Smear yourself, twice-born, in convulsive mud.

And at last coordinate, lakeside conifer,
Your ambiguous tensions of crest and trough)

Here is the second sonnet:

Hiatus irrationalis

Choses, que coule en vous la sueur ou la sève,
Formes, que vous naissiez de la forge ou du sang,
Votre torrent n'est pas plus dense que mon rêve;
Et si je ne vous bats d'un désir incessant,

Je traverse votre eau, je tombe vers la grève
Où m'attire le poids de mon démon pensant.
Seul, il heurte au sol dur sur quoi l'être s'élève,
Au mal aveugle et sourd, au dieu privé de sens,

Mais, sitôt que tout verbe a péri dans ma gorge,
Choses, que vous naissiez du sang ou de la forge,
Nature,—je me perds au flux d'un élément:

Celui qui couve en moi, le même vous soulève,
Formes, que coule en vous la sueur ou la sève,
C'est le feu qui me fait votre immortel amant.
(in Allaigre-Duny, 29)

(Hiatus Irrationalis

Things, whether sweat or sap flow in you,
Forms, whether begotten from forge or flood,
Your stream is not denser than my dream;
And if I do not beat you with unceasing desire,

I cross your water and fall to the shore
Pulled by the weight of my thinking demon
Left alone to fall on hard ground from which being rises,
On evil blind and deaf, on god meaningless,

But, no sooner have words perished in my throat,
Things, whether begotten from blood or forge,
Nature,—than I lose myself in elemental flux:

Fire smouldering in me, the same fire lifts you
Forms, whether sweat or sap flow in you,
It's the fire that makes me your eternal lover.)

If we did not know who the respective authors of these sonnets were but just knew the dates of their composition, between 1929 and 1930, it would be tempting to attribute them to the same poet. Perhaps not the most gifted poet, but still a writer capable of displaying an astonishingly wide range of philosophical allusions and of coining startling metaphors. Some mistakes in diacritics betray the fact that the author of the first sonnet was not a native speaker, which is not the case for the second. The signature of the author of the second poem gives it away immediately, for it follows the text: it is signed Jacques Lacan, whereas the first poem is by Samuel Beckett, and has remained uncollected (in an anthology) for a long time.

'Tristesse Janale' belongs to the cycle of Beckett's work on an imaginary poet and philosopher named Jean du Chas, the immortal inventor of a movement called concentrism. This means that the sonnet is pure parody. The second poem, however, is serious and comes from a moment when Lacan was flirting with mysticism, Jakob Bœhme's kind in particular. The two poems posit seriously—and in a very similar manner—important themes for the work to follow: the primacy of desire and the domination of irrationality in our lives.

The first poem was intended as an exhibit, a proof that someone like Jean du Chas existed and wrote poetry. Of course, Beckett had invented him so as to present his work as a spoof of French literary criticism. His witty essay, 'Le Concentrisme' (*Dsj*, 35–42), was read by Beckett at the Modern Language Society of Trinity College in 1930. Inspired by Normalien *canulars* (their farcical practical jokes), 'Le Concentrisme' sends up the mannerisms of contemporary literary criticism. The verve with which it sketches the career of Jean du Chas, a fictional nobody with a strong suicidal bent, is infectious. Sharing Beckett's date of birth, Du Chas functions as a parodic alter ego in a satire reminiscent of André Gide's *soties*. Du Chas's literary movement, concentrisme, is loaded with puns (*con*: 'cunt' or 'moron') while tending towards its own disappearance. Du Chas's invented 'Discours de la Sortie' ('Discourse of the Exit', 41) would provide a *reductio ad obscenum* that would send up academic discourse and not even spare Proust, quoted as saying that he never blew his nose before six a.m. on Sundays! Jean du Chas's *con*centrism also rhymes with the *con*cierges of the first line: these Parisian janitors or doorkeepers are presented as an obsessive theme in his work. *Du Chas* calls up *chas* (eye of a needle)—a term for the feminine sexual organ in libertine literature. With extreme gusto Beckett debunks the tired tropes of French biographical criticism, while conveying doubts about the very essence of literature.

Beckett mimes and debunks the logorrhœa he had observed among the disciples of *transition*, a magazine in which the genre of the manifesto had been raised to the heights of self-parody. However, he participated in this genre when he co-signed the 1932 manifesto 'Poetry is Vertical', as if a fictional concentrism then gave birth to a parallel verticalism. Du Chas would have brought the touch of humour lacking among the avant-gardist apostles of the revolution of the word. Du Chas, born in Toulouse—because he was destined from birth 'to lose'—launches an inverse verticalism well limned in the author's biography:

> [...] une de ces vies horizontales, sans sommet, tout en longueur, un phénomène de mouvement, sans possibilité d'accélération ni de ralentissement, déclenché, sans être inauguré, par l'accident d'une naissance, terminé sans être conclu, par l'accident d'une mort. (*Dsj*, 38)

> ([...] one of these horizontal lives, without a summit, all drawn out lengthwise, the phenomenon of a movement that cannot accelerate or slow down, triggered without being inaugurated by the accident of a birth, terminated without being concluded by the accident of a death)

Du Chas sums up his wisdom as 'va t'embêter ailleurs' ('Go get bored somewhere else'). This plebeian turn of phrase tells us that if *tædium vitæ* cannot be eliminated, at least one can always go elsewhere, which rephrases Baudelaire's aspiration to go 'Anywhere out of the world' (356–7) while anticipating its own exhaustion.

In the thirties, Beckett had not yet opted for the vernacular of the Paris *con*cierges. He was still stuck in academic verbiage, no matter how close he felt to concierges, already thematically linking Descartes and Du Chas in quest of paternity.[2] The hesitation between the high and the low returns in 'Les Deux besoins,' a serious 1938 manifesto written directly in French. It splices together Racine, Proust, and Flaubert, beginning with an ironical epigraph from *The Sentimental Education.* Astutely distinguishing between the need to have and the need to need, Beckett offers a diagram inspired by Pythagoras, in which the infinity of human desire leaves room for art (see Rabaté, 1996, 153–4). There again, the style is epigrammatic: 'Préférer l'un des testicules à l'autre, ce serait aller sur les platebandes de la métaphysique. À moins d'être le démon de Maxwell' ('To favour one testicle over the other would mean trespassing on the flower-beds of metaphysics. Unless you are Maxwell's demon', *Dsj*, 55–6).

---

2 See 'Whoroscope': '[...] so I'm not my son / (even supposing I were a concierge) [...]' (*CPo*, 42).

For a perfect and synthetic analysis of 'Les Deux besoins', let me refer you to the book that follows. Brown shows expertly how Beckett states once and for all a fundamental irrationality that will be the foundation for his entire œuvre, and that he will begin exemplifying with his first two 'heroes', Belacqua and Murphy. The French essay mentions an 'enfer d'irraison d'où s'élève le cri à blanc, la série de questions pures, l'œuvre' ('hell of unreason whence arises the blank cry, the series of pure questions, the work', *Dsj,* 56). One might say that Beckett's work is underpinned by an 'hiatus irrationalis', a yawning gap that can generate the 'chaos' in which Murphy disappears before engulfing Watt, Molloy, Malone and all the other 'creatures'.

At the same time, by an interesting and not so surprising chiasmus, the spurious mythological allusions of Beckett's poem lead us back to Lacan. In the sonnet he might have attributed to Jean du Chas, Beckett displays his culture, from the two-headed Roman god Janus to the songs of Bilitis made famous by Pierre Louÿs's Lesbian hymns. He includes, moreover, the Telephus who appears in the first page of the *Proust* book and Mallarmé's famously erotic poem, 'Une Négresse', along with other allusions. The sequence of mythological characters peters off in an anti-climax, a desperate call for order facing a feminine chaos of drives, which reminds us of Murphy's initial request that Neary should help him appease the terrifying jumps of his 'irrational heart' performing 'like Petrouchka in his box' (*Mu*, 4). A few years later, using a different mythological figure, but with similar overtones in mind, Lacan would slip a hidden, cryptic poem at the end of one of his lectures—'The Freudian Thing', subtitled 'or Meaning of the Return to Freud in Psychoanalysis', a highly rhetorical speech given in German in Vienna in 1955. Lacan sounded the leitmotiv of a 'return to Freud' against the deviations in Freudian doctrine or the drift to ego-psychology then prevailing in the United States. When the lecture was published in 1956, it ended with a paragraph concealing a submerged quatrain, again those rhyming alexandrines, but this time disguised as opaque prose:

> Actéon trop coupable à courre la déesse,
> proie où se prend, veneur, l'ombre que tu deviens,
> laisse la meute aller sans que ton pas se presse,
> Diane à ce qu'ils vaudront reconnaîtra les chiens...[3] (Lacan, 1966, 436)

Using Bruce Fink's translation, one would have this:

> Actaeon, too guilty to hunt the goddess,
> prey in which is caught, O huntsman, the shadow that you become,
> let the pack go without hastening your step,
> Diana will recognize the hounds for what they are worth. (Lacan, 2006b, 362–63)

It is easy to recognise the invocation to universal desire deployed in 'Hiatus irrationalis', but undercut by a weird humor that erupts here and there. Acteon was changed into a stag when he saw the naked goddess of love, and was devoured by her hounds. Lacan hints that classical psychoanalysts, too prudish to even dare look at her, did not realise that they had been turned into her hounds. A joke transforms the expression 'reconnaîtra les siens' ('tell her own from the others') into 'reconnaîtra les chiens' ('recognise the hounds'). The obscure 'trop coupable à courre la déesse' echoes with 'chasse à courre' ('fox hunting') and 'coureur de déesses' ('womaniser seducing goddesses'). Lacan takes his favorite posture as a joking poet-philosopher of psychoanalysis, a Heideggerian thinker of the Unconscious progressing via opaque and multi-layered epigrams, his opened-ended and literary mode of writing being a pre-condition for a programme aiming at revolutionising psychoanalysis.

Let us return to 'Hiatus irrationalis', a poem dated August 1929 but published in 1933 in the last issue of the surrealist journal *Le Phare de Neuilly* (see Barnet). The journal only saw three issues from

3 I reproduce the text as verse while it is laid out as prose in the original.

1931 to 1933 and was edited by Lise Deharme, mentioned as 'The Lady of the Glove' in André Breton's *Nadja*. Lacan's Petrarchan sonnet in well-balanced alexandrines does not look like a Surrealist text, often marked by wild metaphors and free verse. Its classical rhyme scheme adds an interesting constraint: the B rhyme echoes with the author's name, which immediately follows the text. It looks as if 'Lacan' provides an extra rhyme to 'amant'.

The sonnet's main source is Alexandre Koyré's book on Bœhme's philosophy. *La Philosophie de Jacob Bœhme* (*The Philosophy of Jacob Bœhme,* 1929) comments on the theosophist's sentence 'In Ja und Nein bestehen alle Dinge' ('In Yes and No are all things constituted'). For the German mystic, nature was a dynamic synthesis of affirmation and negation, both implying each other dialectically. This monistic theory of Nature reconciled affirmation and negation via a universal Fire, in which one can see the agency of desire (Koyré, 393–94). Lacan's sonnet, entitled 'Panta Rhei' in an earlier version from 1929, was rewritten for publication in 1933. The title had morphed from Greek to Latin, as if to signify that Heraclitus was to beget Bœhme.

'Hiatus irrationalis' evinces the influence of Paul Valéry's neo-classical style, with echoes of Arthur Rimbaud. Indeed, one overhears 'It is the fire that rises again with its damned soul'[4] (Rimbaud, 1986, 317) from *Season in Hell.* Lacan posits desire as a universal principle that runs through nature: both a Heraclitean stream and a Bœhmean fire. In order to attain the *Mysterium Magnum*, the poet undergoes a moment of muteness, which is why the first tercet evokes speechlessness. Bœhme's mystical vision foreshadows an absolute Other. Its silence lets nature disclose its hidden secrets. 'Hiatus irrationalis' combines Heraclitus' *panta rhei* ('all things flow') with Bœhme's philosophy of fire, less to posit the domination of mutability than an all-consuming desire. Lacan's starting point is Spinoza's *Ethics*, with echoes of Descartes' *malin génie*, which leads to the idea of a *Natura naturans* underpinned by a desire traversing all things.

4 Modified. In French: 'C'est le feu qui se relève avec son damné' (Rimbaud, 1992, 147).

'Hiatus irrationalis' is a phrase that appears in Georg Lukács's *History and Class Consciousness,* an influential book published in German in 1923. It was read by Lacan along with Koyré's work; at the time, Lacan was discovering both the Marxist tradition and German mysticism. Lukács examines the peasants' rebellions in Germany, especially Thomas Münzer's revolt. Münzer was executed in 1525. Lukács links his doctrine of a hidden god (*deus absconditus*) with religious utopias launched by thinkers who had an impact on Jakob Bœhme, born fifty years after the death of Münzer. Lukács notes that Münzer's actions betray a 'dark and empty chasm', the '"*hiatus irrationalis*" between theory and practice' that defines 'a subjective and hence undialectical utopia' (Lukács, 192). Lukács had discovered the expression in the works of Johann Gottlob Fichte. For Fichte, it referred to an irreducible gap between thinking and reality: a yawning abyss between theory and praxis. The visionary mysticism of Bœhme disclosed the truth about desire but stood as a theoretical displacement of the doomed pre-communist utopia.

Lacan's sonnet was contemporary with his first attempts at allowing the insane or the psychotic to speak. Having frequented the surrealists, Lacan agreed with their thesis that everyday language is structured like poetry. This insight came to fruition in his observation of 'inspired speeches' produced by raving patients. In 1931, Lacan co-authored with Lévy-Valensi and Migault an essay entitled 'Inspired Writings'. The three psychiatrists analysed the ramblings of a young female teacher who had been hospitalised at Sainte-Anne. She used to write in a psychotic style, inventing her freewheeling verses marked by bad puns. As the psychiatrists observed, the function of rhythm was dominant, with echoes from popular sayings, borrowings from famous poetic quotes, automatic expressions, proverbial idioms slightly distorted. Such stereotypic echolalia was self-consciously presented as 'poetry' by the psychotic patient.

The grammatical analysis of mad utterances acknowledges pioneering work done by the surrealists a few years before. The authors, who quote Breton's first *Manifesto of Surrealism,* could have looked at the many issues of *transition,* the avant-garde magazine edited by Eugène and Maria Jolas, for which Beckett translated texts regularly, and in which quite a number of his first essays and poems were published. Whereas Jolas and his friends were examining the medical literature about the verbal productions of psychotics, Breton and Éluard went further by imitating different types of delirium. This gave the five psychotic 'imitations' from *The Immaculate Conception* (1930), a text quoted by Lacan and his collaborators in a note (see Lacan, 1980, 379–80). In 'Possessions', Breton and Éluard (51–78) reproduce types of psychotic styles from 'Mental debility' to 'Acute Mania', 'General paralysis', 'Interpretive delirium', and 'Dementia Præcox'. In the introduction, Breton and Éluard explain that they are not indulging in facile pastiches of clinical texts, even though they looked at authentic archives of 'alienated' or insane patients. Their aim is to prove that the poetic faculties of any so-called 'normal' writer will allow him or her to reproduce the most bizarre, paradoxical and eccentric verbal productions, the texts of those who are deemed to be 'insane'. Breton and Éluard disclose a poetic programme, obviously a provocation addressed to literary critics: the ravings of the insane offer new criteria, new poetic forms that will replace traditional genres. They state:

> Finally, we declare that this new exercise of our thought had brought pleasure to us. We became aware of new, up to then unsuspected, resources in us. Without anticipating the conquests of the supreme freedom that this practice can introduce, we take it, from the point of view of modern poetics, as a remarkable standard of value. Which means that we would gladly suggest the generalization of this exercise, and that for us the 'attempt at simulation' of the diseases of those who are locked up in asylums could advantageously replace the ballad, the sonnet, the epic, the improvised poem and other obsolete genres. (Breton, 849)

Thus, an identical point of departure is shared by Beckett and by Lacan. It led Lacan to state that the Unconscious was 'structured like a language', a motto repeated in countless seminars and essays.

Such a thesis then found a confirmation in readings of poems by Victor Hugo, Paul Valéry, T. S. Eliot, Paul Claudel, and many others (Rabaté, 2001). All poetic metaphors disclose an 'involuntary Surrealism' which can inhabit the ravings of the mad, as Paul Éluard had said when praising Lacan for a dissertation in which he quoted the delirious writings of his patient whom he called Aimée. Poetry reveals the essence of language in such a way that there is no distinction between prose and poetry, since both are formations created by a general rhetoric of the Unconscious.

This is a view with which Beckett agreed, as the remarkable book by Llewellyn Brown amply shows. His effort at reading Beckett via Lacan leads him to highlight the theme of the voice, which proves to be most productive. As Maurice Blanchot and Michel Foucault saw, Beckett has changed our views about the links between the voice and writing, between the speaking subject and the notion of the author. I shall quote in conclusion the third 'Text for Nothing', which develops aporias explored at some length in *The Unnamable*:

> What matter who's speaking, someone said what matter who's speaking. There's going to be a departure, I'll be there, I won't miss it, it won't be me, I'll be here, I'll say I'm far from here, it won't be me, I won't say anything, there's going to be a story, someone's going to try and tell a story. Yes, no more denials, all is false, there is no one, it's understood, there is nothing, no more phrases, let us be dupes, dupes of every time and tense, until it's done, all past and done, and the voices cease, it's only voices, only lies. (*CSPr*, 109)

It may matter here that it should be Llewellyn Brown who articulates his *pas de deux* between Lacan and Beckett, and who manages to blend their voices, but never innocently, never naively. One cannot remain naïve about the issues of the voice, of writing and of the origin after one has read Lacan and Beckett. Lacan famously punned on his own discovery of the key to the symbolic realm, the *Nom du Père*, a. k. a. the *Non du Père* (the Father's *No*, or the laying down of the prohibition of incest), when he pluralised it and let it resound as *Les Non-dupes errent.* Like Beckett before him, Lacan pointed to the fact that as soon as we are in language (and we always are, even when we are silent), no 'lie' is possible any longer, for truth obeys the structure of fiction. The illusion would be to try and get rid of the illusion; those who try to be 'not dupes' err all the more. What is the solution, then? Trust the voices, and first, listen to the voices: here is our true point of departure.

Jean-Michel Rabaté
University of Pennsylvania

The Voices of Samuel Beckett: Introduction and First Approaches

The voice is situated at the heart of Samuel Beckett's work, both as a motif and as a structuring element. Its importance has already been pointed out: describing its innumerable occurrences and forms, Chris Ackerley and Stanley Gontarski recognise its centrality ([eds.], 607–18). A simple listing of a few examples can allow us to grasp the constancy of this theme in Beckett's work. As of *Mercier et Camier* (written in French in 1946), the characters state that they hear voices; the narrator of *The Unnamable* is traversed by them, to the detriment of any corporeal presence, and that of *How It Is* claims to content himself with repeating what he hears, regularly punctuating his discourse with 'I quote'. In the plays, Estragon and Vladimir describe 'dead voices' (*G*, 58), and Winnie declares that 'those are happy days, when there are sounds' (*HD*, 162). As for Krapp, he listens to successive recordings of his own voice, by means of a tape recorder. And yet, it is in the later plays that the striking use Beckett makes of this motif can be appreciated: spectral voices constitute the essential part of the theatrical premise used by *That Time* and *Footfalls*. We must not, of course, forget the radio plays—starting with *All That Fall* (1956)—where the voice is heard in a very pure form, unburdened by any visual components. Turning to the narrative texts where the voice apparently occupies a secondary place—being limited to the status of a simple motif—it can be noted that the voice never ceases to be present in a more subtle form, since it supports the narration in its entirety. This fact is confirmed by the reading or reciting of these texts in public, by actors such as Pierre Chabert or Sami Frey. Ludovic Janvier emphasises the crucial nature of the voice in the composition of the prose works, as he noticed when working on the translation of *Watt* from English into French:

> Each time a passage was accepted, Beckett placed it on a pile and in the end he rewrote it all by hand, in small notebooks, so that it

> would all pass via the voice. This transposition from the hand to the voice was necessary so that *Watt* in French would be really intimate for him: the resumption by his gesture and his own vocalisation of the translation in its final state. (1999, 34)

He continues:

> Everything passed through the mouth, as for an actor. Vocalisation was for him the guarantee of the writing subject, the anchoring of the text in a physical rhythm which was that of the voice. It is no mere chance if, since *Molloy*, the theme of the voice has appeared as a priority, as a major part, pervading right through to the last texts that are pure vocalisation, devoid of any support.

Listening

This brief sampling suffices to grasp the crucial importance of the voice for Beckett, to the point where the practice of writing cannot be dissociated from its aural and vocal dimensions. As a young man, Beckett was fundamentally inhabited by listening, a disposition that was not exclusively reserved for his creative activity. Anne Atik records how he gave his interlocutors the remarkable impression of being the object of extremely attentive listening (14, 33). Simple sounds could have a persecuting impact upon him, as his official biographer, James Knowlson, notes:

> He was hypersensitive to sounds. His cousins [...] recalled him coming to the family home [...] for the wake of their mother's funeral, and sitting with his head down at the kitchen table, their mother's hanging wall clock ticking noisily away behind him. He seemed dreadfully disturbed, then finally blurted out: 'Look, I can't go on another minute with this clock. You'll have to stop it ticking!' (1997, 614)

Paradoxically, listening to the most minute sounds also represented an activity in itself for Beckett, as Charles Juliet reports: 'I asked him if he always remained for hours silent and inactive, listening to and observing what spoke and took place within himself. He repeated that hearing was becoming more and more important compared to the eye' (Juliet, 42). In his house at Ussy-sur-Marne, in the Île-de-France region, he appreciated the emptiness and the silence of the countryside, responding as follows to a question asked by Charles Juliet: '– Mais quand rien ne se passe, que faites-vous? / – Il y a toujours à écouter' ('But when nothing happens, what do you do?' 'There is always [something] to listen to', Juliet, 49). Listening thus appears to be inseparable from the background silence that gives form to sounds. James Knowlson observes: 'Beckett is, after all, the great poet of silence, a silence which allowed him to listen to that internal voice murmuring away relentlessly in his head or which emphasised so dramatically the little sounds that so often pass unperceived. A fly buzzing around his worktable, for instance, was to make a companionable appearance later in his prose text *Company*[1] [...]' (2010, 19). Far from being impoverished manifestations, sounds seem to contain a whole world, as Beckett observes in the work of Proust:

> Withdrawn in his cool dark room at Combray he extracts the total essence of a scorching midday from the scarlet stellar blows of a hammer in the street and the chamber-music of flies in the gloom. Lying in bed at dawn, the exact quality of the weather, temperature and visibility, is transmitted to him in terms of sound, in the chimes and the calls of the hawkers. (*Pr*, 83)

For Proust, as for the Beckettian character, the existence of the world is not considered as a compact whole that could be explored in its material breadth but, on the contrary, as being dependent on the sounds that communicate its essence: even visibility has no existence

1 The presence of the fly is a means envisaged to 'bonifier l'entendeur' (improve the hearer, *Cie*, 37–8).

outside of the sounds that pass through it. It is thus that Proust resembles numerous Beckettian characters: lying—in the manner of a recumbent statue (*Company*)—and absorbing the voice that comes to him in the dark.

Other characters echo this practice of listening that Beckett shares with Proust. The narrator of *Malone Dies* explains:

> When I stop, as just now, the noises begin again, strangely loud, those whose turn it is. So that I seem to have again the hearing of my boyhood. Then in my bed, in the dark, on stormy nights, I could tell from one another, in the outcry without, the leaves, the boughs, the groaning trunks, even the grasses and the house that sheltered me. Each tree had its own cry, just as no two whispered alike, when the air was still. I heard afar the iron gates clashing and dragging at their posts and the wind rushing between their bars. There was nothing, not even the sand on the paths, that did not utter its cry. The still nights too, still as the grave, as the saying is, were nights of storm for me, clamourous with countless pantings. These I amused myself with identifying, as I lay there. Yes, I got great amusement, when young, from their so-called silence. (*MD*, 200)

Silence offers exceptional conditions that reveal the richness of sounds. When the outer husk of existence loses its consistency, an infinity of sounds comes to life. Winnie also appreciates these sounds that help her to fill in her time between waking and sleep: 'They are a boon, sounds are a boon, they help me… through the day. [*Smile.*] The old style! [*Smile off.*] Yes, those are happy days, when there are sounds' (*HD*, 162). Or the blind man in *Rough for Theatre I*: 'I can stay for hours listening to all the sounds' (*RT I*, 233).

The relationship between writing and the voice goes much further than the desire to feel at ease with the materiality of words, as Ludovic Janvier emphasised. Beckett's relationship to the voice is manifestly far more intimate and—for this reason—fundamental. James Knowlson notes that Beckett was 'obsessed by the way that he heard the text in his head' (1997, 502). This preoccupation led him to a concern for exactness that could make his experience of listening more difficult during performances of his plays. Regarding a staging of *Endgame*, Beckett asserted: 'It will never be the way I hear it. It's a cantata for two voices' (in McMillan and Fehsenfeld, 163). This musical metaphor suggests that the text, in its very essence, is of a vocal nature—it is elevated to the dignity of a piece of music—and for this reason, it possesses a quality that persists in the realm of the author's intimate experience, so that no punctual recreation can equal it. Beckett's attention to musicality also enabled him to ascertain the exactness of a text's rhythm, when it was translated into Hebrew (Atik, 74). His cousin John Beckett also testifies to Beckett sounding a gong for the recording *MacGowran Speaking Beckett.* He played the instrument 'with terrific concentration', producing a sound of 'a gong in a house', but heard as if it came from another room (in Tucker, 379).

The idea of the voice is not a figure of speech used to translate the author's attachment to the sounds of words. Oriented by listening in his practice of writing, Beckett heard voices in the most literal sense of the word, and he gave form to them in his works. Mary Bryden notes, following André Bernold's testimony, that Beckett declared 'that he heard all of his texts in advance of writing them'[2] (2010, 364). Indeed, when Beckett objected to Albert Finney playing Krapp in December 1972, he pointed to the crucial question of the voice, declaring: 'You hear it a certain way in your head [...]' (in Knowlson, 1997, 596). By contrast, according to Deirdre Bair (491), 'Beckett told Magee that he was astonished when he first heard him speak because Magee's voice was the one which he heard inside his mind'. Stanley Gontarski

2 While this statement may be true, Bernold's account seems to be slightly different, since he actually reports Beckett saying: 'J'ai toujours écrit pour une voix... *La Dernière bande* a été écrite pour la voix d'un acteur que je ne connaissais pas, entendue à la radio... (5 juillet 1982)' ('I have always written for a voice... *Krapp's Last Tape* was written for the voice of an actor whom I did not know, heard on the radio... (5 July 1982)', in Bernold, 107). That is to say that the actor's voice gave the impulse to the work of creation: it was the latter's *cause.*

remarks, about the composition of *That Time*: 'First, the earliest drafts of the memories were recorded in near final form, perhaps because Beckett was recording his own inner voice or unconscious' (1985, 151). Martin Esslin describes this process more precisely: 'When I once asked Beckett about his method of work, he replied that, having attained a state of concentration, he merely listened to the voice emerging from the depths, which he then tried to take down; afterward he would apply his critical and shaping intelligence to the material thus obtained' (379–80). The process described here is not simple, since Esslin reveals three stages, each separated by a gap, by an essential rupture: the original voice emerging spontaneously, followed by the version noted down, then finally, the literary form. This is comparable to a patient in psychoanalysis recounting a dream: whereas the latter represents the 'utterance', what is crucial is his *enunciation*, the subjectivity that enters into play when one recounts and assumes a particular position with regards to this utterance (Lacan, 2013, 166). This ethical position enlarges the question of vocality in Beckett's work beyond its sonorous quality. Mladen Dolar thus correctly emphasises: 'Beckett's literature, written as literature is, is at the same time the literature of the voice as no other, not only by virtue of its being close to the spoken idiom, but also by being sustained merely by pure enunciation which propels it forward [...]'[3] (2010, 58).

Beckett's listening to what could be called 'pre-existing' or 'proto-texts'—communicated from somewhere beyond prosaic reality—leads to texts where the narrators claim they content themselves with quoting the voices they hear, without assuming their content. Thus, in *The Unnamable*, the narrator declares: 'But I don't say anything, I don't know anything, these voices are not mine, nor these thoughts, but the voices and the thoughts of the devils who beset me' (*U*, 341). In *How It Is*, we read: 'then on my elbow I quote I see me prop me up thrust in my arm in the sack' (*HI*, 8). These narrators

3 This notion formed an essential part of our demonstration exploring the scission between seeing and saying in Beckett's fiction (2008, 27 *sqq.*).

appear to reproduce the attitude of Beckett listening to his inner voices to transpose them in written form.

A Complex Field

If the various questions outlined here highlight the importance of voice, sound, and listening for Beckett and his work, they also give an idea of the complexity of this field, its apparently multidimensional nature. It is therefore necessary to determine the different parameters of the question.

Let us start from the word *voice*, which has multiple meanings. It can refer to the sound produced by the throat of a human being, reverberating without. As a result of catachresis, the same phenomenon is recognised in birds or even other animals. The poet Lamartine speaks of 'the voice of dogs' (*la voix des chiens*), in the 1849 Preface to his *Méditations poétiques.* Inversely though, uncertainty remains since for Aristotle, voice requires the presence of a soul (Connor, 2009, 24). Steven Connor (2010) adds, however, that the voice does include the inanimate. The dictionary offers the following definition that highlights the physiological production: 'A series of sounds produced by the larynx, when the vocal cords start vibrating under the effect of rhythmical nervous excitement; effects produced by these sounds' (Rey). This field thus concerns all—or almost all—creations for the theatre. Does an emitter suppose the existence of a receptor, according to the norms established by communication theories? *Not I*, for example, provides for the presence of an Auditor on stage. However, rhetoric reminds us that the presence of a physical person is secondary when it comes to uttering: the function of the address is a factor inherent in all language, as the figure of *allocution* demonstrates.

The voice also supposes the source of an utterance: a character, a narrator. However, our conception of the voice is transformed when the latter becomes multiple. The theories of Mikhail Bakhtin regarding *polyphony* in the novel are well known. Concerning Dostoyevsky, he writes: 'He juxtaposed ideas and conceptions of the world that, in reality, were totally separate and that ignored each other, and obliged them to enter into discussion' (133). The *voice* here is thus the simultaneous presence of heterogeneous utterances that can be ascribed to different sources. However, for such a construction to be possible it requires effacing, to a certain degree, the subject[4] conceived as master of the words attributed to him: 'The Dostoyevskian hero, as a man of ideas, is totally disinterested, insofar as the idea has actually taken possession of the deeper core of his personality' (Bakhtin, 128). Such is also the case of a number of Beckettian 'characters' who are not considered as the authors of the utterances they give voice to: we can think of the Unnamable, traversed by words, of Listener in *That Time* who listens, on stage, to the voices that come to him from without. In these conditions, the utterances can no longer be attributed to the subject they affect: the ego is no longer their source. The voices are imposed from without, exposing the impersonal dimension of language, in that the latter pre-exists the subject. Such, for example, are the voices of *How It Is* or *The Unnamable*, which testify to a split in the narrating agent, so that the *I* who, apparently, pronounces the words denies he is their origin.

According to another meaning of the word, the voice is conceived of as an aural phenomenon, independent of any linguistic manifestation. It thus appears in music, in song, or in the sound produced by other musical instruments. Beckett's expression 'cantata for two voices' (in McMillan and Fehsenfeld, 163) to describe *Endgame* is ap-

---

4 Academic trends have followed the strictures elaborated by gender studies, and imposed the anaphoric pronoun *it*, to refer to *the subject*. However, for psychoanalysis, which provides the framework for our study, the subject is never asexual or neutral. There is no sexless 'esperanto' capable of eliminating the dissonance language introduces in human existence. Thus, *he* not only designates individuals who are biologically male, but it is necessary in order to signify a human referent. This pronoun thus refers to a universal, covering—albeit imperfectly—both sexes. By contrast, *it* refers to inanimate entities, not to humans (thus we do not say: *'I asked an individual, and *it* replied…'). We shall study this question of sexuation more closely, *infra*, p. 69–72.

plicable here, as is the 'mixed choir' of *Watt* (*W*, 34). Despite this musical dimension, the voice remains related to language, to speech; Beckett resolutely situated his productions in the literary field based on writing. Indeed, even in music, the voice is not limited to vocalises, but is associated with the words of a text: the beauty of pure sound—the struggle for the supremacy of one or the other aspect of the work, or for their ever endangered balance—is well known. This question can be found in the work of Beckett, in plays—such as *Not I* and *Play* (Germoni, 27–56)—where the intelligibility of the text recedes as a result of the search for a purely aural effect; or in *Words and Music* where both aspects compete with each other (Ackerley, 2011, 57–76).

Beyond the field of sound, the notion of the voice also refers to the pleasure procured by the act of singing or speaking. In this respect one might think of vocal modulation—expressiveness of tone, physical and aural sound—which expresses the body and the affects of the person who vocalises, as Winnie speaks of it in her stereotyped formulation: '[…] song must come from the heart, that is what I always say, pour out from the inmost, like a thrush' (*HD*, 155). It is no mere chance if the notion of the voice arises when it is a question of the way the narrative texts are appreciated for their lyrical qualities, or for the effect they produce on the reader: a certain *je ne sais quoi* emanates from them, which ensures their perceptible logic or cohesion, far beyond the empirical level made up of the syntactical, lexical or even phonetic formulations. It is a matter of a certain fluidity, the impression of a necessity or a driving force, that the reader can only adhere to, suspending his critical judgement. It is the *souffle*—both 'breath' and 'spirit'—which permeates a literary text, as Louis-Ferdinand Céline explained most eloquently with the metaphor of his *métro-tout-nerfs* (underground train-all-nerves, Céline, 543) in his work *Entretiens avec le professeur Y.*

The term *voice* is also dependent on listening: indeed, to speak of a voice supposes an æsthetic judgement that distinguishes it from unimportant sounds, or noise, that one generally seeks to exclude. However, as pointed out previously, what most people consider as background noise is the focus of Beckett's attentive listening. In this domain we must include sounds of all orders: those Malone listens to, seeking to identify them (*MD*, 200), or the bell that persecutes Winnie, penetrating her flesh like a 'gouge' (*HD*, 162). Once these sounds take on a signifying form—as is the case for Malone—they can be associated with the manifestations of a voice. In the same way, it is impossible to ignore the sounds that make the auditor suffer, insofar as they have a particular impact on him. Thus the policeman in *Mercier and Camier*: 'With the hand that held the truncheon he drew a whistle from his pocket [...]' (*MC*, 93). The combined intrusion of the truncheon and the whistle sets off a violent reaction on the part of the novel's two protagonists.

Is the voice limited to the field of the audible? The passage from *Mercier and Camier* draws a parallel between the sound of the whistle and the truncheon, suggesting that these two instruments have a similar function: both violate bodily integrity. If the voice supposes the existence of an auditor, such a restriction may appear to be arbitrary when the reality of the voice is not necessarily perceived by all present. The dictionary offers an 'abstract' definition of the word voice: 'Discourse, speech that a human being feels within himself, that speaks to him, warning him or inspiring him' (Rey). The voice is thus associated with the rhetorical figure of *prosopopoeia*. Towards the end of *Molloy*, Moran describes his voices as follows:

> And if I submit to this paltry scrivening which is not of my province, it is for reasons very different from those that might be supposed. I am still obeying orders, if you like, but no longer out of fear. No, I am still afraid, but simply from force of habit. And the voice I listen to needs no Gaber to make it heard. For it is within me and exhorts me to continue to the end the faithful servant I have always been of a cause that is not mine, and patiently fulfil in all its bitterness my calamitous part [...]. (*Mo*, 126)

The reality of this voice that speaks to Moran cannot be called into question: no indication suggests that it is an invention or fantasy on the part of the character. And yet, the experience Moran describes is totally subjective: it cannot be supposed that others might be receptors of the same speech; no collective audience can confirm the reality of the phenomenon. To these parameters, it is necessary to add this voice's imperative nature: it is the source of the orders Moran obeys. This is the appropriate moment to recall the common origin of the French verbs *ouïr* (to hear) and *obéir* (to obey), in the Latin *oboedire* (to lend one's ear to, to be submissive to), composed from the prefix *ob-* and the verb *audire.* It is worth noting that Lacan emphasises the imperative dimension of language in this respect: 'To listen to words, to lend one's hearing [*ouïr*] is already to be more or less obedient. To obey is no different, it is to anticipate, in a hearing [*audition*]' (1981, 155). Steven Connor shows how a voice without a visible source is—precisely because it manifests itself as *voice*—endowed with a particularly imperative force, with 'the power of a less-than-presence which is also a more-than-presence' (2009, 25).

This aspect of the voice is perhaps not without a certain relationship to the meaning of the word in the field of grammar, which—in Greek—distinguishes the active, passive and middle forms. It is a meaning that belongs to the logic of written language, and not to the phonetic dimension. However this opposition seems to be instructive as regards the manner in which one can be the bearer of an action—or be subjected to it—while still remaining its *subject*, and constrained to 'obey'. Paradoxically, it is the *subject of enunciation* who desires, not the *ego* or the *I* which, as the subject of the utterance, believes himself to be autonomous. It is in this sense that Lacan underscores the equivocation caused by the French preposition *de* (of), between the objective and subjective genitives: '[…] a person's desire is that of the Other, where the *of* gives the determination grammarians call subjective, that is to say that it is as Other that he desires […]' (1966, 814). Contrary to the *I*, the subject submits to the determination that originates in the Other.

Where does this voice come from? What is its origin? Its source of emission? If the voice appears to be naturally anchored in the body, one may be astonished to notice that the voice Molloy and

Moran perceive is detached from any visible source. In fact, the voice Molloy hears is in his *head*:

> But it is not a sound like other sounds, that you listen to, when you choose, and can sometimes silence, by going away or stopping your ears, no, but it is a sound which begins to rustle in your head, without your knowing how, or why. It's with your head you hear it, not your ears, you can't stop it, but it stops itself, when it chooses. It makes no difference therefore whether I listen to it or not, I shall hear it always, no thunder can deliver me, until it stops. (*Mo*, 36)

This voice appears to come from without—it intrudes on Molloy—but it is also located within the character. The same principle applies to Beckett's 'listening' to his 'inner' voices when composing his works. Instead of passing via the organ of hearing, they arise in the mind and nothing can oppose them: there is no obstacle, and the will is powerless to silence them. For this reason, the *head* should be conceived of as a metaphor expressing the absolute nature of this possession that leaves the subject no reserve, no shelter. The voice is an *external* influence that annuls any interiority.

In this tangle of heterogeneous aspects of the voice, silence cannot be ignored: in the terms of a paradoxical formulation, the voice is silence. Firstly, sounds are heard because they interrupt silence and appear to be embedded within the latter. Next, writing is also a medium of the voice insofar as it is language; it is however penetrated by silence, in that it is not addressed to hearing: in modern reading practice, written words are not usually pronounced out loud, and do not necessarily reach us via the ear. Such is the paradox that Louis-Ferdinand Céline put to work in his novels: '*The emotion of spoken language through writing!*' (498). The same localisation of the voice is evoked: 'The reader who reads me! it seems to him, he would swear it, that someone is reading in his head!… in his own head!…' (545).

Not only does writing ignore the ear, but words can sometimes appear to be impregnated with silence, as the narrator of *The Unnamable* observes: '[…] the words are there, somewhere, without the least sound, [...] drops of silence through the silence, I don't feel it' (*U*, 376). As Charles Juliet reveals, recording Beckett's words, there is a very fine dialectic between speech and silence: '– L'écriture m'a conduit au silence. / Long silence. /– Cependant, je dois continuer' ('"Writing led me to silence." Long silence. "However, I must continue"', in Juliet, 21). One listens to silence, since it is founded on language. Silence is written, albeit with words. And yet, nothing guarantees that silence is actually soundless, that it is the embodiment... of silence. In this sense, Beckett's writing offers us these paradoxical formulations: '[...] this deafening silence' (*TFN* VII, 129); 'screaming silence' (*TFN* XIII, 154); 'mute screams' (*HI*, 46); 'Silence at the eye of the scream' (*IS*, 58); 'No sound. [*Pause.*] None at least to be heard' (*Ff*, 402). If one turns to silence to escape sounds, and the latter remain the manifestation of an unbearable voice, where can a way out be found? As Emil Cioran indicates, for Beckett '*there was no difference between the fall of a bomb and the fall of a leaf...*' (49). What this formulation emphasises, notably, is that the voice often escapes any objective quantification.

A final aspect that merits evoking in this survey of the complexity of the notion of voice, is its dissociation from its physiological source as a result of its recording by a mechanical medium. The voice, which has its origin in the body, and which also involves the affective dimension of the speaker's character, can also be separated from the latter, without ceasing to be a voice. The intervention of technology concerns a whole portion of Beckett's work, starting with *Krapp's Last Tape*—where the present Krapp listens to his old *personæ*—through to his late plays (*That Time*, *Footfalls*, *What Where*), including works for the radio. By means of recording, one can hear the voice of beings who have long since disappeared, and through the radio one can have access to absent voices. The technological support seems to give Molloy's invisible voices their concrete reality. The difference is however inherent in the change of literary genre: by choosing to mobilise technological means, Beckett deliberately places the spectator/auditor in a position comparable to that of his characters, so that the voices impose themselves in their full reality: it is no longer possible to reject them or to relativise them as being the effect of some 'hallucination'.

Thus the voice reveals itself to be of a great complexity, combining personal and impersonal, objective and subjective, corporeal and mechanical, sound and silence, language and its beyond. Faced with this fundamentally paradoxical nature, we have to determine the approach that will enable us to study it, while binding these diverse elements together.

Lacan and the Voice: A Preliminary Overview

The enigmatic nature of the voice requires to be approached in a coherent manner, with adequate conceptual tools which, as this study will endeavour to demonstrate, are offered by the theories of the French psychoanalyst, Jacques Lacan. Indeed, among the particular innovations Lacan contributed to psychoanalysis after Freud—and which is particularly enlightening for Beckett—is the very concept of the *voice*. While the latter has been firmly established as a concept in Lacan's theoretical developments as a whole, Mladen Dolar rightly points out that in his early elaborations, it often took second place by comparison with the gaze,[5] even though it 'can be seen as in some sense even more striking and more elementary' (2006, 39).

Lacan specifically situated the voice among the 'objects' that a subject uses to give a grounding to his reality, in an effort to hem in and keep at bay an uncontrollable force. The voice is thus not an abstract notion, nor is it a neutral phenomenon: it is a material element situated at the very heart of a subject's existence. More precisely, it is

---

5 While the imaginary register is associated with the mirror starting with Lacan's optical diagram (1975a, 126, 220), the gaze is specifically treated in *Seminar XI* (1973, 63–109)—commenting Maurice Merleau-Ponty's developments on the subject—in the unpublished *Seminar XIII*, 'L'Objet de la psychanalyse' (1965–6), a response to Michel Foucault's reading of Velásquez' *Las Meninas*, and in his text on Marguerite Duras (2001, 191–7).

inherent in the fact that the subject is founded in language, the consequence of which is that saying—or *enunciation*—is distinct from the *utterance.*

This grounding is crucial, but Lacan also renders possible the further discrimination between the voice that insists as the hidden and unconscious side of speech, and its complete exteriorisation for the psychotic (1998, 480): the ever-present threat of it forcefully intruding and destroying any coherent subjective reality. This will be apparent in the *vociferation* of the superego: that is to say, the fact that language, in the universal logic it imposes, is experienced in the form of an imperative that, in its ultimate consequences, demands the subject's complete suppression. In a movement that counters such an extreme outcome, Lacan situates *enunciation* as the way a subject 'gives voice' (*donner de la voix*) in order to silence this destructive Other. An additional contribution Lacan makes regarding the structure of the voice, resides in the fact that language does not form a complete and totalising system, but is affected by an insurmountable *hole*, with the consequence that nothing can ultimately silence the voice by enclosing it within the bounds of a final naming. In both of these cases, the subject is obliged to *invent*, which is where the work of creation intervenes.

Lacan and Beckett: Affinities?

The *voice* is thus one crucial psychoanalytical category developed by Lacan, whose theoretical elaborations, such as this one, have largely surpassed the notions used by other schools of psychoanalysis; the latter having, in general, adopted a number of Lacanian concepts. This situation is particularly true as a result of Lacan's deepening of Freud's findings and insights, oriented towards the real, that is to say, a dimension that resists any circumscribing by a subject's personal 'world view', or by the regularity of fixed laws. While post-Freudian theories often remain caught up in the confined sphere defined by the 'Name-of-the-Father'—the agent presiding over the family-centred Œdipal scenario—Lacan ended up reversing his own notions of the unconscious 'structured as a language' whereby strict rationality appeared capable of accounting for a subject's destiny. Hence it would appear that to limit one's scope to earlier theoretical elaborations would be comparable to studying physics from exclusively Newtonian laws. These considerations, alongside factors such as intellectual trends of the moment, have doubtless led a number of critics to integrate Lacanian findings into their works.

It is indeed true that a number of psychoanalytical notions—starting with Freud, but also including various aspects of Lacanian theory—are regularly quoted in academic publications. Surprisingly however, looking at critical studies on Beckett more closely, it seems clear that Lacan's effective presence has been minimal. One reason for this situation in France is that Lacan did not devote full articles to Beckett, as he did to writers such as Marguerite Duras, Paul Claudel, Jean Genet or James Joyce. In spite of this, it can be asserted that Lacan's work—particularly in its later developments—is singularly relevant to the reading of Beckett. Indeed, Suzanne Dow, for example, has seen in him a 'silent partner' of Lacan, 'in the sense that he functions in the period 1968–71 as a figure aligned with psychoanalytic discourse as a "discourse without speech"—that is, the obverse of the discourse of the master [...]' (14).

A brief enumeration of points of convergence will give an overview of their affinities. Both were concerned with the part of existence that lies beyond the comforting *fundamental fantasy*—fiction, or world view (*Weltanschauung*)—that supports the ideals, the goals and meaning most people claim to see in life. Lacan oriented his work towards surveying the screen of the fantasy, then grappling with the dimension of the real that never ceases to overthrow laws and logic, that resists the production of meaning and the elaboration of knowledge; the field where there is no Other capable of providing a guarantee. Beckett's work too discounts verisimilitude and meaning. As Martin Held reports: 'He said that Krapp is not a way of looking at the world (*keine Weltanschauung*), and that in fact answers everything. No, this is just Krapp, not a world-view'[6] (in Hayman, 67–70). The constant calculations Beckett undertook when composing many of his works were destined to reveal the place where language finds its roots in silence and absence of meaning.

This orientation is also manifest in the many statements made by Beckett that resemble Lacanian axioms by virtue of their extreme degree of logical precision.[7] Among these statements, an expression such as 'the absolute absence of the Absolute'[8] (*Dsj*, 33), that Beckett applies to Joyce, recalls Lacan's 'there is no Other of the Other'[9] (1966, 813), and defines Beckett's experience of the radical absence of any transcendent authority endowing existence with a form of coherency. The same could be said of his remarks concerning silence, or the *impossible* (another Lacanian category).[10] As the narrator of *The Unnamable* declares: 'That the impossible should be asked of me, good, what else could be asked of me?' (*U*, 331). Is not this the experience that Beckett describes, when he explains to Charles Juliet, his lack of interest in Oriental philosophers: 'Ils proposent une issue, et moi, je sentais qu'il n'y en avait pas' ('They offer a way out, and I felt that there was none', in Juliet, 20)?

---

6 Here we disagree with Lois Oppenheim who, in a post-Freudian and humanistic perspective, ascribes a 'world-view' (2001, 781) to Beckett: the latter explicitly states, for example, that the painting of the van Velde brothers 'contient plus d'humanité vraie que toutes leurs processions vers un bonheur de mouton sacré' ('contains more true humanity than all their processions towards a sacred sheep's happiness', *MP*, 46).

7 We should add that this logical rigour is totally distinct from what Nina Power and Alberto Toscano call Alain Badiou's 'formal systematicity' (in Badiou, 2003, XVII): the approach that the philosopher imposes on—or reads into—Beckett's work.

8 See *infra*, p. 96–99.

9 The absence of an Other to ensure an ultimate guarantee to existence has been reformulated, by Jacques-Alain Miller, as: 'The Other does not exist', notably in his unpublished course of 1996–1997.

10 Jean-Michel Rabaté points out that Beckett found this term in Maurice Blanchot and Georges Bataille (Rabaté, 2014, 137; 2012, 62–3).

Beckett's denouncing the 'loutishness of learning' (*CPo*, 55)—in spite of being steeped in bookish or verbal culture (Connor, 2014a, 152–75)—is not foreign to Lacan's depreciation of knowledge—including psychoanalytical 'lucubration' (1975b, 127)—when faced with the real. This attitude regarding signifying leads to the rejection of any metalanguage: that is to say, the possibility of an objective, distanced language purported to master what remains structurally refractory to naming (be it in order to interpret a work of creation, or explain symptoms). Displaying an extremely coherent mind, Beckett thus refused to comment on his own work, writing to Michel Polac about *En attendant Godot*:

> Je ne sais pas plus sur cette pièce que celui qui arrive à la lire avec attention.
>
> Je ne sais pas dans quel esprit je l'ai écrit [*sic*].
>
> Je ne sais pas plus sur les personnages que ce qu'ils disent, ce qu'ils font et ce qui leur arrive. [...]
>
> Quant à vouloir trouver à tout cela un sens plus large et plus élevé, à emporter après le spectacle, avec le programme et les Esquimaux, je suis incapable d'en voir l'intérêt. (*L2*, 315)

> I know no more about this play than anyone who manages to read it attentively.
>
> I do not know in what spirit I wrote it.
>
> I know no more of the characters than what they say, what they do and what happens to them. [...]
>
> As for wanting to find in all this a wider and loftier meaning to take away after the show, along with the programme and the choc-ice, I am unable to see the point of it. (*L2*, 316)

What is insistent—or what Beckett pounds out!—in this passage is the assertion 'I do not know': as writing does not belong to the domain of the signified, it is not related to any knowledge. The creator possesses no viewpoint superior to that of the reader, simply because *such knowledge does not exist*: the creation of the work coincides with its accomplishment. As Steven Connor points out, concerning Beckett's refusal (Beckett 1998, 24) to 'explain' *Endgame*, Beckett 'takes no responsibility' for facilitating interpretation, 'because this would loosen the lock of the predicament he is attempting to state, both with extreme simplicity and "as fully as possible"' (2008b, 43).

The subject's absolute singularity—'Impossible de raisonner sur l'unique' ('Impossible to reason on the unique', *MP*, 32), as Beckett says—is precisely what psychoanalysis aims to produce as 'absolute difference' (Lacan, 1973, 248). Beckett's concern with an æsthetics of 'failure' and the 'worst' is in complete harmony with Lacan's dismantling of ideals (such as 'humanity'), to replace them with their counterpart as the *a* object: the subject's destiny as waste or refuse, excluded from the Other. Such precise echoes are neither common nor anecdotal—one would not find such equivalents in the other authors Lacan has commented on—and they merit closer examination.

If Beckett and Lacan seem to share so many points in common, it is undoubtedly for structural reasons. Their rigorously logical approach to their respective domains—unencumbered by trivial concerns that serve to dissimulate a dimension escaping all control—leads them to encounter the same structural points of impasse in language. Of course, this in no way suggests a strict overlap of two heterogeneous fields. If Beckett's work often echoes Lacan, it is in the distinct field of *creation*; as such, it gives a totally new and singular form to these principles, a form that it is impossible to assimilate to any conceptual 'equivalent': their impossible point of convergence, is also, necessarily, a point of *dispersion*.

It is from this point of view that it would seem preferable to consider any links between Beckett and Lacan, rather than in the light of the history of ideas. Of course, it is known that Beckett not only read considerably in the field of psychology and psychoanalysis (Feldman, 2006), but that he also had first-hand contact with what is at stake in these disciplines. In this regard, it would be useful to broach the use of the term *psychoanalysis* in relation to Beckett's experience with Wilfred Bion (1934–1935), which will also pave the terrain for our developments. This term has been contested, on sociological grounds,[11] that Bion had not himself been analysed (Oppenheim, 2001, 768); some however maintain the idea of *therapy* while still paradoxically calling Beckett an *analysand* (Feldman, 2006, 93). To set a conceptual framework, it should be noted that Lacan defines psychoanalysis as a *discursive structure* (one of 'four discourses') that founds transference,[12] in the same way as the classroom produces the pupil/teacher relationship, whatever may be the latter's qualification, professional qualities, or lack thereof. The question becomes more complicated if the *psychic structure* of the patient is taken into account. The 'normal' or neurotic patient will see the analyst as endowed with a certain authority, considering him as having knowledge regarding the patient's most intimate questions. The psychotic patient, however, who can somehow see himself as being his 'own other' (*R*, 441), will certainly not adopt the same position in analysis.

Finally, while ruling out the questions of mutual 'influence', if one considers the 'before' and 'after', it is reasonable to conclude that a real encounter took place between Beckett and Bion. Some do note the improvement experienced by Beckett (Feldman, 94), as did Beckett himself (Beckett, 2009, 258–9, 300). Some psychoanalysts thus do not hesitate to point out the importance of Beckett's analysis (Kaltenbeck, 2005, 193). Bruno Geneste (2015) conjectures that psychoanalysis may have helped Beckett detach himself from the symbolic register experienced as rigid and petrified. Steven Connor's evaluation is similar: 'Analysis provided a kind of mythical scene which allowed Beckett to separate himself from the language of the interpreter, and language as such insofar as it was split off and lodged in the person of

11 We could also add that while he founded institutional mechanisms of recognition, Lacan defined the analyst by strictly internal criteria, as one who 'authorises himself' (2001, 243, 307), in other words in relation to his own experience as analysand, for the logical reason that 'there is no metalanguage' to found authority (Lacan, 1966, 867–8). Luke Thurston undertakes a thorough study of these methodological questions.

12 See *infra*, p. 320 *sqq*.

that interpreter' (2008c, 20; *cf.* Feldman, 2006, 94–5). It would therefore be legitimate to reverse the initial objection and state that Beckett's case demonstrates that psychoanalysis is not simply the effect of institutional authorisation or training; on the contrary, Beckett's work seems to evidence the best one could hope from psychoanalysis. The effects thus produced—and Beckett's relation to language—are what interest us primarily in any consideration on this score, and with regards to the voice.

The Limits of Certain Uses of Lacan

The points we have just outlined would seem to justify entertaining the appropriateness of a Lacanian reading of Beckett. However, investigating existing critical readings more closely, one can observe that their relevance is rather uneven, according to the specific orientation adopted. This is so in the English-speaking world, because critics have essentially limited their readings of Lacan to his early structuralist developments, which have in turn been filtered by the preoccupations of so-called studies of 'French theory'. Thus it is that various critics of Beckett cite the notions of the *barred subject*: the subject understood as simultaneously determined and excluded by the signifier, both represented by language, and devoid of any specific identity; *metaphor*: the function of naming that brings a halt to *metonymy*, defined as perpetual sliding from one signifier to another, entailed by the impossibility for language to name its own anchoring point. These approaches also evoke the authority embodied by the *Name-of-the-Father*,[13] and undertake its deconstruction, to show its powerlessness to account for the real complexities of existence. Although these categories remain important, they belong to the period of Lacan's 'return to Freud' (Lacan, 1966, 405): his determined efforts to reclaim psychoanalysis from Anna Freud's 'ego-psychology', and to give it a firm conceptual grounding.

13 We undertake to define this term *infra*, p. 58–60.

The limits of these approaches to Beckett's creation can be seen in the works of a number of critics. Julia Kristeva's 1976 essay, 'Le Père, l'amour, l'exil' is often cited as an important reference with regards to Lacan and Beckett. However, Kristeva limits the scope of her psychoanalytical framework by subordinating it to her ideological preoccupations: the study of Beckett's literary construction suffers as a result. Her reductive reading of *First Love* and *Not I* treats the two 'characters'—one 'obsessional', the other 'psychotic'—as pathologically absorbed by their indefectible attachment to the dead father (without indicating where the reader should locate the latter in the text of *Not I*), considered as the founder of social bonds. She asserts that in European civilisation, the 'religion of the father' has resulted in the 'maternal repressed-feminine',[14] that is held back under the 'veil of sacred terror' (266). This leads her to call for the reintegration of 'the joyous serenity of incest with the mother' (266). Such a promotion of what constitutes the most universal interdiction in human society does seem strange, even if Kristeva is referring to the realm of cultural productions. Basically, she calls for a form of *jouissance* (considered exclusively as pleasure, it would seem) as a form of compensation for this mortification. Kristeva's analysis appears simplistically binary, aiming—through creating a 'balance'—at reinstituting a harmonious civilisation—necessarily based on the Name-of-the-Father—via the union of maternal and paternal agents. This composition fails to explore in what way, in creation, a subject deals with the fundamentally problematic nature of existence. It must also be added that the entire field Kristeva associates with a supposed reliance on the 'Name-of-the-Father' needs to be reassessed when studying Beckett.

Some critics adopt a voluntarily simplified version of Lacan's theories. David Watson admits resorting to 'an "appropriation" of certain (simplified) concepts as a pretext for a critical discourse' that he considers may be of use (35). This utilitarian approach would seem to

14 We shall explore Kristeva's ideas further in relation to *Not I*. See *infra*, p. 122–4, 136.

recognise Lacan's importance, without really undertaking any consequent reflection on his elaborations: psychoanalysis thus appears as a convenient product of cultural accumulation, rather than being put to the test in relation to clinical findings, of which creation forms a part. Symptomatically, Beckett is seen as illustrative of deconstruction since, by 'stripping away the remaining debris of narrative forms' (33), he concentrates, particularly in *The Unnamable*, 'on the enunciating voice itself, on the act of narration'. Following deconstructionist tendencies, Watson accepts the notion of the subject as reduced to negative qualities, as being 'founded on a lack' (38). This calls for the notion of desire—understood as the 'search of the ultimate object which would make good the lack'—'rides along metonymic chains of signifiers in the attempt to "speak" that object'. Such continual sliding from one signifier to another does provide a starting point, at least for apprehending the dynamics of the voice understood as a deficiency of meaning.

Catharina Wulf follows the same notion, working from Lacan's oft-quoted elaboration of the imaginary register in the form of the 'Mirror stage', where the small child's identity is established by his recognition of his reflection in the mirror for the first time. She asserts that this structure favours misrecognition, which consequently 'presses the individual during its entire life to search for an ideal ego based upon a fictive unity' (Wulf, 155), and can give rise to 'the infinite displacement of signifiers' (155), such as can be found in the narration of *The Unnamable*. According to Wulf, the virtue of this mechanism is that it leads to 'infinite opening' (73). However, as we have pointed out in a previous study (2010), it is most problematic to apply such a notion to the work of Beckett, particularly since desire itself is dependent on the paternal metaphor, and the latter's ability to confer an overall coherence on a subject's reality.

In spite of this absence of such a presiding agent of authority and unity in Beckett—as we shall attempt to demonstrate further on—Watson reproduces the Œdipal story (Watson, 48)—the transgression of an interdiction in an effort to return to the mother—which can only appear trivial with regards to the real questions raised in Beckett's writing. For example, when Watson speaks of a desire to attain silence (44), one may ask *why? What* silence is at stake? It can hardly be a 'symbolic' silence that, by definition, is tightly circumscribed within an overall dialectic. If the Beckettian subject's desire aims to attain the 'ultimate Real' (50), the latter requires to be understood as an ever-present *cause* that continually resounds in the act of enunciation. Through this approach, Watson cannot account for the Beckettian subject's absolute solitude: the absence of any form of interlocutor must be an essential point of reflection, in order to grasp something of the voice.

Hwa-Soon Kim also avowedly makes limited use of Lacan (8). By choosing to study Beckett's characters—who 'are not the patients in a clinic'—she pushes aside the place of the subject who creates, and the resulting dimension of *writing*. Her approach thus suffers from psychologising when she evokes, for example, the idea of Winnie's self-delusion, rather than the difficulties involved in her actual production of speech. As Kim remains strictly on the level of utterances, she ignores the part that necessarily escapes naming. Thus, she sees Winnie's mound as 'her visual resistance against the discourse of the Other' (70), embodying the heap of her 'failed words'. However, she does not take into account the Möbian structure of the play: the fact that nothing stops the course of the unceasing *drive* that leads to Winnie's ultimate burial, and that implacably continues its course behind her abundant use of sterile clichés (Brown, 2011a). While Kim speaks of the concomitant failure of Winnie's words and those of Beckett, with regards to communication, she neglects the fact that failure is inherent in language and subjective structure, and is the very *object* of creation.

Michel Bernard (31) also studies the 'barred subject' and the notion that the subject is spoken by language as *other*. Although they are justified, such notions risk leading to an analysis of Beckett that simply illustrates or confirms Lacan, since these structures are universal and govern all subjects. What is elided is the *literality* of Beckett's writing, the creation of a literary form, in relation to an irreducible real.

One problem—already encountered diversely with Kristeva and Watson—is that Beckett's writing is studied in relation to the normality entailed by the Name-of-the-Father, not with the latter's problematic nature. As Bernard does not raise the question of the vital dimension of existence, the Lacanian play on words *tu es/tuer* (you are/kill) is not related to the effect of the insatiable and tyrannical *superego*. Indeed, although Bernard does speak of the Freudian and Lacanian 'Thing'—related to the lost origin functioning as a cause of discourse (114, 137, 140)—his analysis remains abstract, dematerialised, for want of any notion of traumatism, torment or anxiety. In other words, the part of the subject that seizes him in his flesh, that he has no control over, and alienates what is most vital to his being.

Finally, as a result of their partial use of Lacan, some critics find themselves obliged to overtly supplement their psychoanalytical approach with other tools: Catharina Wulf resorts to Schopenhauer's 'will', which she could usefully have linked to the Freudian and Lacanian notion of the *drive*; Michel Bernard calls on Deleuze, to account for a continuous and unlimited temporality in Beckett's work. Had they rigorously followed Lacan, they would have been able to weave these other thinkers into a coherent overall logic, as made possible by psychoanalysis.

The concepts developed by Lacan in his early work are certainly useful: it could even be said that they are indispensible to reading Beckett, particularly when defining the voice and apprehending the forms it adopts. For example, one cannot ignore the distinction between utterance and enunciation, the subject's fundamental lack of identity. The problem is that these utilisations of Lacan fit too well: they work like a well-lubricated mechanism based on the assumption that everything in existence is commanded by the supremacy of words capable of banishing any disconcerting or untameable reality. That was precisely the reason for Lacan's popularity in academic circles: the notion of the 'unconscious structured like a language' (Lacan, 1966, 269) supposed the domination of the symbolic register,[15] and the illusion

15 We undertake to define this term *infra*, p. 58.

of mastering the *real*. Linguistic structuring thus offered a vision devoid of any *empêchement* (*MP*)—as Beckett called it—regarding subjective experience. *A minima*, when reading Beckett, that means taking into account experiences of the unbearable that Beckett expresses in 'The Calmative', for example, where he speaks of 'fornication with corpses' (*CSPr*, 61) or 'nightmare thingness' (69): conditions which go beyond anxiety.[16] Various concrete and personal elements in Beckett's own experience remain inherent in creation—as in the writing of *En attendant Godot* as a 'game to survive' (in Knowlson, 1997, 536)—since they are what creation both deals with, and gives form to.

Because of these shortcomings, some note a rise and fall of Lacanian psychoanalysis in literary criticism (Oppenheim, 2001, 780). As a consequence, critics often dismiss such readings off-hand, without having delved into Lacan and studied his later elaborations. Ciaran Ross, for example, noting the logical grounding involved in Lacan's early work, deliberately rejects Lacan as being representative of producing a 'formalist' Beckett, an *abstracteur*, at the expense of any emotional dimension (14). Moreover, in areas where Lacan provides specific tools (the body, melancholy, Descartes' *cogito*…),[17] his insights are conspicuously absent from critical works. It could be shown that Lacan's discursive structure called 'discourse of the university'[18] is not so far removed from that of the 'master', whence, at the risk of 'boredom' (*Pr*, 19), literary criticism runs the risk of preferring the 'habit' of readily-exploited concepts, to what may challenge strictly conceptual thinking. The paradox resides in the fact that creation is based precisely on what irremediably escapes established categories.

Seemingly in order to counter such objections, other approaches in the 'psy-' field have been called on recently, such as the

16 Lacan, 2004, 91, 185, 279, 360.

17 Steven Connor, for example, rightly refers to Deleuze, as background to his study on repetition (2007), but without mentioning Lacan who, nonetheless, spoke highly of Deleuze's works *Différence et Répétition* and *Logique du sens* (Lacan 2006a, 218, 225, 227), pointing out the way his theories had influenced them.

18 See *infra*, p. 321.

findings of neuropsychology, in an effort to compare (albeit on a metaphorical level) Beckettian characters with pathologies purported to be similar (Oppenheim, 2008; Fifield, 2008, 2009a). Symptoms are enumerated (like dream symbols, or the compilation of potentially numberless items contained in the *DSM*[19]) in an often anecdotic juxtaposition of resemblances, with little or no conceptual or critical stance. These undertakings have little heuristic value, and do not allow one to draw any form of conclusion. For example, how can one learn about what poetry is, or its function, by locating the nerve endings supposed to produce 'coprolalic' speech (Maude, 2008, 163)?

Another problem is that these approaches are based on the conception of an ideal form of developed individual, compared to 'illnesses', 'maladies' one may suffer from (would it be preferable if creators were 'normal', 'healthy' beings?). They are thus inadequate to deal with a work of creation, particularly that of one who was absolutely opposed to the norm (*cf.* Brown, 2013d). Basically, neurosciences evacuate the subject[20]—his absolutely singular relation to speech—replacing it with the supreme authority of science, that is 'supposed-to-know' (to use Lacan's expression that emphasises the artifice of the analyst/analysand relationship) in the subject's stead. One critic claims exorbitantly: 'Neuropsychology, however, with its substantial models and extensive clinical evidence, re-locates the Beckettian post-obit text from its more abstract interpretations into the realm of substantial empirical enquiry' (Fifield, 2008, 170). We find here a throwback to 19th Century scientism, and are left wondering whether Beckett's 'characters' suffer from pathologies, whether they are modelled on descriptions of the latter, or if the author himself suffers from such maladies. These approaches are the exact opposite of Lacan's

---

19 *Diagnostic and Statistical Manual of Mental Disorders* (*DSM*), published by the American Psychiatric Association. It tends to associate mental suffering with the corresponding medical treatment, thus creating potential consumers for pharmaceutical companies.

20 Which is, however, precisely the reproach such authors (Fifield, 2008, 170) make of structuralism!

(2001, 192–3, 2007, 116) and Freud's principle of giving first place to the artist. In this case, it is infinitely preferable to follow psychoanalysis, and to postulate the link in a real that is part of the creator, who deals with it by giving form—setting it to work—in a production which is in no way imitative or reducible to a pathology. Here, were one to evoke a nosographic classification in relation to the creator, it would be immediately necessary to underscore that a structure—such as psychosis—remains a 'paradoxical class' insofar as it denotes an absolute singularity, as evidenced by his creation: '[...] the property that seems to be its principle and its bond is the name that detaches it from properties and bonds' (Milner, 2007, 111). Indeed, Lacanian psychoanalytical practice aims at bringing to light the absolute singularity of the subject. It is, therefore, false to say that it leaves no place for individual creation (Oppenheim, 2001, 781).

'Jouissance': a Factor of 'Empêchement'

Indeed, what often remains ignored by these critics is the evolution whereby Lacan deepened his approach of what he called *jouissance* and the real—both of which involve the voice—to the point where the latter overturn, to a large degree, his original constructions.

The notion of *jouissance* is crucial here, and an attempt is necessary to define this term which will regularly be used in the course of the following pages. Its paradoxical nature creates a fundamental difficulty in translating this notion into English simply as 'enjoyment', since it is the place where pleasure is reversed into displeasure, to an absolutely uncontrollable degree. As Lacan formulates it: 'It starts with tickles and ends with a blaze fired by petrol' (1991b, 83).

In Lacan's early work, *jouissance* was envisaged negatively, associated with the narcissistic pleasure of the image (Miller, 2010–11). As such, it represented an obstacle to the true relation of the subject to the symbolic Other, and the knowledge (*savoir*) the subject is called upon to derive from it.[21] It was consequently destined to be drawn aside, in order to dispel the illusion it created. Further on in his early elaborations, Lacan saw *jouissance* as essentially—and originally—'negativised', as expelled into what is then called the real (Miller, 2010–11): it is by virtue of such a founding extraction (or 'repression': the so-called 'death of the Father') that any representation can take on form, as is expressed in the common saying 'the exception proves the rule'. This founding point of expulsion will, in Lacan's theoretical writings, be marked by the simple letter *a*, in the term: the '*a* object'. What is then experienced as the 'pleasure principle' is considered as the will to avoid *jouissance* by adhering to a rational and realistic conception of existence, in an effort to maintain homeostasis, a minimum of conflict.

Despite the pacifying influence of speech and dialogue, *jouissance* cannot be eradicated, because language is fundamentally flawed, and is therefore incapable of naming the totality of existence: *jouissance* persists, manifesting itself as a form of excess, which Lacan called—following Marx's notion of 'capital gain'—*plus-de-jouir* (2006a, 16 *sqq*.). It is a remainder that cannot be assimilated and, for this very reason, continually acts as the unseen cause which drives a subject's speech and acts.

The stability of language and representation suffers as a consequence. Insofar as they are marked by error and falsehood, words cannot be relied on to determine ultimate truth: the signifier produces the subject as 'a logical inconsistency' (Miller, 1994b, 13). This is what is often pointed out in deconstructionist thinking, as the inability to pin down a subject within any single or definitive identity, or the difficulty of stating any universal truth. However, this vision ignores the reverse side of the subjective equation since, by contrast, as Jacques-Alain Miller points out, 'on the level of what Lacan calls *plus-de-jouir*, there is no contradiction. The *plus-de-jouir* is always true' (1994b, 13). *Jouissance* testifies to a logical consistency, a fixed point that insists through the subject's repetition of acts and situations.

---

21 This conception is related to the well-known apologue of the 'Mirror Stage'. *Cf. infra*, Lacan's '*Schéma L*', p. 85.

However, the limits of even this conception of *jouissance* appear in the fact that it remains subservient to a dialectic whereby the subject refuses it, in order to attain it on a superior level, through *desire* (Miller, 2010–11, 52, 53), which is a notion previous critics have often relied on. That is to say that from this perspective, *jouissance* only temporarily disturbs the logic of the symbolic, since it is destined to be surpassed, and drawn into harmony with the symbolic law anchored in a lack. In his final work however, Lacan reversed his conception of the negative quality of *jouissance* and gave it a positive value. Following Heidegger (Miller, 2010–11), Lacan linked it to *existence*, as designating all that can be known of the living: the part situated before and beyond *being* which, ever since Aristotle, has remained bound up within the limits of meaning (Miller, 2010–11).

To sum up, what needs to be drawn from this notion of *jouissance* at this stage is, in particular, its positivity, the fact that it represents a fixed point which cannot be assimilated or reduced by naming, and resists any interpretation: no knowledge (*savoir*) can be drawn from it. As concerns our present field of investigation, the *voice* is—alongside the Freudian objects such as breast and faeces—one form of *jouissance*, by means of which the subject gives his existence consistency, when faced with that which, in language, refuses to be named. It is absolutely *singular*, since it marks the subject's response to the absence of any Other[22] (embodied by the 'Name-of-the-Father', for example) capable of founding an ordered reality by means of naming and fixed laws: *contra* Badiou, it is in no way 'generic'.[23]

These developments regarding a dimension that refuses to enter any harmonious whole point out an aspect that is manifestly missing from a number of critical works that use Lacan's theories. This shortcoming is also apparent in postmodern discourses, which superficially seem to be related to Lacanian psychoanalysis. By insisting on

---

22 The juridical use of the term (comparable to *usufruct*) is enlightening, since it refers to the right to use property that belongs to another.

23 Resorting to a metaphysical framework, Badiou claims that Beckett's writing somehow involves 'a generic truth of Humanity' (2003, 16).

supporting an ideological position, postmodern elaborations are often determined to combat anything that might appertain to the idea of truth, which they diversely call 'molar' (Deleuze and Guattari, 47), 'patriarchal', 'phallocentric', normative entities. To these enemies, that are deliberately caricatured—and whose defeat is quite simply prompted by the triumph of capitalism and globalisation—they oppose perpetual difference/deferral, or supposedly minority entities, or the reign of the multiple, and which, if one examines them closely, are no more than the undifferentiated. To the oppression of the One, they oppose the right to polymorphous enjoyment, without hindrance. This perspective admits no point of opacity, no unassimilable element: everything is destined to become transparent, basking in a generalised optimism supported by an ideology of progress.

Psychoanalysis is, of course, linked to these preoccupations to a certain extent, and which can be found in a number of critical uses of Lacan's theories. Indeed, in the second half of the 20th Century, intense and most fruitful intellectual exchanges took place between Lacan and figures such as Claude Lévi-Strauss, Émile Benveniste, Michel Foucault, Jacques Derrida, Gilles Deleuze, Roland Barthes, and numerous others, resulting in the development of structuralism and post-structuralist thinking.

With regards to Beckett, it would seem important to point out what distinguishes psychoanalysis from deconstruction. As seen in the uses of Lacan's early theories, deconstruction adheres to the notion of the subject as being without any fixed identity and obliged therefore to follow the metonymical chain of signifiers. Shane Weller points out that critics such as Steven Connor, Leslie Hill, Carla Locatelli, Thomas Tresize and Richard Begam aim to show that Beckett is 'deconstructive', in the sense that he 'is seen to submit all metaphysical oppositions to a differing-deferring that anticipates the *différance* first theorised by Derrida in the 1960s' (Weller, 27). Daniel Katz, for example, follows this path. Adopting Derrida's theories, he presents the deconstruction of *The Unnamable* as showing 'a shift from a binary oppositional structure of presence and absence into a differential or supplemental schema' (Katz, 96). The difficulty here is that Katz's analysis consequently remains on a verbal level where the subject's absence of coincidence with himself produces a supplement of the same order. It is true that, on a *literary* level, Beckett plays with the effect of paradoxes such as presence/absence, appearing/disappearing (99), thus producing 'double bind' situations that Katz regularly identifies. However, by calling on this notion, his deconstructive approach risks simply miming Beckett. When studying *The Unnamable*, Katz points out the paradox whereby the narrator's 'delegates' are both 'that which speaks *to* the voice' (104) and 'that which gives the voice what it has to speak'. This formulation describes a specular relationship between the two parties, but what is lacking is a material conception of *address*. It could be said, in this respect, that the external voices speak first, and the subject speaks in turn, in order to silence them and to endow himself with an existence and an identity.[24] Such an analysis would have enabled Katz to move beyond the paradox of endless specularity.

Deconstruction is also preoccupied, for example, with showing that the subject is not the conscious author of his utterances: the subject is indeterminate, making it impossible to clearly identify the one who speaks. Thus Katz notes that in the '*Trilogy*', the citational schema 'destroys any possibility of expression as the totalized outpouring of a fully present, interior self-consciousness' (91). He thus promotes the idea that *différance* is the embodiment of a salutary alterity.

However, as we have just seen, while psychoanalysis confirms the subject as empty (a logical inconsistency), on one side, on the other, can be found not simply an open, indeterminate space, but an opaque constant, which we have associated with Lacanian *jouissance*. The subject is both 'barred' (excluded by the signifier that represents him), and in a singular relationship with the *a* object: he is both free

24 See *infra*, p. 118–9. It is true that Katz does raise the notion of address, but he does not develop its consequences beyond the deconstructive or linguistic framework. He speaks—as we shall do so later—of the *I* as posterior to the *you* (Katz, 107, 127, 141), and of the narrator's discourse as a response to the Other (109).

to follow the endless signifying metonymy of identifications, and riveted to a fixed point. In the 'between'—where no identification is adequate—something of a subject's very being remains at stake: there is a vital and absolutely singular *enjeu*[25]. It is therefore essential to take into account both sides: undertaking deconstruction (a negative approach) is necessary in order to move on to the second stage, and ascertain how a subject's identifications are a *vital construct*. In this respect, deconstruction remains strictly one-sided, as it can say *what is not* (identity, origin, belonging, authority…) but not *what is (jouissance)*, because it considers what *is* as being determined by a tyrannical Name-of-the-Father or the individual's *ego*, and hostile to the perpetual metonymy of *différance*. One could say that it is profoundly 'logo-centric', not in spite of but because of its very protestations.

Indeed, metonymy would seem to be an unsatisfactory way of undoing, as it is not only purely verbal, but it is secretly dependent on a (metaphysical) guarantee. It is the latter which enables the proponents of deconstruction to deny any notion of a breaking point (that Freud calls 'castration') where the subject would find himself responsible and, possibly, destitute, in the *absence* of any Other. Deconstruction thus manifests a radical refusal of 'alterity'. For psychoanalysis, examining *what is not* serves to reveal an irreducible positivity, an experience, an existence and a subject. This idea is missing when Katz states that 'subjectivity—as a discrete "substance" capable of existing outside of language and *deixis*—is also rejected' (144). The idea of an *existence* requires to be asserted and developed in its *real* consequences. Deconstruction needs to be followed by the analysis of what purpose any illusory construct serves for the subject.

Of course, there is an on-going debate regarding whether Beckett should be classified as 'modern' or 'postmodern', and the predilection of deconstructionists would seem to favour associating him with the latter. Steven Connor describes postmodern works as concerned with 'emergent force rather than completed form, working out

---

25 The term designates what is 'at stake'—what can be lost or gained—in gambling.

rather than completed work' (2005b, 66). Postmodern preoccupations with the limits of language also give rise to 'a chattering polyglossary' (70), and such texts are 'excited by the prospect of the illegitimate, the unspeakable, and the unknowable'.

For the purposes of our analyses, a broader definition of modernism would be more useful, going back to the emergence of the modern subject. The latter can be related to Descartes' *cogito*—minus the telescoping of its two segments, as Lacan has shown—or in the history of perspective painting since Leon Battista Alberti (1404–1472). As Gérard Wajcman (2004) demonstrates, the frame of a painting operates in the manner of the signifier, founding the subject as invisible or excluded from the representation he contemplates: in a word, as endowed with an *unconscious*. In this context, 'modernism'—since the invention of psychoanalysis by Freud—points to the will to reveal the subject as a construct. Such a critical view point was made possible and necessary by the advances of science and capitalism, as can be seen in Lacan's development of the 'four discourses' starting in 1969: the modernist movements of the 20th Century simply pursue and accentuate the same logic. However, the *unlimited*[26] metonymy of a borderless world, with its intrusive networks—governed by the principle of universality—destroys the subject's intimacy and negates his singularity, submitting him, for example, to an almost total surveillance and determination by science (Wajcman, 2010; 2012). Our study shall attempt to show that while Beckett's work deals constantly with an unlimited dimension, the latter is in no way endowed with a value or promoted as a source of pleasure and optimism: it is, on the contrary, eminently opaque and potentially traumatising. His creation therefore deals with this in a 'modernist' fashion, for example, in the very *framed* and concise structures of his late drama—including his recourse to technology—the use of discursive structures based on what Lacan called the 'discourse of the master'.[27] More fundamentally,

26 We shall study this term in a conceptual approach further on. See *infra*, p. 67 *sqq*.

27 See *infra*, p. 321–3.

Beckett's work deals with the subject's absolute singularity involved in Lacan's concept of *jouissance.*

Further Developments Referring to Lacan: A Change of Orientation

Because of the central place given to the radical level of malfunctioning designated by the term *jouissance*, Lacanian psychoanalysis aims go beyond the status of a conceptual corpus. It involves a question of *orientation* that places at the centre of its enquiries the radically dispersing dimension of the *real*, understood as that which negates all conceptualisation. Lacan's concepts are often not taken seriously when, rather than putting them to work to see how a subject deals with the unbearable that founds his existence, they are used as convenient tools. Lacan declared that psychoanalysis originally caused a scandal because it showed sexuality to be 'so "intellectual"' (1966, 523). If that means that it is grounded in an implacable logic, it should be noted that Lacan's thinking progressively undoes the pre-eminence of logic and places it in perspective. And here, one would find Beckett admiring the 'illogisme brûlant' ('burning illogicality', in Juliet, 72) of the mystics, and the flame 'qui consume cette saloperie de logique' ('that consumes this filthy logic'). The two opposing dimensions show how psychoanalytical notions require to be perpetually confronted with the 'burning illogicality' at the heart of existence and, therefore, of creation.

In this respect, it is crucial to counter one inevitable objection: the idea of 'applying' a set of psychoanalytical categories to something as complex as a work of literary creation that, by definition, escapes rigid conceptual bounds. Some will doubtless suspect the trap of seeking to have a work of literature 'confirm' prior theoretical notions. Such a fear has been expressed in another field, for example, by Lance St. John Butler and Robin Davis, seeing Beckett as 'programmed [...] for a Derridian treatment' (in Katz, 4), and deconstructivist *avant la lettre.* These conceptions represent a strange reversal, suggesting that a work of creation might serve to 'prove' a theory. Indeed, and by definition, creation will still question us long after the fads of academia have passed by. It is no chance that psychoanalysis was invented at a time when science was extending its empire, revealing our existence to be determined by universal laws. Indeed, it was to preserve subjective singularity from the crushing effects of universality that Freud centred his findings on speech, since the latter testifies to the way the subject continues to escape such determinisms. For that reason also, no work of creation can be said to be 'more appropriate' than another for psychoanalytical investigation. In order to be effective, and to detach itself from ideological concerns, psychoanalysis is obliged to approach a subject's creation on his own terms, whatever culture or period may be concerned (Mediæval, Renaissance, French classicism, romanticism…). Psychoanalysis deals with what is radically refractory to norms: a position that distinguishes it from therapies, which aim at adaptation, at easing suffering by helping a person to fit into pre-set identifications. The subject is, by definition, what is capable of saying 'no' to what is imposed on him, and by creating his own, singular, response.

Consequently, psychoanalysis does not intervene as a pre-fabricated body of knowledge that could be simply imposed on a text, as a grid of established interpretations. It only has any value if it incites us to listen more closely to the text, to define more precisely what is at stake in the latter's existential dimension. Since, moreover, the theoretical is never dissociated from the clinical with its necessarily unknown dimension, there is not *one* Lacanian reading, but as many (useful or otherwise) as there are readers. And since there is no metalanguage (Lacan, 1966, 813), the latter always speak of themselves as much as they do of Beckett.

The preceding development aimed to show that what is at stake in Beckett's treatment of the voice escapes what can be mastered by concepts: the voice comes to the fore when, in human experience, language fails to signify, to appear 'transparent' as a result of confirmed meanings. This is not a negligible secondary characteristic of language but a central one for Beckett. It shows 'failure' to be at the heart of his experience: a split or a scission whereby language invariably vehicles a resolutely inscrutable dimension. The 'failure' of meaning leads to the dimension of what Lacan associated with the category of the 'impossible', as we shall see in due course.

In the Anglophone realm—and by contrast with the previous critics cited—Slavoj Žižek has opened up a more coherent and enriching approach to Beckett in a Lacanian perspective, precisely as a consequence of his close relation to Lacanian circles in Paris. His short text on *Not I* offers a reading totally opposed to that of Kristeva, since he works from the notion of the absence of the Other, and does not subordinate Beckett to ideological considerations. He points out a useful parallel between Beckett's experience of being impelled to 'go on' and Kant's categorical imperative. The virtue of this is to show up the dimension of the universal and the superego.[28] Going further than previous critics, he draws on the notion of the *drive* manifest in Mouth, who appears as the 'barred subject', devoid of the protective construction of the fundamental fantasy or vision of one's 'self'. The movement of the play shows Mouth—after a first 'epiphany'—as experiencing the fall of the authority of the Other: both Mouth and Auditor embody this 'failure' of meaning. Žižek thus not only introduces the notion of *addressed* speech, but excludes Kristeva's claim that Mouth would somehow be perpetually attached to the dead Father.

The notion of the Other as radically absent is thus crucial to approaching the voice in Beckett's work, in order to avoid enclosing it within fixed confines which ultimately prove to be redundant, because they largely leave aside the problematic nature of creation. However, the majority of critical literature adhering to this orientation is to be found among clinical psychoanalysts whose findings are absent from academic debate. These critics are doubtless ignored also because they deal with concepts that cannot be easily put to use without having committed oneself to a serious study of psychoanalysis.

---

28 In this respect, Daniel Katz (145) points out a difference: contrary to Kant, Beckett encounters the impossibility, the absence of means to go on. Lacan deals with Kant in his text 'Kant avec Sade' (1966, 765–90).

This absence of the great Other—guarantee of a coherent 'world view' or fantasy, of a law governing events and endowing them with stable meanings—is brought into account when Monique Liart studies the function of creation for Beckett, noting that the latter's 'work and life are one' (2012, 181). She associates him with the schizophrenic form of psychosis[29] (181–2), showing his writing to be situated beyond the neurotic fantasy which is bounded and organised by the paternal metaphor: 'on the border of utter destitution' (1999, 29). Indeed, Lacan's earlier work—*Seminar III*—defined psychosis as resulting from the *foreclosure* of the Name-of-the-Father and the absence of a reigning dialectic (Lacan, 1981, 31). On this point, she specifies in Beckett's case the absence of a pathological form, characterised by delirium, which would have marked a radical detachment from the symbolic Other. Here, following Lacan's work on Joyce, Liart points to writing as a substitute (*suppléance*) for the Name-of-the-Father. Writing thus replaces Beckett's psychosomatic problems, which previously acted as a substitute (2012, 182)—but a much less convenient one—since they attached the body to the latter's image as an organic whole. Finally, she considers that the motif of the unborn being, expounded by Jung,[30] gave Beckett 'a sort of rational explanation for his relationship with his mother' (177).

Other psychoanalysts resolutely ground their studies on the Other that, as Michel Bousseyroux states, in relation to *Endgame*, is 'desperately absent' (2000, 177). In this perspective, there can be no question of *desire*, since the latter is necessarily founded on the reassuring existence of the Other. This does not entail contempt for life on the part of Beckett but an extreme attachment to it, because 'what shatters him is precisely life that has gone away, life that is missing, irreparable loss' (Nguyên, 2010b, 112). Such an attachment to life entails dealing with the untameable *real* in language; that means not being

29 Here we can put aside the various identifications with the *neurotic* structures of obsession and hysteria (Kristeva; Bernard, 1992; Sardin, 2009), which suppose the pre-eminence of the Father.

30 See *infra*, p. 75 *sqq*.

simply a 'man of letters' and defined by his position within society but '*being* a poem', which is 'to reduce the religion of desire by greater flexibility regarding the intrusions of the real' (Nguyên, 2010b, 138). This is, of course, contrary to Alain Badiou's insistence on identifying Beckett's will to go 'on' as the supposed expression of 'desire'. Founding his position on the silence of the *drive* (Geneste, 2008, 151)—in the absence of the Other—Beckett manifests lucidity and determination (Nguyên, 2010a, 86), rather than the enthusiasm that colours desire by authorising the multiplicity of ever-renewed meanings.

This absence is linked to a structural *hole* in language which, as Albert Nguyên states, 'confirms the absence of any support to be found by the subject in the Other, in any Other, at the moment when that which of his [fundamental] fantasy has capsized, is almost shipwrecked, that is to say worsens, propelling him toward the worst, that is to say the impossible' (2010b, 123). In these circumstances, language can signal (*faire signe*) without displaying *meaning* (Bousseyroux, 2000, 177). This entire aspect cannot be dealt with by the earlier approaches we examined, since they limit their conception of language to the words written on the page, and that are linguistically addressed to an interlocutor. Thus, as Bousseyroux points out (2000, 193), the appeal to the Other may very well be silent, not just situated within verbal formulations: like the image in *Nacht und Träume*, for example. The fundamental hole—that, as opposed to the *lack*, is not circumscribed—involves a point in language situated beyond meanings, on the verge of *non-sense*, a total absence of meaning. This gives the voice a completely different resonance, more compatible with Beckett's notion of clawing, for example (Beckett, 1998, 11).

The practice of language, as explored by these critics, thus concerns the voice in the function of *phonation*. Indeed, the superego—characterised by its *vociferation*, and which Marie-Hélène Brousse hears in the capricious commands and imprecations of Hamm[31]—presented

31 '[...] what appears in the place of the King [Œdipus] is the Voice, whence the central choice of the actor who plays Hamm and who is only a voice in a body that is being effaced' (Brousse). The actor alluded to here was

the risk of confronting Beckett with the powerlessness to attenuate its effects: '[...] the voice of regulation covering the saying of love, there is nothing left but submission to the negativities of language, without the resulting constitution of a subject, without a fantasy or desire to assuage the pure pain of existing' (Geneste, 2015). However, Lacan's work on Joyce shows how the *jouissance* of language, which undoes meaning (and which he then calls *lalangue*, in one word[32]), is capable of palliating the insatiable superego, transmitting the function of the missing Name-of-the-Father (Lacan, 2005a, 76[33]). In this context, the superego acquires a salutary function, appearing as the agent that commands to 'go on' (Geneste, 2008). Rather than being entirely subordinated to the mortifying effects of such an imperative, Beckett proved capable of producing a salutary *hiatus*, 'an impossible that cannot be obstructed by obeying the superego's petitions' (Geneste, 2015). This function of the hiatus goes far beyond the notions of *lack*, *desire* and Derridian *différance*, since it articulates language and the question of existence: the space where a subject is able to create a vital living-space. Each of these readers thus sees Beckett's work on language—and, consequently, the voice as situated beyond meaning—at the heart of his creation.

Psychoanalysis, Beckett and the Voice: An Outline of Concepts

This study aims to show how Beckett's work as a whole can be read as an expression of various aspects of the voice. To do so, we shall use both Lacan's earlier and later developments. Regarding the voice, two aspects need to be taken into account. Firstly, the voice manifests a certain degree of independence in relation to the purely literary field. As Beckett points out: '[...] quand on s'écoute, ce n'est pas de la littérature qu'on entend' ('[...] when one listens to oneself, it

---

Serge Merlin, whose remarkable voice indeed occupied the entire stage area.

32 See *infra*, p. 99 *sqq*.

33 See also Nguyên (2011, 78).

is not literature one hears', in Juliet, 12). Insofar as he composed his works by actually listening, he found his starting point in a 'non-literary' voice. The attentive listening to raw sounds, as undertaken by Beckett and some of his characters, highlights this aspect of the voice. However, the latter goes beyond the strictly literary domain, notably insofar as language is inherent in all human existence. On the other hand, regarding creation, each manifestation of the voice is conditioned by the frame of a particular work, marked by its literary genre (fiction or drama, and such) and by the aspect of subjective experience that the author chooses to develop or to create through specifically literary means. Synchronic structural features—that, by definition, are irreducible—consequently occupy different positions and functions, for example, in *The Unnamable* and in *Texts for Nothing*. These two exigencies are important in order to avoid annexing literary creation to a field of investigation taken as an *a priori* and imposed in an arbitrary manner.

Psychoanalysis offers us the means to approach the question of the voice, notably enabling us to avoid subjecting our study to the constraints of sociological realism or communicational symmetries.[34] It also allows us to not limit our investigation to phenomenological or realistic manifestations of the voice but, on the contrary, to articulate it to written production, whose complexity we have outlined. Above all, Lacanian psychoanalysis is the only discipline to have defined the voice as a specific *object*, insofar as the latter is determined by the division that founds the subject of the unconscious. This is the aspect that needs to be examined more closely at present, in order to give an overall definition of the *voice*—providing the conceptual tools that will

---

34 Lacan and Beckett have in common the rejection of the ideology of communication. In *Proust*, the latter writes: 'The artistic tendency is not expansive, but a contraction. And art is the apotheosis of solitude. There is no communication because there are no vehicles of communication' (*Pr*, 64). And Lacan asserts: 'Indeed, it is not as all or nothing that something signifies, it is insofar as something that constitutes a whole, the sign, is there precisely to signify nothing. The order of the signifier begins here, insofar as it is distinct from the order of signification' (1981, 213).

serve in the analyses that follow—and its relation to Beckett. Each of the elements we evoke in this brief survey will return in the course of our study.

First of all, psychoanalysis asserts that language pre-exists the subject: the latter finds himself caught up in discourses imposed by his first Others. Language is not a device that the subject can institute by virtue of his own authority, and which he can dispose of at will. Beyond this 'grammar',[35] it is by means of the signifier that 'the unconscious is the discourse of the Other' (Lacan, 1966, 524). That is to say that behind what one consciously intends to say a pattern can be discerned, revealing that the subject's objective utterances often obey quite a different logic that escapes the speaker much in the same way as the characters of a novel are unaware of the structure that presides over their destiny. And since words are predetermined by the infinite resonances imposed by their history, by previous uses, for example, and by their very intimate encounter with the subject, the latter does not master all the consequences of his utterances: something else—called the Other—speaks through the subject. Beckett's work explores this structural truth in various ways, and gives it astounding material consistency, from the narrators of *The Unnamable*, *Texts for Nothing* and *How It Is*—who insist that they are incapable of personal speech, and are therefore constrained to quote (with or without a physical mouth)—through to Winnie's accumulation of clichés. One can also think of the figures of the *dramaticules* who, immobile or pacing back and forth, strain to hear a voice off stage, from which they are apparently excluded, while being subjected to it: for example, the voices using three different tones, in *That Time*. In the same way that the subject does not control the complete scope of his words, the Other that is addressed is not a physical person but an agent inherent in language,

35 Jacques-Alain Miller notes: 'Grammar seals the servitude of language' (1997, 87). The opening up of language to the dimension of the *unlimited* (see *infra*, p. 67 *sqq.*) accomplished by modern linguistics, undoes this servitude.

which is why, in Beckett's work, figures address imaginary 'delegates' (*The Unnamable*) or some invisible agent (*How It Is*).

Language is therefore commanded by its own logic, by its own necessity, to the point of abolishing any division between inside and outside: 'This so-called interior monologue is in perfect continuity with the external dialogue, and it is for this very reason that we can say that the unconscious is also the discourse of the other' (Lacan, 1981, 128). The structure of language does not allow for a break between the idea of an internal realm (strata of the unconscious, the object of 'depth psychology') and the exteriority that makes up the 'world'. The subject is not faced with an environment to which, for example, he would have to 'adapt' himself. Words, actions, ambient structures are an integral part of the subject, who cannot dissociate himself from them. *The Unnamable* provides an impressive demonstration of this interior/exterior continuity: what belongs to pure language is not the expression of a subject who is conscious of himself, it is not the manifestation of an intimacy set apart from the world. If Beckett banishes the representation of 'traversable space' (*TFN* III, 111) considered as the simulacrum of an external reality, it is not with the aim to reveal writing as being purely literary, but to show how the subject intimately grapples with words whose hypothetical 'meaning', which is generally accepted by all, can in no way provide the shelter of an 'objective' reality situated at a comfortable distance. On the contrary, from a topological point of view, we have to admit that the most internal is, precisely, the most external: what Lacan calls, in a portmanteau word, the '*extimate*' ('*extime*', 1986, 167; 2006a, 224). From this point of view, it can only be the object of misunderstanding (*malentendu*).

Consequently, the subject cannot be identified with the ego as conscious author of his saying. The subject remains radically decentred in relation to the language that represents him, according to the Lacanian axiom: '[…] a signifier is what represents the subject for another signifier' (1966, 819). Because of this structuring, a signifier can never exhaustively express the subject's being: a substantial portion will continue to escape naming. The status of truth is thereby relativised: the subject is situated in a place where he does not think, in his absence from himself, as can be seen, for example, in the *act*, which—according to Lacan's conception—goes beyond conscious intentions. Beckett's narrators who cite voices they hear, who use words while denying they understand their meaning—as in *How It Is* and in *The Unnamable*—are perfect examples of this demolition of the Cartesian *cogito*, and which reveals the presence of the voice in enunciation.

What psychoanalysis calls a *signifier* is not to be confused with the use of this term in the field of linguistics: it is not a simple lexeme. Of course, Lacan takes his starting point in Saussure, defining the signifier in terms of its differential nature: 'In the symbolic order, each element derives its value from its opposition to another' (1981, 17). In Beckett, this differential nature of the signifier leads to the point where Malone can assert: 'Everything divides into itself, I suppose' (*MD*, 176). Thus it is that the register of the signified is downgraded to the status of the *imaginary*, the domain where one seeks to establish a stable equivalence between signifier and signified, according to the logic of semantics. As Lacan explains in this colourful definition of the phallus: 'It then becomes the bar which by the hand of this demon strikes the signified, marking it as the bastard progeny of its signifying concatenation' (1966, 692). The signified is labile, never ceasing to slip, whereas the signifier pins down, operating as binding point in the real. Therefore, the conventional pairs signifier/signified, word/thing, are only an illusion, since, in psychoanalysis as in literature, 'there is no metalanguage'[36] (Lacan, 1966, 813, 867; 2001, 412): that is to say, it is impossible to say the truth about truth, to conduct a 'discourse on' something, insofar as all language is affected by *équivoque* or ambiguity, with regards to which it is impossible to prevail oneself of a position of exteriority. As Beckett states it in relation to the painting of Henri Hayden, in the subject/object crisis, 'confondus dans une même in-

36 Concerning this principle, Évelyne Grossman sees a close relationship between Lacan and Beckett, with regards to the indeterminate subject, and the oscillation of the psychoanalyst 'between theory and practice, discourse and method' (Grossman, 2005, 152).

consistance, ils se désistent de concert' ('confounded in the same inconsistency, they desist with one accord', *Dsj*, 146). This occurs because the signifier is grafted onto the real, onto that which exceeds it. More precisely, the signifier *founds the real* as its own exterior. While he turned his back on Joyce's accumulative writing, Beckett worked on language as marked by equivocation. This can be seen in the destruction of meaning, as well as in the innumerable subtle intertextual allusions revealed by historicising readings. For example, such plays on words as found in *Endgame*—*extinguished* referring to Mother Pegg or to her light (*Eg*, 112)—where meaning vacillates, are pushed to their extreme limit in *Worstward Ho*, with oxymorons such as 'Better worst' (*WH*, 98), or in 'None but the one where none' (*WH*, 83), where *one* and *none* appear as not just as contraries, but as two sides of the same Möbian fabric (Brown, 2008, 81–2). Another example would be the palindrome *no/on* studied by Shane Weller[37] (2010, 127). *Équivoque* results from the absence of any external reality accessible by signification: 'Car chaque fois qu'on veut faire faire aux mots un véritable travail de transbordement, chaque fois qu'on veut leur faire exprimer autre chose que des mots, ils s'alignent de façon à s'annuler mutuellement' ('For each time you want to have words do a true work of transferral, each time you want to make them express something other than words, they line up so as to mutually annul themselves', *MP*, 28).

This is where Lacan's 'objet *a*' intervenes: this letter that is devoid of signification, and is identical to itself; an object that is situated at the point of its own exclusion by the signifier. It is here that the subject localises his being, in order to give consistency to the radical absence of the Other. However, starting from the point where this Other exists—ordaining representation and meaning—it can be noted that the subject is instituted by the latter, within a dynamics of anticipation: 'The meaning [*sens*] always goes towards something, towards another signification, towards the closure of the signification, it always

37 Or again the expression *to go on* alternating between the modalities *can* and *shall*, in their use successively in *The Unnamable* and *Company* (Katz, 169).

refers to something which is ahead or which turns back on itself' (Lacan, 1981, 155). It is at the precise place where this closure operates—the final punctuation of a sentence or a narrative—that one finds excluded, as a persistent remainder, the *a* object, which 'is situated at the point where every signifying chain honours itself by closing off its signification' (Lacan, 1966, 818). The *a* object can thus be conceived of as the result of its exclusion by signifying constructions. Such an operation founds a subject's reality as a whole: '[…] the field of reality […] only supports itself by the extraction of the *a* object which however gives it its frame' (Lacan, 1966, 554). Understood in this perspective, the object points to a point of exception—or, in anthropological terms, the sacrificial victim or scapegoat founding the community—that ensures the consistency of the Whole that is reality, or a subject's 'fundamental fantasy': it thus 'confirms the rule'.

Paradoxically however—and in a reversal of the preceding perspective—the *a* object also appears to undo any signifying construction, since it inscribes a point of non-sense that escapes nomination, and that Beckett's writing makes palpable when *équivoque* breaks up the structuring chain of the 'well-built phrase' (*Mo*, 27); when the narrator experiences an endless voice that refuses to be contained by the closure of a sentence that could give it meaning (*TFN* VII, 131); or in the consequent fact that the Beckettian voice rehearses without ceasing, not only in *The Unnamable*, but also in the repetitions suggested by *Play*, for example. This paradox can be visualised by situating the *a* object at the intersection between two opposing dimensions:

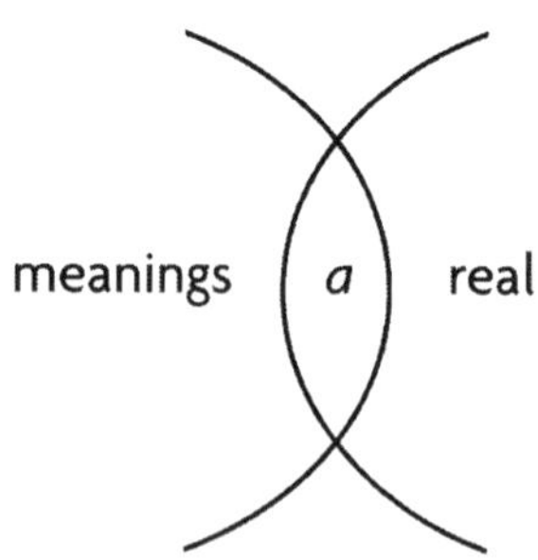

On the nether side, the object opens up to the *real*: it serves the incessant, indomitable and radically inhuman *drive*. The latter takes on form by accomplishing a circular movement, making a detour via the partial object—breast, faeces, gaze, voice—that also localises its action. These '*a* objects' give consistency to the 'erogenous zones', and are qualified as being 'metonymical' insofar as their physical identity is secondary. Lacan speaks of 'this object, which is in fact only the presence of a hollow, a void that is occupyable, as Freud tells us, by any object, and of which we only know the instance in the form of the lost *a* object' (1973, 164). For example, the *drive* can be satisfied indifferently by eating, by conflict, by creation... The subject can grasp his existence in its oscillating movement between complementary functions, such as the inspiration and expiration that open and close *Breath*, separated only by the vision of detritus, which reveals existence as reduced to the status of the *a* object. The extremities of the digestive tract could also be mentioned: 'What matters is to eat and excrete. Dish and pot, dish and pot, these are the poles' (*MD*, 179). Other orifices—such as the eyes and the mouth—can prove to be equivalent: '[...] the sentences, the syllables, the tears, I confuse them, words and tears, my words are my tears, my eyes my mouth' (*TFN* VIII, 131). In *Footfalls*, May nourishes herself not with food but with the story she invents (Asmus), while the narrator of *Ill Seen Ill Said* speaks of 'devouring' the vision of the sky and the earth (*IS*, 78).

Thus, as a localised but basically indifferent entity, the object testifies to what the subject can never assimilate, or what represents his negation: the part of the drive that remains radically impossible for the subject to assume, and which remains definitively assigned to the Other. If Hamm remains immobile, keeping Clov attached to him, and if no decisive action takes place in *Endgame*, nonetheless, Clov observes: 'Something is taking its course'[38] (*Eg*, 98). The indefinite 'something' cannot be reduced to the simple and objective flow of time, nor

38 This phrase, repeated in the play, was adapted as the title of a work by Edmond Jabès—*Ça suit son cours* (Montpellier: Fata Morgana, 1975)—

will its 'nature' be elucidated. It will still move on as implacably as the force that absorbs Winnie into her mound in *Happy Days*. If according to Clov, regarding the objects that clutter up our lives, there is 'no more' (Winnie only has a set number of them in her bag), there is—'still stirring'—this persisting existence of the drive. As for Mouth, the latter causes the total abolition of her bodily consistency.

Thus, more than a simple lack, language suffers from a gaping hole, from a radical failure that founds 'the absolutely heterogeneous' (Milner, 2007, 25), as Jean-Claude Milner points out: 'No signifier is apt to grasp it, since it is foreign to any chain: in other words, the signifier that would suffice is the very one that, for structural reasons, is lacking.' This gaping hole belongs to the real, if we understand the latter as being 'the domain of what subsists outside of symbolisation' (Lacan, 1966, 388). In this case, far from pacifying, language in its entirety places the subject in the presence of this hole that can never be filled. Language borders on this space, where the subject is equivalent to 'l'incommensurabilité de la diagonale de carré avec le côté, sujet sans nombre et sans personne' ('the incommensurability of the diagonal of the square with the side, a subject without number and without a person', *Dsj*, 56). As the narrator of *How It Is* states: 'infinitum alone commensurate with us' (*HI*, 120).

This point is tightly bound up with writing and creation, insofar as, according to Lacan: 'All art is characterised by a certain mode of organisation around this void'[39] (1986, 155). Such an organisation is given a visual form in the 'E supposed a danger zone' (*Q*, 453) of *Quad*: the point where the dancers, executing their series of permutations following a quincunx form, must dodge the central point, in order not to collide with each other. The dancers' movement gives consistency to this location: topologically, it both opens up to and encloses the invisible that surrounds the representation (Brown, 2011d, 128). More generally, the scenic space of Beckett's plays creates the

---

who however dialogues with Blanchot, Lévinas and Derrida, rather than with Beckett.

39 *Cf.* Regnault, 1997, 9–32.

void surrounding it; the narration of *The Unnamable* causes to *resound* the absence of any Other beyond all the ephemeral 'delegates' that appear. Creation is, as the word indicates, something absolutely new, that emerges *ex nihilo* and that is in no way provided for by any supreme 'Creator'. As an object therefore, writing marks the location of this void, which cannot be absorbed by language and speech. If the *a* object is waste that falls off as a result of the operation of signifying, *writing* is the inscription of *jouissance* in the body or on the page. Jean-Claude Milner demonstrates that if, of the real, 'no property precedes it, but moreover, no property follows from it' (2007, 24)—it cannot be caught up in any chain of signifiers—then 'of the Real, nothing is written'. That is to say that the real cannot be recognised as resulting from given circumstances or producing them, since such a construction would suppose its subservience to convenient binary distributions, for example the one separating the *same* from the *other*, with their attendant discernable properties. However, writing marks the *edge*: where the limit is inscribed, eroded, by the unlimited, the latter being understood as where: 'Nothing or no one exists with regards to which the function ceases to make sense' (Milner, 2003, 23).

Structure of Our Study

The points outlined here now require to be studied one by one, in connection with the voice as an object. In our first chapter, we shall seek to establish the terrain of our research by defining the voice: exploring its structure and its characteristics, as we encounter them in Beckett's work. The voice will be heard as a result of the *division* produced in the subject through his representation by the signifier. Here, not only is naming imposed by pre-constructed language—the 'Other'—but the subject has to deal with a fundamental lack of a signifier to name his being, with an absence of meaning. This lack is produced when, in reversing the imposition of language, the subject silences the Other by *addressing* him. Although this structuring means that the subject may encounter the intimate and sometimes traumatic aspect of the voice, the latter's uncontrollable manifestations often remain limited by means of the 'paternal' function, which unifies reality. We shall then suggest that Beckett's work involves a much vaster dimension since, when the 'Name-of-the-Father' is excluded, the subject can find himself exposed to a hallucinatory and persecuting voice.

At this stage, it will be necessary to reverse the initial perspective, so the analysis will not be limited to this negative slant, determined by its reference to 'normality'. It will therefore be important to consider the fundamentally 'unstillable'[40] nature of the Beckettian voice, resulting from the dimension of the unlimited, which ignores unity: the confrontation with a fundamental hole in language.

This structural foundation to our study will make it possible to associate the part of language that cannot be included in representation, with the Beckettian 'unborn' being: a motif that traverses his work, and which can also be studied in relation to the problematics of testimony, as defined by Giorgio Agamben. The 'unborn' being will then be seen as connected to an impassive maternal figure incapable of inscribing the subject in relation to linguistic semblances. The Beckettian subject thus finds himself devoid of any symbolic Other capable of responding and enclosing the subject's existence within the bounds of dialogue form or a dialectic. As a result of its very structure, such a voice cannot be situated within geometrical space: it comes both from within and from without, revealing its very material quality. The voice therefore remains *real*, since the symbolic structure of language cannot always attenuate its dissociation from the register of meaning, and its possibly brutal impact. Linguistic articulation is prone to breaking down, revealing the radically differential nature of the signifier, expressed by Beckett in vocables such as *perhaps* and *neither*.

In our second chapter, this impossibility of unified naming is explored in relation to the use of pronouns, particularly in the consistently problematic nature of the first person *I*, ordinarily identified with the subject of enunciation, but often replaced in Beckett's work by the

40 A term used by Beckett in his *Production Notebook* of *Eh Joe* (in Ackerley and Gontarski, 162).

third person. Here, pronouns appear not to be unified within a form of grammatical whole where each one completes the other and so combine to form a believable reality, but as irremediably distinct, disjointed, leaving an unbridgeable gap wherein lies the unnameable subject. Not only does the first person *I* fail to institute the subject as the conscious agent of his own speech and acts, it also appears, structurally, as a secondary stage, following an inaugural *you*, which crushes any singularity. *Not I* offers a striking example of the voice as *real*: Mouth appears as inhabited by the acephalous *drive* depriving her of the bodily consistency that one usually grasps in the image of one's body as a whole. The reality of this traumatic effect can be experienced by the actress charged with embodying the role. Since the 'Auditor' on stage is not the object of address, both figures are powerless to institute a form of verbal exchange. Although Auditor appears as the possibility for Mouth to accede to an *I*, he remains associated with the imperative force of the superego, insofar as Mouth's existence lies exposed to the gaping hole of language. Thus the true expression of her being is to be found in her violent ejaculation: 'she!…'.

While *Not I* bases its construction solely on the third person, *Company*, influenced by Beckett's work with radio, unfolds the attempt to bind the *you* and the *he* within the dialectics of an exchange, to produce an *I*. The pronoun *you* is heard—without being addressed—by the 'unborn' subject of this text, in order to make the latter assume the personal history related. A ratiocinating voice, a prey to doubt, is referred to as *he*: this entity is devoid of any concrete existence as a person, having no anchoring point in a subject, such as the one provided by *deixis*. The use of the third person produces a form of multiple and endless inclusion in the figure of the 'Devised devisor'. This construction can be conceived positively as producing a voice that provides 'company', in the absence of any dialogical structure. In *A Piece of Monologue*, *he* represents the Speaker who apparently speaks of himself in the third person. And yet, in the absence of linguistic binding or articulation to unite the two, the identification remains impossible. The action described in the play allows the speaker to be 'born' each night as a spectral being: it can be understood as a ritual addressed to an absent Other, in order to acquire, in return, a tangible existence. In these problematic elaborations structured by pronouns, the *voice* can be heard at the intersection of these agents: it is what supports them, and constitutes their driving force in a work of creation, understood as enunciation.

The third chapter is concerned with topological figures of the voice. First of all, the subject experiences his exposure to unstoppable voices, appearing as a 'fundamental sound' that is impossible to eliminate since it is inherent in existence itself. The voice assumes the form of a continuum that appears to be unbreachable by any subjective enunciation. It also manifests itself in the persistence of 'dead voices'—particularly present in the earlier works—that express a state of mortification and exile from any desire. The subject thus risks experiencing a state of being one of the 'living dead', without even the minimal support afforded by anxiety.

In this topology, the subject nonetheless succeeds in creating a breach by means of *invocation*, by addressing the Other. This is how Beckett creates a 'stain' on silence, piercing the ferocious voice of the superego, which appears both as vociferation, or opaque silence, and which demands the subject's elimination. In *Eh Joe*, however, the male figure encounters persecuting 'dead voices', precisely because he is powerless to assume any enunciation. This is correlated with his formerly narcissistic position, and imagined mastery of language. His efforts to stifle the voices into silence simply testify to his powerlessness to impose his own voice. Paradoxically, the voice torments him, but he remains dependent on it to relive his love, and to thereby derive a semblance of existence.

In a marked contrast with the continuous aspect of the voice, *interruption* is a fundamental characteristic of Beckett's writing, which can be considered, along with continuity, as the apparent faces of a single Möbius strip. The interrupted, fragmentary nature of utterances reveals the subject's powerlessness to find a place within discourse where phrases are linked and articulated together. The breaks intervene both as opaque obstacles and an uncontrollable force, where the subject encounters the incommensurable abyss within language. The motifs of bells or 'knocks' mark the breaks, and are destined to be heard by the Other, as well as by the subject, in order for the latter to experience some consistency.

In the interruptions can be discerned the imperative voice of the *superego*, impelling the subject to go 'on' at a point of impossibility. Here, the subject encounters a dimension beyond any law: a *real* governed by wild caprice that threatens to overthrow any form of regularity. The subject responds to the intrusion of the voice by efforts to achieve a physical inscription, in the body, that will impose limits on it. In *Footfalls*, the apparently minimal motif of the pacing constitutes the essential anchoring point of the play, offering a means to impose a limit on the void. At the same time, it enters into a form of counterpoint with the lyrical expansion of the text.

Two responses to the violence of the voice are examined in the following parts of this chapter. The first one is 'doing the image', as is expressed in the short text 'The Image'. This production enables the subject to engender some form of Other, to raise a reliable barrier to silence the invasive voice. The example of *Rough for Radio II* reveals the verbal image of an 'unborn' brother, which arises as a totally detached motif that cannot be rationalised, and that comes in lieu of an impossible naming. A second response to the voice is the adoption of a 'reading voice'. Here, the subject attempts to endow himself with an Other by playing both sides of a fabricated dialogue for want of having been instituted in relation to such an agent on the symbolic level. The 'reading voice' provides an appearance of regularity and solidity: a substitute Other.

Finally, our fourth chapter is devoted to the voice in its exteriority, as exemplified by the recorded voice and the incidence of technology. Language appears as what Lacan called an intrusive 'parasite', creating disorder at the heart of the speaking being. The objects produced by science and technology give a remarkable extension to this subjective or linguistic experience. In *Krapp's Last Tape*, the tape-recorder serves to produce the character's voice as an object. In denigrating his own recorded voice, Krapp relays the scornful judgement originating in his superego: the recording produces his imbecile self that is incapable of equalling his ideal. Considered as a whole, Krapp's annual 'ritual' is offered up to the Other, as a desperate defence against imminent death.

The encounter with radio shows how technology has a real impact on the form of the voice by completely detaching it from the body and making it transmissible, abolishing the usual hierarchies of time and space. It destroys the imaginary association of the voice with the embodied image of the 'person' who is considered to be its source. Situated outside of the body in the radio set, the voice functions as a 'need' or an organ, for the auditor. The latter may then appear as playing the role of 'sound editor', passing between two irreconcilable polarities: from one voice to another, from 'words' to 'music'. Here, instead of creating or producing, the subject plays a crucial structuring role. In *Play*, this function is assumed by the spotlight, which appears to be tyrannical but which, in the absence of any dialogue, is as dependent on the overall setup as are the figures in the urns, in its quest for truth. The 'voice of Bam' is 'editor' in *What Where.* The permutation of the other spectral figures reveals the subject as equivalent to a gaping hole. In *Cascando*, Opener is editor and, as they have their own distinct reality, the voices provide 'company'. Opener's secret fear is that they might completely fade away. In *Words and Music*, the paired elements underscore an absence of resolution, of any constitutive unity.

Finally, forms of 'apparatuses' the subject uses to contain the voices are examined. Ostensibly revealing their geometrical and artificial nature, these structures resemble Lacan's 'four discourses', composed of the functions—four terms arranged in a square pattern—that allow for the production of speech and creation. They give form to what Beckett called the 'mess', by partially circumscribing it. These forms can be observed from *Murphy* (in the MMM) through to *What Where.* Along with the roles of 'witness' and 'scribe', it is important to discern the crucial causal function assumed by the invisible 'master': Youdi (in *Molloy*) or the unnamed committee in *Rough for Radio II.* These structures also reveal a point where the voice appears as torture: where language marks its physical hold on the body. This expresses the function of the superego, considered as an emanation of the universalising aspect of language that can, when pushed to extremes, lead to a subject's abolition. And yet, as in *How It Is*, torture can be seen as a way to inscribe the voice, so the subject feels endowed with his own bodily consistency. In *Rough for Radio II*, the discursive apparatus acts as a substitute form, in the absence of the corresponding subjective structure. As an artifice, it shows itself to be flawed, marked by splits that hinder its efficient functioning. In *What Where*, the response sought repeatedly borders on an impossible, and the torments suggested by the text do not succeed in abolishing the subject's resistance. In their formal quality, these 'discursive apparatuses' would seem to represent a counterpart to the disjointed arrangement of pronouns.

I — The Voice and Its Structure

Initial Concepts

Faced with the multiple facets of the voice—and their apparently mutually exclusive nature—a logical approach allows us to grasp the latter as a phenomenon marked by a scission that is at the basis of enunciation. Of course, Winnie expresses a naïve conception of the voice, which she sees as the direct emanation of a living being when she declares: '[…] song must come from the heart, that is what I always say, pour out from the inmost, like a thrush' (*HD*, 155). Song—an idealised version of the voice—appears here as a univocal outpouring, unmarred by the presence of an auditor that it would be necessary to influence or seduce.

In order to set a solid conceptual basis for our approach to Beckett's voices, we shall start by studying the latter's structuring with regards to language. This opening part of our chapter will involve the exploration of essential theoretical considerations, which will be covered in a progressive manner. Firstly, the distinction between *utterance* and *enunciation*—that is a consequence of the subject being represented by language—will show the voice as a remainder that escapes tight structuring within names and meaning. Despite this breach, an overall unity of representation is still possible here, owing to the effective presence of a dialectical mechanism. We shall then see, however, that Beckett's voices resist any enclosure, a fact that will require us to consider the *unlimited* quality thus introduced, firstly in negative terms (as an absence of unity), then in positive ones (as a boundless dimension). Having laid this theoretical foundation, it will be possible to examine the experience of the Beckettian subject as 'unborn', faced with an absent Other, and in the presence of voices considered as touching on the 'real'. The conclusion will show how this aspect of the voice makes the latter impossible to locate, and endows it with its irreducible subjective reality.

Since a number of specialised psychoanalytical terms will be referred to and explored in the course of this chapter, it will be useful to undertake an initial clarification of concepts that are of more general import. The first of these terms—the symbolic, the Name-of-the-Father, the phallus—are associated with the constitution of an ordered system but, as will be seen, the dimension of the *real* proves to be the definitive obstacle: it is the dimension that orients Lacan's elaboration in its ultimate consequences. What is called the *symbolic* can be understood—following the discoveries of Ferdinand de Saussure—as referring to the inherently *differential* nature of the signifiers that represent the subject. That is to say, a signifier only names and conveys meaning by virtue of the oppositions that determine it in relation to other signifiers, not by any 'natural' link to external reality. To this well-established notion, Lacan adds that a 'signifier is what represents a subject for another signifier' (1966, 819). The subject is thus identified in relation to the Other, whose role is to ensure the validity of this naming.

It is necessary, however, to note an evolution in the use of the term *symbolic* since, in the initial stages of Lacan's thinking, this word points to an orderly system, where positive and negative mutually reinforce each other. As a result, for example, Lacan declares: 'In the symbolic order, the empty spaces are as significant as the full ones [...]' (1966, 392). Within representation, gaps or differences, the said and the unsaid, provide an indispensable effect of scansion, rendering a sentence legible. In this context, the symbolic is understood as being governed by a dialectical logic, compatible with coherent linguistic articulation. This order will however be called into question when the symbolic is understood as being anchored in the *real*, that is to say, a dimension that ultimately escapes all order, all linguistic concatenation.

As long as an orderly construction reigns in Lacan's theory, what is called the *Name-of-the-Father* presides over the symbolic register. The 'father' here is not the biographical person, but the function he represents in language. He intervenes as the agent who separates the child from the mother, through what is generally known as the Œdipal interdiction of incest. That is to say that the child is no longer left exposed to the mother's caprice, since he sees that only the father is capable of satisfying her: the presence of the father diverts the mother's exclusive investment in her child. The term *metaphor*, in this context, indicates the fact that the father intervenes as a symbol that offers a substitute for the mother's desire (Lacan, 1994, 13). The Name-of-the-Father—with its eminently religious overtones—'has the function of signifying the whole of the signifying system, of authorising it to exist, to make of it the law' (Lacan, 1998, 240). Once again, this power to govern an orderly system of representation will be put to the test by Lacan's later elaborations. It can be noted, at this point, that the presence of the Beckettian father is singularly evanescent. The flight of the Beckettian character when confronted with childbirth illustrates the problematic nature of this function[1] (*FL*, 45; *Co*, 7–8).

Indeed, by virtue of the signifier's retroactive mechanism, childbirth instates the subject as a father in turn. The child is not simply an imaginary rival with regards to the mother but, as a result of his presence, the subject is called upon to be the donator of the name, and obliged to respond to the enigmatic desire of the Other. The child thus embodies the subject's own unspeakable singularity. However, for want of an effective inscription in relation to the Name-of-the-Father, the subject will be forcibly confronted with the gaping hole of his being: he will have no means to experience the legitimacy of his own paternal function, or endow his child with the habiliment of a promising future. Thus, examining the end of *First Love* in the light of Otto Rank's theories, Paul Stewart points to the irremediable rupture that appears for the protagonist, who is 'expelled into the world once again [...] as if the hope of a return to the womb had been shattered by the emergence of new life into the light' (2011, 112). This is also why the child embodies the continuation of suffering (113, 128), which some characters would prefer to avoid, an attitude reflected in what Paul Stewart terms Beckett's 'misopedia' (120–34), and in the

1 See also Weller, 2009, 42–3. On the father's nonetheless salutary function, see Geneste, 2008, 153.

eminently problematic question of producing further generations. The torment occasioned by this experience is poignantly expressed by the child's cries that resound at the end of *First Love.*

The third term in this triptych of agents guaranteeing stable representation is what psychoanalysis calls the '*phallus*': this is not the bodily organ but, following its use in Greek comedy for example, it is the detached symbol, in other words, what can go missing. That is to say, it constantly designates its reverse side as *lack* (called 'castration'). It certainly represents the norm which, in its linguistic usage, can be defined as 'the signifier destined to signify as a whole the effects of the signified' (Lacan, 1966, 690). Comparable to the conventional motif of the cornucopia, it is distinct from the Name-of-the-Father in that it presents an abundance of *meanings*, behind which it usually remains 'veiled' (692). Lacan points out that while the name 'calls [one] to speak', 'the privilege of the phallus is that one can call on it desperately, it will still say nothing' (2007, 172). For the purposes of comedy however, it no longer remains silent and veiled, but is revealed as pure artifice, being condemned to repeated and derisive failures. It is also exemplified in a modern literary work: *Le Balcon* (1955–56), by Jean Genet.[2] In this play, the clients of the brothel, where the action takes place, admire themselves, draped in phallic insignia such as the clothes of a bishop, a judge or a general. As for the head of police, he entertains the idea of appearing as a phallus—of the same stature as himself—in order to publicly represent the image of his power. In Beckett's work, the phallus also is of doubtful efficiency since, in order for the sexual act to be accomplished, the male partner has to believe in his own virility. As is well known, the narrators of *First Love* (*FL*, 42), *Molloy* (*Mo*, 51–2) and Macmann in *Malone Dies* (*MD*, 253) have the most extreme difficulty aligning their basically inert organs with the demands of this function. Beckett also expressed his feeling of inadequacy in relation to the phallus when he wrote to MacGreevy: 'All the

2 Lacan approaches this play in terms of the structure of perversion (1998, 263–8).

on & up is so tiresome also, the determined optimism à la Beethoven [...]' (7 August 1936; *L1*, 368, n. 8).

What undoes these agents that reputedly give grounding to a coherent world, or an orderly whole called *reality*, is the *real*: reality finds its roots in this dimension which constitutes its negation, since it escapes naming. The real is 'what subsists outside of symbolisation' (Lacan, 1966, 388). Once again, a distinction is required here. In his earlier works, Lacan saw the real as supporting the existence of the symbolic register. That means that in a differential system, any assertion owes its meaning to the corresponding negation: to say what something *is,* is to simultaneously say what it *is not*. The 'real' thus appears as an integral part of the signifying structure of language, even if it resists the latter: it can still be relied on since, for example, it 'always returns at the same place' (Lacan, 1973, 49). To paraphrase Einstein's phrase: like God, the real 'does not play dice'. However in Lacan's later elaborations, the real comes to be seen as what is detached from all possible naming or linguistic articulation; it obeys no law of regularity. Lacan says: it is 'always a piece, a stub' (2005a, 123) and 'is not linked to anything' but, rather, touches on a gaping hole in language. Henceforth radically detached from any notion of unity, it becomes multiple, so that psychoanalysts speak today of *a real*, with the indefinite article. For that reason, it involves the most elusive and profoundly problematic part of existence. At this stage of our study, another technical term will be explored: *lalangue*, a vocable in which the definite article and the noun (*la langue*: 'language') are telescoped together, pointing to the part of language that remains impregnated with *jouissance*, and refractory to any linguistic articulation and meaning.

Voice and Retroaction of the Signifier

To address the question of the voice as enunciation, it can first be noted that the complexity of the voice is due to the fact that, since it results from the structure of language, it testifies to the effect of a topological torsion that relativises the register of signification.

Speech follows a double movement: whereas discourse follows a *diachronic* progression, meaning results from a movement of *anticipation*, whereby the subject addresses the Other. Speech aims to reach this Other who, by setting a point of closure or punctuation—what Lacan calls a '*point de capiton*' (a 'quilting' or 'anchoring point', 1998, 196)—returns the utterance back to the subject in the form of a 'reversed message'. This is an everyday experience: when speaking (even to oneself), we hear our words in the way we think the interlocutor may receive them. The narrator of *Texts for Nothing* recognises that 'it's the end gives meaning to words' (*TFN* VIII, 131): the conclusion to a sentence or a story determines the signification of the whole. In this way, the signifier testifies to the effect of *retroaction*. Thus it is, for example, that a child's cry has no signification before someone comes to lend it the intentionality of a *call* (Vives, 2012, 39); since at the beginning, one only finds 'the subject of *jouissance*'[3] (Lacan, 2004, 203), devoid of any tangible existence. The Other, here, institutes the signification by 'acknowledging receipt' of the message, as Lacan specifies (1981, 213). This response institutes the *symbolic* dimension of language.

To define more precisely the subject's position in language with relation to his Other, it is necessary to move one step further. Indeed, this relationship does not remain at the level where an all-powerful Other determines what is henceforth understood as the subject's demands. It soon appears that the Other does not know everything; that language suffers from a fundamental lack. From this point, the subject is constituted by his *address* that aims beyond the linguistic code. The subject both uses the 'treasury of signifiers' (Lacan, 1966, 806) instituted by the Other, but he also *divides* the latter, since the act of addressing reveals a field where the Other is incapable of providing an answer, and is thus reduced to silence. It is here that the subject's message comes back to him not as an answer, but as the question '*che*

3 For Lacan's successive definitions of this term, see *supra*, p. 28–30.

vuoi?[4] (what do you want) concerning his desire. Consequently, a crucial dimension remains without any possible answer. Jean-Michel Vives analyses this mechanism, emphasising that 'the field of sound is itself organised around a deaf spot' (2012, 37). The repression that produces this point of deafness is precisely what enables the subject's voice to not be 'totally drowned by that of the Other' (36). Having first been exposed to the voice of the Other, the subject has to extract himself in a contradictory movement since, 'after having resonated to the tone of the Other, the future subject both assumes it and rejects it' (39). This truly founding act is realised in the *address* by which the subject 'seeks out the ear of the Other to obtain a response. [...] the subject institutes an Other who is not deaf and is capable of hearing him.' In this way, the *invocating subject*, instead of remaining dependent on the Other, appears as the product of a *separation* (Vives, 2015).

It is crucial to note that this operation necessarily includes a certain failure: at the very point of closure operated by the response, can be found, on its external side, the *a* object that 'is situated at the point where every signifying chain honours itself by closing off its signification' (Lacan, 1966, 818). The voice thus appears as a *remainder* which never ceases to return within the enunciation, constituting its substratum: it marks an anchoring point that can never be assimilated. In his analysis of its use in cinema, Michel Chion thus describes the voice as a subversion of the 'umbilical' closure that marks the separation with the mother (61–2). As a consequence, any *said* contains its share of *unsaid*, any *saying* will seek to reach what can only be contained within an utterance, any poetic construction will seek to reintegrate the part beyond meaning that may be heard in rhythm and sounds. The *voice* signals that the signifier/signified couple—instituted by the mechanics of communication—is insufficient to account for the subject in his articulation with language.

4 Lacan borrows this formulation from Jacques Cazotte, *Le Diable amoureux* (1772).

The 'Buffering' Effect of the Paternal Metaphor

In order to define more precisely the status of the Beckettian voice, it is necessary to clarify the register that this operation opens up for the subject. At the beginning, the intervention of the signifier produces a radical split. On this point, Lacan asserts that if the subject 'appears on one side as meaning [*sens*], produced by the signifier, on the other, he appears as *aphanisis*'[5] (1973, 191). This alternative integrates a '*lethal factor*' (193) that can be ascertained in the expression 'liberty or death', where choosing *liberty* fatally imposes, at the same time, the second member of the alternative. This stage constitutes what can be called a 'primary negativising' (Rey-Flaud, 19) or extraction of *jouissance.*

However, the process requires to be repeated in order to evacuate this alienation, so that the subject is no longer entirely exposed to the threat of his annihilation, the latter henceforth being taken charge of by the Other. *Aphanisis*, or the radical 'fading' of the subject is lodged with the Other and, at the same time, the *libido* is embodied and localised in the lost *a* object. Thus the paternal metaphor is produced, which 'substitutes [the Name-of-the-Father] at the place initially symbolised by the operation of the absence of the mother' (Lacan, 1966, 557). The signifier introduced by the maternal Other becomes the enigmatic *x* of its desire, repressed and replaced by this new signifier that causes an effect of *separation.*

The subject is thus endowed with a unified representation so that, instead of feeling the exorbitant weight of his singularity, he can now count himself as *one* among those of his kind: of his 'species' (*W*, 85) or 'kith' (*Dsj*, 149), as Beckett would say. The Other becomes the guardian of the unbearable in existence, offering a barrier against the sudden appearance of the unnameable: the 'Name-of-the-Father' evacuates the threatening, persecuting *voice*, relegating it to an *outside* that no longer threatens to invade the subject. In its stead, a dialectic

---

5 The term *aphanisis* is derived from the works of Ernest Jones.

allows the latter to negotiate the unimaginable, to relativise it, to set it into perspective.

The subject henceforth has a buffer—diversely called 'fundamental fantasy', 'reality', *Weltanschauung*—against the unbearable, which the naked signifier threatens to confront him with. His existence can be integrated without too much difficulty within an overall reality that appears acceptable for all. In his works of the 1940s and 1950s, Beckett often describes this dimension as the space his characters are excluded from. It is what he calls, on various occasions: 'traversable space' (*TFN* III, 111), the 'outer world' (*MD*, 215, 230), the 'big world' (*Mu*, 6), 'life above in the light' (*HI*, 127). The existence of this space allows the subject to ignore the structuring framework that gives consistency to his 'world':[6] the stability of the latter remains guaranteed by a reliable Other, so that any unforeseen event rapidly finds its place within an overall order. Thus, the *chattering of the signifier* covers up the *unbearable nature of the voice*: the vociferation or the inexhaustible 'rustling' which originally characterises it.

'Foreclosure' of the Paternal Metaphor

If the *voice* appears as the part that is excluded from the representation of the world as a coherent whole, it also supports the latter, in the same way as it can be said that 'the exception *founds* the rule'. However, it is now necessary to analyse the specific manner in which Beckett's work resolutely turns its back on chattering, on the metonymy of discourse nourished by meaning.

Indeed, in cases where the *separation*, or second extraction of *jouissance*, has not taken place, the subject can find himself incapable of facing what he encounters, unable to respond to an unbearable imperative that can, sometimes, cause his world to collapse. Such, for example, was the situation that caused the delirium of President Schreber,

6 For a detailed study of this question of the way reality has been considered as a tableau ever since Leon Battista Alberti, see Wajcman (2004, *passim*).

as studied by Freud, when he was unexpectedly called to a position of great responsibility (Lacan, 1981, 124–5). Another example: Janet Frame, whose crises were initiated by a teaching inspection (*An Angel at my Table*, 1984). In both cases, the subject found himself in a position of having to respond to a call that revealed his very real destitution, the fundamental nothingness of his being. It is a matter of 'a certain call to which the subject cannot respond' (Lacan, 1981, 289). At this moment, as Alain Vaissermann explains, the subject 'feels himself singled out, aimed at, in this point, which poses an insoluble enigma for him' (4–6).

In these cases, it is no longer a matter of the *repression* that founds the symbolic register, but of a rejection that Lacan defines in the form of an axiom: '[…] everything that is refused in the symbolic order, in the sense of *Verwerfung*, reappears in the real' (1981, 21). Contrary to what happens in repression, what returns at this point 'reappears in another place, *in altero*' (120), coming from without, in its brute force, so that the subject has no means at his disposal to deal with it. It is no longer the signified but the *signifier* that conveys this unbearable effect, pointing to 'the limit where discourse' (157) leads to 'something beyond meaning', that is to say to 'something of the signifier in the real'.

Thus it is that President Schreber—whose case Lacan studied in his Seminar *Les Psychoses*, of 1955–1956—experienced 'a radical submersion of all his categories' (1981, 99). Such an experience can lead to a generalised contamination of one's existence, to the point of 'threatening the whole edifice'. A distinct echo of this experience can be heard in the sentence of *Malone Dies*: 'I know those little phrases that seem so innocuous and, once you let them in, pollute the whole of speech. *Nothing is more real than nothing.* They rise up out of the pit and know no rest until they drag you down into its dark' (*MD*, 186–7). The damage that a single phrase can lead to is not limited to an isolated and manageable zone, but can extend to a subject's entire existence, for want of a function capable of serving as a barrier. Arthur Rose brings up a crucial distinction here, pointing out that 'Schreber's instability […] is mimicked in *The Unnamable*', and that there is no equivalence between the two: 'Schreber's hallucinations come from an unstable vision of the world as such, while the narrator's hallucinations come from its efforts to stabilise the free reign of textual possibility [...]' (221). This is precisely what separates a clinical document from a work of creation: we shall return to this dimension in order to develop it further.

The Model of the 'Pastout' or the 'Unlimited'

Even if one encounters expressions evoking a 'lack', a flaw, experienced by the Beckettian subject, it is important to nuance this model. Indeed, the first teachings of Lacan—where he develops the concept of 'foreclosure' of the Name-of-the-Father—tend to approach the question of psychosis in the perspective of a deficiency: according to this perception, the psychotic is someone who does not have access to Œdipal structuring and the norm it institutes. However, Lacan's later work reverses these presuppositions, allowing us to conceive this experience differently, somewhat in the way the theory of relativity situates Newtonian physics in another framework, without disqualifying it.

Lacan centres his later theoretical elaborations on the question of *jouissance* ('enjoyment', is a pallid literal translation) rather than desire. If this term has no single definition,[7] our earlier development on the question can be summarised by noting that it expresses the fact that the subject's relationship to language goes beyond any metonymical 'pleasure principle' (supposing minimal tension). Vitally anchored in the body, it entails displeasure (maximal tension) and marks the breakdown of any signifying. The novels of Sade are a prime example: they show how what at first appears as pleasure progresses to a breaking point where it turns into horror, revealing the unspeakable dimension that structurally supports it. As it is an equivocal term, *jouissance* designates the way—specific to each person—a subject deals with the

7 Jacques-Alain Miller (1999) develops six paradigms of the term in Lacan's theory. See our more detailed development *supra*, p. 28–30.

impossibility for language to name his existence. What is particularly important is Lacan's work on feminine *jouissance*—in books XIX (*...ou pire...*) and XX (*Encore*) of his Seminar—which sheds light on a part that remains resistant to the Law of the Father and the phallus (Miller, 2010–11), and that concerns not only the psychotic but, fundamentally, each speaking being.

Lacan draws up a tableau containing four formulæ, which can be described as follows (the letter *F* signifying 'function'[8]). On the masculine side: *For all x, Fx.* That is to say, each one is subjected to the universal validity of the phallic law. Then: *There exists an x for whom not Fx.* Here, an exception bounds or limits the whole, insofar as it represents the latter's negation. As such, this exception *founds* the universal law (the *a* object is thus the corollary of castration). Everyday use of language shows us, for example, that any assertion entails—implicitly, but nonetheless clearly—its corresponding negation. Politically, *limited wholes* define a logic whereby a homogeneous group is governed by a Master who, as such, occupies the place of an *exception* since the force he exerts—by means of secret agents, for example—is anchored in a realm beyond the legality applying to all. In such a régime, a 'scapegoat' such as Œdipus—as author of deeds he was unaware of—is expelled to ensure the unity of the *polis*. That is to say, *limited wholes* are based on exclusion and repression of the exception; master and scapegoat are two sides of the same coin.

On the feminine side however, there is not a simple negation—such a convenient symmetry would make of it an essence—but a contradiction: *Not for all x, Fx*; and: *No x exists for which not Fx*. The existence of *one* that may escape the universal law finds itself con-

8 To introduce his demonstration, Lacan used the letter *F* (2007, 110–1) as does Jean-Claude Milner (2003, 18). He later replaced it by the letter Φ (for phallus). We previously developed this presentation in a study of *L'Innommable* (2013e).

fronted with the *negation of any such possibility*. It is thus that not-all (*'pas-tout*'[9]) is inscribed in the universal phallic law. The negation that founds the latter encounters a dimension that it is impossible to negativise or extract, that is not subjected to castration. This concept substitutes an *unlimited* (Milner, 2003, 19–20) whole for the *limited* one governed by the Name-of-the-Father. It is appropriate to add that *limited* and *unlimited* are not equivalent to *infinite* and *finite*,[10] since a value may be infinite, while still being based on the defining exclusion of an element (Milner, 2003, 19). Jacques-Alain Miller explains as follows how the *unlimited* escapes the closure of dialectical mechanisms: 'What Lacan calls a special *jouissance* reserved for women is precisely the part that exists without being subjected to a prohibition, that is not caught up in the [binary] system of prohibition/recovery and its *Aufhebung*' (2010–2011). This category has become crucial to our modern world ever since the decisive events of World War One (the eruption of total warfare) and the *Shoah* (total extermination of Jews), which have succeeded in abolishing the order guaranteed by the reign of limited wholes.

It needs to be pointed out that Lacan's analysis of what he calls '*sexuation*' is distinct from the ideas developed in gender studies. The idea of gender is in agreement with the findings of psychoanalysis insofar as it does not consider sexual identification as a natural given, imposing a set of standard characteristics. Where it parts from psychoanalysis is in its ideological aims to 'deconstruct' patterns of 'domination', seen as constructs on a social level (Weller, 2006, 161). What Lacan calls the 'discourse of the master'—the structure that allows any

9 On the difficulty of translating this term, and the formulæ used in the following paragraphs, see (Grigg, 53–65).

10 Steven Connor deals with the notion of the finite, but without recourse to the structuring possibilities offered by the question of *jouissance* and the *real*. He does, however, point out the separation from the dimension of *limited wholes* guaranteed by the Name-of-the-Father, when he states: 'The point of Beckett's finitude is to resist being drawn out [...] into validation, promotion, authorisation, exculpation, explication—into public relations' (2008b, 44).

human group to function on an institutional level—is seen, by proponents of gender, as a form of conditioning imposed on individuals by society. This vision leads to the creation of simplistic binary notions: masculine/feminine, dominant/dominated (Weller, 2006, 162).

One of the by-products of this view is to reject the masculine as a neutral universal, and to demand the pairing of 'masculine' and 'feminine': public speeches will address '*Françaises et Français*'—as if referring to two distinct peoples—and the anaphoric pronouns for the word *subject* will follow suit, or will be neutered as *it*, a pronoun previously reserved for inanimate objects. In this spirit, Éliane Viennot criticises the masculinisation of the French language where it is commonly said '*le masculin l'emporte*' ('the masculine prevails'), particularly whenever gendered nouns or pronouns refer to a mixed group. To support her analysis, she points out that before the 17th Century, masculine and feminine remained distinct, and were treated as equals. However, as her primary concern is an ideological combat, she sees the evolution of linguistic practice purely as an effect of the male will to dominate, rather than the result of a much broader logic, as can be seen in the field of æsthetics. Indeed, during the Middle Ages and the Renaissance, painting and theatre allowed for the juxtaposition of diverse components according to the logic of the polyptych. Gérard Wajcman explains how the evolution starting with Leon Battista Alberti (in his 1435 work *De Pictura*) led to the unifying of space according to the laws of perspective, with the consequence that 'from Mediæval space to perspective space, we move from a system opposing great/small to a system opposing whole/detail'[11] (2004, 143). The three unities (action, place, time) in classical 17th Century French theatre, for example, result from this rational structuring of modernity on the basis of a purely pictorial model (288). This process was accentuated by the spread of rationalism and science, so that what prevails thereafter is clearly the logic of *limited wholes*: a coherently organised

11 Art historian Daniel Arasse (to whom Wajcman dedicates his book) is an indispensible reference on this question. See his study *Le Détail.*

discursive machine, functioning according to the law of a single signifier, and founded on the exclusion of an element. As a result, contemporary gender demands can in no way be considered as being formulated in the ancient context of a cosmic order governed by God, but emanating rather from one where science and capitalism are triumphant and claim to satisfy everyone's slightest whim. The æsthetic paucity of such narcissism becomes clear when gendered utterances in written French are regularly presented in 'kit' form, for example: '*étudiant-e-s*', to allow for simultaneously masculine, feminine, singular and plural readings. A similarly ungainly formulation is embodied by the title of the 'LBGT' movement. These initials would seem to lend themselves to an indefinite extension, inviting the addition of other letters of the alphabet, according to any diverse sexual identifications demanding public recognition.

Thus, notions of gender work on a specular logic implying that there be explicit mention of two (or more) identifications, or of none, on the pretext that each person will thus find some form of completeness through social recognition. By contesting the norm, such a stance aims to disqualify the category of the 'abnormal', with the consequence of encompassing it within a new all-inclusive version of the norm. The latter as *limited* is abolished, and is replaced with its reinforced and *unlimited* equivalent, on the rhizome model of financial capitalism and information networks, for example.

In questioning social reality, gender theory excludes from its field of investigation the fact that matters of masculine and feminine remain intrinsically bound up in the construction of the subject as a result of language. The ideological stance adopted therefore involves a deliberate refusal to raise the question of what is at stake for the subject: what *jouissance* or unbearable is dealt with by the latter's sexual choices and constructions. As a result, gender theory simply returns the question—often in the form of a complaint—to society, challenging the constraints that the latter imposes on individuals: the group is considered responsible for the subject's suffering or feelings of inadequacy with regards to representations or roles. In other words, the notion of gender leads to a preoccupation with adaptation and adequacy, ignoring what remains to torment the subject who, structurally, is radically excluded from any representation.

Contrary to this postmodern vision, and according to Lacan, social structures find their origins in language, while evolving according to the society and the period studied. The impact sexuation has on the subject consists of *dividing* him in relation to an irreducible *real*. It is therefore in reference to the constraints of language that a subject originally situates himself: he makes the unpredictable choice of his sexual preferences and the satisfaction (that may paradoxically involve suffering) he derives from them. The specificity of the feminine, as Lacan points out, is to involve the *pastout*: *unlimited jouissance* that escapes naming. However, while Lacan inscribes a bar over the definite article of *La Femme*—showing that no signifier exists for this dimension[12]—the latter necessarily preserves its reference to the universal masculine, which represents the norm. Both *limited* and *unlimited* thus accompany each other, which is why, for example, the hysteric tends to confirm the place of the Master, while deriding his shortcomings. Gender theory can only ignore the dialectic founded by this logic, such as the one that Pierre Corneille develops in his tragedies founded on what François Regnault calls the 'knot of glory' (1996, 59–69). His heroes seek the *impossible* conjunction of the universal phallic register—embodied by ancestry or State—with the irreducibly singular dimension represented by the choice of a love relationship. The dilemma that unfolds in Rodrigue's *stances*, in *Le Cid*, offers an outstanding representation of this dialectical logic (Regnault, 2006).

As a result of this structuring by the *unlimited*, the minimal differential relationship between two signifiers (which can be noted, following Lacan: S_1–S_2) places the subject directly in the presence of a dimension that *naming can never silence*. Thus, Lacan asserts: 'The ears are, in the field of the unconscious, the only orifice that cannot be closed' (1973, 178). This statement does not simply concern anatomy

12 If 'Woman' does not exist, Lacan adds: 'Inexistence is not nothingness [*néant*]' (2011, 53).

but the subject's relationship to language, whereby, in the context of *limited wholes*, the 'deaf point' that structures the field of sound is never guaranteed, since the subject is never completely sheltered from the *voice*. What Steven Connor points out about the cinema concerns the voice as a structure:

> But sound in the cinema, like sound in the world, has no frame [...]. It is a world rather of events, which are both continuously about-to-be, for one cannot listen away as one can look away, cannot ever stop hearing, and also, so to speak, continuously intermittent. There is no background, no firmament, only figures which start forth from their own ground. (Connor, 2005a)

The voice is perpetually ready to suppress all distance, to invade the subject's intimate space, to the point, sometimes, of abolishing all subjectivity.

It is in the perspective of the *unlimited* that it is useful to approach the specificity of the Beckettian voice, insofar as it cannot be silenced by a nomination within which the subject could lodge himself. This conceptual framework can shed light on what Jean-Michel Rabaté, for example, sees as the persistence of Beckett's 'ghosts': '[...] the "ghost" has to be described by a voice which reiterates its insistent drone in the "skull", while asserting a difficulty to become visible' (1996, 33). That is also why objects never really disappear in Beckett's creation, but perpetually return to haunt the subject (Hill, 71): as there is no definitive extraction of *jouissance*, the voice remains forever present as a background noise that accompanies and parasites all representations. As a result of the voice, the subject also experiences a radical *scission* that 'leaves the "I" dangling in the middle'[13] (Rabaté, 1996, 33): a point that we shall return to.[14]

Beckett's early novels in particular bring to light the tension between the imperative to name and the impossibility of doing so. As

13 See *infra*, p. 134.

14 See *infra*, p. 335 *sqq.*; where the Unnamable encounters this problem.

a result, the quest for naming appears as being supported by a substitutive and arbitrary justification. Thus, the following explanation appears in *The Unnamable*:

> All this business of a labour to accomplish, before I end, of words to say, a truth to recover, in order to say it, before I can end, of an imposed task, once known, long neglected, finally forgotten, to perform, before I can be done with speaking, done with listening, I invented it all, in the hope it would console me, help me to go on, allow me to think of myself as somewhere on a road, moving, between a beginning and an end [...]. (*U*, 307–8)

The narrator evokes his aim of attaining a nomination: one that will allow him to enclose his *saying*, his *uttering*, within the bounds imposed by a final punctuation. And yet, he finds himself incapable of believing such a perspective is possible: the idea of a nomination indeed exists in language, but it has no grip on this subject's real existence. So much so that he suggests that this punctuation might simply put an end to his speaking! In reality, this nomination—were it to exist for him—would shelter him from the *unlimited*. However, the unbearable voice persists behind any pretexts he may latch on to, as he asserts: '[...] it's myself I hear, howling behind my dissertation' (*U*, 308). The subject is thus situated at the most acute point of the separation between the 'whole' composed of names and statements—and which, for him, remain devoid of meaning—and the *pastout* or the *unlimited*, that nothing can pacify or endow with meaning. It is precisely at this point that the narrator feels the necessity of speaking:

> I have to speak, whatever that means. Having nothing to say, no words but the words of others, I have to speak. No one compels me to, there is no one, it's an accident, a fact. Nothing can ever exempt me from it, there is nothing, nothing to discover, nothing to recover, nothing that can lessen what remains to say, I have the ocean to drink, so there is an ocean then. (*U*, 308)

Only the existence of *sense* or meaning could allow him to envisage a concordance between the necessity and the means. In the absence of such a register, the subject cannot be exempted from the necessity of saying: on the contrary, the constraint becomes all the more imperious.

Thus, far from the structure of the Beckettian voice reposing on the conception of an aberrant or anomalous 'deficiency', it preserves its reference to the register of *limited wholes*, while revealing the *unlimited* as the dimension that underlies human experience of language.

An 'Unborn' Subject

The experience of such a subject excluded from common representations is expressed throughout Beckett's work by the metaphor of one who is 'not born'. Beckett's experience when he undertook psychoanalysis with Wilfred Bion from 1933 to 1934 can be read in this perspective:

> I certainly came up with some extraordinary memories of being in the womb. Intrauterine memories. I remember feeling trapped, of being imprisoned and unable to escape, of crying to be let out but no one could hear, no one was listening. I remember being in pain but being unable to do anything about it. (in Knowlson, 1997, 177)

What this description brings to light is that Beckett felt, intensely, the condition of being deprived of any symbolic link to an Other. The image of the intrauterine condition expresses a total enveloping that excludes any dialectical opening through speech. The uterus appears as a metaphor of a topological form where nothing intervenes to inscribe the place of a structuring breach or exception. The subject's cries convey the failure of the *invocation* by means of which he can impose silence on the Other. Beckett pointed out the precise link between this experience and the imperative to create when he responded to Martin Esslin's question 'What motivates you to write?' He replied:

'The only obligation I feel is towards that enclosed poor embryo' (in Knowlson and Knowlson, 151). He added: 'That is the most terrible situation you can imagine, because you know you're in distress but you don't know that there is anything outside this distress or any possibility of getting out of that distress.' In order to grasp the specific extension Beckett gives to this condition in his creation, it is useful to recall what he states in 1949, regarding the painting of Pierre Tal Coat: 'The expression that there is nothing to express, nothing with which to express, nothing from which to express, no power to express, no desire to express, together with the obligation to express' (*Dsj*, 139). It thus comes as no surprise to find Beckett particularly sensitive, in 1937, to the painting *Resurrection*, by Dieric Bouts the Elder, where he discerns, in one character: 'The remoteness almost of schizophrenia' (in Knowlson, 1997, 256). The same radical experience of being cut off from the world was underscored by Beckett when explaining to Patrick Magee how to read *Texts for Nothing*, in the recording he was undertaking for the BBC:

> In order to explain it to Pat, 'Sam said: You see this is a man who is sitting at an open window on the ground floor of a flat. He is looking out into the street and people are passing a few yards away from him but to him it is as if he were ten thousand miles away?' So it was a description of schizophrenic withdrawal symptoms. (Esslin in Knowlson, 1997, 605)

It is well known that Beckett read Otto Rank's investigations of the 'intrauterine situation' (in Feldman, 2006, 107; Herren, 2014), but this evocation seems to find its origins in what Beckett heard at the third conference given by C. G. Jung at the Tavistock Clinic in 1935, in the company of Wilfred Bion, where the famous psychologist described a young girl who had 'never been born entirely' (in Pountney, 107). In his conversations with Charles Juliet, Beckett describes Jung speaking, at this conference, of a young girl; then, 'comme se parlant à lui-même, étonné par la découverte qu'il faisait, il ajouta: /– Au fond, elle n'était jamais née' ('as if speaking to himself, astonished by the discovery he was making, he added: "Basically, she had never been born'", in Juliet, 15). Clearly, Beckett identified with this young girl, as can be seen in the sentence that follows this recollection in Juliet's book: 'J'ai toujours eu le sentiment que moi non plus, je n'étais jamais né' ('I have always had the feeling that I too had never been born'). This experience can be understood as a state of mortification from which the subject is incapable of breaking free, as can be seen in the remarks that precede this sentence: 'J'ai toujours eu la sensation qu'il y avait en moi un être assassiné. Assassiné avant ma naissance. Il me fallait retrouver cet être assassiné. Tenter de lui redonner vie…' ('I have always had the feeling that there was an assassinated being within me. Assassinated before my birth. I had to find this assassinated being. Try to give life back to him…').

Rosemary Pountney (129) enlighteningly compares this image of the unborn twin with Stevenson's *Dr. Jeckyll and Mr. Hyde*. Critics have sometimes tended to extend this motif beyond Jung, to include a supposed relationship—of varying degrees—between Bion and Beckett. Although Matthew Feldman (2006, 85) has noted a lack of documentation about Beckett's time in analysis, some have pointed to possible influences or a community of interest. Following Bennett Simon and Didier Anzieu, Angela Moorjani traces the prevalence of this motif—among others—in Beckett's creation, as evidenced in his 'pseudocouples', for example (2004b, 30–1; 2004a, 177–8). Others even claim—in a conception incompatible with psychoanalysis' postulate of the misunderstanding (*malentendu*) inherent in any human exchange—that Jung offered Bion and Beckett a path to mutual 'understanding' (Miller and Souter, 90). More seriously, Monique Liart makes a precious clinical remark, considering that this motif had a beneficial effect as a 'delirious metaphor' helping to stabilise Beckett (1999, 30; 2012, 177). As such, it intervenes as an *image* that is endowed with the capacity to give form to the unnameable, in the absence of the Name-of-the-Father.

Indeed, the notion of an unborn twin—present in *Rough for Radio II*, for example (Lawley, 1988)—requires to be approached from a structural point of view. Beckett's use of *seeing* and *blind* pairs of characters, which Angela Moorjani (2004b 30) associates with this motif, can be considered as the manifestation of a radical scission that admits of no dialectical synthesis, that maintains maximal tension. Indeed, any evocation of opposed terms in Beckett reveals the very *real* hole in language that cannot be filled in or subsumed by linguistic articulation. It is to such a structural antithesis that Laura Salisbury gives metaphorical importance when she quotes Beckett, who once stated that the 'writer's best chance' is 'gazing into the synaptic chasm' (in Salisbury, 2010, 213). Jean-Michel Rabaté also sees the presence of the 'unborn' motif throughout Beckett's work, calling such manifestations 'ghosts' (1996, 33). He states that after the 1940s, ghosts 'appear as the nothing that is more real than Nothing, as a resilient "lessness" that manages to survive erasure and oblivion' (28). Leslie Hill (105) emphasises the role of language in this state: 'The failure to be born and therefore to die [...] is consequently a failure attributable in part to the function of the name.' This assertion is true, insofar as a *limited whole* is governed by the name. However these occurrences of the unborn testify to what æthetically enables Beckett to deal with the part that remains constantly present, in all its positivity, as *unlimited.* It is because the latter is structurally at the centre of Beckett's work that all his characters, or figures, can be described as 'unborn'. As Lacan explains in relation to the ghost in *Hamlet,* the intolerable loss of an other causes a 'hole in the real' (2013, 397), bringing to light the radical absence of a signifier, so that, as Beckett expressed it, it 'pollute[s] the whole of speech' (*MD*, 186). The consequences are clear, for example, in the many spectral figures of the *dramaticules*, and in the constructions on radio and television that make them appear as such.

Dan Mellamphy associates the unborn being with the 'non-conceptual and non-conceptualisable non-being: a non-existent existence, or what Emmanuel Lévinas would call an "existence without existent"' (492–3). Lévinas also calls this impersonal state the '*il y a*' (there is), which he describes as follows:

> Essence stretching on indefinitely, without any possible halt or interruption, the equality of essence not justifying, in all equity, any instant's halt, without respite, without any possible suspension, is the horrifying *there is* behind all finality proper to the thematizing ego, which cannot sink into the essence it thematises.[15] (Lévinas, 163)

This condition can be understood in its specifically subjective significance in terms of Lacan's idea that once a subject is postulated by the signifier, he 'can no longer destroy himself' and 'enters an unbearable chain' (2013, 114) where he encounters the 'eternalisation of his desire' (1966, 319). This is to be understood as the 'structuring, signifying necessity that forbids a subject to escape the concatenation of existence as it is determined by the nature of the signifier' (2013, 118). Here, for example, Hamlet's dilemma—'to be or not to be'—reveals that he is irremediably bound within the signifying chain (2013, 293): there is no possibility for him *not to be*. Lacan describes, as follows, this implacable binding that weighs on Hamlet's existence: '[…] being remains identical to everything that he has articulated through the discourse of his life. There, there is no *To be or not to be*—whatever the circumstances, the *To be* remains eternal' (2013, 314). That is to say that in this condition, no element of *exception* exists to contradict the mortifying function of language, in order to allow the subject a space to *breathe*.[16] This is what the Unnamable encounters in the impossibility of opting for speechlessness, since he risks being 'punished for having gone silent' (*U*, 388). From this point of view, the 'unborn' also

---

15 Yoshiki Tajiri also points to Maurice Blanchot's reading of Lévinas' *il y a*, opposing it to Heidegger's subordination of beings to Being (Tajiri, 2012, 161–5).

16 'Ça n'a pas d'importance de n'être pas publié. On fait cela pour pouvoir respirer' ('It is of no importance not to be published. One does it to be able to breathe', in Juliet, 43). For want of such a vital breach, some do end up literally stifling themselves.

expresses the inability to die, to attain an ending, whence the encounter with the terrifying state of 'nightmare thingness' (*CSPr*, 69) and perpetual mortification.[17]

This allows us to further nuance our analysis of the *unlimited*. As has been pointed out (Geneste, 2015), a distinction needs to be made between the unlimited dimension as the 'unstillable' voice which Beckett uses, in his later work, to maintain himself in relation to the symbolic register by creating an hiatus or a blank in language, and the earlier impasses he encountered, and where he found no consistent means to extract himself from the ceaseless voice.

That is to say that the formulæ of sexuation bring into play the role of the *phallus* which functions as a veil over the symbolic structuring, and gives access to the effects of the signified. Lacan points out that Hamlet finds himself excluded from this register of phallic semblances that motivate Fortinbras' heroism, the desire for revenge, the possibility of loving Ophelia: all things that inspire adhesion or belief, and give its grounding to desire. Indeed, the collapsing of the phallic function leaves him unable to see any way out of his eternal inscription in the signifying chain: he has no guarantee that death will actually bring an end to his existence. His condition is therefore contrary to that of the neurotic (or 'normal') subject, for whom the inevitability of death is paradoxically reassuring, insofar as it marks the presence of the Other as a *guarantee*: the condition whereby the Other endows the signifying chain with an end, a cutting-off point.[18]

Hamlet, however, experiences 'the dread of something after death' (Act III, sc. 1, l. 78) which paralyzes him and excludes all possibility of any act of revenge. He only acts once he sees Laertes—his specular double—demonstrating his grief for the death of Ophelia. This intervention of the imaginary allows him to at last see the latter as an objet of love and mourning: as a *lost object*. 'In sum, it is insofar

---

17 See *infra*, p. 159 *sqq*.

18 Lacan explicitly states that in the initial situation of *Hamlet*, as distinct from that of Œdipus in *Œdipus the King*, is the absence of *castration* (Lacan, 2013, 296).

as Ophelia has become an impossible object that she becomes once again the object of his desire' (Lacan, 2013, 396). Lacan shows that Hamlet finds himself exposed to the pure 'pain of existing' (1966, 777). Indeed, contrary to Œdipus—who is blissfully ignorant of his past and his incestuous relationship with his mother (2013, 293)—Hamlet *knows* right from the start (2013, 293, 351): the words of the ghost are of the sort that 'rise up out of the pit and know no rest until they drag you down into its [speech's] dark' (*MD*, 186–7). Hamlet knows full well that falsehood is present everywhere, that there is no (paternal) guarantee: '[…] there is no Other of the Other' (Lacan, 2013, 384). He is like the one whose 'greatest offense / Is that he has been born' (Calderón, in Schopenhauer, 254), since he is summoned to pay for the sins that his father—'cut off even in the blossom of [his] sin' (Act I, sc. 5, l. 76)—did not expiate (Lacan, 2013, 294). This brings into play an unlimited state, which is also expressed in terms of Beckett's 'dead voices',[19] and which contrasts with the use he makes in his later works of the symbolic in its vivifying relation to *jouissance*, a practice that involves a breach in language—the structural silence where the Other does not know—so that the subject is no longer subjected to the pure mortification inflicted by the signifier.

It is thus possible to situate more precisely the status of the unborn subject in its structural setting. Firstly, as Arthur Rose (216) points out, the unborn subject is counterbalanced by the assertion of birth. Malone speaks of 'being given […] birth into death' (*MD*, 276), as he emerges from 'the great cunt of existence'; and the Unnamable remarks that it is far too late to regret entering life: '[…] I'm looking for my mother to kill her, I should have thought of that a bit earlier, before being born […]' (*U*, 385). This wish to kill his mother appears as a direct response to the impression of having been 'assassiné' (in Juliet, 15) before birth. Such metaphors lead to a feeling of guilt for having 'been born'. The Unnamable asserts he is ignorant of what he is 'guilty of' (*U*, 362), suggesting: 'I was given a pensum, at birth perhaps, as a punishment for having been born […]' (304). As Malone

19 See *infra*, p. 159 *sqq*.

emphasises, while living is itself punishment, it cannot be considered 'a sufficient atonement' (*MD*, 233). However, enduring continuous punishment, accompanied by shame,[20] is nonetheless a way of palpably experiencing one's existence as a subject, in spite of the absence of any mark of approval forthcoming from an Other.

Indeed, in the works of Beckett's middle period, the voice is dead: it is in no way vivifying, leading to the paradoxical expression of birth as an entry into death. The Unnamable speaks of 'giving up the ghost be born at last' (*U*, 336). The words of others—the 'dead tongue of the living' (331)—are viewed as oppressive: 'Another trap to snap me up among the living' (339). They also appear as a form of persecution, comparable to being scourged (347). And yet, such strenuous resistance means that the subject can indeed envisage the other side of words: it is precisely because he knows of it that he is all the more unwilling to assume its discourse. It therefore provokes his visceral rejection: 'It is they who dictate this torrent of balls, they who stuffed me full of these groans that choke me. And it all pours out unchanged [...]' (329). What he calls 'it all' remains 'unchanged' precisely because he is unable to clothe it with the phallic brilliance of desire.

On the other hand, the status of being unborn can be seen as involving the very real *creation* of a double, a 'brother' or 'twin' (*RRII*, 279). Indeed, in Beckett's remarks to Charles Juliet, it appears that to state that the double is *unborn* suggests that it may be possible, somehow, to give birth to the latter, to endow him with some identity, with a visage: the unborn double acts as a veil over the void. Locating the hole in language in the figure of this double is a means by which the writer succeeds in endowing himself with a certain *maternal status*, as being charged with giving birth to the unborn one, as is clearly described by Fox in *Rough for Radio II*.[21] This creation thus retroactively affords the subject a means of existing. The paradoxical expression 'The child is father to the man' sheds light on this mechanism, since it

---

20 We shall return to this crucial notion *infra*, p. 86–7 (regarding the notion of testimony) and p. 374.

21 See *infra*, p. 231–2.

can be understood as signifying not only that the child grows into the man, but that, on the level of the signifier, the arrival of a child retroactively causes a man to become—and assume the role of—a father. Here, Beckett's 'unborn' double *engenders the subject*, since the latter experiences the consequent obligation to care for it, to endow it with a life that will respect its full integrity: such is the function of literary creation. At the same time, the unborn double represents a cause for not succumbing to the imperative to return to silence, to abolish one's own existence.[22]

The maternal function with regards to the 'unborn' twin is made clear in the split between the 'assumed voice' and the 'normal voice' (in Pountney, 95) in the 1963 'Kilcool' manuscript, that preceded the composition of *Not I*: the 'normal voice' is an unborn being, recounting from beyond the grave, and who speaks of: 'Someone in me, trying to get out, saying let me out…' (in Pountney, 98). The former voice, however, enjoins her to 'go out, live!' (in Pountney, 96). Such is also the role of the perspective Beckett maintains of a future naming, as Leslie Hill (106) points out, speaking of a name that may come to replace the fundamental absence of one: 'But it is no exaggeration to say that the project of Beckett's writing, throughout the trilogy and beyond, is an attempt to spell this cryptic other's name.' Literary creation assumes this very role: the created object comes in the place of the name that does not exist within language. Instead of being perpetually glued to his own mortification—in the 'fornication with corpses' (*CSPr*, 61)—Beckett succeeds in giving life, in his work, to his experience of the *unlimited*. In the same way as Murphy is unable to join Mr Endon (Rabaté, 1996, 29), Beckett cannot draw any knowledge from his eternal and unknowable brother whom, however, he preserves and gives existence to within his creation.

From this coexistence of being 'born' and 'unborn' results the Beckettian form of undecidability, expressed emblematically by the adverbs *perhaps* (in Driver, 23) and *neither*[23] (*CSPr*, 258) in relation to

22 See *infra*, p. 161.

23 See *infra*, p. 109–10.

the signifying chain. It is also what leads to the creation of doubles, such as the following: '[...] and who is this clot who doesn't know where to go, who can't stop, who takes himself for me and for whom I take myself [...]' (*TFN* XI, 146). Of the two figures evoked, one is alive, or enrolled in conventional human existence, while the other feels he has not yet come to existence. Such imaginary doubles offer a form of discursive structuring[24] allowing the subject to situate himself, instead of being helplessly 'scattered by the everlasting words' (*TFN* XI, 144).

This motif of the unborn twin raises the problematic question of testimony, dealt with by certain critics. Daniel Katz picks up Yeats' notion of symbolism giving 'dumb things voices' (11), stating that with Beckett, 'it is the "poet" who is voiceless' (14), and his narrators' desire is not to accept the bestowal of the voice, but 'only to divest themselves of this poisoned gift' (12). This eliminates the notion of self-expression in *The Unnamable*, for example, because 'it is not a self that is doing the expressing' (15). Katz thus suggests the term 'autoprosopopeia, in which every thetic statement is presented as borrowed, non-originary, indebted, and imposed, although the concept of any exterior, antecedent origin is equally rejected' (16). He deconstructs the 'identity' of the narrator in *The Unnamable* as follows: '*The Unnamable*, however, not only has no name by which "it" could be referred to, or refer to itself, but in addition *it cannot even refer to "itself" through the use of a pronoun*' (80). To describe the state of radical separation from linguistic identity, Giorgio Agamben refers to Giorgio Magnanelli's notion of 'homopseudonymy' (130), a term designating the use of a 'pseudonym' that is identical to one's own name: a practice which reveals the strangeness that can arise between such a 'proper' noun and the subject it is supposed to name.

In *The Unnamable*, Katz asserts that 'the "I" is simultaneously asserted and effaced, in a double bind' (82), and that this *I* is not replaced by any 'impersonality or neutrality', while it does not recover its place either. This evaluation may be true on the level of the text's

---

24 Discursive structuring is the object of our final chapter, *infra*, p. 320 *sqq*.

material expression, however what it ignores is the place of *jouissance*: the *voice* that, contrary to infinite verbal metonymy, remains a constant. The actual existence of a subject risks being evacuated by situating one's analysis purely on the level of words, as found in the famous paradox of the Cretan liar. Lacan (1973, 127–8) approaches this question by differentiating between the enunciation and the utterance: the sentence *I lie*, pronounced by the subject, comes back as the 'reversed message' from the place of the Other, who is then able to retort: *You are telling the truth*. The mechanism at work can be visualised by adapting Lacan's '*Schéma L*'[25] (1966, 53) as follows:

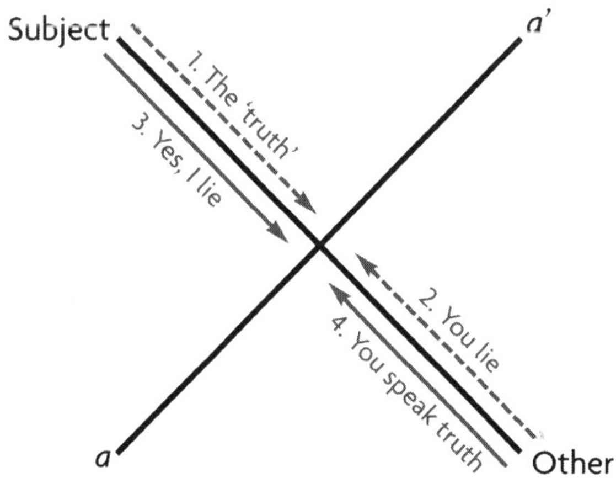

The dotted arrows indicate the level of *enunciation*, while the continuous ones represent the effective utterances. As the paradox is usually conceived, the Other—like the spotlight in *Play*—is condemned to search along the imaginary axis (from *a* to *a'*) among utterances that are invariably false: all Cretans are liars, including he who says 'I am lying'. In the meantime, the subject remains totally ungraspable. In reality however—as shown in the diagram—the subject, on the point of lying (no. 1) anticipates the interpretation coming back from the Other (no. 2). He then confesses the falsehood intended (no.

25 We return to this diagram in our study of *Play*. See *infra*, p. 288–91.

3) and, finally, the Other confirms the truth of this statement (no. 4). By contrast, the strictly verbal aspect of the paradox that neglects this movement between the interlocutors is present when Katz notes (76) of Moran's contradictory final statement, that it 'prevents the temporality of what is narrated from ever catching up to and coinciding with the temporality of the narration'. Such a paradox is situated only on the imaginary level—that of the reality represented—and not on that of the *voice* that narrates, that stands behind the writing.

It would therefore seem obvious that in a work of creation, there *is a subject*: be he obscure and unknowable, he embodies an eminently *positive* existence. Developments given to the notion of testimony are most useful here. Russell Smith approaches this question by criticising Maurice Blanchot and Michel Foucault who, he asserts, abolish the place of the speaker. He states: 'In each case the *écart* that separates the subject and its utterance is not merely widened, it is sundered, and the ethical dimension of enunciation, its "obligation to express," is elided' (2007, 348). Both Russell Smith and David Houston Jones study the question of testimony in the light of Giorgio Agamben's book *Remnants of Auschwitz: The Witness and the Archive*, which explores the case of the *Muselmänner*, described by Primo Levi in *Se questo è un uomo* (1947): these prisoners in the Nazi camps, who were reduced to a state of total inhumanity, and radically deprived of any means of expression. Such an abyss between a mute existence and speech is literally insuperable, placing the one who seeks to transmit in the position of one who betrays an impossible truth, as Thomas Tresize says (in Jones, 64), and as we ourselves found necessary to express it, in our own work of testimony *Savoir de l'amour* (2012, 157). Indeed, what right does anyone have to assume sole responsibility for someone who alone has authority to account for his existence? At the same time, the obligation to speak is equally imperious. In this process, Agamben ascribes a crucial role to shame, which simultaneously produces a condition of subjectivation and desubjectivation (106). As a result, testimony has a very real function, and cannot be confused with betrayal. Agamben asserts: 'Testimony takes place where the speechless one makes the speaking one speak and where the one who speaks bears the impossibility of speaking in his own speech [...]' (120). This gives the witness authority, when he speaks '*solely in the name of an incapacity to speak—that is, in his or her being a subject*' (158). Agamben points out that in testimony, one specifically bears 'witness to his incapacity to speak', so that this language that 'survives the subjects who spoke it coincides with a speaker who remains beyond it' (161–2). Testimony thus divides the subject, and supposes that the one who is incapable of speech remains present insofar as he acts henceforth as a *cause* of speech (Brown, 2012, 160–1). In such a case, to speak *of* the person is also to speak *for* him (161), and thus give him existence through speech.

The scission experienced between the one who is mute and the one who speaks occurs within the same person in the case of the 'survivor', who speaks of himself as he was when a *Muselmann* (Jones, 64). Smith concludes therefore:

> The speech of Beckett's characters is always chained to the embodied voice, a body that is often mutilated or deformed, but never dematerialized, never able to celebrate the blissful dissolution of the subject in the anonymity of a murmur. That is why the modality of enunciation in Beckett is not one of indifference, but of shame. (Smith, 2007, 352)

Shame maintains the subject's division, manifesting the impact of the 'master signifier'—one that determines his existence—as represented by an ideal, as Suzanne Dow has pointed out in her remarkable reading of one of Lacan's rare allusions to Beckett.

The motif of the unborn subject and the failure of birth is explicitly mentioned in several texts that span a large period in Beckett's work. The Addenda of *Watt* contain the fragment: 'never been properly born' (*W*, 248). In *Footfalls*, in order to avoid associating the notion of birth with her daughter, May's mother uses a circumlocution: 'The same where she began. [*Pause.*] Where it began. [*Pause.*] It all began' (*Ff*, 401). Walter Asmus reports Beckett's comments on this expression: 'She was going to say: "...the same where she was *born*".

But that is wrong, she hasn't been born. She just began. "It began. There is a difference. She was never born"' (in Asmus). The narrator of *The Unnamable* is another who was not born: 'I'll sham dead now, whom they couldn't bring to life [...]' (*U*, 319).

In other texts, the character expresses regrets concerning his coming into the world, as in 'From an Abandoned Work': '[...] all I regret is having been born, dying is such a long tiresome business I always found' (*CSPr*, 158). This regret is nothing other than the avowal of his failure to 'be born', and that can only be the result of the manner in which the subject has been—or rather, has not been—instituted by a symbolic Other. In this respect, it is useful to notice the passive structure of the English verb *to be born*, which supposes the preeminent role played by the Other: the subject can never 'bear' himself. By denigrating his own birth, the subject echoes the judgement formulated by his Other. Molloy also declares, about his mother: 'I know she did all she could not to have me, except of course the one thing, and if she never succeeded in getting me unstuck, it was that fate had earmarked me for less compassionate sewers' (*Mo*, 14). In an ironic tone, Molloy seeks excuses for she who, by begetting him, manifested a moment of weakness; and, in order to correct this error, he hastens to recall that he will nonetheless end up in the same hole: the tomb, rather than the sewer where he would have fallen, had his mother succeeded in aborting him. Here, the French uses the term *fosse d'aisance* rather than *sewer*: the word *fosse* echoes the *fosse commune* (common grave), confirming the association with the tomb.

This insistence requires us to look more closely at what is at stake here for the subject. Since the latter is represented by a signifier for another signifier, Lacan notes that 'once the signifying battery is given [...] nothing is lacking' (1991a, 281). How can a subject come to existence if everything—the totality of available signifiers—is already provided in an immutable manner? Lacan continues:

> [For something to] be subjectivised is [for it] to take place in a subject considered as valid for another subject, that is to say to move to the most radical point where the very idea of communication is

> possible. Any signifying battery can tell you that what it cannot say will mean nothing from the place of the Other. Now, everything that signifies for us always passes via the place of the Other. [...] At what moment does the lack of a signifier, possibly, begin to appear? In this dimension that is subjectivised, and that is called the question. (Lacan, 1991a, 281)

In this passage, Lacan points out that the subject can come to being from the moment its Other—the authority owing to which the subject is instituted in language—manifests a *lack*; this is possible in the structuring dimension offered by the *question*. It is the existence of a lack in which the subject can be inscribed in reference to the Other by returning a question back to him: at this point, the Other is incapable of providing a total response regarding the subject's desire.

If, according to Lacan, 'the subject's desire is the desire of the Other' (1991a, 212, 314; 1975b, 11), it is crucial that the Other himself be inhabited by a living desire, in order for the subject to desire in turn: that is to say, the Other is not self-sufficient but ignores something essential about himself. Lacan explains that insofar as the mother is 'the first symbolised object', 'her absence or her presence will become, for the subject the sign of the desire that his own desire will latch onto, and will make of him, or not, not simply a satisfied child or not, but a desired or undesired child' (1998, 257). From this perspective, the child does not relate to the mother as such, 'but to the mother's desire. It is a desire for desire' (198) which alone allows the child to make the choice to live. The desired child has the possibility to be represented 'by one signifier for another': the child represents something for this Other, who is aware of his own incompleteness.

What makes the subject's inscription in reference to his Other problematic is when the latter manifests no desire, when nothing names the desire that brought the child into existence. Beckett's *Not I*, for example, describes how the desire that caused the parents to unite vanishes into inconsistency, leaving the tiny girl with a future that remains uncertain with regards to her own existence: 'parents unknown ... unheard of ... he having vanished ... thin air... no sooner buttoned up his breeches… she similarly…' (*NI*, 376). Lacan notices the effects on the child to come who, not endowed with the appearance of a person, in the mother's mind, can only be a soulless *thing*:

> […] what the mother of a schizophrenic articulates regarding what her child was for her at the moment when he was in her womb—nothing but a body inversely convenient or cumbersome, that is to say the subjectivisation of [the] *a* [object] as a pure real. (2004, 140)

The child has no symbolic consistency for the mother if she is not capable of *clothing* him with the imaginary: creating for herself representations that will enable her to admire this new being, to desire a future for him, to assign him a place within the family circle.

If he is not established by maternal desire, the subject can only see himself as fallen from a totally intact Other, as Molloy expresses it:

> And if ever I'm reduced to looking for a meaning to my life, you never can tell, it's in that old mess I'll stick my nose to begin with, the mess of that poor old uniparous whore and myself the last of my foul breed, neither man nor beast. (*Mo*, 14–5)

The subject's life can have no 'meaning', insofar as the latter must be bequeathed to him by the Other. Molloy has no 'breed' because he has not been inscribed within any lineage: he has only been engendered, in the purely biological sense of the term. For want of being named in the desire of his Other, he is nothing more than a *thing* that has fallen as scraps or refuse—the *a* object—the (unnameable) piece of flesh that has no cause to live. This allows us to read the following statement by Beckett not as a vague and commonplace expression of 'otherness', but to discern its association with the *real*: 'The artist who stakes his being is from nowhere, has no kith' (*Dsj*, 149).

An Impassive Mother

The child thus only comes into existence—is 'born', according to the Beckettian metaphor—if language (*langue*) has a breach in it: if the mother has some bodily object to give up, such as a breast, a voice, a gaze (Borie, 115). Psychoanalyst Jacques Borie sheds light on this principle when he reports and comments on a patient's words:

> 'My baby's mouth closed on no breast to grasp. I clench my teeth and let fly a mute scream. When confronted with the slightest problem, I fall back on this basic scene. No breast to grasp, it leaves you voiceless, unless you bite.' This construction, which is perfectly logical, shows how, in an instant, the encounter with another who has nothing to let go of, has the consequence of leaving the subject with a mouth that cannot divide itself between speech and orality, and has no use for the organ other than for self-devouring. (Borie, 151)

If such a cession does not take place, the child has no breach in which his existence can be inscribed: he finds himself faced with a completely smooth wall that leaves nothing to latch on to. It is crucial to note however that this should in no way be understood as some sort of line of conduct a mother would be required follow in order to fulfil her role. On the contrary, no rule can prescribe something that can never be ordained: nothing can dictate what a mother spontaneously invests—or is capable of investing—in the life of her child.

This inability to give up something for her child is precisely what characterises the Beckettian mother.[26] An evocation of this aspect can be found in *Company*, where mother and child walk on in

---

26 Our analysis thus excludes any psychological or sociological dimension. We can also note the extreme compassion Beckett expresses for the 'savage loving' (letter to MacGreevy, 6 October 1937; *L1*, 552) of his own mother, and which we find in his later representation of maternal figures. For example, in the image of the mother in mourning (*cf.* Baker, 153), in *Ill Seen Ill Said.*

silence, 'through the warm still summer air' (*Co*, 5): 'Looking up at the blue sky and then at your mother's face you break the silence asking her if it is not in reality much more distant than it appears. The sky that is. The blue sky.' Here, it is the child who takes the initiative of breaking the silence, not the mother: the burden rests entirely on him.

In his question, the child establishes an equivalence between the 'blue sky' (*Co*, 5) and his mother's face: both are distant, impassive. It is precisely this inscrutable nature that the child seeks to breach, in order to find a place in relation to his Other. The lyrical stereotype 'ciel d'azur' (*Cie*, 12)—elsewhere called 'the blue celeste of poesy' ('Lessness', *CSPr*, 199)—expresses an æsthetic and self-sufficient uniformity that nothing can traverse. Here the child's question concerns the distance he is unable to evaluate: having never been inscribed in his mother's desire, he is unable to enter the three-dimensional space that the fundamental fantasy produces (Brown, 2007, 15–7), as supported by the universal phallic register. The immeasurably close and the infinitely distant converge in this indeterminate space, and the child remains uncertain as to the place he occupies with regards to his Other. Beckett plays on the equivocal nature of the pronoun *it*, which necessitates the ensuing hyperbaton in order to 'specify' his meaning: 'The sky that is' (*Co*, 5). This uncertainty engenders anxiety, and the child repeats his question, in a symmetrical formulation: 'Receiving no answer you mentally reframe your question and some hundred paces later look up at her face again and ask her if it does not appear much less distant than in reality it is' (5–6).

This problematic is reminiscent of the one dealt with by Descartes, in *La Dioptrique* (1637). The philosopher notes that 'all the means we have to know distance are most uncertain' (Descartes, 159). He points out therefore that the distance of objects is estimated not in relation to the size of the images they produce in the eye but with reference to one's 'knowledge' or 'opinion' of them (155). Indeed, images can lead to error, as a result of variations in colour and lighting conditions. By contrast, the sensorial impression made by the nerves allows a blind person, for example (150–1) to determine the coordinates of an object situated beyond the range of his hands, and geometrical calculations allow surveyors to situate an inaccessible point *X* (153). The presence of these reliable references means that such a subject has already been instituted by his Other, and thus has access to geometrical space, determined by the laws of perspective. Beckett evokes the same problematic as Descartes in relation to the question of an enigmatic Other, whom he associates with the 'sky whence cometh our help' (*HI*, 15), in other words with what for him remains the Other's eternally enigmatic and speechless desire.

In these passages therefore, the mother's response leaves no place for an explanation that might attenuate its brutality. What this about-face reveals is that the signified can in no way palliate the dimension external to speech: the brute signifier, which remains unarticulated but cuts into the flesh. This mother who does not respond with words is comparable to the father Nagg who, indisposed by his son Hamm's cries, refuses to respond—and so transform the cries into *calls*—but who places the source of this 'noise' at a convenient distance: 'Whom did you call when you were a tiny boy, and were frightened in the dark? Your mother? No. Me. We let you cry. Then we moved you out of earshot, so that we might sleep in peace' (*Eg*, 119). The child remains plunged into the greatest of solitudes, without any response that might enable him to name what torments him.

The episode from *Company* can be found in two other texts. In 'The End', the narrator is expelled from an institution, and the irony directed against Mr. Weir—qualified as '[v]ery friendly' (*CSPr*, 81)—is emphasised by the association of the 'empty cloudless sky' after the rain (evoked in the present tense) with the memory in the form of a small narrative in the past: 'A small boy, stretching out his hands and looking up at the blue sky, asked his mother how such a thing was possible. Fuck off, she said.' The violence of the reply[27] (reinforced by the alliterative chiasmus /f/ and /k/) contrasts with the child's ex-

27 It would seem that the 'fuck life' (*R*, 246) of *Rockaby* offers a response to this violence (*cf.* Brown, 2013c, 200–1).

pression of innocent perplexity and amazement. In *Malone Dies*, a complex succession of remarks and memories underscores the extreme anxiety caused by an apparently neutral reaction on the part of the mother. At an air show, the son is not afraid, while his mother exclaims: 'It's a miracle, a miracle' (*MD*, 261). If however the boy 'changed [his] mind', the reason becomes clear when he jumps to the memory of his asking his mother: 'The sky is further away than you think, is it not, mama?' By contrast with her exaltation—seemingly expressive of belief in the celestial status of the flying machines—the mother's rely, in this version, expresses inflexible impersonality: 'It is precisely as far away as it appears to be.' The suffering occasioned is conveyed not only by the boy's reaction ('I was aghast') but also by the insistence: 'She replied to me her son [...].' The mother's phrase fundamentally points to her rejection of any maternal presence that leaves the narrator exposed to the anxiety of the gaze. Indeed, on their way 'home from the butcher's', the narrator finds himself indelibly marked by presence of a blind point: 'I can still see the spot, opposite Tyler's gate. A market gardener, he had only one eye [...].' Having left the butcher (who can be associated with 'Abel'), he is confronted with a 'Cain' that recalls Victor Hugo's famous verse from *La Légende des siècles*: 'L'œil était dans la tombe et regardait Caïn' ('The eye was in the tomb and was watching Cain').

Insofar as creation is a way of dealing with what exceeds the nameable, this voice—manifesting an absence of vocal modulation—is transposed to the toneless voice that Beckett sought to obtain in many of his theatrical creations. In *Berceuse*, the voice is '*Blanche, sourde, monotone*' ('colourless, dull, monotonous', *Ber*, 55). In *Eh Joe*: 'Low, distinct, remote, little colour, absolutely steady rhythm [...]' (*EJ*, 361). In the rehearsals for *Comédie*, in 1964, the actors tried to achieve this voice: 'They concentrated on acquiring what Beckett described as a "recto-tono", a tone not unlike that adopted by monks as they read from sacred texts at mealtimes' (Knowlson, 1997, 515). This was precisely the effect that Beckett wished for, as he indicated to Alan Schneider: 'Voices grey and abstract as the faces, grey as cinders [...]' (Beckett, 1998, 145). Again, in *Come and Go*, Beckett asked for: the

'Same toneless voices save for "Oh!"s' (Beckett, 1998, 417). The colourless voice represents a means of achieving the anonymity inherent in the attitude of a mother confronted with the enigma of her child's existence, which she herself is incapable of naming. Through his creation Beckett confronts this impassivity, he gives form to this *absence*, rendering it present, which is why he told André Bernold, in 1981, that the mysterious 'voix blanche' (colourless voice, in Bernold, 105) was his ultimate aim. He later defined it as follows: 'Il faudrait trouver une *ombre vocale*, me dit Beckett le 12 novembre 1981, une voix qui soit une ombre. Une voix blanche' ('We would need to find a *vocal shadow*, Beckett told me on 12 November 1981, a voice that is a shadow. A colourless voice', Bernold, 108).

This voice, devoid of any expressiveness, is somewhat reminiscent of Mariko Hori Tanaka's (110) description of dance in Japanese theatre: 'The supreme goal of *ma*[28] as temporal space is the complete stillness that is highly respected in Noh; the culminating moment of a Noh play is a dance called *i-guse*, the "completely still dance."' In other words, it is the manner in which the actor's presence approaches the point where it is entirely subjected to the *voice* as silence: the *subject*, where he appears as the *object* of his Other and, paradoxically, where his silent but irreducible existence is essential for the latter's existence, and vice-versa. The toneless voice is thus somewhat comparable to the mask of Noh theatre, a tradition from which Akira Kurosawa drew a lot of inspiration, putting it to use in some of his films. In *Throne of Blood* (1957)—based on *Macbeth*—he told actress Isuzu Yamada: 'You have to be like a Noh mask, so you must not blink. Never blink' (Kurosawa). Her face had to remain motionless, leaving her to find expression through her gestures and her body. The mask effaces the contingent personality (the ego) and brings to life the subject's essential bodily existence in relation to artistic form. In his old age, Kurosawa wrote a script for a documentary called *The Beauty of Noh*, in

28 *Ma* literally means the 'space' or 'vacuum' (Hori Tanaka, 109), and refers to moments that are 'more important than the emotional utterances of the protagonist [*shite*] sung either by him or by singers' (108).

which he observed: 'The Noh mask is neither an accessory nor a work of art. When the actor dons the mask, he begins to live. It is a mysterious creature' (*idem*).

It is, therefore, not astonishing that it is in empty space—similar to that of Japanese *ma*—that Beckett finds reassurance, as he expressed it in 1981, since its nature is the same as that of the atonal voice: 'My only desire for weeks to come is to sit quiet contemplating my old friend, empty space…' (Beckett, 1998, 403). This reassurance represents a manner of entering into harmony with his enigmatic Other, as is suggested by this echo from *A Piece of Monologue*: 'Backs away to edge of light and stands facing blank wall. Covered with pictures once' (*PM*, 426).

The mother's impassivity, that is echoed in the atonal voice, can only be understood as a dead desire, in the way Clov expresses it: 'I love order. It's my dream. A world where all would be silent and still and each thing in its last place, under the last dust.'[29] (*Eg*, 120). By assuming such a desire, the subject finds a form of reconciliation with the unnameable.

A Nonexistent Other

As is illustrated by the figure of the impassive mother, the Beckettian Other is fundamentally absent, one who does not exist, according to the structure that Lacan expresses in the axiom: '[…] there is no Other of the Other' (1966, 813). Ordinarily, this absence is dissimulated behind the appearances of a coherent 'world': a subject who has been instituted by the paternal metaphor benefits from an inscription in reference to the Other who, whatever the circumstances may be, ensures the stability of the subject's existence, and places all invasive *jouissance* at a distance. Words can consequently appear as tools

29 As Thomas Cousineau has demonstrated (28), in a very fine analysis, the character Clov is, with regards to Hamm, an inversion of the maternal figure.

that allow the subject to deal with the unknown by means of a dialectic: words that name or explain have a pacifying effect. Because they only name incompletely (belonging to the register of *limited wholes*), words rely upon each other, leaving a place whereby the subject can continue to explore the question of his desire.

The Beckettian subject, however, finds himself radically alone. In an axiomatic formulation which enters into resonance with that of Lacan,[30] Beckett states that Joyce's work is 'purgatorial' because it reveals 'the absolute absence of the Absolute' (*Dsj*, 33). This form of expression is similar to that of the 'bull', the characteristics of which Shane Weller identifies in the phrase '*Nothing is more real than nothing*' (*MD*, 186). He notes that the 'radical paradoxicality' of this sentence 'detaches the nothing from itself, opens a space within it, even as it posits the nothing as that which lies beyond all affirmation and negation'[31] (2006, 121). Frédéric Pellion observes similar paralogistic formations in relation to melancholy, where 'it is only as an object that the subject of an eventual enunciation is evoked' (264). This foregrounding of the object, in subjective experience, can also make us think of Beckett's 'accusative I' (*TFN* IV, 114). In Beckett's remark about Joyce, *the Absolute*—a God who exists, for example—is struck with a nonexistence that is as immense as the faith that is ordinarily invested in him. Hamm expresses the idea eloquently, after a collective effort to address a prayer to the divinity: 'The bastard! He doesn't exist!' (*Eg*, 119). It is not without importance that, immediately after this exclamation, Nagg speaks of his refusal to listen to his child's cries. Rather than asserting nonexistence outright however, Beckett reinforces the paradoxical construction by means of Clov's immediate response to Hamm: 'Not yet.' The Beckettian heavens are absolutely

30 Lacan also expresses this idea in the form of the barred letter A (for *Autre*, 'Other'): 'Placed across the great A, this bar says that there is no Other who could respond as a partner' (2005a, 127).

31 Working from Christopher Ricks, Paul Stewart also sees the 'inexpressible change' experienced by Arsene in *Watt* as 'in the same world as the bull, a world in which congruity and causal relations are not apparent' (2006, 69).

empty, and cannot inspire the slightest belief in a universal order. As Lacan says, concerning the disappearance of the Other in the modern era:

> [...] the vault of the heavens no longer exists, and all the heavenly bodies, that are the best guides, appear as if they just as well might not exist—their reality is essentially marked, as Existentialism says, by its artificial nature, they are fundamentally contingent.[32] (1986, 147)

All that remains possible, in Beckett's work, is to evoke the 'inviolable zenith where for amateurs of myth lies hidden a way out to earth and sky' (*LO*, 207).

Conscious of the radically contingent nature of existence, the Beckettian subject is completely alone, without any Other (Brown, 2011e). This leads to an absence of any real dialogue, a state that is palliated by the existence of 'pseudocouple[s]' (*U*, 291), or the diverse forms of monologue (*Rockaby*, *That Time*). It is this experience of the total absence of the Other that led Beckett, in 1952, to point out that in the subject/object crisis of modern art, some artists latch on to one of these two terms in order to ensure a form of stability. He defines the specificity of Henri Hayden's painting as residing in the fact that 'ils se désistent de concert' ('they withdraw jointly', *Dsj*, 146): nothing can guarantee them any common ground. The absolute solitude described in a number of prose texts, such as *The Lost Ones*, is exemplified in the *explicit* of *Company*: '[...] labour lost and silence. And you as you always were. / Alone' (*Co*, 42). The isolation of the final vocable, highlighted by the new paragraph,[33] gives material representation to this

32 François Regnault deals with this theme in relation to *Ill Seen Ill Said* (Regnault, 2007).

33 Precisely, the grammatical status of the last word of *Company* appears to be rather uncertain: is it an attribute situated within an elliptical construction? an epithet?

solitude. It is less a matter of the idea of 'failure'—with its moral connotation—than a manner of emphasising the perennial nature of this solitude, its unbreachable character. Beckett gives this situation a precise and succinct formulation, in *Le Monde et le pantalon*: 'Impossible de raisonner sur l'unique' ('Impossible to reason on the unique', *MP*, 32). Indeed, one can 'reason' only if one is sure that meanings enjoy a certain degree of stability, if words lend themselves to concatenation. Once the signifier becomes detached from the chain, the subject experiences his existence as excluded from any community, making reasoning or knowledge no longer valid: he can only *create*.

The Voice: Real and 'Lalangue'

It is with regards to this absolute solitude that the place of language for Beckett can be situated. In the following passage, Lacan defines two faces of the symbolic register, in terms that set the context for the impact of the signifier in Beckett's work:

> In the symbolic order, the empty spaces are as significant as the full ones; it seems indeed, in reading Freud today, that it is the gaping emptiness [*béance d'un vide*] that constitutes the first step of any dialectical movement.
>
> That is what explains, so it would seem, the insistence with which the schizophrenic reiterates this step. In vain, since for him all the symbolic is real. (Lacan, 1966, 392)

The 'gaping emptiness' evoked here is situated prior to the discrete spaces that make up the symbolic order, and that allow for dialectical articulation. If the real 'is the field of that which subsists outside of symbolisation' (Lacan, 1966, 388), it belongs to the realm of the unnameable. Lacan also asserts: 'The real is either the totality, or the vanished instant' (2005b, 53). That is because, to the extent that the real is correlated with the logical category of the 'impossible',[34] it is both

34 Lacan, 1994, 20; 1973, 152; 2005a, 37, 64, 65, 125; 2001, 408, 506.

the unbearable (*insupportable*) and that by virtue of which the subject 'bears' his own existence (*se supporte*): that in which he is grounded. The correlation of the Lacanian *real* with the impossible leads Jean-Claude Milner to declare that it cannot be grasped by the symbolic, since the specificity of the latter is to produce an inscription: '[...] of the Real, nothing is written'[35] (2007, 24).

If, in Lacan's statement, the empty spaces of the symbolic register are 'as significant as the full ones', it is because they belong to a dialectic that confers meaning on them. One can say that the spaces operate a scansion allowing us to read words by means of the differential system they institute. The 'gaping emptiness', on the other hand, is radically irretrievable: nothing can endow it with meaning. For this reason, Jacques-Alain Miller qualifies the schizophrenic as 'the only subject who does not defend himself from the real by means of the symbolic' (1993, 5). If the neurotic—instituted by the paternal metaphor—can defend himself from the real by means of language, it is because the latter offers him a dimension that gives words the quality of 'semblances'. Words allow him to negotiate the unbearable, to set it at a distance: he can sidestep, when faced with the non-negotiable.

When a dialectic is lacking,[36] the subject finds himself faced with the isolated signifier that excludes any metonymical relay. Jacques Borie notes that this is a paradox, since the signifier is by definition—ever since Saussure—of a differential nature; it only exists by virtue of its difference from another signifier:

> There is an equivalence between the signifier by itself [...] and the organ, the object, which Lacan writes as $S_1 = a$. In schizophrenia,

35 We can add this particularly precise formulation: 'No signifier is apt to grasp it, since it is foreign to any chain: in other words, the signifier that would suffice is the very one that, structurally, is missing' (Milner, 1983, 25).

36 '[...] he is inaccessible, inert, stagnant in relation to any dialectic' (Lacan, 1981, 31).

> the word is no longer thought out in the register of representation—which implies a reference—but approached from its phonetic equality with another. In itself, the thing is included in the word.[37] (Borie, 79)

The signifier, thus isolated as a material *thing*, confronts the subject with an absence of representation, which is manifest in the thematic of the degraded body in Beckett's '*Trilogy*'. Thus, not only does Molloy declare that he is 'onelegged' (*Mo*, 31), but his very existence is uncertain: 'Yes, there were times when I forgot not only who I was, but that I was, forgot to be' (44). Far from being a quip, this remark shows how the *real* hole appears in the place of a *rejected* signifier, which springs up without being linked to anything, since it is inaccessible to any dialectic (Lacan, 1981, 99); consequently, the subject has no means at his disposal to deal with it. The presence of this dimension of the impossible involves the signifying system in its entirety—it 'pollute[s] the whole of speech' (*MD*, 186)—directly confronting the Beckettian subject with the *voice object*.

The voice is not an object in the ordinary sense of the word: one which 'is determined by a relation' (Lacan, 2005a, 120). It is an object in the sense that it is excluded from any dialectic. That is also what gives it its status as a real: 'The real […] is always a piece, a stub. […] its stigmata—that of this real as such—is that it is not linked to anything' (Lacan, 2005a, 123). The real of the voice therefore manifests itself at moments when the signified collapses. It is then no longer dissimulated behind the network of diverse meanings—that are always uncertain, both jointed together and labile—but is revealed in the open. In the reality of the novels—*Mercier and Camier*, *Watt*, *Molloy*—it breaks out from time to time, but it conditions the reality of the *dramaticules*: in these plays, the spectator finds himself directly subjected to the incidence of the voices.

---

37 Borie approaches this question by using Freud (Freud, 1968, 65–123). In this passage, the signifier is detached from a dialectic, which would be noted as S_1–S_2.

It is however necessary to make a distinction here. The *real* is fundamentally ungraspable: it is necessary to understand it as being on the horizon of any signifying elaboration since the latter involves articulation which, as such, falls into the realm of the *imaginary*. In Beckett's work, the subject consistently encounters the symbolic as grafted onto a real: it regularly entails a dimension that is unbearable and untameable. What disappears is the body as signified, as the image of a whole: as supported by the phallic register. While Molloy, echoing *Hamlet*, forgets 'to be', the Unnamable disappears physically, remaining only as 'the thing that divides the world in two' (*U*, 376), so that he has 'two surfaces and no thickness'. He is therefore present solely in a structural way, in relation to the symbolic function of language. That is why he persists in the famous *clausula* faced with an impossible: '[…] I can't go on, I'll go on' (407). The Beckettian subject thus finds himself confronted with the symbolic in its differential and unappeasable nature as *voice*, while being imperiously obliged to work with the symbolic. In this way, he indeed insistently defends himself with the symbolic, which is why the latter is brought to the fore throughout Beckett's work.

It is with regards to language's relation to the voice that Beckett's 'attacks on linking' can be considered. The latter is a concept developed by Wilfred Bion in the course of the 1950s, and which concerns the rejection, by certain patients, of the integrative or linking function of language.[38] The latter can be defined as the way language—when it is guaranteed by the Name-of-the-Father—allows the *imaginary* register to assume consistency, so the subject is able to confront any traumatising event. In Beckett's art, such attacks aim manifestly at creating a 'literature of the non-word' (Beckett, 2009, 520) or drilling holes into language (518), as he expressed it in his 1937 letter to Axel Kaun: in short, anything that contributes to destroying language as meaning or communication. While Steven Connor sees such an approach as a possible consequence of psychoanalysis (2008c, 19–

38 Steven Connor provides a detailed study of the evolution of this question (2008c, 16–20).

20), Évelyne Grossman suggests that the original violence came from Beckett's 'dead mother tongue' that obliges the writer 'to say everything while hindering him from doing so, since it literally incarcerates him in the shackles of its imposed structures' (2000, 194). Both these views would seem to be valid. Connor continues:

> [...] throughout the texts of the 1950s and early 1960s, Beckett elaborates his attack on the symbolising, integrating functions of language, and the concomitant claims of the analyst or interpreter. [...] The struggle against language is identified with a struggle against a series of mysteriously oppressing tyrants, whose motivation appears always to be to force a coherent ego or human nature upon the speaker of Beckett's fictions. (Connor, 2008c, 22)

Éric Wessler confirms this perception, pointing out that up until *The Unnamable*, 'the more speech becomes difficult and illegitimate, [...] the more the narrators' historical, and particularly literary, knowledge becomes cumbersome, hampering, and singled out as being the burden that they need to be rid of' (2009, 187). As for the analyst, he can sometimes indeed be experienced as a factor of persecution: a *superego* that commands the preserving of links (Milner, 2007, 12), in a neutral and absolute fashion, similar to the Kantian 'categorical imperative'.

Connor rightly extends this principle: 'It is not too much to say that there is a horror of universal association that matches the horror of eternal life in Beckett' (2008b, 45). Indeed, Beckett goes far beyond attacks that can be noted, for example in *The Unnamable*: his work ends up dealing more basically with what Lacan calls *lalangue*.[39] Indeed, in his later work, Lacan severely relativised the importance and the artificial coherency of the symbolic register—as supported by the Name-of-the-Father—and the unconscious rigorously 'structured like a language' (2001, 498), stating that the latter can only be 'hypothetical with regards to what supports it, that is to say lalangue' (1975b, 127). He thus brings to light the dimension that never ceases to escape being

39 Transposed in English as *llanguage* (Dolar, 143).

ordered by notions such as metaphor and metonymy. In fusing the definite article *la* to the noun it usually determines, Lacan points to an aspect of language where grammar and linguistic distinctions cease to operate.

The word *lalangue* can be associated with 'lallation', baby-talk that is devoid of the symbolic structuring of language, and that materially marks—as a form of writing—the impact of the signifier on the body, producing *jouissance* (Nguyên, 2010a, 75). Michel Bousseyroux points out that the effect of sense [*sens*] here is 'the very present real of lalangue, and not the effect of the signifier's temporal retroaction in the symbolic' (2014, 53). Indeed, such a retroactive mechanism supposes the presence of an Other to provide a final punctuation, and thus ensure meaningful linguistic articulation. In *lalangue*, such pairing does not exist, as Jean-Claude Milner asserts: '[…] lalangue is what makes a language incomparable to any other, in that precisely it has no other, also in that what makes it incomparable cannot be said' (1978, 22). It thus entails the perpetual *équivoque* of language, the impossibility of effacing the differential nature of the signifier, as the narrator of *Malone Dies* expresses it: 'Everything divides into itself, I suppose' (*MD*, 176).

To grasp the importance of this evolution, and to place it into perspective, it is worth making a distinction regarding *équivoque*. Lacan has often been associated with plays on words and the regular use of homophones. Thus, the play on *tuer* (to kill) and *tu es* (you are), defines the lethal aspect involved in naming a subject (1998, 201). The reciprocal relationship expressed by the superego's imperative *Jouis!* (enjoy), and *J'ouis!* (I hear, Lacan, 1966, 821) reveals the consequent response whereby the subject can only *obey* (according to the etymology shared by the two verbs). These examples show homophones as a function of the articulation inherent in *addressed* language: the way speech returns to the subject in the form of a 'reversed message' (Lacan, 1966, 9). The unexpected meanings revealed by homophones bring to light the way the subject is determined by language in relation to the Other, beyond any conscious intended meaning. However, a problem arises here, insofar as psychoanalytical interpretation that relies solely on meaning risks reinforcing the symptom as 'truth' (Bousseyroux, 2014, 58).

Lacan's later uses of homophones diverge from such tight structuring, and it is here that parallels can be drawn with Beckett. One example from Lacan is the notion of a 'master signifier' (commanding a chain of discourse) noted by the symbol S_1. Written as its homophone *essaim* (a swarm, Lacan, 1975b, 130), it is divested of its power to command, and revealed as being exposed to an uncontrollable multiplicity. That is to say, if a signifier is defined by its difference from another, the latter will no longer guarantee any ulterior unification: the signifier (S_2) charged with opening up a dialectical relationship and stable significations is suddenly pronounced *est-ce d'eux*, raising the question *is it of them*... that one speaks? or: what is the object of communication: conventional reality, or *jouissance*? (Lacan, 1975b, 126). In the same way, the singular Name-of-the-Father is expressed in the plural, and written as *les non-dupes-errent* (Lacan, 2001, 516): those who refuse to be 'dupes' of the paternal artifice are prone to 'err' or 'wander'. Such multiplicity reveals the resolutely singular responses each subject invents to deal with the real, in the absence of any norm. In these later developments, it is clear that Lacan is working with language in its material dimension, where it cannot be limited to, or enfolded within a single meaning.

Henceforth, Lacan renounced turning psychoanalysis into a 'garden *à la française*' (2001, 457) and, as Jean-Claude Milner has pointed out, broke with the notion of *style*, that he originally defined—adapting a phrase by Buffon (1707–1788)—as 'the man... whom one addresses' (Lacan, 1966, 9): one is symbolically defined by the Other to whom one's speech is fundamentally addressed, thus bringing into play one's intimacy. Lacan chose rather to 'brutalise' language (Milner, 2011, 63), creating an 'exostyle' (Milner, 2011, 64) that ignores the intimate. This approach recalls Beckett's 'I'll fix their gibberish for them' (*U*, 318).

Lalangue brings into play incessant *non-sense* (Lacan, 2001, 513) where the *unlimited* multiple breaks up discrete units of meaning. One point of particular interest in the case of Beckett is its absolutely singular relation to the mother tongue (Lacan, 1975b, 126): Beckett's regular navigation between two languages serves to reveal the hole inherent in both of them. Lacan pointed out the absence of any authority in the terribly infinite anagrams of Saussure, where no divinity could guarantee that they were actually intended by the author (in Depelsenaire, 33). However, the negative formulations here require to be reversed, since Lacan points to language itself as being a place of knowledge (Depelsenaire, 35), to the detriment of the subject, insofar as something can be said 'without any subject knowing it' (Lacan, 2001, 336). Both Lacan and Beckett deal with this dimension of language, in their respective fields. Like Beckett, Lacan deals with the part that never ceases to 'ooze' (*WH*, 98), and where words 's'alignent de façon à s'annuler mutuellement' ('line up to mutually cancel themselves out', *MP*, 28). The importance of the voice for Beckett—understood as the signifier devoid of meaning—is illustrated by his suddenly asking André Bernold the meaning of a nonexistent word (Bernold, 100). That is to say, he was clearly convinced that such a word did exist, but that its meaning had simply slipped his mind: the force of such a word was independent of any given signifier.

It is well known that, in this respect, Joyce made the choice of accumulation, so that in his work: 'The signifier stuffs [*vient truffer*] the signified' (Lacan, 1975b, 37). Opting for the opposite path, Beckett also worked with language as devoid of subjectivity and 'style', causing the voice to resound in the absence of the Other, in the absence of any final punctuation or possible meaning: his language is continually open to '*soubresauts*' or 'stirrings still'. In this respect, Catherine Laws points out the importance of 'unheard sound' in Beckett's work (2013, 229). This is quite different from the endless voice in works such as *Texts for Nothing*, as she notes: 'The manuscripts show that Beckett vacillated for some time whether the steps of the Figure in *Ghost Trio* should be audible [...]. In the end he made them soundless [...]' (2013, 229). This manifestation of the voice is that of the 'unheard footfalls only sound' (*CSPr*, 258) of 'neither', or in the conclusion to *Footfalls*:

'No sound. [*Pause.*] None at least to be heard' (*Ff*, 402). Laws comments:

> [...] the apparent persistence of a desire for silence is less significant than the insistent, if shadowy, presence of unheard sound, or of hearing nothing. Beckett seems here to focus not on silence or absent sound, but on a kind of 'leastness' of sound [...]. (Laws, 2013, 230)

It is necessary to add that the silence in question is what Bruno Geneste (2015) defines not as being silent (*tacere*)—of refraining from uttering—but 'the silence said to be "of nature" or "of divinity" (*silere*), that is located on the fringes of the void'. This dimension is brought to the fore insofar as such a silence is inherent in the very structure of language—in its dividing and fragmenting—resulting in its impossibility of attaining any ultimate silence. Such silence only exists inasmuch as it is circumscribed by words pushed to their breaking point, which is another way of stating its structural status, far beyond any quest for silence considered as a straightforward progression.

For this very reason then, it is impossible to reduce Beckett's creations to some purely imaginary and arbitrary 'latent poem' (Badiou, 2003, 41): a Platonic perspective that resolutely ignores the materiality of language. If images are encountered in his later works—in *A Piece of Monologue*, *Ill Seen Ill Said*, at random—they are effects of language and *enunciation*: they do not constitute a reference to any stable 'reality' but remain grounded in the incessant *lalangue*, as can clearly be seen, for example, in the permutations of the dancers in *Quad*, or that of the sentences in 'Lessness', which undermine meaning. It is with this practice of language that Beckett succeeds in giving the symbolic its positivity. It should be added that his complex use of images suggest that the question of the Other—as capable of instituting 'traversable space' (*TFN* III, 111), in the works of the middle period for example—can be situated in relation to the phallus, thus placing his work at one remove from foreclosure. That is to say that Beckett's expressions which seem to refer to such structuring would doubtless belong not to psychosis but to a transposition of such motifs into the realm of melancholy, where what remains problematic is the absence of a founding 'assent of the Other' (Lacan, 1991a, 414). So, for example, the expression: '[...] but I could employ fifty wretches for this sinister operation and still be short of a fifty-first, to close the circuit [...]' (*U*, 332). One may be tempted to interpret this lack of a signifier as the description of foreclosure. However, the very fact of *formulating* something similar to this notion means that it enters signifying representation, that it is not radically excluded from the latter. Nonetheless, Beckett's extremely acute relationship to language enabled him to conceive its subjective impact in rigorous formulations that bear conceptual resonance, causing some readers to detect their metaphysical or philosophical implications. As regards the symbolic, it is worth noting that in *Texts for Nothing*, the narrator found himself in a position where words and the material dimension of the letter left him no salutary breach wherein to experience his existence as a subject: '[...] it's forever the same murmur, flowing unbroken, like a single endless word and therefore meaningless, for it's the end gives meaning to words' (*TFN* VIII, 131). By contrast, it is by following the razor-edge of the symbolic—as grafted onto the real—that Beckett succeeds, in his works as of *How It Is*, and most spectacularly in *Worstward Ho*, in creating a breach, a *blank* or an hiatus capable of endowing him with a positive existence as a subjective singularity. Here, as Bruno Geneste points out, Beckett succeeds in moving beyond his aggressive use of 'nominalistic irony' (*L2*, 520) to attack links, working towards the '*most real of the Symbolic*' (Geneste, 2015).

The 'attacks on linking' here are thus largely distinct from the violent rejection of the language imposed on the narrator-subject of *The Unnamable*: 'It's a poor trick that consists in ramming a set of words down your gullet on the principle that you can't bring them up without being branded as belonging to their breed. But I'll fix their gibberish for them' (*U*, 318). Éric Wessler (2015) notes that as of 'From an Abandoned Work' (1954–55), Beckett's writing changed: his style became more contracted, centred on fixity, an orientation that enabled him to transform violence into poetry, in a context where the bodily image was dispersed by the gaze of the Other (intervening in the character of Balfe). In the same vein, Cécile Yapaudjian-Labat demonstrates how, in *Worstward Ho*, the violence of the universal dimension of the signifier—the *logos*—ends up turned against itself as a result of a counter-violence that it itself engenders, so that in breaking up signifying units, it reveals the irreducible presence of the subject. In this way, the latter is no longer simply revolting against the tyranny of the signifier, nor is he lamenting language's powerlessness to endow him with being, as he does in *Texts for Nothing*. A contrast can be heard between the latter position, and Beckett's declaration to André Bernold, after speaking about his work with Jim Lewis and the Süddendeutscher Rundfunk: 'Il me faudrait des acteurs-substantifs' ('I would require substantive-actors', in Bernold, 65). Such a declaration may seem paradoxical, regarding the spectral figures Beckett was producing for the television. And yet, in 'From an Abandoned Work', rather than rejecting words, he is able to declare his attachment to them: '[…] words have been my only loves, not many' (*CSPr*, 162). Indeed, in *How It Is*, the subject acquires consistency by latching onto signifiers while breaking them up. P. J. Murphy points out: 'The ultimate paradox of *How It Is* is that the syntax of weakness enables the narrator to find a language that has the strength to command being' (75). Here, the absence of punctuation breaks up the text, producing a state of perpetual *équivoque*: a syntax that is rigorously constructed, but where the point of attachment of each member of any given utterance remains uncertain. Thus the reader is forced to mime 'the extortion of voice, or the forcing of the text into vocality' (Connor, 2014b, 277) experienced by the painfully uttering subject.

This dimension of language sets the Beckettian adverbs *perhaps* (in Driver, 23) and *neither* (*CSPr*, 258) in their true perspective, that is to say, in relation to the real. The hole inherent in language leaves the subject (term that Lacan finally replaces by *parlêtre*, to place it in relation to *lalangue*) alone to grapple with language as bordering on the *real*. That is precisely why Beckett declared: 'I take no sides' (in Worton, 75). Taking sides can only testify to the unstable imaginary register, where one endorses the numerable predicates of a party or a clan. Beckett's position brings to the fore the absence of guarantee in language: the nonexistence of any law capable of giving meaning an irrefutable foundation.

The perception of this dimension of language seems to have caused the exemplary reversal of Steven Connor's position, from seeking to show 'the ways in which Beckett's work dissolves the claims of presence' (2008b, 42)—which he admits was an 'evasion' (47)—to at last recognising Beckett's 'effort to find his way to a presence, though a presence denuded of all determinations'. This allowed Connor to comment on the poem 'comment dire'/'what is the word' (*CPo*, 226–7, 228–9) as 'a frantic splintering under the extreme stress of ostension' (2008b, 41), an interpretation that thus moves closer to that of Michel Bousseyroux (2000, 199), who centres his approach resolutely on the relation of the symbolic and the real.[40] Thus the 'attacks on linking' go far beyond the particular difficulties encountered by Beckett's narrators in the '*Trilogy*'—with their aggressive irony—and can be found in a remarkable form in *Worstward Ho,* to take just one notable example (Brown, 2008, 78–88).

The Hallucinated Voice

One crucial aspect of the Beckettian voice that critics have already noted is the complexity of its location. Chris Ackerley has pointed out as much, showing the difference between *Murphy* and *Watt*, the latter offering 'a classic case of the schizoid voice' (2004, 42). He also asserts that the voice fading and coming back is the origin and nucleus of *The Unnamable* (2004, 46). He evokes, in this respect, the uncertainty principle:

---

40 We could also distinguish this reading of 'comment dire', that includes *jouissance* and the real, from that of Deleuze, who speaks of stuttering (*bégaiement*), whereby Beckett 'makes the sentence grow out of its middle' (Deleuze, 140): it is crucial to give to this splitting its material—and thus problematic—*content.* See also Luke Thurston on the syllable *ma* and the name as underscoring the failure of the signifier.

> [...] be it in terms of Bohr's notion of complementarity and/or Heisenberg's Uncertainty Principle, which suggest that it can be heard but not located, or vice versa, but not heard and located simultaneously. Thus the antimony of the 'I' and the 'Not-I' must remain absolute, in the same way that Murphy cannot apperceive himself in the dark part of his mind: one cannot be conscious of being unconscious. (Ackerley, 2004, 47)

Indeed, as we have previously pointed out (2008, 13–6), it is the paternal metaphor as instituted by a separation that founds three-dimensional reality, opening up the coordinates of 'traversable space' (*TFN* III, 111), the supposedly objective world where the *voice* remains veiled behind imaginary representations. Beckett's voices, however, remain in the open, embedded in incessant language whose flow cannot be stemmed by naming.

It is thus precisely because his voices are manifestations of the *unlimited* that they cannot be contained within the bounds of a recognisable world: that they cannot be limited, for example, to a specific source or origin. Ulrika Maude states that 'a sound without a source' would be unbearable (2009, 50). Moving closer to the structural dimension, Steven Connor notes that there are no sound objects:

> [...] objects are only the occasions for sound, never their origins. And there is no sound that is the sound of one object alone. All sounds are the result of collisions, abrasions, impingements or minglings of objects. (2005a)

Mladen Dolar comments on Michel Chion's study of the *acousmatic* voice—one that can be heard, but whose source remains hidden—pointing out that '*there is no such thing as disacousmatization.* The source of the voice can never be seen' (2006, 70). The voice, as such, cannot be situated within specific coordinates, a fact which leads Ulrika Maude to point out that the sense of hearing 'enables the auditor to traverse obstacles the other senses cannot overcome' (2009, 52), and that sound 'surrounds us with a 360-degree range, instead of only facing us, as vision does' (58). The voice thus appears as an *a* object: one that has fallen off, that emanates from between signifiers or other nameable objects but in no way belongs to them.

Conversely, however, concrete objects mobilise something that, as a *voice*, concerns the hearer intimately, as in John Donne's famous sentence expressing the wilful misapprehension of what is, in reality, immediately grasped by the subject: '[...] never send to know for whom the bell tolls; it tolls for thee.' The bell's voice *necessarily* resounds for me, from a subjective point of view, even when this statement may be objectively inexact. The *voice* reaches the subject via a unilateral movement that the latter has no mastery over, because it strikes him in a part that irremediably belongs to the Other. The only way to intervene then is to speak oneself.

The divorce from concrete, 'traversable space' (*TFN* III, 111), can go even further. For example, where is Mouth located, during *Not I*? Invaded by the voice, she is nothing more than the latter that drives her to speech[41] and that, for the spectators, is situated in the visible mouth, and in the tormented rhythm composing the play as a whole. The most extreme diminution of any spatial reality is without doubt to be found in the play *Breath*, where no human figure appears, but which unfolds in a total duration of thirty-five seconds, between the scansion marked by the poles inspiration/expiration. The entirety of *existence* is contained here, in the absence of anything that could be called *being*.[42] The perception of this dimension in Beckett's work led Hélène Cixous to say: 'To make one step of a centimetre, of a millimetre, of a word, of three dots, a nuclear energy is necessary, to *make* an image, to do, the slightest do, to do' (29).

---

41 For a detailed analysis of this play, in relation to the drive, see *infra*, p. 120 *sqq*.

42 In his later work, Lacan distinguishes between *being* (which remains attached to the register of signification) and *existence*, which is not a preconstituted physical being (contrary to Existentialist thinking) but belongs to the original encounter of the 'speaking being' with language (Miller, 2010–11).

As the voice cannot be located, it often appears as a hallucination. In his description of the frightening slipping occurring in language, Watt makes an essential remark when he declares: 'And I have little doubt that I was the only person living to discover them' (*W*, 43). Watt asserts the reality of the *voice*, without claiming that this reality can be generalised, or that others could hear it. This position contrasts with the judgement made by Ada, in the radio play *Embers*. Beckett remarks that this text is based 'sur une ambiguïté: le personnage a-t-il une hallucination ou est-il en présence de la réalité?' ('on an ambiguity: is the character having a hallucination or is he in the presence of reality?' in Zilliacus, 83). Ada is far more peremptory when she evokes the manner in which the protagonist, Henry, persists in talking to himself, in order not to hear the sound of the sea: 'It's silly to say it keeps you from hearing it, it doesn't keep you from hearing it and even if it does you shouldn't be hearing it, there must be something wrong with your brain' (*E*, 260). She also protests: 'I don't think you are hearing it.' Ada refuses to recognise the slightest reality—other than medical or organic—in the auditory phenomena experienced by Henry. Speaking from a firm foundation in common sense, she is determined to remain impermeable to any idea of a subjective experience that, in her opinion, has no concrete existence.

The status of the voice thus proves to be problematic. Insofar as it constitutes an effect of language, it engages a subject's entire reality. It affects the part that founds the latter in his singularity. For this reason, it can be distinguished from an 'objective' event that, as such, can be observed by a third party. Mercier and Camier encounter a similar phenomenon:

> I hear singing.
> They halted, the better to listen.
> I hear nothing, said Mercier.
> And yet you have good ears, said Camier, so far as I know.
> Very fair, said Mercier.
> Strange, said Camier.
> Do you hear it still? said Mercier.

> For all the world a mixed choir, said Camier.
> Perhaps it's a delusion, said Mercier.
> Possibly, said Camier. (*MC*, 16)

If it seems plausible that the members of this 'pseudocouple' represent two faces of a single subjectivity, this passage can be understood as the staging of an internal debate bearing on the reality of the voices. Here, while Camier declares that he hears singing, Mercier hears nothing. The voice is thus situated on a purely subjective level. A second stage is indicated by Camier's remark concerning Mercier's hearing. Since the latter's aural faculty is unimpeded, one must conclude that the voice does not belong to the sensory field: what one *hears* has no need to pass through the medium of the body in order to exist and produce an effect on the subject. If such were the case, the voice would be of a purely objective nature, belonging to shared reality. To take an example from outside the field of literature, the experience of Beethoven, who became progressively deaf after 1796, is instructive. Indeed, according to André Bernold, Beckett envisaged devoting a play to Beethoven deaf, and which 'simply consisted in making heard the absence of a voice' (Bernold, 53). Such an allusion appears relevant, in the light of Beckett's reference to this composer, in his famous letter to Axel Kaun:

> Is there any reason why that terrifyingly arbitrary materiality of the word surface should not be dissolved, as for example the sound surface of Beethoven's Seventh Symphony is devoured by huge black pauses, so that for pages on end we cannot perceive it as other than a dizzying path of sounds connecting unfathomable chasms of silence? (9 July 1937, Beckett, 2009, 518–9)

To dissolve the surface of words and meaning is to find oneself in the presence of the *voice*. The importance of the dialogue form, used by Mercier and Camier, consists in maintaining the voice's uncertain status: one cannot simply declare that Camier is hallucinating, and so deny the voice any reality, in the same way as it cannot be claimed that the voice belongs to an overall, objective existence.

This hesitation is essential to emphasise the fact that the subjective dimension of the *voice* is in no way incompatible with its reality. As Lacan points out: '[…] truly, the madman does not believe in the reality of his hallucination' (1981, 87). However, if the subject by no means claims that the voices that assail him are an objective phenomenon, the way he experiences them testifies to a *certainty*: it is precisely because the voice intrudes like a 'foreign body' (313), and the *ego* finds itself 'expelled from its home', that the subject no longer doubts. It is therefore important to distinguish *certainty* from simple *belief*, which rests on an identifiable truth. As Lacan specifies concerning the one who experiences auditory hallucinations:

> But contrary to the normal subject for whom reality is directly served up to him, he has a certainty, which is that what is happening—from the hallucination to the interpretation—concerns him.
>
> It is not a question of reality for him, but of certainty. (Lacan, 1981, 88)

Thus it is that Glenn Clifton can say of *The Unnamable*: 'While the speaker of *The Unnamable* is not fully present to himself in the sense that Derrida deconstructs, he is also completely unable to get away from himself; the contact between the speaker and the voice remains unquestionable' (165). If the subject cannot perceive himself in the mastery of his own speech, he can in no way dissociate himself from the voice, since this impossibility constitutes the latter's very reality. The voice touches on a real that, as such, remains impervious to any effort to pin it down. The certainty thus bears on the incidence of the voice on the subject, and on the latter's existence.

The reality of the voice as an object, and its very real impact on the body, are thus determined by the impossibility for language to fully represent the subject. The Beckettian subject in particular finds himself grappling not only with a signifying lack in language that is capable of supporting the metonymical movement of one signifier to another, that characterises desire, but with an *unlimited*, incessant dimension that refuses to be contained within naming and representation, and that will not allow itself to be forgotten or ignored. It is possible to observe the precise way in which a subject is inscribed in language through his relationship to the pronouns that determine his existence, insofar as the specificity of deictic pronouns consists in pointing to the part of a subject's being that remains excluded from the signifying chain.

II — Disjunction of Pronouns

To explore the voice as involving the real for a subject, it is necessary to study the way in which the latter is situated with regards to the pronouns that structure language. Here, we shall start by examining the first person pronoun that constitutes a subject as *enunciation*, insofar as it only partially covers or represents the latter's existence. This is particularly true since, in terms of its logical construction, the *I* represents an attainment that authorises the subject to speak in his own name, and to converse with others. We shall then turn to the example of *Not I*, where the first person pronoun is vigorously rejected by Mouth. This refusal to say *I* will be analysed as a consequence of the insatiable *drive*, a term that it will first be necessary to define. However, the interpretation advanced will state that far from being absent, Mouth is most *present* in her very insistence on pronouncing the pronoun *she* in the fiction she relates.

Having established the refusal of the *I*, Beckett's use of the third person singular *he* will be addressed. Firstly, *Company* will show the fictional effort to bind the *you* and the *he*, in order to produce an *I*, but which stumbles on a structural impossibility that confirms the subject's solitude. Finally, *A Piece of Monologue* will reveal the subject speaking of himself as *he*, but whose spoken 'ritual' constitutes his address to an absent Other.

Metaphorical Formation of the 'I'

Pronouns reveal a systematically problematic nature in Beckett's work, in the narrator's refusal to say *I* (*The Unnamable*, *Texts for Nothing*, *Not I*), in the failure to produce an *I* in *Company*; or in the use of the third person for the narrators of the *dramaticules* (*A Piece of Monologue*, *Footfalls*); or, yet again, in the insistent use of *you* in *Company*, *That Time* and *Eh Joe*.

Among pronouns, the third person—the 'non-person', excluded from communication—which generally functions as an anaphoric pronoun, is usually distinguished from the first and second—deictic—persons, pointing to actors engaged in conversation. The two latter groups are directly articulated with extra-linguistic referents. Indeed, in order to consider language in its material quality, it is indispensable to take into account a point situated outside of representation, a point of cessation that does not enter the representation and is not subordinated to linguistic logification. It is an ultimate point marked by the *impossible*, leading Jean-Claude Milner to assert that in cases such as that of oaths, insults and indirect speech, among others, it is necessary to posit the dimension of the subject:

> In all these cases, we can point out the given of an impossible, whose explanation demands we resort no longer to a speaking subject that is symmetrisable and non-desiring, but to a subject of enunciation, capable of desire and non-symmetrisable. (1978, 46)

On a structural level, the subject cannot be completely identified with the pronoun *I* which, far from expressing him exhaustively, can only represent him. Thus this subject does not fit in with its usual meaning as a conscious and autonomous agent of his acts. Lacan's definition—'[...] a signifier is what represents the subject for another signifier' (1966, 819)—brings into account the distinction between *utterance* and *enunciation*. The subject cannot be grasped in the signifying chain, in the same way as the Unnamable is heard as the voice that bears his utterances, without ever being named by the words he proffers.

To enable the subject to dispose of the *I*, an operation of separation is necessary, since originally, the signifier's retroactive effect produces the subject as *you*, marking his alienation to language:[1] the mortification of a *you are* which, in the French *tu es* can be heard as the

1 See *supra*, p. 104, 307–8.

infinitive *tuer*, 'to kill'.[2] Lacan indicates that primitive identification 'consists of this exchange that makes the I of the subject come to being in the place of the mother as Other, whereas the mother's I becomes his Other' (1998, 201). The subject's *I* is inscribed in relation to the mother: the subject thus acquires an existence by taking a signifier from the Other. But, instead of being entirely alienated to the latter, he finds the mother's desire directed elsewhere. This diverting makes the latter forever enigmatic, causing the subject to identify with it. Instead of being assigned to the place designated by the *you*, the subject will *assume the lack* that appears in the fact that the Other desires, and is already *other to himself*. Thus, after *alienation*, the operation of *separation* founds the subject—once and for all—in relation to the paternal metaphor. This separation also founds the address to the Other. To sum up, it can be said that the *I* unfolds according to three registers:

The *I* is *imaginary*, insofar as it is materialised in the empirical phrase, where one's *I* is opposed to others in a verbal exchange. It is what could be more appropriately expressed by the pronoun *me*, where each person considers he is identical to himself, master of his utterances.

The *I* is *symbolic*, giving expression to the desiring subject faced with a missing Other: it is the subject of enunciation. By virtue of this, the subject no longer keeps an eye on the conformity of his utterances, according to received and collective criteria, but accepts the risk of unveiling the signifiers that determine him (Lacan, 2006a, 19).

Finally, the *I* is *real*, insofar as it is the 'unborn' subject, who remains excluded from access to the paternal metaphor. Thus it is that Beckett could say to Charles Juliet: 'Il n'y a pas de pronom… Le *je*, le *il*, le *nous*, rien ne convient' ('There is no pronoun… The *I*, the *he*, the

---

2 Lacan states that the *tu* 'is the other insofar as it is caught up in ostentation with regards to this *all* that the universe of discourse supposes. But at the same time, when I take the other out of this universe, I objectify him' (1981, 340). The *tu/you* thus has a dehumanising effect similar to that of the insult. *Cf. infra*, p. 307–8.

us, nothing is appropriate', in Juliet, 67). This gaping hole in language leads to the conclusion: 'Rien n'est dicible' ('Nothing is speakable').

Beckettian texts accentuate this inadequacy between the subject of the utterance and the subject of enunciation, insofar as they appear to seek out or to display an impersonal dimension: their narrator regularly rejects pronouns, denouncing their insufficiency. These processes lay bare the structure of language, stripping down imaginary identifications. It is precisely in this context that writing gives voice to the dimension of the subject as *real*: to the latter's impenetrable, 'unnameable' nature. Such a subject is completely engaged in enunciation, in that he can be heard struggling with the *impossible* dimension of his existence. In Beckett's work, what is absent is the symbolic *I*: of course, occurrences of the pronoun *I* can be found in the texts, but the character or the narrator never ceases to deny any palpable or necessary link between this pronoun and himself as a subject: no *I* allows for the establishing of a dialectic between the subject and an Other marked with a lack. For this subject, who is faced with 'the absolute absence of the Absolute' (*Dsj*, 33), the dimension of address is radically absent. It is therefore not astonishing to find evoked, in *Texts for Nothing*, 'a voice that makes no sound because it goes towards none' (*TFN* IV, 115). The Beckettian voice appears as 'a pure enunciation without a subject, or an enunciation in search of a subject' (Dolar, 2010, 58).

'I' and the Drive: 'Not I'

Beckett's exploration of the complexity of the pronoun *I* assumes emblematic importance, not only in *The Unnamable* (Brown, 2011b), but also in the *dramaticule* whose title gives a central place to this pronoun: *Not I*. This play's construction invites us to situate the subject in a context where the deictic pronoun *I* is forcefully rejected. The dimension of the voice is massively present in what assumes the form of an irrepressible logorrhœa. The monologue that composes this play has been situated in its filiation with *The Unnamable*: '[…] the dominant inspiration for the work, partly perhaps visual as well as verbal, seems to lie in *The Unnamable*, which Beckett himself referred to as a major source' (Knowlson and Pilling, 197; *cf.* Knowlson, 1997, 590). It is true that as in *The Unnamable*, the voice of *Not I* is not one that the feminine subject has at her disposal but one that traverses her, as with Neary, in *Murphy*: 'Neary began to speak, or, as it rather sounded, be spoken through' (*Mu*, 133). Given over to the voice object, she finds herself in a position of radical exteriority, instead of being enveloped and gently rocked, as is the case in *That Time*, *Rockaby* and *Footfalls*. In *Not I*, the voice is a torment, not a source of reassurance.

However, substantial differences exist between *The Unnamable* and *Not I*. Instead of relentlessly striving to avoid being caught up in naming that she rejects, Mouth is striving to thread together a narrative: like the characters of *Play*, who seek refuge from the spotlight in 'the shade of words' (Lawley, 1984), Mouth constructs herself as the unknown being, embedded in the 'shade' of her fiction. Also, the rigorous structure of this *dramaticule* is based on rhythm: repetition of motifs, punctuation by the five vocal ejaculations and fading. By contrast, *The Unnamable* is dominated by its linear structure, as it moves forever 'on'. The subject of *Not I* gives form to battles with language in an effort to lodge herself in relation to the incidence of the signifier on her body, not in order to tear herself away from it. This play thus comes in the wake of *How It Is*, when Beckett moved past the lack of being he experienced so acutely in *Texts for Nothing*. This vital link to existence in language is why Éric Wessler (2009, 164–5) can note—even in this play dealing with what seems to resemble a form of intense delirium: words imposing themselves as foreign and uncontrollable—that Beckett multiplies the indirect references to his work and to words springing up like a Proustian revelation. Catherine Laws thus correctly points out:

> [...] the 'musicality' of Beckett might be seen to lie less in a drive towards the abstracting of language or pure self-reference than in the interplay between subjective agency and the concretising im-

> pulse of form and structure—a characteristic more truly attributable to music than either pure abstraction or absolute expressivism. (Laws, 2013, 252)

This remark is perfectly in harmony with the conception of the voice in its relation to language and the signifier. *Not I* shows most eloquently that language is material, situated on the incalculable border between meaning and absence of meaning, graspable and ungraspable, with the consequent effects on the body. Mouth also appears to be grappling with the incommensurable effort to produce form, to latch on to words, while revealing the impossibility for signifiers to enclose her being, since the latter remains the opaque existence revealed where meaning breaks down and provides no shelter. In respect of the latter, *Not I* can also be read in the light of an irrepressible movement aiming to suck the spectator into a 'rioting and rambling hole', as Billie Whitelaw experienced it (1978, 118). This perception is close to Mladen Dolar's interpretation of Edvard Munch's painting[3] *The Scream* (1893), where the landscape 'eddies into the black hole of the mouth' (Dolar, 2006, 69). In *Not I*, endless metonymy is replaced by a precise and dangerous localisation.

Among the various analyses given of the pronoun *I*, Lois Oppenheim offers a normative point of view, situating Mouth in the light of pathology and impairments (2008, 193–4) that supposedly hinder 'the self's extended consciousness' as an ideal of humanisation. Such an approach ignores *jouissance*: the question of what inhabits the subject and is *at stake* for him. Ulrika Maude evokes Tourette's syndrome, which evacuates subjectivity and mobilises 'coprolalic' language. However the ideological notion that the use of such vocabulary might be capable of contesting the 'guarantors of will and agency' (2008, 165) seems insufficient.

Elizabeth Barry gives credence to Julia Kristeva's conception of Mouth's desire to retain the Law of the Father, purported to have

3 Beckett was enthusiastic about Munch's paintings when he discovered them during his trip to Germany (Vilar, 692).

'repressed the feminine voice' (Barry, 2006, 159). Mouth is said to be an 'impossible subject', in relation only to a great Other—God—for want of 'a "he" or a significant other to whom to relate' in dialogue. However, it is difficult to know what this 'feminine voice' might be, other than the result of an operation of *separation*, a second extraction of *jouissance* which, precisely, institutes the Name-of-the-Father. At this stage, 'dialogue'—involving symbolic retroaction—would come into existence, and it would then be possible to speak, on this derivative level, of 'gender performance'. That means that any notions of a masculine and a feminine 'gender' are of a purely *imaginary* or specular nature, dissimulating the way sexuality is structured by language. Indeed, Kristeva does not take this dimension into account, since she considers masculine and feminine as symmetrical and complementary terms. It is clear, however, that dialogue—as a symbolic construction, with the locutor's words received back from the Other as a 'reversed message'—is not present in Beckett's work, because he is working with that *real* part of language that escapes dialectical binding.

And yet, working within such a strictly binary conception (masculine/feminine, father/mother), Kristeva sees Mouth as a counterpart to the narrator of *First Love*, in the sense that she considers them both as being morbidly attached to the 'dead father', the founder of social bonds. She links Mouth to writing, in her will to retain the father:

> […] the act of writing, without I nor you, will be precisely this obstinacy to not relinquish the third person: the outside of discourse, the third, the 'he [or it] exists', the anonymous, the unnameable 'God', the 'Other'—the axis of the pen, the Death of the father, outside of locution, outside of subjectivism, outside of psychologism. (Kristeva, 262)

It is far from clear what 'dead father' figure Kristeva might be referring to in the text of *Not I*. However, she sees Beckett as expressing a son's attachment to death through this feminine mouth (263).

Basically, since Kristeva's thinking is entirely bound up in the notion of the Œdipal father figure, she totally ignores the dimension of the *unlimited* and the absence of any Other that marks Beckett's work. She develops her ideas much more in relation to the dual notions inherent in the theory of 'gender', rather than to a psychoanalytical problematic. This position leads her to call for a reassuring balancing between father and mother figures. The 'mother' supposedly bringing 'the echolalia of intense pre-Œdipian symbiosis, anterior to the father' (Kristeva, 267); this would be 'admittedly a copy of the 3rd person', 'but also the bursting of the object through the seen and the said in the rhythm: polymorphic, polyphonic, serene, eternal and inalterable *jouissance*'. Such a perception, which she draws from Joyce, has little to do with the relation to the real that Lacan studied in the great writer's work, since she describes it as being purely pleasurable and exalting; in other words, subordinated to ideological criteria. Contrary to Kristeva, our reading will aim to show that it is precisely in the 'not I'—in her effacing—that Mouth actually asserts her existence.

Beckett evoked a real episode as a source of the play:

> I knew that woman in Ireland… I knew who she was—not 'she' specifically, one single woman, but there were so many old crones, stumbling down the lanes, in the ditches, beside the hedgerows. Ireland is full of them. And I heard 'her' saying what I wrote in *Not I*. I actually heard it. (in Brater, 1987, 24)

Two things appear to be of particular interest in this remark. Firstly, the reference to an event that really occurred (once, several times…), that is to say, Beckett provides a clinical dimension that sheds light on literary innovation. This aspect can be distinguished from sociological approaches: that is to say, here it is in no way a matter of simply reflecting a reality observable in 'marginal' individuals, but of highlighting a subjective position with relation to speech. Secondly, by evoking a multitude of old women, Beckett affirms that he heard what he wrote: what arises from this experience explicitly belongs to the realm of the voice, and to the one that speaks in *Not I*. In other words, there is a movement towards a voice that is embodied in the author, who acts as a 'scribe'.

This text has also been associated with the remark Beckett made to Pinter: 'I was in hospital once. There was a man in another ward, dying of throat cancer. In the silence I could hear his screams continually. That's the only kind of form my work has' (in Bair, 528). These screams—emanating from someone approaching death, and suffering from excruciating pain caused by the disintegration of his body—are assuredly enlightening for the question of the Beckettian voice as a whole: structurally, the *voice* touches on this unbearable suffering, where the bond between the subject and his body is at stake.

In Beckett's original intention, the fragmenting of the body is correlated with the incidence of the voice: 'Ruby Cohn recalls Beckett's interest in a talking mouth a bit earlier, in the summer of 1971, when he asked her, "Can you stage a mouth? Just a moving mouth, with the rest of the face in darkness"' (Gontarski, 1985, 132). The invasion by the voice is inseparable from this evacuation of the unified body: the person is reduced to a simple mouth, in a transformation apparently inspired by Caravaggio's painting entitled *Decollation of Saint John*, in Valletta Cathedral, Malta (Knowlson and Pilling, 196). In addition to this, Peter Fifield sees a close connection between Beckett's mouth and those represented in Francis Bacon's paintings (Fifield, 2009b, 63). This production of an acephalous subject is closely linked to speech that seems emancipated from any intentionality. Enoch Brater notes:

> In a discarded piece entitled 'Kilcool' he was already preoccupied with the image of a severed head and the theme of involuntary speech: 'every word is mild torture I would give all I have to stop, but I have nothing, nothing left, or there are no takers.' (Brater, 1987, 24)

The mouth represents a portion detached from the body, and that appears as obscene refuse. Beckett explains to Alain Schneider: 'Her speech a purely buccal phenomenon without mental control or understanding, only half heard. Function running away with the organ' (Beckett, 1998, 283). The existence of 'mental control' or 'understanding' would confirm the existence of a subject who is sufficiently identified to be capable of clear intentionality. The subject of *Not I* knows no such security. In a manuscript, Beckett emphasises once again the dimension of such an experience as *real*: 'The sheer terror of being run away with by a bodily function' (TCD 10971/7/2, in Feldman, 2006, 100). Terror invades the subject from the moment the latter's body no longer offers any barrier against overwhelming *jouissance*.

This 'bodily function' is none other, in the final analysis, than the voice that manifests its autonomy. In *Not I*, language speaks alone. *Ça parle/It speaks*: 'and the brain… raving away on its own… trying to make sense of it… or make it stop…' (*NI*, 380). Steven Connor sees the isolated mouth as challenging 'the proposition that speech comes "from" the mouth, or the body' (2007, 180). Indeed, as early as his conception of the 'mirror stage', Lacan demonstrates that the existence of the 'body' is due to specific conditions resulting from inscription in language. Jean-Claude Milner notes that, contrary to Freud—who supposed an entity called 'sexuality' that he then projected onto anatomy—Lacan 'operated a series of uncouplings' (2011a, 109). Consequently, for the psychoanalyst, 'there are no sexual organs', in the same way as, for linguists, there are no 'speech organs'. The relevance of this structural principle appears with force in Beckett's construction of the *voice*.

Far from being a neutral phenomenon, a pure question of literary formalism, the *ça parle/it speaks* is a terrifying experience which assumes reality in the very staging of the play, allowing us to measure the dimension of the voice as real. Beckett affirmed as much several times: 'I'm not unduly concerned with intelligibility. I want the piece to work on the nerves of the audience' (in Ackerley and Gontarski, 411); or: 'I hear it breathless, urgent, feverish, rhythmic, panting along, without undue concern with intelligibility. Addressed less to the understanding than to the nerves of the audience which should in a sense *share her bewilderment*' (Beckett, 1998, 283). The 'sharing' that takes place in the theatrical experience is thus situated in this turmoil that destroys all meaning. It is at this point that the spectator finds himself radically confronted, for example, with the two irreconcilable aspects of the play: the beauty of the written text, in contrast with its unbearable nature which appears when it is staged, where the words disintegrate into non-sense and unintelligibility. As an effect of the *voice*, the faculty of understanding is reduced to almost nothing. At that moment, it can be noticed that language does not act as 'representation' but brings to the fore, precisely, the signifier as *devoid of meaning*. Actress and spectator are thus united in a dimension of the real.

Billie Whitelaw's experience of acting this play is perfectly exemplary of the dimension where the symbolic is bound up in the real, and also of the distinction according to which while Joyce 'enjoys *lalangue* as a thing',[4] 'for Beckett, writing must have an effect on the body' (Geneste, 2014). As Rosemary Pountney observes: 'The actor in fact "tunes in" to Beckett rather than creating his own character' (185). The reverse movement proves to be complementary, since the actor's function, in turn, is not to simply comply with the strictly written formulations of a pre-established text, or any prior authorial 'intention' or 'meaning'. Matthieu Protin (2014) shows in great detail how Beckett's work with actors started precisely with what is absent from the play as written. As stage director—in *Endgame*, for example—Beckett first worked on achieving a convincing bodily posture, the latter involving the character as speechless, that is to say, as isolated in his relationship to the signifier devoid of extension in meaning or naturalistic characterisation. This modelling of the body consequently governs the character and his sensations during the performance. Protin highlights the 'attention given to vocal and bodily exteriority, seemingly to the detriment of a psychologising or hermeneutic approach' (2014, 294). As result, the actor's lines are worked on as pure 'sound material' dependent on a *deixis* that endows it with its singularity, rather than as utterances anchored in the emotional history of a character. According to John Calder, it was the sound of Whitelaw's voice that Beckett carried in his head (Whitelaw, 1996, 117). The exemplary

---

4 For the use of this term *lalangue*, see *supra*, p. 99 *sqq*.

communication at work here is remarkable: one actress quoted by Billie Whitelaw stated that the only perfect Winnie was Beckett himself (153). It is also worth noting Beckett's fear of having his own voice recorded—projected outside of himself (137, 140)—and the *physical* suffering he experienced if his text was not reproduced in its most minute musical details (151).

When she read *Not I* for the first time, Billie Whitelaw explains she was seized by an 'inner scream' (1996, 116), and when she performed it: 'I wanted to be left with nothing but my centre, my core, which seemed to be situated somewhere around my gut—the little flame I needed' (128). She had no existence other than the imperative flow of the words, to 'get to the point where I opened my mouth, and this stuff just poured out of me, like some sort of verbal diarrhœa' (122). This is the point where the actress is given over to the *drive*, which abolishes the rest of her body as a unified image. The consequences were inescapable; not only ill health caused by each successive play, but after *Not I*: 'The play had touched terrors within me that I have never come to terms with' (131). This perfect conformity of *jouissance* and text could also be observed in the æsthetic achievement of *Footfalls*, under Beckett's painstaking and demanding direction:

> Whenever the shape and the movements were finally right, I found that a surge of energy would start to go through me. [...] It became the only possible shape. I knew when the shape was not right, because my body felt dead, lifeless. (Whitelaw, 145)

As for the body, Billie Whitelaw expressed the trauma she experienced when she performed *Not I*: 'I went to pieces. I felt I had no body; I could not relate to where I was; and, going at that speed, I was becoming very dizzy and felt like an astronaut tumbling into space. I swore to God I was falling' (1978). This experience constitutes the dimension of *enunciation* that dominates this play: where language is anchored in a bodily real.

This enunciation rests on the incidence of the *drive*, and the manner in which the latter accomplishes the subject's fading, excluding any possibility of attaining the *I*, a state which Elizabeth Wright rightly situates in relation to the subject's first entry into language (in McMullan, 76). This approach shows the drive as a positive, living force, inherent in each subject, rather than as a pathological deviance, or as a simple location in the hypothalamus, as neurosciences often promote it.

Lacan originally situates this term in relation to an unconditional and imperative *Demand*, where the subject is effaced (a condition called *aphanisis* or *fading*). He states that the drive is 'what becomes of the demand when the subject disappears in it' (1966, 817), adding that what is left is the cut (*coupure*). The drive thus produces an 'acephalous subjectivation, a subjectivation without a subject, a bone, a structure, a tracing' (1973, 167). Jacques-Alain Miller provides a useful analogy: 'It is the knife without a blade, from which the handle has been removed' (2010–11).

Jacques-Alain Miller sees an evolution in Lacan's conception of the drive when he describes it as simply a vector, accomplishing a binary movement, or an open/close alternation, tracing a loop that circumscribes a central void (Lacan, 1973, 163). This circular movement can only be apprehended in a topological perspective, as being situated on an edge, a slit, or the *cut*, identified with the '"erogenous zone" that the drive isolates from the metabolism of the function'[5] (Lacan, 1966, 817). Here the drive can be grasped as 'partial', that is to say as being centred on various replaceable, 'metonymical' objects, none of which can claim any pre-eminence (Lacan, 1973, 163). The object is only what the drive can circumscribe and localise, without in any way satisfying the latter. As a result of the drive, the *object* is emp-

5 Symptomatic of many usages of Lacan's theories in critical studies, while Anna McMullan quotes this very passage (72–3), she draws no conclusion from it, returning to the works of more conventional academic theoreticians (Kristeva, Irigaray).

tied of all substance, so that the only thing we know of it is 'the instance in the form of the lost small *a* object' (164). Thus it is that the visible object gives way to the invisibility of the *gaze*, and the audibility of speech is effaced, to the benefit of the voice's 'screaming silence' (*TFN* XIII, 154).

As it is situated outside the empirical articulation offered by the symbolic, the drive cannot be tamed. However, when Lacan finally states that the drives are 'the echo in the body of the fact that there is a saying' (2005a, 17), he completely detaches them from any linguistic articulation, leaving the impact of the signifier on the body, the effect of *jouissance*, where there is no subject and no Other.

If the identity of the object is of no importance in itself, the election of one object in particular—following an initial evacuation of *jouissance*—allows the subject to consolidate his 'world'. In *Not I*, however, nothing can bring the verbal flow to a halt. Orality prevails over any consideration of bodily unity: 'whole body like gone... just the mouth...' (*NI*, 380). This orality is fundamentally problematic. Firstly, the isolated mouth reveals the slit that becomes obscene, since it effaces the image of the body as a constituted whole, revealing the object. Secondly, a pulsating movement dominates the drive, as is shown by the succession of prepositions *on/off*: 'groan... on and off' (378); 'just the eyelids... [...] on and off...' (378); 'and the beam... flickering on and off...' (381). If the mouth is central to the play, it enters in resonance with the other orifices that are aligned in the same series without distinction, as Peter Fifield (2009b, 65) and Steven Connor (2007, 179) both note. Thus: 'just the eyelids... presumably... on and off... shut out the light... reflex they call it...' (*NI*, 378); 'for she could still hear the buzzing... so-called... in the ears...' (377); 'stream of words... in her ear... practically in her ear...' (380). Mouth desperately seeks to evacuate the voice that is engulfing her, that she feels to be a substance, waste that she must expel in order to find relief: 'she'll be purged...' (381); 'nearest lavatory... start pouring it out... steady stream... mad stuff...' (382). In this respect, tears follow the same path as her words: 'no sound... just the tears...' (381). Mouth herself has always been situated in a 'hole', ever since birth: 'tiny little thing...

before its time… godforsaken hole…' (381). While watching a version of the play filmed by the BBC, Beckett realised that the mouth resembled a vagina[6] (Knowlson and Pilling, 200).

However, Keir Elam's notion of the mouth being 'a corporeal and semantic (black) hole onto or into which the spectator may project any number of literally organic senses' (151) seems inadequate since, as a consequence of the drive, nothing can integrate this gaping hole within a dialectic: Mouth has never been 'born'. It is because of its status as a partial object that the mouth commands space. Steven Connor points out that 'this is not an organ that exists solidly in space, but is itself the space in which solidity and vacancy are produced and reproduced' (2007, 179). Peter Fifield notes the 'combination of pushing itself out towards its observers, and drawing inwards with that dark central cave' (2009b, 64). It is precisely this combination that reveals the mouth's status as partial object: its abstraction as well as the concrete presence of flesh and the *jouissance* it embodies, without any attenuation provided by the specular image of the body as a whole, and which supposes a comforting, pacified integration.

Mouth finds herself carried away by an irrepressible metonymy, so that it is impossible for her to situate her corporeal functions within a hierarchy. Her body is devoid of any consistency: 'all the time the buzzing… so-called… in the ears… though of course actually… not in the ears at all… in the skull…' (*NI*, 378). Her body registers no sensations, and all sexuality is evacuated: 'when clearly intended to be having pleasure… she was in fact… having none… not the slightest…' (377). Indeed, only the paternal metaphor can eroticise ('phallicise'[7]) the body and thus limit and localise *jouissance*, transforming it into an experience of pleasure. However Mouth feels no sensation that could allow her to situate herself in a body: 'no part of her moving…

6 The performance given by Lisa Dwan indeed bears out this strong visual dimension of the play (*Not I*, *Footfalls* and *Rockaby*, directed by Walter Asmus, Athénée-Théâtre Louis-Jouvet, Paris, 11–15 March 2015).

7 For a definition of phallus, see *supra*, p. 60.

that she could feel…' (378); 'and now this stream… not catching the half of it… not the quarter… no idea… what she was saying…' (379).

In the published version of the play, Mouth's irrepressible speech is not situated in a total void but in connection to an 'Auditor'. What takes place is not a dialogue—that necessarily reposes on a dialectical structure—but a sort of sharing which, paradoxically, sheds light on the non-negotiable chasm separating the two figures. For Mouth, no real address is possible, insofar as she is *spoken* by the Other. Thus, the Auditor is not designated by a deictic pronoun (*you*) but his presence is heard in the interruptions present in Mouth's discourse, in the questions or objections that are not verbalised by this Other. Beckett emphasises the form of exchange between the two in his analysis of the first version of the play, and where he designates Auditor as 'interrupter' (RUL 1227/7/12/1, in Tonning, 111). Beckett noted, in his drafts, that Mouth is 'denied by interrupter' (in Pountney, 100), and Rosemary Pountney comments that 'the interrupter is that part of the consciousness continually trying to prod the voice into self-acceptance, signified by the question "what?".' Thus, in spite of his silence—according to the spectator's perception, at least—for Mouth, Auditor appears sometimes as an unbearable *voice* that she must expel.

United on the stage, these two figures compose a chiastic relationship. On one hand, Mouth is entirely speech: her body is fragmented, and her sexuality is undone. On the other hand, Auditor has no speech; he possesses a unified body, but appears anonymous and sexless.[8] He is presented as follows: '[…] tall standing figure, sex undeterminable, enveloped from head to foot in loose black djellaba, with hood […]' (*NI*, 376). The two figures represent an extreme polarity, so that no exchange is possible, no speech can pass from one to the other, and each one has a monopoly over the characteristics he presents. On one side, Auditor is only the closure of meaning, with no access to enunciation; on the other side, Mouth is enunciation without an *I*, without any passage to a closure productive of meaning.

---

8 Of course, Beckett adds: 'It is not stated, though suggested by the masculine "auditor," that it is a man' (1998, 283).

Slavoj Žižek considers the role of the Auditor—'a silent impotent witness' (Žižek, 2009)—to be related to that of the great Other, to whom Mouth's discourse is addressed. At regular intervals, Auditor makes 'a gesture of helpless compassion'[9] (*NI*, 375). This description invites us to situate the place of the Other in a position analogous to that occupied by the gaze of E ('Eye') at the end of *Film*: '[…] neither severity nor benignity, but rather acute *intentness*' (*F*, 329). That is to say that this maternal figure (be it played by a masculine character), for want of instituting the child within speech expressive of desire, is unable to formulate an attitude in words, but can only manifest a vague reaction which remains marked by *équivoque*. In *Not I*, in particular, the author attributes to Auditor a compassionate attitude, by means of which both figures share their powerlessness. Auditor occupies the place of a parent contemplating a scene that escapes him: his child who, at the bottom of a hole, is struggling with forces beyond his power to combat.

However, as mute and powerless as he may be, the presence of this Other enables Mouth to pronounce her discourse: whether he be visibly present or not (he is generally excluded from stage productions), Auditor remains essential from a structural point of view, since he represents the only possibility for Mouth to have access to an *I*. Nonetheless, the vacuity Mouth suffers from cannot be diminished as long as her Other remains self-sufficient, unmarked by any lack, such as would be embodied in addressed speech. As presented here, the situation suggests no way out.

The place of the pronoun *I*, which Mouth rejects with such violence, has yet to be defined more closely. The discourse of the play as a whole unfolds in an impersonal mode: Mouth can only refer to

---

9 We find the same gesture in a short text of 1929: 'He sketched a tired gesture of acceptation […]' ('Assumption', *CSPr*, 5). The character makes this gesture when hearing the woman talk, except that in this text, the woman's discourse is calm and smooth, expressing her indifference to the torment of the one who is listening to her.

herself by means of the delocutive pronoun *she*, who is an actor of the narrative. This situation can be summed up in the following diagram:

story	>	she (representation)
(absence of a story)	//	(*I*) (unrepresented)

As a subject, Mouth has no story at her disposal: she is little more than a gaping hole. The creation of a fiction creates a scene that allows her to come to being as *she*. This pronoun appears in the place of an *I*: the outcome aimed at by this operation, but which remains ever virtual. The oblique double bar indicates the impossibility for the product of this operation to merge with what causes it, except that it would be necessary to situate, in this point, the complete *scission* between the two tiers of this structuring.

For Mouth, the *I*—the sign of a *divided* subject—is out of reach: she only knows the *split* that definitively excludes her from nomination. Remaining on the side of the impersonal and the gaping hole, she unfolds her third person discourse, whose function is comparable to the stories read by Beckett's characters, like May, in *Footfalls*.[10] Indeed, nothing indicates that Mouth's story is not an invention, a desperate effort to endow herself with the personal history that she is lacking. The spectator has no reference to measure the 'veracity' of the events related. Basically, in the construction of this play, the story covers a real: the impossibility for Mouth to assume a story that may be hers.

Insofar as it designates the delocutive person, the anaphoric pronoun *she* is homomorphous with the other pronouns in the story. However, it acquires a crucial importance in Mouth's five exclamations—'what?... who?... no!... she!...' (*NI*, 377, 379, 381, 382)—each of which appears as a response to Auditor's mute invitation to proffer the pronoun *I*, since his gesture follows a pause. The fifth time, however, the pronoun is printed in (small) capitals—'what?... who?...

10 See *infra*, p. 220–1.

no!… SHE!…' (382)—and Auditor remains still, as if Mouth had definitively rejected the invitation to pronounce *I*, and Auditor himself had decided to abandon his vain efforts. This relation appears in the title *Not I*, which can be read as equivalent to Mouth's protests; but with this reserve, that the expression *not I* comes not from Mouth but from the author, as if the latter, occupying a place similar to that of Auditor, were compensating for Mouth's powerlessness to express herself.

In these circumstances, it is appropriate to re-evaluate the status of this *she*, and to see to what extent this pronoun offers a substitute for the *I*, operating somewhat paradoxically as a form of deictic. Indeed, the exclamatory *she* appears to be symmetrical to Auditor's gesture: it is a verbal sign that could be interpreted as 'she, over there, that I named in the story'. The pronoun *she* would thus have the function of designating the strangeness of the voice, the Thing that cannot be assumed by the subject as *I*.

Between the pronoun *she* and the absent *I*, it is important to discern a rupture analogous to the one that constitutes the 'fall' evoked in the story:

> nothing of any note till coming up to sixty when–… what?… seventy?… good God!… coming up to seventy… wandering in a field… looking aimlessly for cowslips… to make a ball… a few steps then stop… stare into space… then on… a few more… stop and stare again… so on… drifting around… when suddenly… gradually… all went out… all that early April morning light… and she found herself in the—… what?… who?… no!… she!… [*Pause and movement 1.*]… found herself in the dark… (*NI*, 376–7)

During the first part of her life, Mouth moves with no hitch in 'traversable space': an 'objective' realm, equivalent to the spring fields of Crocker's Acres. Suddenly, without any circumstance enabling her to foresee, to explain or identify it, an event occurs that plunges her into a hole characterised by the absence of light: the 'godforsaken hole' (*NI*, 381) that marks the total absence of any Other. It is this event that sets off the rest of her story. Some critics, intent on replacing the literary construction by a realistic justification to fill in the disquieting lacunæ, have suggested the idea of a rape.[11] Slavoj Žižek (2009), however, speaks of an 'epiphany'.

The absence of an *I* should thus be associated with this fall into an absolute absence of an Other. In the 'Kilcool' manuscript which Beckett wrote in 1963, and which paved the way for *Not I*, two voices can be observed: the 'normal voice' and the 'assumed' one (in Pountney, 95). In one fragment, it would seem, the 'normal' voice avoids the *I* (Pountney, 97), trying to convince itself of a fiction, as does Mouth in *Not I*, while the 'assumed voice' enjoins it to 'go out, live!' (in Pountney, 96). In the hypothesis that Mouth may have, in the past, used the pronoun *I*, this possibility is henceforth prohibited, as the voice is no longer shared between two agents. The subject revealed by Mouth is not specularisable: a fact that can be associated, for example, with the picture turned face to the wall in *Endgame* (*Eg*, 92), or the torn up photographs in *A Piece of Monologue* (*PM*, 426). If Auditor demands that she proffer the pronoun *I*, Mouth can in no way grant this demand, as she has never benefited from a structuring *separation*—or second extraction of *jouissance*—which could have instituted her in reference to the paternal metaphor: at the corresponding point, she only finds an abyss. She cannot confess the words demanded by the Other, since she is incapable of considering them as semblances: such a confession would cause her abolition.

Here we can push further our critique of Kristeva. For Lacan, the feminine as non-totalisable retains a relation to the universal—a notion absent from Kristeva's text—and which, in the absence of the Name-of-the-Father and its attending dialectical mechanism, gives rise to the exorbitant place occupied by the superego. What Mouth refuses to relinquish is her singularity: to give this up would mean suppressing

11 'When Alan Schneider asked whether or not "she" had been raped in the field, Beckett said he was surprised by the question; however, he didn't say yes and he didn't say no' (Interview with Jessica Tandy, in Brater, 1987, 32).

her very existence. In that case, the effect of this text is to give voice to this singularity: far from being repressed, her 'feminine voice' is embodied in the terrible combat inherent in her pure enunciation, and which can be linked to Lacan's development on calligraphy.[12] In his text 'Lituraterre' (1971), Lacan states that in Japanese calligraphy, 'the singular of the hand crushes the universal' (Lacan, 2001, 16), since the line traced (or *trait*) gives existence to the subject's absolute singularity as barred or divided, as only partially represented by the signifier: 'Pure *litura* is the literal. To produce it is to reproduce this half without a pair from which a subject subsists' (Lacan, 2001, 16). Pierre Skriabine points out here the effect of a 'paradoxical disjunction' separating 'the extreme of the universal'—such as the form imposed by science, for example—'the pure function of the cut operated by the signifier' and, on the other hand, what 'belongs to the register of its singular materiality, which affects a being and its jouissance' (Skriabine, 37). The subject thus surges up from this pure *cut*—previously associated with the drive—being both a product of the universal and what radically rejects it. It is in this context that Lacan (2001, 11, 16) explicitly refutes Derrida's claim of a trace purportedly existing prior to the signifier (Lacan, 2007, 64–5, 78). Mouth's 'assumed voice' is thus marked by the superego: 'life'[13] entails the possibility of being integrated into discourse (as universal), but it supposes the death of the unspoken being, as pure enunciation and subjectivity (absolute singularity). Hence Mouth's choice to enunciate in the third person, to lodge herself within the fiction created, to be the unspoken author of the fiction: such is the only binding possible, that is to say, within this split or scission as written or inscribed.

Paradoxically therefore—and like in the 'fuck life' (*R*, 246) of *Rockaby* (Brown, 2013c, 200–1)—it is in the assertion of *she* that the

12 We pursue this question of inscription further; see *infra*, p. 213 *sqq*.

13 This voice is comparable to the one in *A Piece of Monologue*, that also urges to opt for 'life': 'Move on to other matters' (*PM*, 428, see Kaltenbeck, 2010, 91–2).

subject is most present: in this violent rupture.[14] On this point—and in reference to Beckett's evolution following *Texts for Nothing*—Éric Wessler observes that 'after having been *for nothing*, the self-referential text, in Beckett, is more and more often dictated to say *not I*' (2009, 199). That is to say that the forceful cry *not I* is a form of assertion: it is the means by which the subject here comes to existence. It is possible to further adapt Wessler's remark concerning the pronunciation of exclamations in *Come and Go*. He notes that 'in the rounding of their mouths required by their pronunciation, the image returns of an empty circle—but not all that empty, since it henceforth obeys a principle of differenciation' (331). Thus, the apparently empty hole of the exclamation presents the positive presence of an indefinable but irreducible subjective singularity. In the forceful negations of *Not I* too, such a singularity is brought to the fore. Indeed, Mouth does not say *it is not me* (the French would resort to the fully articulated two-part negation: *ne… pas…*, giving: *ce n'est pas moi*): she does not formulate such a radical disqualification of her subjective being. Rather, she says, as the title emphasises: *It is 'not-me'*, or *It is: 'not I'*. Mouth asserts herself on the level of the drive; she resists the language of the Other (the 'treasury of the signifier' that designates her as excluded) by asserting herself in her very exclusion, by demanding her death as a symbolic subject. *She* is the ejaculation that designates the subject as powerless to assume an *I*, with the result that she comes to being in the energy of this very ejaculation, in this proof of life that, paradoxically, designates her as 'unborn': the subject is situated between the level of the closed utterance (*she*)—thus resembling the hooded Other—and the abyss where she remains impervious to any naming.

The Quest for a Binding: 'Company'

If the complexity of the pronoun *I* is explored in several texts—being situated in relation to the third person, as noted previously—the second person pronoun *you* is much rarer, being found

---

14 Erik Tonning associates the line in *Rockaby* with the maternal figure 'rail[ing] at the source of all life' (*IS*, 45, Tonning, 2010, 234).

mainly in *That Time* (written 1974–1975), where three voices address the figure present on stage. *Company* (published in 1980) is remarkable for the use of a device where *you* and *he* are heard alternately, thus calling into question their impossible articulation. The treatment offered here is calmer, and marked by a much more measured pacing than *The Unnamable*. This text seems to have been strongly influenced by Beckett's work with electronic media, as Steven Connor suggests:

> The voice which 'comes to one in the dark' throughout this text has many of the qualities of the voices 'coming out of the dark' of radio drama and the details of the listener's position remind us remarkably of the listening face of *That Time*, a stage play that itself uses some of the properties of radio drama. (2007, 166)

The first version of this text is found in an abandoned manuscript entitled 'The Voice', which bears the indication 'Paris, Jan. 1977' (Ackerley and Gontarski, 618). This work thus deals fundamentally with the voice, not only in the sense that the latter is an 'actor' in the story that unfolds, but also in that this text represents a construction exploring what constitutes the voice in the impossibility of binding the *you* to a *he*.

The *incipit* formulates the question immediately, in a sentence that sets the scene of the narration: 'A voice comes to one in the dark. Imagine' (*Co*, 3). According to Chris Ackerley, Beckett revealed that Jeremiah was behind this voice (2004, 45). The formulation used in this sentence assumes the appearance of an axiom, from which the subject—who could say *I*—is evacuated: on one side can be found a faceless voice, devoid of any identity; on the other side, a subject who is just as anonymous, in a space empty of any reference point. This utterance sets the scene. At the opposite pole of the book—in the conclusion—the result of the discourse unveils the vanity of this undertaking: 'The fable of one fabling of one with you in the dark. And how better in the end labour lost and silence. And you as you always were. / Alone' (42). In its unfolding, the 'fable' is divided between, on the one hand, the voice that uses the pronoun *you*—and that relates childhood memories in the form of vignettes—and, on the other hand, the description of the subject, designated by the pronoun *he*, lying in the dark, listening to the same voice.

The use of the deictic pronoun *you* would lead us to suppose the existence of a subject having an *I* at his disposal. However, these two pronouns are not at all symmetrical, as the subject of this story experiences the impossibility of appropriating the pronoun *I*. For this reason, it is of particular interest to examine the way in which the narrator defines his problematic in a logical form: 'The use of the second person marks the voice. That of the third that cankerous other. Could he speak to and of whom the voice speaks there would be a first. But he cannot. He shall not. You cannot. You shall not' (*Co*, 4). The envisaged existence of an *I* is what is at stake in this proposition. The first difficulty resides in the use of the prepositions *to* and *of*, marked by haplology, that is to say, avoiding the doubling of the preposition introducing the indirect complement for each occurrence of the verb *to speak*: **speak to* [*the one*] *to whom the voice speaks*. Then, a scission appears—leading to the absence of an *I*—and which opposes an obstacle, thwarting the efforts to untangle the threads. According to the terms of this scission, the voice has the monopoly of the *you*, while to the 'other' is ascribed the pronoun *he*. However, the narrator avoids articulating the relationship between these pronouns and the instances: for 'marks', the French uses the expression 'est le fait de' (*Cie*, 9) which, contrary to the English, does not signify 'possess' or 'proffer'. In this gap, therefore, an opacity can be observed that drives the text's unfolding. In the apodosis of this passage, the hypothesis of a future binding ends in failure. The voice comes undone and is diffracted because of the absence of an *I*, as a result of its constitutive scission: it thus leaves us with the iterative succession of the pronouns *he* and *you*.

The heart of this formulation therefore resides in the hypothesis: 'Could he speak to and of whom the voice speaks there would be a first' (*Co*, 4). To grasp what is at stake in this phrase, it may be useful to set it in parallel with a formulation—that, at first glance, appears to be similar—by Lacan, in his Seminar on psychoses, concerning the patient in psychoanalysis:

> [. . .] the subject starts by speaking of himself, he does not speak to you—then, he speaks to you, but he does not speak of himself—when he has spoken of himself, who will have appreciably changed in the interval, to you, we will have arrived at the end of the analysis. (1981, 182–3)

As the result of the final binding (*of himself, to you*) indicates, each one of these two aspects contains its qualities and its limits. Thus, in speaking *of* himself, the subject places at a distance the fundamental fantasy that structures his 'world', and that maintains him riveted to his satisfaction (be it dissimulated behind a show of dissatisfaction and displeasure): instead of remaining at the place his original Other assigned him to, he detaches himself to see his position as a construct, not as a fatality. Diverse incidents are then clearly seen as part of a repetitive *series*, not as separate and unrelated. Thus it is that the subject speaks *of himself*, from the vantage point of the Other, in relation to a dimension of universality that produces knowledge.

However, the subject can also consider he is making simple statements that are little likely to call his preconceived ideas into question. He supposes that he alone can say what concerns him, relegating the Other to the simple function of expressing approval. And yet, by speaking *to* the psychoanalyst, the subject can limit himself to the register of the demand, expecting the Other to provide a response to his suffering. The subject supposes that he is powerless to know, instituting his Other in the position of one who can know in his stead. And yet, by addressing himself to the Other, the subject also questions the unknown dimension of the desire of the Other, where language is marked by incompleteness. This lack is returned to him, according to the retroactive logic of the signifier, so that he is made aware of his own solitude; but this time not without the Other. At this moment, the binding operates: the subject can speak of himself (which no one else can do in his stead); but he does so while assuming the risk implied in the confrontation with the radical absence of a response. At this moment, no adequacy is possible: the Other can only acknowledge what the subject alone is able to formulate, assuming the entire risk of his enunciation. This risk supposes an *act* by virtue of which the subject gives up his *jouissance*, his *a* object or his 'pound of flesh' (Lacan, 2013, 387) which is dearer to him than life itself. As Beckett states it, the artist, like the subject, 'stakes his being' (*Dsj*, 149). Speaking, here, is considered as *giving voice*, as an *invocation* whereby the subject gives his 'real weight' (Lacan, 2013, 458).

The structure of *Company* is based on the failure of such a possibility of subjectivisation. The existence of an *I* would suppose that the subject does not remain assigned to a place by the voice's *you*, but that he speaks *to* it. What the subject of *Company* aspires to attain appears to be more of a *false binding*: for him, it is a matter of speaking 'to and of whom the voice speaks' (*Co*, 4). In this way, he imagines he can assume the enunciation from the position of the voice (that pronounces the *you*), and also speak of himself (*he*). This would be, or so he imagines, to situate himself as a *singularity* conveying an interiorised (subjectivised) voice and placing himself on the level of *universality*, as 'one among others'. But the construction described by the narrator represents the contrary of an enunciating *I*: the latter remains unimaginable and out of reach. Indeed, by situating himself in the place he describes, he only reproduces the pattern that already composes the story: combining the *you* and the *he*, that are proffered, in spite of the subject's absolute opacity. The narrator in no way evokes the bi-polar construction (based on the retroaction of the signifier) that consists of speaking '*to* the Other *of* oneself'. On the contrary, what he describes remains in the field of this gaping and unbridgeable hole: *of whom to whom*. Thus continues to be manifest, on one side, the mastery of speech—revealing the imperative power of the voice—and, on the other, absolute silence.

For these reasons, in *Company*, the *I* remains absent: in its place, there is only the presence of an abyss: 'For the first personal singular and a fortiori plural pronoun had never any place in your vocabulary' (*Co*, 41). Such an *I* can only be founded by virtue of a symbolic transmission which, here, is radically lacking. Thus: 'Nowhere to be found. Nowhere to be sought. The unthinkable last of all. Unnamable. Last person. I. Quick leave him' (15).

The *I* does not come into existence in the text, but the *you* is indeed present. This pronoun comes to the 'unborn' subject as a *voice*, conserving the remains of its original imperative force. It is by means of the *you* that the voice composes vignettes that appear as so many images of the past, and which it seeks to make the subject assume. Its 'object' is defined thus: 'To have the hearer have a past and acknowledge it' (*Co*, 22). If the subject could assume a past, with its memories, he would effectively have the pronoun *I* at his disposal: this past would be connected to his present, so that he could pass on his experiences to others. However, in the absence of an enunciation, the voice resorts to monotonous reiteration:

> As if willing him by this dint to make it his. To confess, Yes I remember. Perhaps even to have a voice. To murmur, Yes I remember. What an addition to company that would be! A voice in the first person singular. Murmuring now and then, Yes I remember. (*Co*, 9)

The voice must repeat, as if it could thus penetrate the subject and compel him to recognise the episodes as belonging to his personal past: to make the subject the vector of an enunciation. Such a project is paradoxical, since the production of an *I* testifies to a failure on behalf of the emitter of the *you*: its function consists of *silencing the voice.* The narrator conceives this production of an *I* as a source of 'company': 'What an addition to company that would be! [...] In the end you will utter again. Yes I remember. That was I. That was I then' (13). Certainly, but the idea of 'company' has a very different meaning from what these sentences suggest: if the subject could speak, he would not simply be the voice's double; he would not imitate the latter by telling himself stories. On the contrary he would, as a subject, have a symbolic Other at his disposal; he would be liberated from his profound solitude.

Despite his use of the pronoun *you*, and its function of occupying the subject, the voice remains anonymous, since it is devoid of any address. The subject is in no way capable of knowing if the voice is addressing him: 'Of words murmured in his ear to wonder if they are addressed to him!' (*Co*, 20). Indeed, the pronoun *you* alone does not permit him to determine with certainty if he is the true addressee of the message, an idea which leads him to ask himself if the voice is not speaking *to* another, or *of* another. For want of being able to recognise himself in the images evoked, the subject can hardly discern if the voice is actually speaking *of* him. In the same way, he fails to determine if the *you* is speaking precisely *to* him. Of course, the narrator corrects this error of appreciation, but the subject still feels this uncertainty: 'For were the voice speaking not to him but to another then it must be of that other it is speaking and not of him or of another still. Since it speaks in the second person' (6).

Such an address would have been possible if a proper name had taken form: the latter, like the *I*, founds the subject, once and for all, within the coordinates that determine geometrical space. Indeed, the simple adding of a proper noun enables the subject to distinguish himself from other bearers of the pronoun *you*, to situate himself as a singularity: 'You Haitch are on your back in the dark. [...] No longer any question of his overhearing. Of his not being meant' (*Co*, 20). The proper noun offers the possibility of establishing coordinates: the apposition here posits the identity of the name (shared by a plurality of people, and so belonging to a generality) and the vocative *you*, which marks the address to someone singular, in the place of a third person discourse, where the other would have the status of an object. Were it to be effective, the apposition would confirm a binding of the singular and the universal, by which the subject could count himself as *one among others*: 'So that faint uneasiness lost. That faint hope' (20).

However, this 'hope' concludes in failure, since the name *Haitch/H* does not remain, and the *you* itself is powerless to draw the subject out of his anonymity: 'Then let him not be named H. Let him be again as he was. The hearer. Unnamable. You' (*Co*, 20). If *you* is necessarily the receiver—*the object*—of the voice, he remains anonymous, powerless to appropriate the traits that define him from without. He conserves an impersonal dimension, since the emitter cannot express any desire: the part that is unknown to himself, and that would drive him to address another. Consequently, the subject has no access to the traits by which he could identify himself as *me*. As Lacan emphasises, the pronoun *you* has an imperative quality, as it is 'the other insofar as he is caught in the ostentation with relation to this *all* [*tous*] that the universe of discourse supposes. But by the same token, when I take the other out of this universe, I objectify him' (1981, 340). The *you* thus originally supposes an Other who remains master of discourse, an Other devoid of any lack and whose intervention can only place the subject on the same level as all impersonal words.[15]

The subject of *Company* endeavours to invent the voice announced in the *incipit*. Of course, the latter is not addressed to him: he invents it, and it remains anonymous, since it 'comes to one in the dark' (*Co*, 3). If, however, according to this structuring, the voice aims to have him recognise a past that belongs to him, it is a matter, according to the terms of Beckettian creation, of bringing to life a subject that is 'not born'. In other words, it is a voice that could be called 'maternal' and that, finally, would be capable of transmitting a desire regarding her child. The invented voice replaces the missing maternal one, since like the latter, it is situated: 'Above the upturned face. Falling tangent to the crown' (31). The analogy is made explicit: 'A mother's stooping over the cradle from behind.' Of course, the failure that gave rise to this writing can only reproduce itself: 'She moves aside to let the father look. In his turn he murmurs to the newborn. Flat tone unchanged. No trace of love.' For want of a word of desire, the subject invents for himself 'company' that he has never known.

By inventing the *you* pronounced by the voice, the subject seeks to be instituted by the Other in a desperate effort to produce an

---

15 See *infra*, p. 258.

I by means of the pronoun *he*. In this way, he adopts the view point of the Other, observing his unspeakable being from above: '[...] without a word you view yourself to this effect as you would a stranger suffering say from Hodgkin's disease or if you prefer Percival Pott's surprised at prayer' (*Co*, 41). In the absence of a symbolised subjectivity, the only possible discourse about the subject is the one that the latter must adopt to speak of himself.

In this text, the one who is referred to by this third person is the prey of doubt: he is characterised by ratiocination and a vocabulary marked by logical terms, as in the following passages: '[...] the type of assertion he does not question' (*Co*, 4); 'But company apart this effect is clearly necessary. For were he merely to hear the voice [...]. Or of course unless as above surmised it is directed at another' (5). This discourse procures no feeling of reassurance, since the *he* doubts that the voice is addressing him: 'If the voice is not speaking to him it must be speaking to another' (6). Indeed, despite appearances, the speculations this voice formulates are not of an objective nature; rather, they have a *function* that consists of filling the emptiness. Contrary to the *you*, the *he* has no actual presence: at most, the subject can represent him as a body crawling in the void (31). The *he* does not provide the subject with any concrete existence.

Indeed, for want of a subject capable of incorporating the voice, it is impossible to establish an objective existence or reality: 'There being nothing to show when it describes correctly his situation that the description is not for the benefit of another in the same situation' (*Co*, 29). This impersonal discourse founded on the third person is unlikely to construct a consistent space or reality: 'No that then to compare to this now.' The content of the signified does not suffice to found a reality, in the absence of an *enunciation*, an *I* that can convey his discourse. Of course, the voice sometimes endeavours to articulate both aspects: 'Sometimes the two are combined as for example, You first saw the light on such and such a day and now you are on your back in the dark' (3). By juxtaposing these coordinated clauses, the voice attempts to give the impression that such a unique point exists, but this effort fails since it is founded on no real inscription, but simply on an association of signifieds.

Consequently, the disconnected ratiocination fails, revealing something of the falseness—the *semblance*, as Lacan would say—of all rationality. The narrator admits: 'So with what reason remains he reasons and reasons ill' (*Co*, 6); 'What kind of imagination is this so reason-ridden? A kind of its own' (21). Of itself, reason is powerless to impose an order on the phenomena it describes.

The use of the third person produces an inextricable confusion between *he* and *another*. While the *he* is the mask of the unnameable subject, the latter is designated by the term *the other*: 'He speaks of himself as of another. He says speaking of himself, He speaks of himself as of another. Himself he devises too for company' (*Co*, 16). In passages like this one, the splitting assumes the form of a multiple inclusion: the subject observes himself and intervenes in order to comment on this same observation. To account for this confusion, a model taken from set theory could prove useful. To found a set, it is necessary to start with a *trait* (term understood as a 'line') that can only be described paradoxically: 'The *unary trait* [*trait unaire*, Freud's *Einziger Zug*] only signifies insofar as it is different from any other signifier, including itself' (Bruno, 96). This is what founds Bertrand Russell's paradox:[16] *the set of all the sets that do not include themselves.* So, to describe one's siblings, one will say: 'The three of us are brothers'; by virtue of which the subject sees himself from without, included in the whole. Or: 'I have two brothers'; whereby the subject appears as an exception to the group. However, the following sentence could also be imagined: 'I have three brothers: John, Paul and myself.'[17] This rendering is paradoxical, since the subject claims to apprehend himself within the set, even though the pronoun *I* is incapable of including itself. He who

16 Bertrand Russel reformulated a paradox that had originally been discovered by Georg Cantor, according to Gilles Chatenay (83, n. 3).

17 This example was created by psychologist Alfred Binet (1857–1911) and used by Lacan in order to distinguish the subject of the utterance from the subject of enunciation (2013, 92–3).

proffers this sentence claims to situate himself both within and without. So, whereas the first two formulations suppose a constituted subject that has an *I* at his disposal, the third one manifests the absence of this pronoun. It expresses the position of a subject who is not instituted by the paternal metaphor, thus producing a sentence such as the following: 'Devised deviser devising it all for company' (30). The 'Devised deviser' excludes the evocation of a subject capable of devising it. Behind him, can be situated the subject who is radically excluded: 'Is there anything to add to this esquisse? His unnamability. Even M must go. So W reminds himself of his creature as so far created. W? But W too is creature. Figment.' Here, any attempt at naming must entail the conclusion that the name is little more than a *figment.* Only the subject's *division* could found him on the basis of a point of extraction or exclusion. In the absence of such an operation, it is impossible to designate; it is only possible to line up signifiers that echo each other, in the manner of infinite mirror images: 'Why in another dark or in the same? And whose voice is asking this? Who asks, Whose voice is asking this?' (15).

Thus reigns a confusion which, like the voice that says *you*, serves to extract the subject from his radical solitude, and offers him a form of 'company': 'Confusion too is company up to a point' (*Co*, 16). Ratiocination and the series of doublings are a part of Beckett's poetic objectives. They occupy a function in writing, replacing the impossible nomination, as is specified in *Le Monde et le pantalon*:

> Car chaque fois qu'on veut faire faire aux mots un véritable travail de transbordement, chaque fois qu'on veut leur faire exprimer autre chose que des mots, ils s'alignent de façon à s'annuler mutuellement. C'est, sans doute, ce qui donne à la vie tout son charme. (*MP*, 28)

> (For each time you want to have words do a true work of transferral, each time you want to make them express something other than words, they line up so as to mutually annul themselves. That is doubtless what gives life all its charm.)

The pronoun *he* supports the claim to express an objective reality. However, the words cancel each other out because of the evanescent nature of the signifieds, and in the absence of an element of exception capable of founding the *whole*. This 'charm' is analysed in *Company*: 'In another dark or in the same another devising it all for company. This at first seems clear' (*Co*, 13). The ordering of these terms appears to be 'clear', then it 'grows obscure', because of the underlying and ever present gaping hole. Consequently, this utterance will never be 'clear', it will never lend itself to understanding.

Staging the 'He': 'A Piece of Monologue'

The problematic nature of pronouns appears in *A Piece of Monologue*—written in English from 1977–1979—where *he* is used to express an *I*, as Stanley Gontarski has shown (1985, 155). If the split between the two remains, the tension is much more discrete than in *Not I* and *Company*. The scission produced between the two instances requires close studying, in order to discern its dramatic function. That is to say, how does this construction undermine any semantic transparency to achieve a material quality, in an orientation towards the Other?

Indeed, in this play, the Speaker appears on stage, but discrepancies appear between the gestures he describes and those he executes, aside from a number of points of convergence that serve to maintain the ambiguity of the two registers. In this respect, the *he* of the story appears as a phantom, as a voice that haunts the speaker. The monologue as a whole detaches itself from the figure on stage, who seems to describe the actions of his double. In this way, *he* manifests the detaching of the register of meaning, which cannot be assumed by the speaker. The latter proffers a discourse, but the content of his words is severed from his person, so that he himself is not represented within the story. Not only can it be asserted, as in *Company*: '[…] He speaks of himself as of another' (*Co*, 16), but the relationship between the speaker and his character also appears to echo the one described in *Malone Dies*: 'Nothing is less like me than this patient, reasonable child

[…]' (*MD*, 187). No transparency can be purported between the two registers: between the speaker and his story. However, it is possible to see how the speaker's action of *reciting*, or giving existence to a verbal representation, contributes to create not a diminished reality, but an amplified one, by virtue of the *voice*.

The story as a whole reposes both on the axiom formulated in the *incipit*: 'Birth was the death of him' (*PM*, 425), and on a basic 'unit', composed of the ritual accomplished by the character, and which corresponds to the story's 'present'. For one who is 'unborn', his 'birth' leaves him confronted with death, instead of setting him on the path of life. Far from suggesting that the expanse of life separates the subject from his final death—authorising the protection afforded by structural misapprehension of the *real*—the text asserts the abrupt identity of birth and death: 'Born dead of night' (425). Only the *équivoque* of this sentence makes palpable the inextricably contemporaneous character of these two faces of the signifier. This position of mortification is the one that his Other has assigned the subject to: not in a desire for him to live but in a message of death.

His 'ritual' enables the speaker to relive the night of his birth, from which he cannot—for want of the protective screen created by the imaginary—detach himself. If death is inseparable from birth, the subject cannot identify himself with the character whose actions he evokes. Only the reciting of his monologue can outline the gestures of a ritual that will give his existence some consistency.

In the monologue, the spectator witnesses the appearance of the light that accompanies his birth. The two events thus manifest a form of asymptotic simultaneity. In evoking the moment of his birth, the character is 'reborn' each night, but only as a phantom. The two nights are not only parallel, but are also situated in a metonymical continuity: 'Ghastly grinning ever since. From funeral to funeral. To now. This night' (*PM*, 425). The expression *this night*, in its equivocal nature, refers simultaneously to the night of the character and to that of the speaker on stage. Night is the moment when he comes back to life, giving birth to himself: 'Up at nightfall.' The character wakes up, rises, at the moment when the night falls, in the same way as he is born in the depth of night.

If the ritual commemorates the past by making it present again, the text as a whole produces a symmetrical effect, following a path that leads the character towards death. Whereas the elements that are framed, or presented as a *mise en abyme*, engender a form of fragmentation,[18] the composition of the text describes a single progression that confirms the unity of the theatrical performance. On this level, an acceleration or an intensification of the rhythm can be observed, particularly in the final part, where a conflict appears in the enunciation. Thus, the acute nature of the *birth/death* opposition, their irreconcilable status, does not lead to a standstill or a petrification but serves a dramatic progression that guides the subject in his reflection on death.

This progression can be described as follows. The *first part* of the text situates the scene and the content of the monologue, recapitulating the past. The character's whole life is a ritual. 'Thirty thousand nights' (*PM*, 425) reduce the density of existence to a ceremony that brings him to the present: 'To now.' After the evocation of the family pictures—torn to pieces—the character looks beyond the wall to the east: 'Nothing stirring there either.'

The *second part* offers a summary of the ritual, and brings the character to pronounce the word *birth*. He sees the appearance of a window—a 'faint form' (*PM*, 427)—and a vision of 'that first night'. After arriving at this night of his birth and seeing the lighting of the lamp (427), he pronounces the words anew: 'Birth the death of him' (426). This vision is ephemeral, and its disappearance—'Gone' (428), evoking a sort of 'fall'—leads to the following part.

The *third part* introduces an image of the funeral and the *agon*, composed of questions and answers. The appearance of the image is something new: 'Till dark slowly parts again' (*PM*, 428), and the dra-

18 Stéphanie Ravez provides a detailed analysis of the text's cinematographic 'sequences' (2013, 87–107).

matic intensity increases, since it is no longer just a matter of the character's birth, but of the death of another, whose fate is intimately linked to that of the speaker. On this point, the pronouns create an *équivoque*: 'Loved one… he all but said loved one on his way. Her way' (429). The possessive determinant *his* could refer to the speaker or to another; whereas *her* could be a maternal figure.[19] The mouth from which these words fall, and the mud of the cemetery in the rain, are associated together. In pronouncing the word, the mouth suggests an action of parturition: 'Parts lips and thrusts tongue forward. Birth' (428). The subsequent cry is analogous to that of birth: 'Feel soft touch of lip on lip. Lip lipping lip. Then parted by a cry as before.' Contrary to the mouth in *Not I*, which is carried along by the flow of words, here, the character manifests a *jouissance* that is localised in the mouth,[20] in a movement that impedes his aspiration towards death: in this action, his body takes on consistency, instead of being fragmented. However, his gaze is associated with the end—'As if looking his last' (428)—since the character turns back toward the room which ressembles his future coffin: 'Turn away in the end to darkened room. Where soon to be. This night to be' (428–9).

Finally, the *conclusion* contradicts his efforts to think of 'other matters': his attention is entirely centred on the single question: 'Never were other matters. Never two matters. Never but the one matter. The dead and gone. The dying and the going. From the word go. The word begone' (*PM*, 429). As in the beginning, birth is both the entry to life ('go') and that of abandonment and death ('begone'). The text brings about its paroxysm as an encounter with the unbearable, that nothing

19 See the question of the mother in relation to melancholy, where the son preciously preserves the image of the mourning mother (Baker). Delphine Lemonnier-Texier (71–85) evokes an association with the death of Ophelia in *Hamlet*.

20 We can compare the pronunciation of the word *birth* and that of *spool* by Krapp (*K*, 216). This manner of lallation would seem to recall the formulation taken from Freud, according to whom the oral drive is *the mouth kissing itself*, and which he calls auto-eroticism. We could also, however, draw a parallel with *Eh Joe* (see *infra*, p. 179–80).

can palliate, other than the theatrical setting and the conclusion. The unbearable is what the imperative indicates: 'Move on to other matters. Try to move on' (428). That is also what is expressed by the character's inability to proffer utterances. At this moment, he adopts one of the aspects of Mouth in *Not I*, in the sense that he is inhabited by the voice, to the exclusion of any willpower: 'The words falling from his mouth. Making do with his mouth.'

The protective framework takes on form—at the present moment of the ritual—by means of the forehead brought close to the wall, the latter acting as a 'window' that inscribes a gap between the subject and the darkness beyond: 'How far from wall? Head almost touching' (*PM*, 428). Indeed, the play also relates the encounter with the Other's absence, which is marked by the impenetrable night, where no one is to be found: 'Stands there facing the wall staring beyond. Nothing there either. Nothing stirring there either. Nothing stirring anywhere. Nothing to be seen anywhere' (426). However, in accordance with the Beckettian principle of uncertainty summed up by the adverb *perhaps* which excludes any univocal judgement, a presence also can be discerned: 'Faint light in room. Whence unknown. None from window.'[21] This uncreated light—which one can also suppose to be endless—is opposed to the ephemeral one produced by the matchstick (426), and also to that of the globe which has now disappeared ('gone'): 'The globe alone. Not the other. The unaccountable' (429).

Thus the monologue reveals a character's struggle with his absence of 'birth' and his acceptance of death. However, it is necessary to consider *A Piece of Monologue* not only from the point of view of this *fictional* construction, but as an *acting out* accomplished by the speaker. Like what is described in the monologue, the text constitutes a means for the speaker to endow himself with a birth that constitutes, at the

21 This indication can be associated with certain paintings by Caravaggio—*Calling of Saint Matthew* (1599–1600); *Saint Jerome* (*ca.* 1607–8)—where a divine light appears independently of any visible physical source. We have dealt with the specific structure of this light in relation to Beckett (2011d, 110–1), and also in quite a different context (2012, 6).

same time, the construction of his relationship to death. The ritual shows the image of his disappearance, in order to associate it with the proffering of the word *birth*, and also to bring about the effacing of the speaker from the stage. This same *night* also confirms the disappearance of the speaker as a stage entity, at the moment when the light goes out: 'Such as the light going now. Beginning to go. In the room. Where else? [...] The globe alone. Not the other. [...] The globe alone. Alone gone' (429). In this sense, the stage directions note the simultaneity of the action described and that seen by the spectator: '*Thirty seconds before end of speech lamplight begins to fail. Lamp out. Silence. speaker, globe, foot of pallet, barely visible in diffuse light. / Ten seconds. / Curtain*' (425). However, this simultaneity emphasises—following the linguistic logic of homonymy—that the two are not identical.

This dissociation of the two levels is a part of theatrical representation, the specificity of which consists of being situated in reference to the Other. The *in text* stage directions emphasise the material dimension: 'Hair white to take faint light' (*PM*, 427); this indication echoes the liminal directions describing the speaker: '*White hair, white nightgown, white socks*' (425). In this play, the speaker represents an *I* who offers up an image to his Other, whose presence is outlined by an uncreated light devoid of any discernable source. Or: the character reveals himself, by means of the light he turns on, as a signal addressed to his Other. This reading calls on the meaning of the term *ritual*, which supposes the existence of the Other to whom it is offered up. In this sense, one can hear the *équivoque* present in this expression tinged with religious vocabulary, used to characterise the scene of the burial: 'Seen from on high' (429). The 'on high' suggests a divine vantage point, in the same way as the Beckettian character is often contemplated from a raised view point (as in the staging of *That Time*). This monologue thus has the appearance of a prayer, comparable to the tone that Hamm punctuates with the exclamation: 'The bastard! He doesn't exist!' (*Eg*, 119). If Beckett could, in his youth, see poetry as a prayer,[22] the monologue—confirming the absence of the Other—is nonetheless an 'invocation' (*HI*, 7), according to the terms of *How It Is*: the effort to produce the presence of an Other who, fundamentally, proves to be radically absent and who, as a result, may exist—at least for the duration of the performance—as *divided*, as a subject.[23] This is, once again, a way in which Beckett as creator assumes a maternal position in relation to the 'unborn' subject.[24]

In this play, the character does not espouse a position of denial or rejection of the pronoun *I*, contrary to the narrators of *The Unnamable*, of *Texts for Nothing* or Mouth in *Not I*. The theatrical representation is composed of a character who says *he*, instead of *I*—being unable to assume a personalised, subjective story—and who offers up this *he* by way of a substitutive *I*, to his Other. The subject addresses an invitation to the Other, so that the latter will be able to discern the subject that supports the *he*. This Other is not simply the spectator—the author's fellow beings—however crucial the latter may be to mark the effective reception of the play recognised as a work of creation.[25] As a function of language, the Other is situated beyond the empirical individuals present. The profound uncertainty regarding the very ex-

---

22 On the subject of Thomas MacGreevy's poetry: 'All poetry, as discriminated from the various paradigms of prosody, is prayer' (*Dsj*, 68).

23 It is to this same Other that *Breath* is offered up: instead of presenting a 'character', the play reveals the subject's existence as reduced to the oscillation inspiration/expiration, marked by two identical cries. The subject appears as the pure *cut* that manifests the drive, and which is anchored by the image of the rubbish, as an *a* object.

24 As Beckett stated to Charles Juliet, the creator is simultaneously 'millions of light-years' in the heavens, and on Earth below (in Juliet, 66–7). See *infra*, p. 231–2.

25 Gérard Wajcman (1998, 68) points out that artist, spectator and work are comparable to the three intertwining rings composing Lacan's 'Borromean knot', since they represent 'three functions knotted to each of the two others and among which none of the three can be removed without the two others becoming detached in turn'. These three functions circumscribe the ungraspable *objet*.

istence of this Other necessitates, on the one hand, the use of the pronoun *he* and, on the other hand, the monologue form, where the subject knows he is condemned to speak alone, as he is unable to address an interlocutor. As he is 'unborn', devoid of any 'means' of communication, the subject offers this spectral existence—reduced to words' signified—to the Other, of whom the spectator acts as a substitute. The stage version of *he* gives him his only possibility to exist, to find some extension in reality.

Thus we have seen that the articulation of deictic pronouns *I* and *you* with the anaphoric pronouns *he* or *she* is absent in these texts. Consequently, Beckett's pronouns do not situate the subject in any sort of community with others, nor do they establish, as a consequence, a form of dialogue. This absence does however produce a positive presence: that of the *voice*, which provides these pronouns with their material binding. Mouth's ejaculation *she* is a forceful assertion, whereby the subject situates herself and gives expression to her being. The narration that traverses *Company* is far from simply the failure to have an *I* replace the *you* and the *he*, since the subject that is finally 'alone', has succeeded in producing 'company' in the form of the voice. Finally, the ritual in *A Piece of Monologue*, as a visual and verbal performance, produces the function of the Other by means of the oblique address that a work of creation aims to achieve.

III. — Continuous, Interrupted, Responses

We have seen that pronouns represent a fundamental structuring factor of subjectivity: they found enunciation, whereby the subject is both represented, and excluded from the words charged with representing him; and they situate the subject in relation to others. By contrast with this functional articulation, the Beckettian voice persists as a profoundly unsettling force arising in the gaping holes that this construction fails to contain, undermining any attempt to bind the various pronouns within an overall dialogical context.

It is now necessary to examine both the topological forms of the voice, and the interactions that occur between the subject and the voice's powerful and ceaseless presence. Our approach in this chapter will unfold in two stages. Firstly, we shall study the way the voice combines two apparently opposing—but fundamentally unified—qualities: *continuity* and *interruption*. The voice will appear, in Beckett's earlier works, as a continuous 'rustling', insofar as they are 'dead voices', testifying to the mortifying effect of language on the subject, to the exclusion of any vivifying quality. By way of contrast, the example of *Eh Joe* will show these voices as a continuous persecuting presence. The perspective will then be reversed to show interruptions not as a function of discursive articulation, but as the disquieting presence of the voice that disrupts the narrators' or the characters' speech, and which can bring its weight to bear on the subject in the form of a persecuting and capricious *superego*.

To provide a preliminary definition of the latter,[1] it can be pointed out that while the superego is often described as a force that commands order in society, Lacan distinguished its action from the pacifying effects ascribed to the Name-of-the-Father: whereas the latter points to a fundamental *lack* in the system of language, the superego denies any such obstacle. Thus, Lacan associates it with a fero-

1 We shall further develop our exploration of this term. See *infra*, p. 336–7.

cious commandment to *jouir* (1966, 821). He describes it as a 'law without dialectic' (1981, 312) and that, like Kant's categorical imperative, is characterised by its 'malfeasant neutrality': it makes no distinctions, admits no attenuating circumstances. If it appears to be an agent of virtue in, for example, demanding that a subject renounce pleasure, it knows no satisfaction, and any concession to its dictates can only serve to augment its ferocity.

To account for another point of extreme tension in Beckett's writing, the term *alienation* will be used to shed light on the original impact of the signifier on the subject.[2] This notion refers to the fact that the subject, originally, is marked by the mortifying effect of the signifier, with the consequence that 'if he appears on one side as sense [*sens*], produced by the signifier, on the other he appears as *aphanisis*' (Lacan, 1973, 191) or as *fading*. This imposes a radical alternative, so that whichever of the two terms one chooses—sense or being, one's 'life' or one's 'money'—the subject will be inevitably evacuated from representation. In this perspective, the subject is considered as empty, only represented by the signifier (Miller, 1999, 15). The '*lethal factor*' (Lacan, 1973, 191) involved here is attenuated with the following operation, called *separation*, that institutes the symbolic Other, and produces *jouissance* in the form of the lost object. The story of Genesis provides a picturesque example of this logical succession: following the encounter with the serpent, Adam and Eve are declared mortal, and discover their nudity, that is to say, their sexuality; their expulsion from the garden of Eden—which is forever lost to them—confirms their existence as autonomous beings.

In the second part of this chapter, two responses the subject elaborates to the voice—in an effort to place the latter at a distance and reduce it to silence—will be observed: firstly, the subject's attempts to produce a salutary *inscription* and, secondly, the protective function of the *image*. Inscription will be seen as representing a subject's response to the voice, in order to anchor the latter in the body,

2 For the purposes of this chapter, we reformulate here the definition given *supra*, p. 64.

thus silencing its incessant and uncontrollable clamour. In *Footfalls*, May's pacing will be seen as representing a form of physical 'inscription' that provides the play with its fundamental structuring. While this can be understood as one possible recourse for the subject, the corresponding pole, in the verbal realm, is the creation of an 'image', which can assume the form of the 'unborn twin' in *Rough for Radio II*, or the adopting of a 'reading voice', whereby enunciation serves to attain the stability of a written text.

1. The Continuous

Multiplicity and 'Dead Voices'

In the narrative works of Beckett spanning the period from 1946 (*Mercier et Camier*) to 1960 (*Comment c'est*), the voices take the form of a continuous sound that cannot be silenced, an 'unstillable'[3] murmur or rustling that constitutes the underlying substance of reality. Sometimes the presence of the voices is described as being pushed to the background; at other times it comes to the fore, determining the narrator's speech, as in *The Unnamable*,

Here, can be emphasised what distinguishes the *voice* from the *gaze*. With the inception of the latter, the *infans* is completely surrounded and enveloped by the gaze of his Other, who watches him from all sides. When it is internalised, this gaze functions as the sign of 'the assent of the Other' (Lacan, 1991a, 414), founding the possibility of desire. It therefore has a comforting and calming influence, as can be seen in the creation of the stage image in *A Piece of Monologue*, for example. As Frédéric Pellion points out, 'the gaze decides on what will be distinguished' by a subject's desire, in relation to truth 'in the hubbub of perceived voices' (115). However, while a child is always able to close his eyes, he is powerless to shut out sound: 'The ears are in the field of the unconscious, the only orifice that cannot be closed'

3 A term used by Beckett in his *Production Notebook* (in Ackerley and Gontarski, 162).

(Lacan, 1973, 178). This physiological fact reveals, on the structural level, that the subject can in no way subtract himself from the effects of the voice, which Beckett often shows as invading the characters' head: from the voice, there is no refuge. It is for this reason that the characters must strive to silence the voices which they know to be unremitting.

The voice thus takes the form of what Roland Barthes calls *bruissement* (rustling) (100), testifying to a fragmenting of articulated language and revealing the impossibility of confining the signifier within stable utterances. Instead of resonating on a background of silence, the voice encompasses all, producing what Slavoj Žižek defines as a 'pre-modern "closed" universe, bordered by a fundamental "noise"' (Žižek, 1995, 84), or what Simon Critchley calls 'a buzzing, the tinnitus of existence' (203). Emmanuel Lévinas identifies this space as that of the limitless and impersonal *il y a* (there is), where 'the imperturbable essence', or being, turns 'into monotony, anonymity, insignificance, into an incessant buzzing that nothing can now stop and which absorbs all signification, even that of which this bustling about is a modality' (163). Thus, Euclidian space is replaced by a curved one, by a topology comparable to that of the Möbius strip which—contrary to the impression that it might be possible to move from a visible side to a hidden one, or vice versa—allows for no breach. It marks the place where the signifier is grafted onto the *real* of the body, as John Cage observed when, seeking a completely soundproof room, he noticed the impossibility of extracting himself from the sounds that are inherent in the body itself (Bryden, 1997, 281; Connor, 2011, 7). Steven Connor evokes such an experience as a result of tinnitus, where the voice assumes the form of sound that is eminently bound up in the real, and thus impossible to eliminate: noise that identifiable sounds only serve to cover up or stifle. He observes that it 'can cause desperation and even suicide' when it intrudes as an external force, 'without any possibility of evading it or putting any distance between ourselves and it. Such sounds are a kind of endogenous, indwelling exteriority, an outside that comes at you from the inside'

(2011, 7–8). This impossibility of creating any distance reveals the imperative impact of the signifier. Thus Dirk Van Hulle points out the irresistible imperative that is associated with the voice, on an intertextual level, in the 'dead voices' of *Waiting for Godot*, since the character Septimus Smith, in Virginia Woolf's novel *Mrs Dalloway*, hears the voices of his dead comrades rustling in his head. The inexorable nature of these voices drives him to suicide (Van Hulle, 2010a, 79–81).

In his well-known 1959 essay 'Où maintenant? Qui maintenant?', Maurice Blanchot describes the endless voice of *The Unnamable*. This voice is unlimited, so that even when it stops, 'it is then that one has to make the terrible discovery that, when it does not speak, it still speaks, when it ceases, it perseveres, not silent, for in it silence eternally speaks' (286). Russell Smith (345) criticises this evaluation of the Beckettian voice, and considers Blanchot's idea of speech 'without a speaker' as problematic. However, it would seem that he does not do justice to this text, confusing Blanchot's notion of language as *voice*—as an impersonal *a* object—and the person: his interpretation supposes that speech can only come from a mouth and an individual, that a subject cannot be traversed by speech he does not initiate.

The problem is that to practice writing as enunciation, is to follow the dictates of language as *other*. Thus it is that Beckett can write as one who is given over to this totally impersonal voice, as Charles Juliet reports: 'Il estime que ce qui est exigé de l'artiste, c'est de disparaître en tant qu'individu de ce qu'il fait' ('He considers that what is demanded of the artist is to disappear as an individual in what he does', 54). Here, Beckett clearly does not mean to disappear as an *enunciating subject*.

It is true that Blanchot pushes aside æsthetics, not abusively—as it might seem to some academics: he does not actually suppose the author has no æsthetic consciousness—but to highlight the *experience* produced by the voice. Blanchot enables us to understand that what may appear as the 'deconstruction' of identities (in a postmodern perspective) reveals something of a positive existence: that of the incessant voice. It is this terrible positivity that appears:

> But *The Unnamable* is precisely an experience lived under the threat of the impersonal, the approach of a neutral speech that speaks alone, that traverses the one who listens, is without intimacy, that excludes any intimacy, and that one cannot silence, since it is the incessant, the interminable. (Blanchot, 290)

Blanchot reveals the *a* object as the cause of writing when he states that it is a matter 'of the pure approach of the movement whence derive all books, of this original point where the work doubtless loses itself, that always ruins the work' (Blanchot, 290–1). In this respect, Shane Weller points out what separates Blanchot from Lévinas:

> [...] whereas Levinas's thought of the ethical relation to the Other is the escape from this irreducible *il y a*, Blanchot thinks literature itself in terms of this voice, and, far from attempting to silence it, he attempts to identify it, disclose it [...]. (Weller, 2006, 12)

The difference here is that creation, as such, works with the dimension that threatens subjectivity with its abolition; this condition, however, becomes a specifically æsthetic object as a result of a subjective act that gives existence to it by means of a distancing. A work of art is thus an eminently subjective expression of *enunciation*. It is only thus that the terrifying *il y a* can be apprehended by the subject, and communicated to others. In the same way, what is important, when a patient recounts a dream to his analyst, is not strictly the content as such (the utterance), but the position he assumes when relating it, and which constitutes his indispensible enunciation (Lacan, 2013, 166).

The experience of an endless voice is particularly acute in the '*Trilogy*': Molloy describes a sound of this nature, calling it 'that rumour rising at birth and even earlier' (*Mo*, 6), and that can be heard each time the husk of reality disappears:

> [...] perhaps the far unchanging noise the earth makes and which other noises cover, but not for long. For they do not account for that noise you hear when you really listen, when all seems hushed.

> And there was another noise, that of my life become the life of this garden as it rode the earth of deeps and wildernesses. (*Mo*, 44)

It is impossible to silence these voices that arise precisely when the reassuring chatter of reality vanishes.

The multiplicity that, in the descriptions of the 'fundamental sound', characterises this *One as real*—a characteristic of the *unlimited*—is understood as the expression of that which, in reality, cannot be absorbed by any nomination or metaphor. This causes the contradictory images generally used to give an idea of this 'One' that is devoid of any properties: '[...] the atom or the fixed star, but also the fine cloud, the pile, the heap [of Democritus], flocculation [...]' (Milner, 2007, 28). Thus, while manifesting itself in unlimited fragmentation, the voice will be endowed with characteristics of the continuous, as Malone describes it:

> [...] the noises of the world, so various in themselves and which I used to be so clever at distinguishing from one another, had been dinning at me for so long, always the same old noises, as gradually to have merged into a single noise, to that all I heard was one vast continuous buzzing. The volume of sound perceived remained no doubt the same, I had simply lost the faculty of decomposing it. (*MD*, 201)

That is to say that at this level, it is impossible for the subject to extract himself from the voice, to attain an external vantage point from which he could situate sounds within a perspective. With regards to this question, Steven Connor refers to Murray Schafer's developments on the 'sonic plenum', in which the signal-to-noise ratio can either allow or exclude the differentiation of sounds, permitting or not perception within a perspective framework[4] (2006). Laura Salisbury also points out that as of *Murphy*, and contrary to Gestaltist theories, with which Beckett was familiar, 'figure and ground convert into one another' (2010, 222), adding that 'the noise and nonsense of sounds and signifiers' are language's 'Ur-condition', which threatens to submerge stable signification (223).

The Beckettian image of the 'dead voices'—the *bruissement* we find evoked in *En attendant Godot* (*G*, 81)—is of particular importance here, and necessitates closer examination. These voices cannot be attributed to a person, since they overtly adhere to their signifying structure: they are therefore not 'expressive', and are incapable of echoing the subject's desire. Robert Kiely's suggestion that such voices—as manifest in the '*Trilogy*'—may be associated with the spiritualist function of a medium goes little further than providing a casual metaphor, not least since the mortified state of the absent emitter is not examined. Rather, this characterisation can be understood as a consequence of the original mortification of the subject by the signifier. Lacan states that 'the symbol is firstly manifested as the murder of the thing, and this death constitutes in the subject the eternalisation of his desire' (1966, 319). However, if the subject as such is mortified, to approach Beckett's creation this operation needs to situated not at the point which founds the Name-of-the-Father but at the stage of 'alienation': the moment of the first 'negativising' or extraction of *jouissance* by the signifier. At this logical stage, the subject finds himself confronted with the *impossible*, before the institution of any prohibition.[5]

---

4 Gérard Wajcman (2004) shows how perspective constitutes a mode of construction of the subject, as can be seen in the development of Western visual art. Perspective is thus dependant on the *gaze*, as opposed to the *voice*.

5 'The prohibition intervenes with the appearance of the third party, when taking the father into account leads the child to suppose that this Thing that has been signified for him as impossible is perhaps not so for everyone, that there is perhaps at least one who has it' (Rey-Flaud, 296). At this moment, the Other is instituted, and the subject can find himself unburdened of his unspeakable singularity; he can then open himself up

In this perspective, the persistence of 'dead voices' results from the absence of the subject's inscription in relation to the Other: nothing has allowed the subject to lodge himself in the fracture of an Other marked by a lack that causes his desire. Thus it is that the narrator of 'From an Abandoned Work' (written 1954–55) evokes his voices. During his wanderings, he talks to himself, but the voice is not his: '[…] the sound of my voice all day long muttering the same old things I don't listen to, not even mine it was at the end of the day, like a marmoset sitting on my shoulder with its bushy tail, keeping me company' (*CSPr*, 159). He describes this dissociation as the result of the absence of any vivifying exchange with his parents: 'Perhaps I should mention here that I never talked to anyone, I think my father was the last one I talked to. My mother was the same, never talked, never answered, since my father died.' The absence of verbal exchange signifies the nonexistence of the structuring *separation* that causes people to address each other, to turn to their interlocutor—to whom they ascribe a certain knowledge—for the answer they cannot find by themselves.

The 'dead voices' thus seem to find their origin in the absence of a vivifying address. Beckett associates them with the image of leaves, found in Paul Verlaine's poem 'Chanson d'automne':

> ESTRAGON: All the dead voices. […]
> VLADIMIR: They all speak together.
> ESTRAGON: Each one to itself.
> VLADIMIR: Rather they whisper.
> ESTRAGON: They rustle.
> VLADIMIR: They murmur.
> ESTRAGON: They rustle. […]
> ESTRAGON: They talk about their lives.
> VLADIMIR: To have lived is not enough for them.
> ESTRAGON: They have to talk about it.
> VLADIMIR: To be dead is not enough for them. (*G*, 58)

---

to the metonymy of desire, that is to say to the succession of desirable objects.

Like the 'fundamental sound', these leaves do not participate in articulated discourse but manifest characteristics that are contradictory, mutually incompatible, thus engendering a gentle cacophony.

These leaves 'speak', only to express the subject's state of mortification; and he who hears them is incapable of detaching himself from them, since they give no access to a point of punctuation and silence. According to the characteristic structure of Beckett's writing: since these voices have never lived, they cannot die. This fact inspires an exclamation such as: '[…] Blessed be the dead that die!' (*MC*, 91).

Indeed, the symbolic 'dead father'—instituted as a pure signifier, according to the principle 'the word is the murder of the thing' (Lacan, 1966, 319)—represents the contrary of the alienation to a morbid figure: it consecrates the creation of a space of liberty where the subject of desire can come to being. Owing to the repression of the oppressive and all-powerful figure of the father (Freud's mythical 'Father of the primitive horde' in *Totem and Taboo*), the subject becomes free to take any signifier as the equivalent of the unattainable Thing, according to Lacan's definition of sublimation.[6] For want of such an operation, the subject experiences a state of mortification; a condition that is reflected in the image of the raincoat that 'dies', in *Mercier and Camier* (originally written in French in 1946): 'Let it lie where it is, said Camier. Soon no trace of our bodies will subsist. Under the action of the sun it will shrivel, like a dead leaf' (*MC*, 48). As a result of this mortification, the characters envisage allowing everything to be effaced, instead of burying what already resembles a shroud: in French, a 'linceul' (*MC*, 106); in English, it 'looked flayed' (48). This effacing (whose Möbian reverse side is the ceaseless *voice*…) occurs in the absence of an original extraction of *jouissance*: without any inscription in life, the subject is reduced to the state of refuse, to dust.

6 'And the most general formulation that I give you of sublimation is this—it raises an object […] to the dignity of the Thing' (Lacan, 1986, 133).

In the works of this period, the word *life* does not mean the liberation of the subject, his access to a feeling of autonomy, but points to the state of mortification expressed by the voices that resonate in him. This is why the narrator of *The Unnamable* speaks of 'this dead tongue of the living' (*U*, 331), which he desperately seeks to escape, viewing it as the imposition of an unbearable constraint that will continue to destroy his 'unborn' being. Speaking of the contents of their raincoat's pockets, Camier does not envisage the traces of a meaningful life but, on the contrary, inert objects incapable of giving any meaning to reality: 'Punched tickets of all sorts, said Camier, spent matches [...], dust. Life in short. / Nothing we'll be needing? said Mercier. / Did you not hear what I said? said Camier. Life' (*MC*, 49). All the metonymical objects that may quicken one's desire are here reduced to lifeless forms, devoid of substance. Nothing is capable of infusing the subject with enthusiasm, as Molloy declares: 'All I know is what the words know, and the dead things, and that makes a handsome little sum, with a beginning, a middle and an end as in the well-built phrase and the long sonata of the dead' (*Mo*, 27).

This evocation of a retroactive linguistic structure—tracing the curve of a well-constructed phrase—does not allow the subject to attain a belief in the verisimilitude of such a form, to extract himself from his state as a cadaver, from the reality of this mortification as a consequence of the signifier. Such is the destiny of all linguistic construction that, for the narrator of *Texts for Nothing* (originally completed in French in 1951), is incapable of having any real or structuring impact on his existence: '[...] nothing has stirred, no one has spoken. [...] And the voices, wherever they come from, have no life in them' (*TFN* III, 113); '[...] what a blessing it's all down the drain, nothing ever as much as begun, nothing ever but nothing and never, nothing ever but lifeless words' (*TFN* XII, 151). Of course, the narrator can, in a moment of 'weakness', give in to the attraction of signifiers, as can be seen in this exclamation where the narrator responds to his own utterance: 'Vile words to make me believe I'm here, and that I have a head, and a voice [...]' (*TFN* XI, 145). Fundamentally, the subject is incapable of attaining a belief that supposes the existence of a symbolic Other capable of inspiring confidence. In the absence of this Other, the narrator can only speak of a 'phantom' of belief: one suggested by the meaning of words, but which can never take on existence and establish him among the living.

Such an experience is expressed in a particularly vivid form in 'The Calmative', written in 1946, and where the narrator speaks of 'fornication with corpses' (*CSPr*, 61), and encounters 'nightmare thingness' (69). Indeed, in this condition—characteristic of melancholy—nothing intervenes to attenuate the 'pure pain of existence' (Lacan, 1966, 777). Deprived of any 'elsewhere', the subject is confined to a perpetual and oppressive present, to 'the prison of this cursed one who is the living-dead' (Didier-Weill, 147), and who is thus unable to die. Since, contrary to what one may spontaneously think, the fact of being mortal, of being destined to die, is what makes human existence bearable.[7] This condition is seen as resulting from the absence of an original affirmation coming from the Other who institutes the subject as such, by naming a desire for him, and in his stead (Nguyên, 2010a, 96; Geneste, 2013, 33; 2015). It should be added that such a state goes beyond anxiety (Kaltenbeck, 2006, 17) which, as Lacan emphasises, is not devoid of any object, contrary to what is commonly asserted (2004, 91, 185, 279, 360). Indeed, insofar as the *a* object is defined as the part that is cut off or extracted to produce a *limited whole*, anxiety has the quality of providing such an anchoring where any *lack* is… lacking (Lacan, 2001, 573). Franz Kaltenbeck (2006, 19) has shown one such encounter, for example, in the disintegration of the corporeal image in episodes of 'The Calmative' and *That Time*. Anxiety thus appears as a fundamentally stabilising factor (Geneste, 2013, 45–6), providing the subject with a certain consistency when

---

7 This is how Lacan analyses the dilemma of Hamlet. Even the act of suicide is powerless to abolish a subject's definitive inscription in language, so that 'being remains identical to everything that he [Hamlet] articulated through the discourse of his life. There, there is no *To be or not to be*—whatever the circumstances, the *To be* remains eternal' (2013, 314).

faced with this stifling condition that constitutes the dimension of the *real.*

In other texts, this condition can be agonising, as Mr Rooney remarks to his wife, in *All That Fall*: 'Do you know, Maddy, sometimes one would think you were struggling with a dead language. / Yes indeed, Dan, I know full well what you mean, I often have that feeling, it is unspeakably excruciating' (*AF*, 194). For Mrs Rooney, this dead language—'like our own poor dear Gaelic'—is a veritable torment which, precisely, is close to what cannot be said ('unspeakable'). The adjective *excruciating* can be etymologically associated with the crucifixion,[8] to which Molloy compares union with his sexual partners (*Mo*, 54): the incestuous adhesion he experiences when he confuses the latter with his mother inspires him with horror.

More generally, the Beckettian subject, in these texts, finds himself unable to 'experience' his own life. The petrified voices appear to be ancient, as does the life to which they are attached: 'You know the faint imploring voice, said Camier, that drivels to us on and off of former lives? / I confuse it more and more, said Mercier, with the one that tries to cod me I'm not yet dead' (*MC*, 44). The *voice* assigns the subject to his place, and the words it conveys do contain fragments of meaning that belong to life. And yet the subject can no longer feel that these 'former lives' are his, since he is fundamentally detached from them, as Estragon exclaims: 'No, I was never in the Macon country. I've puked my puke of a life away here, I tell you! Here! in the Cackon country' (*G*, 57). The historical reality of such a trip is of little interest: what alone counts is the immutable rooting of the character's existence in this 'closed' space—suggested in the French by the suffix *-cluse* in the toponym *Vaucluse* (*G*, 80)—that language assigns him to. Of course, these signifiers come back, in the manner of Virgil's voice—'that voice ruined from such long silence' (*HI*, 91; *cf.* Ferrini, 219–52)—but they remain a 'dead letter' (*lettre morte*), similar to the loss of meaning that occurs in the episode of the Galls, in *Watt*: '[...] this seemed rather to belong to some story heard long before, an instant

8 On this motif, see Leslie Hill (92, 97, 97).

in the life of another, ill told, ill heard, and more than half forgotten' (*W*, 74).

As for the present, the Beckettian characters resemble the 'as if' subjects described by Helene Deutsch (Grossman, 1998, 77–8 ; *cf.* Mével, 327–8), as Miss Fitt expresses it in *All That Fall*: 'I see, hear, smell, and so on, I go through the usual motions, but my heart is not in it, Mrs Rooney, my heart is in none of it' (*AF*, 183). Words signify, they indicate the way to live, but in this state, the subject is incapable of getting fully involved in living, while being aware that he has no choice but to adhere to the outward forms prescribed by language, as Estragon explains: 'We always find something, eh Didi, to give us the impression we exist?' (*G*, 64).

Creating Silence

Structured by the *unlimited*, it is impossible to bring the voice to a halt, to assign limits to it, to situate it within coordinates defining an 'emitter' and a 'receiver'. The voice intervenes as *tone*, as defined by Jean-Michel Vives: 'Tone is the negation of the symbolic by the real or, in other words, it is what escapes the power of symbolising and remains untranslatable' (2012, 221). Whereas *tone* is discernible in classical singing and allows for the identification of a singer's singularity, it is also the very essence of 'techno' music, where it no longer appears as a limited, circumscribed phenomenon.

This question is particularly present in Beckett's earlier works, exemplified by *The Unnamable*: '[…] the words are there, somewhere, without the least sound; […] drops of silence through the silence […]' (*U*, 376). They are also present in the voices heard by Mercier and Camier, by Molloy and Moran, and by Malone. *Texts for Nothing* also shows the impasse encountered by Beckett at this period, in the impossibility of finding an opening, a breach that would allow him to extract himself from the voice. As Jean-Michel Vives notes: 'In order to use one's voice, it is in fact necessary to not be totally submerged by that of the Other' (2012, 36). It is through the use of one's voice—by *invocation* (Vives, 2015; Lacan, 1998, 151) or by *enunciation*—that a subject reduces the voice of the Other to silence, creating an inhabitable void, instead of being drowned out by an incessant clamour. Thus, contrary to Derrida's deconstruction of the voice as imaginary presence (*cf.* Dolar, 37–42), Lacan states that the voice gives 'the weight of the subject, his real weight' (2013, 458): the subject's enunciation makes possible his intimate confrontation with the absence of the Other. Such is manifestly the case, for example, when the subject is called to speak in traumatic circumstances, and finds himself unable to utter a word.

Something of this subjective 'weight' can be measured in the rift produced by creation with regards to the imperative voice of the Ego Ideal, whose exigency Beckett memorably formulated in the sentence: 'Every word is like an unnecessary stain on silence and nothingness.'[9] The word *stain* expresses the demanding point of view of an absolute Other: the authority that passes a pejorative judgement on language, the latter being purportedly insufficient with regards to absolute perfection. Such an exigency is of an infinite nature: it escapes anything that could enter the domain of language understood as expressivity, ordered articulation, dialectics of form and content, signifier, signified and enunciation. This point can be illustrated by the exorbitant demands expressed in the examples of *Ubu roi*, by Alfred Jarry, and the Reign of Terror inaugurated by Robespierre, as commented on by Henri Rey-Flaud:

> Confronted with the infinite demands of the Law any real fault, be it virtual or supposed, effectively becomes worthy of capital punishment. Only the guillotine is capable of liberating the Law from the signifier, since to extricate the Law from all the imaginary ideals, one must start by killing everybody. (Rey-Flaud, 204)

9 Interview in *Vogue* (after Beckett's being awarded the Nobel Prize), December 1969.

The establishment of a signifying chain necessarily supposes that such an absolute ends up being marred and relativised, insofar as no signifier is self-sufficient, but necessarily refers to all the others:

> Any order, from the moment it is instituted, cannot help but secrete signifiers, produce new ideals that are as many offenses to 'the purity of non-being'. This absolute Law thus supposes a world without History either preceding it—since it requires a *tabula rasa*—nor following it—since it requires extirpating any 'descendants' (*Abkömmlinge*) that may arise from what was originally repressed. (Rey-Flaud, 205)

These reflections draw our attention to two consequences of this ideal for the Beckettian subject. On the one hand, the latter—particularly in the earlier works—experiences a generalised feeling of guilt: 'The tragic figure represents the expiation of original sin, [...] the sin of having been born'[10] (*Pr*, 67); '[...] that obscure assize where to be is to be guilty' (*TFN* V, 117). This guilt assumes an infinite and impregnable form, since it cannot be attributed to any precise 'fault': incestuous desire, in the Œdipal structure, for example...

On the other hand however, if Beckett asserts that writing led him to silence, and if he denounces words as offending the purity of nothing, such a position can only be paradoxical, since Beckett never gave up literary creation. In Art Spiegelman's book *Maus II*, the character Art speaks to his psychiatrist, and remarks: 'Samuel Beckett once

---

10 Mark Nixon (2012, 31) notes Beckett's interest in Otto Rank, whose book *The Trauma of Birth* opened with the classical epigraph '*Optimum non nasci, aut cito mori*', that Beckett had already copied from Burton's *The Anatomy of Melancholy*, into his *Whoroscope* notebook. Schopenhauer—whom Beckett read in 1930, while preparing to write *Proust*—picks up this motif from Calderón: 'The true sense of the tragedy is the deeper insight that what the hero atones for is not his own particular sins, but original sin, in other words, the guilt of existence itself [...]' (Schopenhauer, 254).

said: "Every word is like an unnecessary stain on silence and nothingness."' Then, after a pause, he adds: 'On the other hand, he said it' (45). The first utterance contains a fundamental contradiction, since it illustrates the fault it claims to denounce. Jim Lewis, filming *Nacht und Träume*, reports that Beckett said that it was 'difficult for him to keep writing words, without having the feeling it was a lie'[11] (in Kalb, 1989, 98). Beckett made other similar formulations which, instead of suggesting the will to preserve silence, emphasise the *necessity* of violating the absolute: his duty to place a 'blot on silence' (in Kalb, 1989, 233). Beckett thus characterised his work, paradoxically, as 'a desecration of silence' (in Van Hulle, 2010b, 209). Far from considering himself obliged to respect or to reinforce this silence, Beckett deliberately profanes it: these phrases continue to assert the absolute nature of silence, while positing creation as an indispensible breach of it.[12]

This determination to contradict the imperative of silence is vital, as it is productive of the subjective dimension: precisely, the subject signals his presence by leaving a 'stain' on perfection. This is what Bruno Geneste (2015) sees as the creating of a vital and salutary *hiatus* or blank in the potentially absolute nature of the signifier. Whence Beckett's complementary remark: 'I couldn't have done it otherwise. Gone on, I mean. I could not have gone through the awful wretched mess of life without having left a stain upon the silence' (in Bair, 640). Such an act allows the subject to live, as Lacan notes:

> I am in the place where is vociferated that 'the universe is a flaw in the purity of Non-Being.'
>
> And not without reason, since as it is guarded, this place has Being itself languishing. It is called *Jouissance*, and it is that whose lack would make the universe void. (Lacan, 1966, 819)

11 '[...] c'était difficile pour lui d'écrire encore des mots, sans avoir le sentiment que c'est un mensonge.'

12 Bruno Geneste (2015) points out that while the Ego Ideal, correlated to the fantasy, demands stasis and silence, the superego does not aim at finishing off the symbolic register.

A subject's *jouissance* is a perpetual obstacle to the perfect assimilation of the subject to the signifier,[13] since the purity of the latter embodies silence beyond any meaning. This impossible fusion is, for example, at the basis of the ceaseless alternation in Beckett's work between dark and light, and of the importance of the adverb *perhaps*, which points to the ultimate impossibility or achieving any resolution.[14] The manipulation of words violates silence as a form of totality: it belongs to the realm of refuse, of scraps, while placing an incommensurable rift at the very heart of the work of creation. Beckett cannot resort to the ignorance authorised by art considered as the concrete realisation of an absolute, that is to say communicating the impression that 'this is *it*'. He continues precisely at the point where words are gutted of any meaning they may promise—where they border on meaninglessness, non-sense—but where he is in no way able to abandon them by succumbing to the imperative of silence. This is where he must continually—and vitally—resort to the symbolic in its dimension of impurity, thus working with what Bruno Geneste (2015) calls '*the most real of the Symbolic*'.

The Dead Voices in 'Eh Joe'

Eh Joe was Beckett's first piece for television (composed in 1965), a work Marie-Claude Hubert describes as being 'a play where a disembodied voice questions a voiceless character' (Hubert ed., 354).

---

13 The extension of the *unlimited*, in the 20th Century, was manifest in the Nazi extermination camps which, as Alain Finkielkraut observes, were '*laboratories of humanity devoid of men*', aiming at, 'beyond the *physical* annihilation of the Adversary, the *metaphysical* disappearance of the Multiple in the One' (111). He indicates, by way of contrast, that Antonin Artaud declared: 'As long as someone exists, humanity is imperfect'.

14 Arthur Rose shows that this tension is manifest in the two endings Beckett successively prepared for *L'Innommable*. The first one (evoked in 1949, *L2*, 160/162) expresses the aim: '[…] pour n'avoir plus rien à dire, plus rien à entendre, avant d'être mort' ('to no longer have anymore to say, anymore to hear, before being dead', in Rose, 212). The well-known *explicit* retained in the final edition asserts the necessity to 'go on'.

However, whereas the 'dead voices' of Beckett's novels of the 1940s and 1950s were associated with an incessant flux that rendered any extraction or separation unimaginable, the voices in the teleplay *Eh Joe*, are called 'dead' not because they are inert but rather because they are associated with the departed. Their intervention is conditioned by the television medium which, because of the concrete, performance framework involved, imposes a halt, contrary to the potentially endless metonymy of written prose. Rosemary Pountney (131) shows that although the confined situation of this play prolongs the one seen in *Film* with the room as a trap,[15] in this work 'the entire text is confrontation'. Indeed, while the earlier 'dead voices' were an expression of the subject's mortification and his inability to detach himself from the dejection (which can be heard, etymologically as being 'thrown down', from the Latin *dejicere*) that strikes his being, here it is possible to note the operative presence of a separation. The incidence of the persecuting superego has the effect of situating the subject with his feelings of guilt. Contrary to the incessant dead voices in the earlier works, the subject here is called into being, he is summoned to respond.[16] It should also be pointed out that this text is quite distinct from a play like *That Time* since, here, the voices do not at all permeate the character's consciousness: they inflict a stabbing action, nourishing the feeling of remorse emanating from the superego. Joe also appears as the opposite of Mouth in *Not I*, since he is present rather than reduced to a bodily fragment, and he seeks to still the voices, rather than to thread together the components of a narration.

---

15 Beckett remarks : '[…] cet endroit est un piège préparé pour lui et tout ce qui s'y trouve est piégé. Tout, dans cet endroit, est destiné à le prendre au piège' ('[…] this place is a trap prepared for him and everything that is there is a trap. Everything, in this place, is designed to trap him', in Fehsenfeld, 365).

16 This ontological function—or, as Lacan spells it '*hontological*' (*honte* meaning 'shame', 1991b, 209)—of language is developed *infra* in relation to Beckett's discursive structures (p. 374). See also Dow (13). As it dissolves narcissistic identifications, shame brings a subject to the point where *being* collapses.

Critics show a certain hesitation in determining the nature of the voices that persecute Joe, often seeking to situate them within a classification. Stanley Gontarski notes:

> These voices, which Beckett's characters at times try to quell but at other times embrace, are finally the creative manifestation of the subconscious, and quieting them is Beckett's famous pursuit of silence, an artistic suicide. (1985, 114)

The Grove Companion puts forward a somewhat diverging opinion: 'The voice that assails him is neither external, nor memory, nor the subconscious, but imagination, or creativity' (Ackerley and Gontarski, 164). Or: 'Despite the assault of Voice, Joe strains to hear the whispered words that assail him, for these are the creative fountainhead' (Ackerley and Gontarski, 165). These evaluations end up replacing the question of the *voice* by allegories, by anagogical interpretation. But the protagonist of this play is not primarily an artist, and he does not seek to return to silence: Joe is persecuted by the voice in a passionate manner.

Some readers hesitate with regards to the personal dimension of the voice. Graley Herren asserts: 'Voice is based upon a real person who existed in a real past, but her present reincarnation is entirely distinct from, and develops independent of, any past reality' (2007, 56). It can be said that this independence simply results from its quality as an unstillable *voice*, from its subjective dimension: it is not the representation of a *person*. Some have also tried to discern the characteristics opposing Joe and the voices: 'Voice in "Eh Joe" is less Joe's dark or evil side than his opposite: feminine, constant, secure and irreligious, to Joe's masculine, lecherous, dishonest, but (surprisingly) religious self (or selves)' (Ackerley and Gontarski, 163). The problem with this characterisation is that it does not really shed light on the question of the *voice*.

In the same spirit, some critics raise the question of the source of the voice, following a realistic interpretation. Graley Herren asserts that the voice emanates 'not from without but from within' (2007, 54).

Marie-Claude Hubert sees a similarity with 'the interior voice that, from the first narrative texts, obliges the character to speak' (ed., 353). Of course, the text insists on localising the voice in Joe's head: 'The whisper in your head.... Me whispering in at you in your head...' (*EJ*, 364); 'You know that penny farthing hell you call your mind.... That's where you think this is coming from, don't you?...' (362). Beckett also specifies: 'A dead voice in his head' (Beckett, 1998, 201). However, in spite of these metaphorical indications, the inside/outside polarity only exists with reference to an instituted reality, and disregards the nature of this voice as bordering on a *real* that is consubstantial with the subject's existence. Locating the voice in the head essentially serves to emphasise the impossibility for the mortified subject to detach himself from it, to withdraw himself and find a shelter.

Marie-Claude Hubert submits a complementary idea:

> It is impossible to reduce, as Martin Esslin does, this voice that resounds in the consciousness, to an 'internal monologue [that] is identified with the eye of the camera' [...] insofar as the man perceives the voice from without. [...] Even though Beckett suggests by these words that it is hallucinatory, [...] it nonetheless has a real existence. (Hubert ed., 354)

Indeed, it is necessary to accept the separation between the eye of the camera and the voices: 'Each move is stopped by voice resuming, never camera move and voice together' (*EJ*, 361). It cannot therefore be supposed that they have a common source. It is more appropriate to state that *voice* and gaze are two forms by which the women—or the Other—persist in Joe's life, once they have departed.

The gaze that weighs down on Joe, through the camera, seems to betray a certain ambivalence, reminiscent of the one described in *Film*: '[...] neither severity nor benignity, but rather acute intentness' (*F*, 329). Joe is initially afraid of an eye that might remain in the dark—'There might be a louse watching you....' (*EJ*, 362)—but as the gaze of the camera acts in counterpoint with the voice, it would seem to have a role somewhat similar to that of Auditor, in *Not I*. Indeed, this gaze appears to intervene for the spectator alone, since Joe himself is preoccupied only by the torment inflicted by the voices. Beckett indicates:

> He does not look directly at camera and is not aware of it. He is aware only of the voice. The eyes are turned inward, a listening look. It is however effective dramatically if at the very end, with the smile, he looks full at the objective for the first time. (Beckett, 1998, 203)

It is at this moment that Joe succeeds in silencing the voices, and he can at last face up to the gaze. Joe expresses his feeling of victory in the direction of this Other, by contrast with the anxiety the voice causes him. As the camera is devoid of speech, it appears as an Other that seeks to capture Joe's reaction to the words spoken. Because of this function, the gaze of the camera would seem to have an enveloping aspect, manifesting a certain affinity with the closed space of the hermetically closed room. On this occasion, Joe enjoys a feeling of victory, of autonomy and perhaps perceives a possibility of recognition from the Other who is watching him.

The split between camera and voice also reveals Joe's relation to language. Joe is silent throughout the play, completely exposed to the assaults of the voice, and inert under the gaze of the camera. It is his silence—his exclusion from speech—that engenders the voice. That is to say that he proves to be powerless to oppose the voice by *invocation*, by creating a breach that will silence the Other and thus allow him to assume his past life, to integrate it as part of his experience. Here, his whole life is borne by the utterances of others. Therefore, the silence Joe seems to impose on the voice at the end of the play is the one in which he is himself immured. His victory will therefore only be temporary, since silence can only be the continuation of the *voice,* whence the ironic ambiguity Beckett maintains: 'I asked in London and Stuttgart for a smile at the end (oh not a real smile). He "wins" again' (1998, 202). By displaying a smile, Joe bathes in the light of the gaze. But his victory will only be temporary: everything can and must be continually reversed.

The 'dead' voices start to speak when no one is present: they never die. Joe can never consider himself to be even with the departed: they will always come back to demand their due. The persecuting dimension of the voice is manifested in the manner in which it attacks the character, according to Beckett's description: 'A dead voice in his head. Minimum of colour. Attacking. Each sentence a knife going in, pause for withdrawal, then in again' (1998, 201). This incisive nature of the voice appears as the reverse side of Joe's use of language in the past, where mastery and an exaggerated opinion of himself betrayed his fundamental inability to proffer subjective enunciation. He is now entirely dependent on a voice that escapes his control.

Manifesting the force of the superego, the voice acts as a Möbian reversal of Joe's past narcissistic position: 'Sit there in his stinking old wrapper hearing himself… that lifelong adorer.…' (*EJ*, 363). The voice demolishes the positive image he entertained of himself. In the same way, Joe is denied his former mastery over language: 'Powerful grasp of language you had.…' (363). The voice suggests that if Joe used to admire the feminine voice, it was because it reflected his own use of words, situating the two lovers in a specular relationship: 'How you admired my elocution!… […] Flint glass… You could have listened to it forever.…' The impenetrable solidity, the inalterability and the transparency expressed by this metaphor have now become a source of persecution. Henceforth, Joe remains confined in a silence that appears to be the cause of the voice that quotes his former sayings: 'The best's to come, you said, that last time.…' (362). The voice adopts a provocative attitude, seeking to drive Joe out of his silence: 'Say it you now, Joe, no one'll hear you.…'; 'Say it you now, no one'll hear you.… Say "Joe" it parts the lips…' (366). The repetition of the utterance 'Eh Joe?' reveals the programmatic nature of the play's title, showing how powerless the character is to assume the utterances proffered by the voice, and to speak in turn, which is the only means by which he could bring about a peaceful silence. This projected parting of Joe's lips points to an envisaged *parturition* evoked in *A Piece of Monologue*, where the central word pronounced by the figure on stage entails the sensual enjoyment of the lips' movement: 'Birth. Parts lips and thrusts tongue between them' (*PM*, 428). By pronouncing the word *birth*—and by speaking, for Joe—the subject attempts to give himself some form of palpable existence.

Brutally expelled from his position of mastery over speech, Joe endeavours to 'kill' the voices: 'Mental thuggee you called it....' (*EJ*, 363); 'Throttling the dead in his head.' Beckett evokes 'a passion to kill the voices which he cannot kill' (in Ackerley and Gontarski, 162). However, he can never 'kill' those who have never been dead, or 'stilled', on a symbolic level. The physical nature of the violence expressed here is thus intended to replace an impossible nomination. However, Joe's efforts only testify to the force of the voice that *causes* its attacks, in the same way as a person, caught up in a delirium, may vociferate, to calm his torment. His attempts to stifle the voices can thus be seen as maintaining the latters' incisiveness, for want of engendering a structural breach. What intervenes here is a reflection of the Ego Ideal, that demands a final ending of all the symbolic (Geneste, 2015), a radical effacing equivalent to suicide, whereby there would be no longer any need to 'go on', to face up to the torment of the voice.

It could also be added that attacking others gives him the impression of somehow being alive: 'What it'd be if you ran out of us....' (*EJ*, 363). To have an Other to kill is still to have an Other, rather than remaining completely alone: the voice torments, but listening to it is a way of continuing to exist. In its narrative function, the voice tells of a life that Joe can no longer really live; one that he was never capable of living: the voice brings back words from the past that remained superficial eloquence, but that Joe was never able to subjectively assume. Thus it is that Graley Herren points out an ambiguity:

> On the one hand, Joe overtly seeks to distance himself from Voice, trying to throttle her into submission like he has her predecessors. On the other hand, as the covert source of Voice, Joe is essentially

> responsible for generating and perpetuating her narrative. So although his mouth says no, his mind's eye says yes. (Herren, 2007, 64)

Joe reveals a structural aspect of the voice: he seeks to exhaust it, while deriving a *jouissance* from it; he lives by means of the voice, hoping it will give consistency to his existence as an unspeakable hole, excluded from any utterance.

Indeed, Joe seeks to preserve the other as an image, whence the *jouissance* he derives from listening to the story of the death of the 'green one': this narration is a way to defensively '*faire l'image*' ('do the image')—as in the story *L'Image*[17] delaying the inevitable encounter with one's self and with the ultimate unstillable *voice*: 'There was love for you....' (*EJ*, 365). The *équivoque* of the words *for you* is perceptible: they can be understood as the expression of a superlative, or as 'that is how love is, what do you expect?', or again as love 'addressed to you' / 'that she bore for you'. Joe's impotence can also be heard in the expression: 'The best's to come, you said, that last time....' (362); 'The best's to come, you said....' (365). This equivocal locution expresses the illusory promises that Joe made to women; it also suggests the death awaiting them all, Joe included. The promises are part of the exaggeration the character used in order to reassure himself with regards to the future.

The story recounted by the voice is a torment because what Joe hears represented is that which he has definitively lost, whereas, at the same time, the voice makes this representation exist again, as if it were still possible to restore this reality. This incompatibility shows that Joe only has access to love in the form of a destroyed love. Amourous attachment exists for him only in the form of a sacrifice: the woman puts an end to her life (her death is the acme of the voice's speech) both out of love and despair. Her act constitutes the proof of the love she bore for Joe, but which was not enough for him. This sacrifice thus reveals Joe's suffering to be derisory: 'Finishes the

17 See *infra*, p. 225–8.

tube.... There's love for you.... Eh Joe?' (*EJ*, 366); 'Till they go.... There's love for you.... Isn't it, Joe?... Wasn't it, Joe? [...] Compared to us.... Compared to Him.... Eh Joe?...' (367). The irony in one formulation, where Joe's suffering is compared to Jesus'—'The passion of our Joe....' (364)—evokes the notion of a *sacrifice* whereby the Other is preserved intact since, once Joe is dead, he will be forever frozen in the demonstration of his love.

By contrast, to succeed in stifling the voices would leave Joe facing the void, alone with his failure: 'Straining to hear.... Why must you do that?... When you're nearly home.... What matter then.... What we mean.... It should be the best.... Nearly home again.... Another stilled.... And it's the worst...' (*EJ*, 364). If the voices finally fell silent, Joe would redouble his efforts to grasp the words whispered by the voice, in the very heart of silence. Thus, he reveals the unstoppable nature of the voice that will never belong to him:

> And now this.... Squeezed down to this.... How much longer would you say ?... Till the whisper.... You know.... When you can't hear the words.... [...] Straining to hear.... [...] If it went on.... The whisper in your head.... Me whispering in at you in your head.... Things you can't catch.... On and off.... (*EJ*, 363–4)

In the discourse proffered by the voice, the meaning at least offers the advantage of allowing Joe to latch onto some form of representation.

However, this voice is 'unstillable', like that of God. Joe aims to evacuate all voices, in order to achieve peace, but at that precise moment, he risks encountering the divinity:

> Silence of the grave without the maggots.... To crown your labours.... Till one night.... 'Thou fool thy soul'.... [...] Ever think of that ?... When He starts in on you.... When you're done with yourself.... If you ever are. (*EJ*, 364)

This divine, unceasing voice escapes all attempts to silence it, since it supposes eradicating the language that is at the basis of his very existence: as if Joe were trying to free himself of his own head. The divine voice is, by definition, what exceeds all efforts to stifle it.

Joe's death constitutes the following stage, once he has succeeded in stifling the voice his life depends on: 'Or is it the heart already?... Crumbles when you lie down in the dark... Dry rotten at last...' (*EJ*, 362); 'Till you join us...' (364). Indeed, the successive voices—which compose a series—show a process of crumbling: 'your father' (363), 'Then your mother', 'All the others'; then: 'the green one', the present voice, eventually the 'slut': 'Unless that poor old slut loves you.... Then yourself.... That old bonfire.... Years of that stink.... Then the silence...' (365). This movement suggests that each voice ends up falling definitively silent, leaving, in the end, the inevitable encounter with one's self, with a remainder that cannot be eliminated. It is as if, having poisoned the lives of others, Joe were condemned to face up to his own inability to liberate himself. The others acquire a new life through the voice, which he must continually stifle, but in the end, he will come face to face with death, his own, which is precisely that of an 'unborn' subject.

The theme of the inordinate guilt that assails him can be explained by the fact that Joe appears as the cause of the others' death. His fetishistic approach to utterances testifies to his efforts to preserve himself from the persecuting dimension he encounters in enunciation. Hence his admiration for the voice's past elocution (*EJ*, 363), or for 'the green one': 'Spirit made light.... To borrow your expression....' (365). These images represent the banishment of all obscurity contained in the gaping hole of the persecuting *voice.* The absence of a symbolic inscription can be observed in the fact that these images are already mortified, rather than being expressive of physical presence. Joe causes the death of the 'green one' as if, when she was alive, she were already a persecuting *voice* for him: 'She went young.... No more old lip from her' (365). The expression 'old lip' seems to suggest that the affection that could be expressed by kissing lips has been transformed into a tormenting voice that echoes the maternal superego (the adjective *old* points to this pejorative judgment). Even if the account of 'the green one's' suicide were an invention—since he could not have been present—the repeated attempts to kill herself represent the means by which Joe perpetuates his own feeling of guilt.

Graley Herren (2012) points out the melancholic nature of Joe's suffering. He reveals the parallels between the story of 'the green one' and Beckett's youthful relationship with his cousin Peggy Sinclair which, in all likelihood, he broke off as a result of his mother's severe disapproval. In Freud's analysis of melancholy, the subject turns against himself the reproaches he feels for the one he has lost, the latter being assimilated to the mother whom the subject feels has abandoned him.[18] As regards Peggy, Herren notes:

> It turns out that the traumatic events from the past which end up haunting most tenaciously tend to be either those events that one did not recognize as traumatic until it was too late to prevent them, or those events which one feels one should have been present for but was absent. (Herren, 2012, 62)

In this case, Beckett only learned of Peggy's death when he was informed after awaking from an operation to have a cyst removed. However, the anecdotal facts are less important here than the structural aspect involving melancholy. Indeed, according to Freudian theory, the lost *a* object can only take on form as a result of repetition, since the first occurrence of a founding event is *real*, and as such, cannot be grasped as an object.

In *Eh Joe*, the 'object' assumes the form of the reconstituted image: the suicide of 'the green one', that no one actually witnessed. This image is thus equivalent to that of the birth evoked in *Rough for Radio II*,[19] intervening as a replacement for something devoid of any existence in factual reality. The image allows Joe to *jouir*, to hold onto the representation of the thing he is incapable of subjectivising, so that

18 Herren resorts to Kleinian theory on this point (Herren, 2012, 50).

19 *Cf. infra*, p. 231–2.

displeasure remains paradoxically bound up in pleasure. The fact that he remains resolutely mute demonstrates that he is unable to address his Other by invocation: he cannot make the subjective leap to integrate this loss as a personal experience, with the responsibility that such an act supposes.

Herren points out that originally, Beckett had envisaged having 'the green one' relate her own suicide, but that he later decided to 'deflect the story onto a third entity by having Voice instead imagine the death of the green one' (2012, 61). The voice intensifies Joe's solitude, since he cannot even enjoy the comfort of the familiar voice: he is forever deprived of that which he was unable to possess. The *voice* thus signifies the reality of this loss. Joe does not rebel because he does not have the subjective means to do so: he knows nothing more than what the voice gives access to:[20] a verbal and visual representation that gives form to the unbearable.

The persecuting voice appears to be that of the maternal superego: the one that enjoined him to be rid of 'the green one'. This tormenting maternal voice rails against both 'the green one' (Herren, 2012, 50–1) and Joe. The latter thus experiences his existence at the place he is assigned to by his voice: where the image comes into being. In other words, Joe exists because the voice continues to look over him, passing judgement on him: the persecution is also comfort, in the same way as a child paradoxically sees punishment as proof of his father's love (Freud, 2002, 219–43). What would be truly unbearable for him would be to be confronted with definitive silence: the disappearance of his Other. Self-flagellation through the assaults of the voice constitutes a means to ensure himself of the presence of an Other: *I am loved because the Other persecutes me; I still have the presence of my mother as a voice, railing the one whom I have lost.* If, as Freud points out, the melancholic knows *whom* he has lost, but not *what* he has lost (that is to say,

---

20 Thus Beckett stated: 'There was some sort of unofficial engagement with his sister Peggy. Then, for some reason, I don't know why, I broke it off' (in Knowlson and Knowlson, 37). This absence of knowing must be understood as authentic, not feigned.

as a subjective function, 2006, 289), the voice at least gives form and consistency to this absence. Moreover, the one that Joe himself no longer has at his disposal is that of 'the green one': she remains only a verbal image. In turn, the spectator finds himself in a similar position to that of Joe: contemplating an image and listening to a voice; he has access to the image of Joe, not to that of 'the green one'. Finally, Beckett presents a facet of himself in this image of one who cannot break out and speak forth in order to silence the voice by subjective means. The televisual device serves to contain and give form to what the author, as a subject, finds unbearable.

Joe's women die because he is fundamentally incapable of supporting a woman's desire: his partners find in him no subjective enunciation capable of instituting them in a loving relationship, and of pacifying their *jouissance*. This can be seen as the cause of his guilt: Joe finds himself powerless to protect his partners since a woman, for him, is exclusively situated either on the side of the mortified image, or of the *voice*. Their death is the expression of the abyss that Joe is incapable of dealing with.

Eh Joe thus brings into play the character's invasion by 'dead voices', testifying to Joe's efforts to escape their unstillable dimension. However, his failure resides in the fact that he only has, at his disposal, means that express his mortification and the supremacy of the persecuting superego.

2. Interruption

Interruption as Absolute

If the voice often imposes itself in the form of an unbreachable continuity, this massive quality is not univocal but is doubled—according to a Möbian logic[21]—by interruption. This characteristic of the voice appears clearly when Steven Connor points out that while

---

21 We have developed more fully elsewhere this topological approach in relation to Beckett (2008) and (2007) to Henri Michaux.

the visible appears as continuous, the 'world of pure hearing' can be considered as '*unremittingly intermittent*' (2009a, 17). Indeed, an æsthetics of interruption pervades the whole of Beckett's work, and is particularly striking in his plays. Thus, speaking of Pozzo, Beckett notes:

> He is a hypomaniac and the only way to play him is to play him mad. [...] Pozzo's sudden changes of tone, mood, behaviour, etc., may I suppose be related to what is going on about him, but their source is in the dark of his own inner upheavals and confusions. The temptation is to minimize an irresponsibility and discontinuity which should on the contrary be stressed. (Beckett, 1998, 6)

Winnie also represents a notable case: 'One of the clues of the play is interruption [...]. Something begins; something else begins. She begins but doesn't carry through with it. She's constantly being interrupted or interrupting herself. She's an interrupted being' (Beckett, 1995, 16). Speaking of Krapp, Beckett emphasises again: 'His whole life has been interruption' (in Lawley, 2007, 90). In fact, the project of rupturing goes back at least to 1937, when Beckett declared: 'I am starting a Logoclasts' League. [...] I am the only member at present. The idea is ruptured writing, so that the void may protrude, like a hernia' (*L1*, 521). Beckett also expressed his ambition of drilling holes into language (*L1*, 518), in his letter to Axel Kaun of the same year. This insistence with which Beckett creates 'interrupted' characters leads us to discern a much deeper disposition—of an existential nature—in these interruptions that, in reality, are present throughout his entire work.

The insistent nature of these interruptions has been noted by critics. Leslie Hill (67) associates interruptions with repetition, that 'multiplies difference and challenges identity'. This deconstructionist perception tends to avoid the problematic presence of *jouissance*, that other readings point to without naming it. Yann Mével (280) sees a tension, in Beckett's evocations, between Gilbert Durand's categories of 'schizomorphic' structures—involving the use of rigid geometrical forms—and 'glischromorphic' ones, implying viscosity, physical proximity and confusion. Ulrika Maude shows how Molloy's compulsive mobility 'is forever threatening to come to a halt' (2009, 91), as a result of 'tics, twitches, jerks, aches and falls'. Such techniques of fragmentation, in *Krapp's Last Tape*, are also seen as 'a major source of dramatic energy' (Hill, 129). In the same vein, Steven Connor asserts that Beckett 'will sometimes borrow the force of interruption, seeking to synchronise with it' (2008b, 91). Elsewhere, he appropriately remarks the importance of 'switches', as a motif expressing interruption throughout Beckett's work (2014a, 76). Hélène Cixous sees the music of *Not I* as residing in what she calls the 'correlation 1/f', which means that 'if you try to foresee the following note you have one chance out of two of being mistaken' (62–3). The consequence is that the 'perfect music of *Not I*' is both 'structured *and* surprising' (63).

However, another dimension requires to be taken into account: an uncontrollable aspect, manifest in the tremor. Steven Connor defines the latter as the encounter and exchange of opposing forces: 'A strength meets a weakness that is not quite weak enough simply to absorb it, to collapse and vanish under the blow' (2008a). Ulrika Maude sees the shaking body as 'a dynamic impetus rather than a passive attitude' (2009, 95). Yann Mével points to the specific dynamics whereby the 'energy invested by the Beckettian character in the demanding minuteness of his intellectual enterprises betrays, *a contrario*, the prescience of their inevitable incompletion' (286). In studying *Ill Seen Ill Said*, Erik Tonning (2010, 234) and Laura Salisbury both evoke the way Parkinson's disease takes hold of the body, producing 'sudden speedings and slowings that quiver between limit instances—extremes of acanthisia (restlessness) and akinesia (profound rigidity and paralysis of will)' (2012, 156). What is described by these critics in the form of an analogy assumes more importance when one considers that it brings to the fore the very real bodily dimension—the *jouissance*—which may remain unnoticed if one concentrated only on the text's apparent 'abstraction'.

At this point, it is worth emphasising Beckett's refusal of the notion of abstraction[22] when writing to Carlheinz Caspari in 1953 about the characters in *Warten auf Godot.* He states:

> Je conçois fort bien votre gêne devant leur peu de caractérisation. Mais je vous engagerai à y voir moins l'effet d'un effort d'abstraction, ce dont je suis peu capable, que le refus d'atténuer tout ce qu'ils ont à la fois de complexe et d'amorphe. (*L2*, 389)

> I can readily understand your unease at their lack of characterisation. But I would urge you to see in them less the result of an attempt at abstraction, something I am almost incapable of, than a refusal to tone down all that is at one and the same time complex and amorphous in them. (*L2*, 391)

While Pascale Casanova speaks of the process of 'abstractivation' (166), referring to the activating of a formal abstraction and 'a methodical and systematic operation of abandonment and "purification" [*épuration*]' in Beckett's work, she also points out that he only undertakes his 'formal revolution by accommodating the necessary and "non-annullable" link between language and the world; even better, he invents abstract art in literature in the tension and the movement towards the impossible extinction of meaning' (167). Indeed, simple abstraction would entail claiming to eliminate the materiality of the signifier. Catherine Laws makes a similar remark: '[…] the complexities of Beckett's uses of music acknowledge the inevitable failure of this drive towards abstraction' (2013, 213). This is why Matthieu Protin points out how, in staging his early plays, Beckett's work on the character always started with the body, not with the written text: with the posture which, precisely, is absent from the latter (2014, 275). Bruno Geneste (2014) emphasises that 'for Beckett, writing must have an effect on the body'. Thus, if 'abstraction' means the elimination of the signified from the signifier, the latter only has any value insofar as

22 See also Rabaté, 2014, 136.

it can be understood as having a very real effect on the subject, not as a purely 'spiritual' or ethereal construction aiming to abolish perpetually problematic corporeal existence. Indeed, Matthieu Protin explains that 'in continuity with this corporeal work, the text itself will be apprehended in its materiality, particularly via a vocal treatment that makes the signifier stand out in relation to the signified' (2014, 296).

Interruption thus needs to be understood not simply as an external motif or theme, but as a characteristic of the signifier which, as a result of its differential nature, produces effects on the body in the form of *jouissance*. The breaks in Beckett's work show up the way the signifier creates—in its links to the *real*—total incompatibilities (what, in Lacan's later work, is called the nonexistence of any 'sexual rapport'[23]), an absence of any dialectics capable of subsuming terms within a *limited* whole. Language thus reveals an incommensurable abyss in its very heart, and which cannot be reduced to a simple anecdotal perception. It is thus necessary to understand Beckett's preoccupation with interruption in terms of the motif of the 'unborn' being, the state of 'the awful acceptance of 2 entities that will never mingle' (*L1*, 540), as he stated in 1937, regarding the painting of Jack Yeats. What separates two signifiers is, fundamentally, the same gaping hole that intervenes between the artist and objects, as 'no-man's land, Hellespont or vacuum' (*Dsj*, 70). Beckett's treatment of this insuperable separation can be seen in his remark made to André Bernold, concerning Jean Genet's 'Quatre heures à Chatila': 'Oui, répondit-il, c'est le même paradoxe que chez Kafka: horreur du contenu, sérénité de la forme' ('Yes, he replied, it's the same paradox as in Kafka: horror of the content, serenity of the form', in Bernold, 81). The 'horror of the

23 The negation of any *rapport* means that there exists no inescapable and necessary link, as there is, for example, in an animal's adaptation to its environment. Any relationship is thus of a purely *contingent* (or 'occasionalist', if we follow Beckett's readings of Geulincx) nature. The absence of *rapport* is what imposes the necessity of repeatedly undertaking *relationships*.

content' is what breaks up any will to signify, and which æsthetic construction brings to light and gives form to by precise use of interruptions.

These effects of *jouissance* require to be taken into account in Beckett's work as stage director. Matthieu Protin points out that where the rhapsodist unifies heterogeneous voices, Beckett introduces multiplicity into the original unity of his monologues, such as those of Krapp and Nagg: fissuring thus replaces structuring (Protin, 2014, 354). This multiplicity is extremely spectacular, for example, in Lisa Dwan's performance of *Not I*,[24] where the breathless succession of broken utterances was combined with constant changes in voice tone, which also resulted in an intensely melodic effect that seemed totally unimaginable when studying the written text.

The interruptions manifest in Winnie's monologues reveal these incompatibilities that testify to the character's desperate efforts to cover up the gaping abyss in language. On the one hand, Winnie's speech is made up of clichés (Barry, 2006; Brown, 2011a)—utterances devoid of enunciation—that constitute the verbal equivalent of the blinding light inundating the stage in *Happy Days*. If they offer a discourse of a dismaying rectitude, it is because their reverse side is continually present: a radical absence of any discursive hinterland. Consequently, the Möbian equivalent of monotony appears as the effect of a total, non negotiable void that is refractory to any will to say.

Winnie's interruptions appear to be partially covered up by the flow of words; for example, in the reversals where she systematically alternates between the smile expressing a calm closure, and the opening up to anxiety: '[…] all comes back. [*Pause.*] All? [*Pause.*] No, not all. [*Smile.*] No no. [*Smile off.*] Not quite' (*HD*, 144). Ordinarily, dialectical speech allows a subject to face the unknown, to find ways to bypass the impossible and reduce its incidence. With Winnie, how-

24 *Not I*, *Footfalls* and *Rockaby*, directed by Walter Asmus, Athénée-Théâtre Louis-Jouvet, Paris, 11–15 March 2015.

ever, the succession of clichés is doubled by her fundamental powerlessness, which can be ascribed to no visible cause. Thus Winnie muses:

> To think there are times one cannot take off one's hat, not even if one's life were at stake. [...] How often I have said, Put on your hat now Winnie, there is nothing else for it, take off your hat now Winnie, like a good girl, it will do you good, and did not. [*Pause.*] Could not. (*HD*, 146)

Both sides—the full meaning of the utterance (the exhortation addressed to herself to put her hat on) and the absolute void (unexplainable paralysis)—relay each other: nothing ensures their mediation or attenuates their implacable alternation. Matthieu Protin underscores the difficulty here for the actress, which he also notes in *Waiting for Godot*. In Lucky's monologue, he shows that the enumeration of sports is particularly problematic if the actor makes a pause, however slight (2014, 302). This question becomes clear when contrasting the respective performances of Madeleine Renaud and Billie Whitelaw in *Happy Days*. The former resorted to the solution of maintaining a conversational tone: the ends of her phrases were tenuous, leaving an opening, as if awaiting a response. Billie Whitelaw however accentuated the interruption, running the risk of losing the thread of her discourse.

Interruption imposes itself in its radical and absolute nature. This dimension of interruption can be grasped in the light of two types of rupture pointed out by Lacan. On this point, Graciela Brodsky distinguishes first a fixed and repressed 'master signifier'[25] (S_1) that

25 A brief definition: in his developments on the 'four discourses' (See *infra*, p. 321–2), Lacan confers a founding role on this signifier that represents the subject—establishing him in discourse—and commands representation as a unified whole, thus instituting the categories of truth and the norm. It should however be added that the function of this master signifier is not abolished in Beckett's work. Suzanne Dow has pointed out how Lacan indicates that Beckett maintains its function, along with the

springs up in the form of the Freudian slip: 'It is a matter of a moment, not of a state; we can suppose that the chain [of signifiers] will link up again with its continuity in the form of "that means such or such a thing…"' (Brodsky, 321). The sudden appearance of the master signifier brings the subject's speech to a halt, making him question what has happened, and driving the search for its meaning. This type of rupture occurs in the context of *limited wholes*, that is to say, in relation to the inscription of the paternal metaphor and the second extraction of *jouissance* or *separation*. In this case, anything new will be interpreted with regards to the general logic anchored in this basic structuring. The subject can restore the scaffolding of his effective discourse (his ideals, his rational justifications, his singular perception): all the components of his world will remain in place, endowed with their own specific meaning and value. Indeed, the paternal metaphor produces a beginning that contains its own ending: the subject is founded by a prior inscription that offers the possibility, by anticipation, of limiting the incidence of any eventual failure.

However, another type of rupture exists, which brings the *a* object into play: this obstacle is embodied by the presence of the psychoanalyst (Brodsky, 315). In Beckett's work, such presence can be found in the opacity of this *drive object*, which he situates at the heart of creation with the term *empêchement* (*MP*, 57). This 'hindrance'—that Beckett evokes in 'Peintres de l'empêchement' in relation to painting—escapes any stability instituted on the side of the eye or the physical object: it cannot be circumscribed or located. Here, the term '*a* object' points not to the object created by lack, but to the one that is refractory to the effects of meaning because it is anchored in the *unlimited*. Thus if the S_1 becomes an *essaim* ('swarm', in a play on homophony;[26] Lacan, 1975b, 130), the value of any given term will perpetually change according to the uncontrollable movements of *jouissance*: no construction will remain permanent.

dimension of *shame*, which is indispensible for a subject to apprehend something of his unconscious.

26 See *supra*, p. 105.

Faced with this abyss, the character can attempt to palliate it with a material object. Some characters stop and, by turning the page, reveal the presence of the text they are reading from. Thus Krapp peruses the ledger enumerating the episodes recorded on his tapes: 'Farewell to—[*he turns page*]—love' (*K*, 217). Here, the effect produced confers an ironic appearance on the evocation of a love that, for the character, no longer has any sublime nature, to the point where Krapp is incapable of completing his own utterance from memory. In *Ohio Impromptu*, Reader hesitates regarding the formulation he reads, and is obliged to verify it:

> After so long a lapse that as if never been. [*Pause. Looks closer.*] Yes, after so long a lapse that as if never been. Now with redoubled force the fearful symptoms described at length page forty paragraph four. [*Starts to turn back the pages. Checked by* L's *left hand. Resumes relinquished page.*] (*OI*, 446)

In these examples, the discourse is consigned to the page, it is externalised, and thus belongs to the Other. It is composed of utterances devoid of enunciation, and the reader's position is comparable to that of the narrator of *The Unnamable*, who will not assume the words he pronounces, or to the one in *How It Is*: 'I say it as I hear it every word always' (*HI*, 42). The subject is manifestly excluded from this reified language: nothing permits him to appropriate the text, to fill in the gap separating him from words.

On this subject, and in relation to Krapp, Steven Connor points to the tension between the written and the spoken, resulting from 'the written text's iterability' (2007, 143). This notion requires however to be linked to the structural fact that in these texts, the symbolic register is not inscribed in the subject: the latter is thus often obliged to seek after his words, as actor Sami Frey showed most remarkably, in his staging of *Premier amour*.[27] The place of the material object thus goes beyond the presence of the written text, pointing to

27 Théâtre de l'atelier, Paris, 2011 and 2013.

the character's need to latch on to an external tangible inscription that will afford him physical support. Such is the vital function that Bruno Geneste (2014) ascribes to the motif of the hand, in *Texts For Nothing* and *How It Is*, and that Marie Jejcic sees in Hackett's bench, described in *Watt* (Jejcic, 165–7). This search for material support also marks the interruptions in Winnie's speech, each time she turns towards one of the objects stowed in her bag or arranged on the mound around her.

In the plays, the breaks often take the form of an auditory manifestation, signalled by the emission of a brief sound: the '*Faint single chime*' (*Ff*, 399) of *Footfalls*, the '*Knock*' of *Ohio Impromptu*, the bell that becomes progressively more tyrannical, in *Happy Days*. M's hiccup, in *Play*, has a similar status; according to Rosemary Pountney, it also 'serves to emphasise the dichotomy of his situation; his request for "pardon" is clearly doubly meant' (33). This splitting is equally present in the contrast between the uncontrollable physical manifestation and the polite expression intended to cover it up. It is important to approach this sound marking the interruption in its relation to language. Chris Ackerley associates Neary's hiccup with Hippasos's betrayal of the Pythagorean Mysteries (2014, 22).

In *Footfalls*, each of the sequences constitutes a whole, totally disconnected from the others (Tonning, 160): it is impossible to articulate or absorb them within a strictly coherent overall composition. The '*chime*' that announces the beginning of each new sequence appears as a pure signifier, devoid of any content, but whose efficiency resides in reactivating the movement of the play. The origins of this motif could perhaps be traced back to *Dream of Fair to middling Women*, where Belacqua's sounding of a bell is associated with a break that appears in Beethoven's Seventh Symphony, the score of which the narrator consequently quotes (Laws, 2013, 93–6). Comparable to the signal that inaugurates a ceremony, it is addressed to those present (here, the spectators), but also to the Other. Indeed, as *invocation* (or the phatic function; Lacan, 2004, 318), it resonates in the emptiness of the Other, creating the space in which the pacing and the dialogue can unfold. It also calls on the latter to be present, to witness the ceremony and thus give it consistency. This is the hypothetical Other who observes May's ceaseless torment, and who wishes that she *may* find peace. The chime thus enters in resonance with the motif of the church, and not merely the one described in the 'Sequel' (*Ff*, 402), but also the idea that such a place might suggest the possible—but ever uncertain—existence of an Other, as represented by the appeal to 'God', in various texts by Beckett. As an anchoring that establishes a form of 'alliance' with the Other,[28] and in its identical repetition, it forms a structuring counterpoint with regards to the metonymical movement of May's pacing and her fiction.

In *Ohio Impromptu*, the *knocks* punctuate a progression that can be established as follows: 1. 'Little is left to tell' (*OI*, 445, 446, 447); 2. 'Nothing is left to tell' (448); 3. '*Knock*' (448); 4. '*Silence*'. Like the 'chime' of *Footfalls*, the *knock* appears as a compact signifier, closed in on itself, opaque, unbreachable—evoking no variation or modulation—contrary to the story, which possesses its lyrical musicality and its articulated evolution. The movement towards silence described here expresses the truth of this sound's structure: the story is drawn towards the end of saying, then the *knock* impels speech again, but is emptied once more, and falls back into silence. Because of this movement, combined with an increase in the intensity of the narration, the story loses its autonomy, to the benefit of its dramatic function: the story is an integral part of Listener's experience, on stage, during the performance. Like May in *Footfalls*,[29] Listener is possibly inventing his story for himself, and his *alter ego* appears to embody this function, conferring on the play its dramatic quality.

---

28 We can point to the theme of the *shofar*, the horn that resounds on *Yom Kippur*, studied by Lacan (2004, 282 *sqq.*; *cf.* Dolar, 52–6), following Theodor Reik, in its link to the murder of the primeval and absolute Father.

29 About May, Walter Asmus notes that in the third part, her voice should be 'a bit more alive' than in the first. He reports Beckett stating: 'One can suppose that she has written down everything which she has invented up to this, that she will one day find a reader for her story—therefore the address to the reader ("Mrs Winter, whom the reader will remember…").'

As a pure signifying intervention detached from any signifier, the knock has an operative, efficient value. Its link to the *real* is signalled by the fact that it 'always returns at the same place' (Lacan, 1973, 49): it is always *other*, it cannot be absorbed within the enclosure of meanings. In the course of the play, Listener remains mute: his knock replaces speech, testifying to his powerlessness to formulate a request and, at the same time, the absence of the dialectic usually associated with the genre of the conversation between two interlocutors. The knock expresses a speechless distress, signalling the urgency with which Listener seeks to attain, by means of this reading, a pacification to calm his torment. The knock marks the point where the outside—'l'insurrection des molécules'[30] ('the insurrection of molecules', *MP*, 35), for example—penetrates the stage area. If the outside is designated by the story, it is in no way exhausted by it, and it can be understood that the 'real' story of Listener will forever remain unknown to the spectator: it will remain excluded from any narrative. The knock thus marks the place where extreme order and extreme disorder meet.

The knock also expresses Listener's effort to assimilate or appropriate the text: he lodges himself in the written text by imposing pauses, as if he were seeking to make the last sentence soak in, instead of leaving the text to unfold without a break. Steven Connor also notes the dual nature of these knocks, whereby 'the listener pauses, perhaps to assure himself of the truth of what he has just heard' (2007, 147), while, at the same time, 'he actually pushes the moment of ending further into the future'. The knock thus has a dual value, being the sign of both a halt and a new start. On one hand—in insofar as it confirms the punctuation and retroactive looping of the signifier—the knock is equivalent to the word *More*, used in *Rockaby*, and *On*, in *Ill Seen Ill Said*, or the word *Again*, in *A Piece of Monologue*, that allow the character to establish an utterance. Like Winnie's '*I say*…', it reveals the effort to latch on to the utterance as such, to the exclusion of any dissimulated

30 On the origins of such molecular and cosmological images in *Dream of Fair to middling Women*, and their relation to music, see Laws (2013, 80 *sqq.*).

or equivocal dimension. Thus: 'Little is left to tell. In a last—/ [*L knocks with left hand on table.*] / Little is left to tell. / [*Pause. Knock.*] / In a last attempt to obtain relief [. . .]' (*OI*, 445). As Marjorie Perloff notes about *Embers*: 'The only way of interrupting the continuity of water and fire sounds, it seems, is to introduce another sound, one that is finite (and hence controllable) rather than continuous' (1999). The intervention of the knock interrupts the text, causing Reader to repeat his first sentence. Only when Listener makes the knock heard once again can Reader resume, repeating the second sentence. The pause thus created allows Listener to assimilate the first utterance, before moving on. In this way, he aligns himself as much as possible with the Other—conceived of as 'treasury of signifiers'—for want of a symbolic inscription as a subject. The story recounted is not his: none can belong to one who is radically devoid of any historicity. And yet, he needs a story that comes from without, which he takes in as best he can: a voice that composes his intimate theatre. The interruptions mark the moments by virtue of which he can appropriate that which he can never really internalise. As in *Footfalls*, the knock acts as a substitute for the *invocation* whose function is to silence the ceaseless voice, and create a space whereby the subject can exist in relation to a symbolic Other.

Imperative of the Superego

Interruptions also testify to the presence of an imperative force. Thus, at the beginning of *Embers*—a play which, according to Clas Zilliacus (89), counts more than two hundred pauses—Henry manifests a scission by means of which he gives orders, appearing as a sort of stage director of himself: 'On. [*Sea. Voice louder.*] On! [*He moves on. Boots on shingle. As he goes.*] Stop. [*Boots on shingle. As he goes, louder.*] Stop! [*He halts. Sea a little louder.*] Down. [*Sea. Voice louder.*] Down!' (*E*, 253). The sea composes the background of this play, producing a sound that Henry finds unbearable, since the sea has taken his father, and Ada it would seem, and threatens also to claim Henry (Pountney, 110). He seeks to stifle it with his speech, but it reappears whenever he falls into silence: '*Sea, still faint, audible throughout what follows whenever pause indicated*' (253). In spite of the incessant and unbearable presence of the sea, Henry must resort to the imperative in order to start moving, leaning on an external element, for want of being able to find the determination within himself. He hoists himself up to the status of an active being, by appropriating the necessary linguistic tools. As the *incipit* of this play shows, it is not sufficient for Henry to utter the order once only: he must reiterate it, louder, in order for the action to take effect. He feels the necessity of uttering these words audibly, so they may act on a body that, since it is devoid of an inscription in the Other, is reduced to a state of inertia.

This imperative is an integral part of the Beckettian necessity to go 'on' precisely at the point where the subject finds himself devoid of any means to do so, as expressed, for example, in the well-known *explicit* of *The Unnamable*: '[…] I can't go on, I'll go on' (*U*, 407). Finding himself in an intermediate zone, with no means at his disposal to say—since everything remains irremediably on the side of the Other—he nonetheless experiences the obligation to say. Here it can be noted that while the works such as the '*Trilogy*' and *Texts for Nothing* situated this effort to move forward in relation to 'traversable space' (*TFN* III, 111) and the endless linear movement of prose, Beckett ultimately turns the drive to go 'on' towards the logic of the symbolic, with its concommitant breaking point. This position 'between' appears as a strictly unbearable absolute. It is in this light that the importance of what Beckett declares about the painter Bram van Velde can be grasped: 'The situation is that of him who is helpless, cannot act, in the event cannot paint, since he is obliged to paint. […] Because there is nothing to paint and nothing to paint with' (*Dsj*, 142). According to Beckett's experience, the artist or the writer finds himself at the precise point between the nothing to express and the duty to express, between *no* and *on*. Majorie Perloff confirms this intermediate position when she analyses the vowel sounds of the *Embers*:

> From 'On' to 'No': this is the trajectory of Henry's speech, his Omega (note that both 'Bolton' and 'Holloway' contain long 'o's as well) in conflict with the Alpha of his wife's name 'Ada,' and the diminutive of Ada in the child's name 'Addie.' (Perloff, 1999)

Beckett's phrases strangely echo this sentence where Lacan shows the inadequacy of the notion of communication with respect to the primitive status of the subject, who 'has nothing to communicate, since all the instruments of communication are on the other side, in the field of the Other, from whom he has to receive them' (2004, 314–5). Finding himself perpetually in such a condition, the Beckettian subject remains acutely sensitive to this state of deprivation that, however, in no way annuls the imperative to say. The narrator of *The Unnamable* cannot ascribe this imperative to any authority other than the existence of language as such: 'Having nothing to say, no words but the words of others, I have to speak. No one compels me to, there is no one, it's an accident, a fact' (*U*, 308). That is to say that *speaking* and *not speaking* impose themselves as absolutes, not as possibilities at the disposal of a subject who, enjoying the position of a third party, would be free to make a choice or express a preference. The imperative involved here is therefore not mortifying but fundamentally salutary.

Interruptions thus situate the subject outside the possible: at a point where signifiers border on the irreconcilable. Shane Weller discerns this experience in the 'pseudocouples' that seek both to advance and attain an end, and who are consequently 'caught within the reversibility of the palindrome "no"/"on"' (2010, 127). The *no*, which expresses the impossibility of advancing, and the *on*, which designates the extreme urgency to move forward, are both equally constraining, imposing themselves on the subject in a univocal manner, allowing for no concession or dialectical compromise. These two antonyms offer no possibilities but compose a dilemma centred on an *impossible*. It is for this reason that Beckett rejects both the negation and the affirmation, considering them equally absurd:

> – La négation n'est pas possible. Pas plus que l'affirmation. Il est absurde de dire que c'est absurde. C'est encore porter un jugement de valeur. On ne peut pas protester, et on ne peut pas opiner.
>
> Après un long silence :
>
> – Il faut se tenir là où il n'y a ni pronom, ni solution, ni réaction, ni prise de position possibles… C'est ce qui rend le travail si diaboliquement difficile. (in Juliet, 68)

> ('Negation is not possible. No more than affirmation. It is absurd to say that it is absurd. That is still to express a value judgement. One cannot protest, and one cannot consent.'
>
> After a long silence:
>
> 'We have to stand where there is no possible pronoun, no solution, no reaction, no taking of position… That is what makes the work so diabolically difficult.')

Indeed, the Beckettian subject is not situated in a place where he can dispose of linguistic means to express himself, he is rigorously correlated with the impossible, as the narrator of *The Unnamable* declares: 'That the impossible should be asked of me, good, what else could be asked of me?' (*U*, 331). Beckett thus confirms Lacan, who defines the impossible as the *real* (1973, 152). The possible belongs to semantics and constructions afforded by linguistic articulation, which is why Beckett criticised Italian painters, who 'never stirred from the field of the possible, however much they may have enlarged it' (*Dsj*, 139). For the *possible* to have any meaning, it must be anchored in what allows it to be defined: in what negates it and which, following a retroactive logic, constitutes it as a *limited whole.*

Here can be measured the existential importance of the absence of a dialectic, the impossibility of making any firm assertion, which Beckett found expressed in the signifier *neither*, as spelled out in the eponymous text: 'To and fro in shadow from inner to outershadow / from impenetrable self to impenetrable unself by way of neither' (*CSPr*, 258). In these circumstances, the alternatives leave no escape route: on either side, the subject encounters the 'impenetrable', the 'shadow'. The alternations *inner/outer*, *self/unself*, do not combine within a hierarchy but are articulated around a radical impasse which is, for the subject, his unnameable being, his 'unspeakable home'. By comparison with the reality expressed by the word *neither*, the terms that make up the alternatives are little more than 'lit refuges', temporary abodes.

It is in relation to this impossibility that the imperative of the superego intervenes to propel the subject to action, insofar as it gives substance (*jouissance*) to the latter's attachment to the signifier (Lacan, 1994, 212). For example, the bell that persecutes Winnie represents a real distress: it intervenes like a violent blow that subjugates her body[31] as much as the tormenting sun. Winnie emphasises this unbearable and physical nature of the bell: 'It hurts like a knife. [*Pause.*] A gouge. [*Pause.*] One cannot ignore it' (*HD*, 162). And yet, this same bell sets her speech in motion.

The violence described in *How It Is* takes the form of inscriptions in the body[32] that are necessary to trigger the production of the voice: 'that's not all he stops nails in armpit he resumes cheers done it armpit song and this music as sure as if I pressed a button I can indulge in it any time henceforward' (*HI*, 64); 'the thump on skull signifying stop at all times and that come to think of it almost mechanically'; 'take the opener in my right hand [...] and drive it into the arse [...] a cheek he cries I withdraw it thump on the skull the cries cease it's mechanical' (67). The 'mechanical' quality of these interventions expresses the impersonal manner in which the subject seeks to prompt the verbal production by means of an instrument of torture: the inscription in the body by use of the can-opener in *How It Is*, the goad in *Act Without*

---

31 It is worth noticing, by way of contrast, that Beckett replaced the alarm clock, present in the original drafts, with this unbearable bell (Gontarski, in Beckett, 1985, 77). Besides having a much gentler sound, the alarm clock allowed Winnie to exert some control over the way she experienced her day.

32 See *infra*, p. 202, 342–4.

Words II, Croak's 'club' in *Words and Music*,[33] the '*bull's pizzle*' (RR *II*, 275) in *Rough for Radio II*, along with the cylindrical ruler[34] and the pencil.

If these motifs of violent intrusion are so prevalent, it is because the imperative superego serves to anchor the subject's inscription in language, in accordance with the double orientation of the signifier: 'The signifier is the cause of *jouissance*. [...] the signifier is what brings *jouissance* to a halt' (Lacan, 1975b, 27). The Beckettian subject finds himself potentially exposed to the imperative contained in the totality of language: one that determines his existence and is marked in his flesh. In this condition where the symbolic borders on the real, the superego manifests itself, as Lacan states, in the form of a 'law without dialectics' (1981, 312), such as is expressed, for example, in Kant's categorical imperative, which admits no exception. However, it is crucial to recall the role of creation here: by producing the expression of this unleashed violence, Beckett transforms it into a localised *cry*, that opens a new space wherein the subject finds existence in his continued treatment of the incessant voice.

Caprice

The imperative thus constitutes one of the causes of interruption in Beckett's work, in a response to the unbearable: it both repulses

33 There is undoubtedly derision in the use of this motif. Everett Frost points out that Geulincx 'recounts the story of Hercules amusing himself by quietly helping a presumptuous dwarf to heft his club, with the result that the dwarf believes he is just as powerfully able to wield the club as Hercules' (Frost, 263, n. 9). We find a very similar image in Robert Browning's dramatic poem 'Paracelsus' (1835), whose visionary protatonist complains about his students: '[...] the best of them / So clumsily wield the weapons I supply / And they extol, that I begin to doubt / Whether their own rude clubs and pebblestones / Would not do better service than my arms / Thus vilely swayed [...]' (64).

34 This cylindrical ruler already belonged to the policeman in *Molloy* (*Mo*, 18), and was originally to be found in the office of Beckett's father (Baker, 28).

the latter and makes its presence heard. Insofar as Beckett's creation is structured by the *unlimited*, the persistence of interruptions reveals a *capricious* dimension that obeys no law. Rosemary Pountney (16) evokes the notion of caprice in relation to the aleatory method Beckett chose to compose 'Lessness', through the mingling of its originally separate sentences. She sees it as the expression of a certain vision: 'Beyond the man-made or imposed order [...] lies an arbitrary and capricious world of chance.' She also cites *All That Fall*, where Mr Rooney is unable to count the station steps, wondering if he is not the victim of some inscrutable malicious will: 'Sometimes I wonder if they do not change them in the night' (*AF*, 189). However, this principle can be extended to the work as a whole, in relation to the question of interruptions, insofar as the intervention of the superego reveals a Möbian equivalence between the demand for absolute rectitude, on one hand, and total caprice, on the other (Brown, 2008, 119). The dimension of the *real* is suggested by the very term *caprice*, which comes from the Italian *capo* (head) and *riccio* (curl, frizzled), describing the hair standing on end in horror. As Jean-Claude Milner points out, horror is structured by the *a* object in its 'harrowing [*déchirant*] asphericity' (2007, 62). Caprice thus reveals, in language, the total absence of any Other to guarantee a fixed law.

Indeed, the existence of any *law* is instituted by the paternal metaphor, which makes signifying repetition possible in the form of regularity: the Law thus has a pacifying influence. According to Lacan, the paternal function—resulting from the mother's relationship to the father—creates a breach in the maternal *jouissance*, so that the child is not totally at the mother's mercy. Thus is made possible an attenuation of the original anomic violence (Lacan, 1998, 191) characterising the mother's 'omnipotence or her caprice' (462). Reversing his earlier elaborations however, Lacan ended up seeing the *real* not as the 'guarantee of the symbolic order' (Miller, 2012, 3)—both as its negation and its anchoring point—but as inherent in *lalangue*, that reveals the fundamental absence of any law underlying language: 'Each language is forged by contingency and chance' (Miller, 2012, 6). The notion of *caprice* is thus intimately linked to this absence of law, which testifies to the structure of the *unlimited*, manifest in Beckett's work.

The Other, for the Beckettian subject, regularly imposes manifestations that escape any law. In *Act Without Words I*, for example, the character is subjected to the torment of seeing objects presented and then withdrawn. Each of these interventions is signalled by a 'Whistle' (*AW I*, 203) that nothing coordinates other than a dimension beyond any meaning, so that, seeing that it is impossible for him to accomplish a completed action, the character ends up ceasing to react. This whistle is comparable to Winnie's bell which, far from filling her day, subjects her to the logic of *caprice*: if the bell rings twice in the first act, it goes wild in the second (*HD*, 160, 161, 162, 164, 168), submitting Winnie's body to its obscure and uncontrolled exigencies.

Company provides a particularly instructive example of the impact of caprice, in the 'vignette' (as we could call it) describing the child who addresses a question to his mother:

> Receiving no answer you mentally reframe your question [...]. For some reason you could never fathom this question must have angered her exceedingly. For she shook off your little hand and made you a cutting retort you have never forgotten. (*Co*, 5–6)

In this passage, the child seeks a rational explanation for the indeterminate distance of the sky, which is enigmatic for him. Instead of the mother being a source of speech, she walks on and refuses to respond. She is impassive, mortified, just like the calm and empty image evoked: in French, the 'blue sky' is designated by the words 'ciel d'azur' (*Cie*, 5), which compose a lyrical stereotype (found in the poems of Verlaine and Mallarmé, for example). The maternal silence is not the only decisive aspect in this episode, since it is broken only by a cruel rejection. Here, any mediation is absent: no word allows the child to determine the cause of his mother's reaction. He supposes that she is moved by a speechless violence—'angered her exceedingly' (*Co*, 6)—that can only be turned back on him. The rejection is felt in the child's body: 'For she shook off your little hand and made you a cutting retort [...].'

Here, nothing regulates the mother's action: she passes from absolute silence to violence, so that the child can in no way attenuate this outburst by recourse to rationality. It is nonetheless in reference to this very violence that the child has to find his place, and he does so in the impossibility of detaching himself from it: it remains 'never forgotten'.

Such an episode was not foreign to Beckett's childhood experience. If biographical fragments are never simply transposed, within a work of creation, from their status as objective experiences, they can reveal or confirm traits that show the subjective resonance of caprice. Thus Deirdre Bair points out that May Beckett 'often suffered from severe tension headaches, dark depressions and thundering rages' (13); adding that she 'could be temperamental, and her moods zigzagged crazily from hilarity at [her children's] pranks and misbehavior to demands for strict silence and immediate obedience' (22). James Knowlson reports that she was 'extremely strict and demanding', but also:

> She used to have moods of dark depression that would last for days on end, when she was extremely difficult to deal with: 'strange', 'ill-tempered', 'bottled up', 'tricky', and 'difficult' were among the words used by those trying to convey this side of her personality. (Knowlson, 1997, 5)

Such violence assumes considerable importance in Beckett's works up to the '*Trilogy*', in relation to the threat represented by specular doubles. In *Mercier and Camier*, the *voice* takes hold of the two protagonists. When a constable seizes Camier physically and delivers him 'a violent smack' (*MC*, 71), he is not moved by some form of professional zealousness but by the will to cause *jouissance* for himself and for others, as can be heard in the irony of the following sentences: 'His interest was awakening. It was not every night a diversion of this quality broke the monotony of his beat. The profession had its silver lining, he had always said so.' The policeman's whistle appears as equivalent to the bell that torments Winnie: 'With the hand that held the truncheon he drew a whistle from his pocket, for he was no less dexterous than powerful' (71). Mercier then kicks the constable in the testicles, causing him to fall 'howling with pain and nausea to the ground' (72). These cries prove to be unbearable for Mercier and Camier, and must be silenced at all costs:

> But Camier, beside himself with indignation, caught up the truncheon, sent the helmet flying with his boot and clubbed the defenceless skull with all his might, again and again, holding the truncheon with both hands. The howls ceased. (72)

Once their work is done, a new form of irony can be discerned in the calm manner in which Mercier expresses himself, describing the dead constable's skull: 'Like partly shelled hard-boiled egg, was his impression.' The dimension of the *voice* appears in that which is unbearable for the characters. Since words remain totally inadequate, they can only speak of what remains in a strangely detached way: it is impossible for them to give meaning to what has just occurred. The cries however, anchored in their flesh, continue long after this outburst of extreme violence:

> On the edge of the square they were brought to a stand by the violence of the blast. Then slowly, head down, unsteadily, they pressed on through a tumult of shadow and clamour, stumbling on the cobbles strewn already with black boughs trailing grating before the wind or by little leaps and bounds as though on springs. (*MC*, 72)

These sounds emanating from the environment echo the voices that torment the two characters, and the alternation between opposed qualities—the branches simultaneously 'trailing' and 'grating […] by little leaps and bounds'—testifies to the impossibility of pacifying the anomic violence.

The structure of caprice gives rise to a series of motifs expressing the fundamental absence of regularity: it is inherent in the question of the 'tremor' evoked earlier in relation to interruptions.

These images are particularly manifest in passages where the body remains exposed to an unrelenting agitation. In *Mercier and Camier*, the cockatoo suffers from erratic breathing that, in the French, is termed 'arythmie' (*MC*, 40): 'Feebly and fitfully its breast rose and fell, faint quiverings ruffled up the down at every expiration' (*MC*, 18). The relationship to its emotional state is underlined: 'Shivers of anguish rippled the plumage, blazing in ironic splendour.' Murphy suffers from an 'irrational heart' (*Mu*, 4; *cf.* Ackerley and Gontarski, 278). Beckett spoke of having similar symptoms, following the passing away of his brother Frank in 1954: '[…] the old heart knocking hell out of me nightly and like an old stone in the day' (*L2*, 531). Herbert Blau describes the very physical feeling of asphyxiation Beckett experienced:

> Beckett, actually, in the panic of similar seizures, for him lifelong, and as he has described it—once in a conversation, suddenly stuttering, when he was writing *Comment c'est*—even more severe. They call it sleep apnea, a blockage of air in the windpipe, which at its worst seems to be caused by the nervous system's not getting an expected signal from the brain, which otherwise never stops, what leaves you breathless in Beckett. (Blau, 38–9)

As in the episode of the policeman's assassination, in *Mercier and Camier*, this oscillation between uncontrollable beatings and inertia show the unity of these two opposed positions within a Möbian topology, as Laura Salisbury has also suggested (2012, 158): the absence of mediation projects the subject, unforeseeably, from one extreme to the other. Before their outburst of violence, Mercier and Camier already methodically allied contrary exigencies. Their 'watchword' is defined by both metonymy and unpredictable rupture: '[…] lente, lente, and circumspection, with deviations to right and left and sudden reversals of course' (*MC*, 49). The French version ascribes the impulse to these deviations and reversals to the 'dards obscurs de l'intuition' ('obscure stings of intuition', 109).

The episode from *Company* articulates caprice with the question of knowledge: the omnipresence of caprice hinders the structuring of *experience*: in this case, the child's effort to evaluate distance. The 'cutting retort' (*Co*, 6) excludes any speech that could aid the character to arrive at an answer. The question of knowing is also central to *Watt*, where the word *caprice* expresses the protagonist's inability to situate the episode of the Galls, in relation to other incidents:

> It resembled them in the sense that it was not ended, when it was past, but continued to unfold, in Watt's head, from beginning to end, over and over again, the complex connexions of its lights and shadows, the passing from silence to sound and from sound to silence, the stillness before the movement and the stillness after, the quickenings and retardings, the approaches and the separations, all the shifting detail of its march and ordinance, according to the irrevocable caprice of its taking place. (*W*, 72)

Nothing allows this episode—nor the others in the novel, for that matter—to attain a form of unity: the innumerable parameters that condition it obey no law, a fact that hinders it from becoming an *event* bearing a subjective meaning: the episode related is conveyed only by the *unlimited* nature of the *voice*.

The violence of caprice leaves the subject in a situation of total dependence. Thus *Endgame* provides an example of the superego's caprice in the character of Hamm (Brousse). In his position as a tyrant, he constrains Clov to obey his every whim. It is precisely his capriciousness that makes of Clov his 'slave', for example when he demands to be placed in the centre of the room:

> HAMM: I feel a little too far to the left. [CLOV *moves chair slightly*.] Now I feel a little too far to the right. [CLOV *moves chair slightly*.] I feel a little too far forward. [CLOV *moves chair slightly*.] Now I feel a little too far back. (*Eg*, 105)

Manifestly, these demands are perfectly contradictory. Just before expressing this dissatisfaction, Hamm had asked: 'Am I right in the centre?' (*Eg*, 104). When Clov says he will measure to be sure of being exact, Hamm responds: 'More or less! More or less!' (105). The sequence is repeated: Hamm demands 'Put me right in the centre!', and when Clov declares he will fetch the tape measure, he responds again: 'Roughly! Roughly!' In other words, in the absence of any principle capable of providing the subject with a believable 'centre', no position will ever be adequate—not even one situated by metrical coordinates—since for the superego, no universal standard can impose a pacifying Law.

In this highlighting of *caprice* and the *unlimited*, Beckett's work gives a glimpse of the link with language as an 'event of the body', such as the idea has been put forward in relation to the later theories of Lacan. In this perspective—and contrary to the development undertaken by Marie-Claude Hubert (1994)—the link with the body does not concern the institution of the image (as in Lacan's famous 'mirror stage'), but rather a contingent encounter that escapes any norm or law, and where 'the body appears thereafter as the signifier's Other insofar as the signifier creates the event' (Miller, 2010–11). The *One* evoked here is related not to a unity that founds circumscribed entities (*limited wholes*), but concerns absolute singularity, which Beckett sums up in the axiomatic formulation: 'Impossible de raisonner sur l'unique' ('Impossible to reason on the unique', *MP*, 32). Thus the Beckettian Other, like that of the later Lacan, is not the pacifying symbolic that evacuates *jouissance*, but the *body*, in relation to a *jouissance* that cannot be mastered, as Jacques-Alain Miller states:

> The value of a body event is opposed to interdiction, it is not articulated with the law of desire. *Jouissance* is of the order of a trauma, a shock, contingency, pure chance, and not the law of desire. It is not caught up in a dialectic, but is the object of a fixation. (2010–11)

The absence of a law—the paternal metaphor—results in the fact that nothing can protect the subject from the shocks caused by the caprice of the Other. All that remains is to seek out responses that will succeed, tentatively at least, to set the torment at a safe distance.

The question of the continuous, incessant voice evolves throughout Beckett's work. If the notion—conceived by Wilfred Bion—of 'attacks on linking' appeared to be particularly important in the novels of the 1940s and 1950s, as studied earlier, it also seems to be associated with the writer's difficulty to extricate himself from the uninterrupted murmur of the *voice*. In this situation, as Bruno Geneste (2014) has pointed out, the voice, devoid of any 'hiatus' (*TPR*, 168), leaves no tracc on thc body, any more than the wind in the leaves. It was therefore indispensable, in order to avoid the fate threatened by a melancholic condition, to create such a breach in the inhuman imperative of the superego. Geneste states that 'what causes the failure of Beckett's melancholy is the writing of the gap, of the *blank*' (2015). Catherine Laws points out how Beckett ultimately deprives music of its metaphysical status as a breachless whole and as a comfortable escape from the contingency of language, so that musicality becomes present in 'structures of repetition and association that foreground the sounding qualities of language' (2013, 213), combined with the 'inability absolutely to divorce individual words from their conventional associations: grammatical, cultural and memorial'. She adds: 'Beckett plays on the very impossibility of treating syllables as musical notes, pushing in that direction but exploiting the minimal conventional meanings that remain' (223).

This is what constitutes Beckett's use of *lalangue*—language as *aporia*, devoid of any ultimate solution—and situates *interruption* as an integral part of language and its musicality; making it the very substance of language and, as such, something that takes on form in writing, rather than allowing its asperities to be attenuated by grammatical articulation. The existence of such an opening would help us to interpret Hélène Cixous' calling Beckett 'the neighbour of zero', when she states: 'Since to be alone, one must be more than one. Only one who is accompanied, surrounded, pressed by solitude feels alone. *Alone* keeps itself company *in the neighbourhood of zero*' (18). If this 'one' is 'more than one', it is owing to the prior presence of a symbolic structure allowing the subject to transform the incessant voices into 'company'. That is possible by virtue of the fact that, logically, zero is what structures any series: this is what distinguishes it from a pure void, as real. As Lacan develops the idea: '[...] the series of numbers, one can only represent it by representing zero, in a more or less latent way. Now zero is the presence of the subject who, at that level, totalises it' (1973, 205).

This discovery or invention of a structuring hiatus is thus decisive for Beckett's creation through to *What Where*, as Michel Bousseyroux has shown (2000). The interruptions thus appear to be much less violent in the later works, as Steven Connor has pointed out, seeing, in the *Nohow On* trilogy, 'a more measured pacing, with the gaps in the text seeming to be filled more with rumination than desperate panicked lockjaw' (2014a, 76). Instead of seeking to aggressively drill holes in language (*L1*, 518) by means of 'ruptured writing' (521), he works on the 'fundamental sounds' (Beckett, 1998, 24)—'accommodat[ing] the mess' (in Driver, 23; *cf.* Dow)—and the *équivoque* inherent in *lalangue*, that inscribes itself in the body (Nguyên, 2010a). Cécile Yapaudjian-Labat thus demonstrates how the violence inherent in the universality of the *logos* is turned against language in *Worstward Ho*, precisely because the affects—*jouissance*—prove to remain irreducible. Subjectivity thus thwarts the *logos*, leading to the creation of a 'minor literature'.[35] Interruption is thus a privileged means whereby Beckett deals with Lacan's fundamental 'absence of sexual rapport' in language, the ultimate nonexistence of determination or metalanguage.

35 Bruno Geneste (2015) also studies this evolution that started in Beckett's more aggressive use of 'nominalistic irony' (*L1*, 520).

3. Inscription

The study of the voice in its topological quality—as continuous and unbreachable, on the one hand, and marked by uncontrollable interruptions, on the other—shows it as a force that largely escapes the subject. We shall now examine privileged ways in which the subject succeeds in responding to the voice by means of producing an inscription, then by creating an image or adopting a 'reading voice'.

Inscription: A Definition

The process of inscription concerns language in the material effects it produces on the body. If, in the context of *limited wholes* governed by the Name-of-the-Father, the subject benefits from a definitive inscription in the register of linguistic semblances, in his confrontation with the *unlimited*, he is obliged to renew and diversify the forms of his *inscription*, with an aim to create an indispensible border. It is therefore a matter of an *action* involving the body, as the encounter with a *jouissance* that is radically 'unstillable'.[36] In this perspective, writing proves to be of a material order, as Henri Michaux remarkably demonstrates in his paintings.[37] While a signifier names, it also points to the place where it breaks down and encounters, not another signifier capable of reviving meaning, by founding a dialectic, but a void that, then, becomes a 'jar ever ready to receive *jouissance*, or at least to invoke it with its artifice' (Lacan, 2001, 19). Writing here comes as a substitute for the symbolic inscription usually afforded by a structuring *invocation.*

As such, it is qualified as a '*littoral*', 'figuring an entire domain made for the other frontier, in that they are foreign, to the point of not being reciprocal' (Lacan, 2001, 14). A frontier, as such, supposes a symbolic operation of exclusion as a result of which the two protagonists—be they enemies—are situated together within a set, and are

36 A term used by Beckett in his *Production Notebook* (in Ackerley and Gontarski, 162).

37 The relationship between writing and painting is manifest in the work of Henri Michaux (Brown, 2007, 173–92).

governed by the same law. The *littoral*, however, supposes a total absence of any relationship: neither of the two entities can function as a border for the other; neither can confer existence on the other as a *limited whole*. In sum, the abyss remains impossible to absorb, to bypass or to completely hem in. This conception of the *littoral* thus points to the subject as reduced to his founding *trait* or *cut*: to the original incidence of the signifier that produced the 'speaking being' (*parlêtre*), in the absence of any symbolic Other capable of inscribing the subject within a dialogical construction. This is where the subject encounters the force of the *drive*—as observed earlier when studying Mouth in *Not I*—in relation to Lacan's demonstration of how Japanese calligraphy provides the conditions for an absolutely singular response to the crushing force of the universal.[38]

The material quality of writing is particularly palpable in *Texts for Nothing* (completed in 1951), where the subject shows himself to be unable to create a distance from the unstoppable *voice*. Indeed, at this stage of his creation, Beckett had not yet attained the structuring hiatus or blank capable of extricating him from the incessant flow of the voice. As Éric Wessler (2015) points out, this renewal was only possible as of 'From an Abandoned Work' and *Comment c'est*. P. J. Murphy also notes: 'The ultimate paradox of *How It Is* is that the syntax of weakness enables the narrator to find a language that has the strength to command being' (75). In *Texts for Nothing*, by contrast, the narrator 'lacks a subject in an ontological sense' (Murphy, 74). Here he describes words not in their signifying quality but as belonging to the realm of waste or refuse, exhorting himself to 'void yourself of them' (*TFN* II, 106). 'Voiding' oneself does not mean to construct a discourse addressed to an auditor, where ideas enter a hierarchy, and words are interpreted according to their differential nature. Rather, it is to eject an excremental object, under the pressure of an unbearable *jouissance*.

In these texts, the materiality of words is manifested by images dealing with bodily secretions, as if there were only the slightest

---

38 See *supra*, p. 137.

of limits between inside and outside. The *voice* that remains inaccessible to the symbolic is heard, in a figurative manner, in this comparison of words with tears: 'I weep too without interruption. It's an unbroken flow of words and tears' (*TFN* VIII, 131). These tears flow in an autonomous fashion, independently of any subjectivity, without being attached to any meaning that would allow them to be seen as the expression of an emotion. Thus, when the body loses its consistency, the functions of the orifices are undifferentiated: '[...] I confuse them, words and tears, my words are my tears, my eyes my mouth.'

The submerging by the *voice* is expressed by a progression towards confusion. Firstly, words are opposed to silence: 'Only the words break the silence, all other sounds have ceased' (*TFN* VIII, 131). Then, the narrator notices the impossibility of achieving a definitive absence of sound: 'But if I were silent the other sounds would start again, those to which the words have made me deaf, or which have really ceased.' The subject's silence is insufficient, because the voice that is stopped by means of words inevitably resumes as soon as the latter come to a halt. Then an about turn occurs, by virtue of which the narrator admits he cannot distinguish between what he utters and his muteness: 'But I am silent, it sometimes happens, no, never, not one second.' To be silent or not are no longer separate, opposed states. Finally, comes the stream of tears: 'I weep too without interruption. It's an unbroken flow of words and tears.' The absence of a break in the duration and in the quality becomes apparent: words and tears are of the same substance, leading to a fusion between the three elements, *silence/words/tears*: 'But I speak softer, every year a little softer.' The lack of distinction between voice, silence and secretion indicates the impossibility of breaking utterances into separate units. The silence is *voice*, and to proffer words is only a way for the *drive*—the inaudible, screaming voice—to circumscribe an object, to localise itself within the body. A marked difference appears here, with regards to the interruptions produced by certain characters. The 'knock' in *Ohio Impromptu*, or the 'chime' in *Footfalls*, operated breaks allowing the subject to find an anchoring point for representation: they functioned as a substitute for invocation. In *Texts for Nothing*, a form of metonymy unfolds whereby the subject is only capable of a minimal inscription that cannot bring the voice to a halt, and create a salutary hiatus.

The *explicit* of *First Love* (written in 1946) describes a somewhat more successful attempt to silence the voice. At this stage in the story, Lulu has given birth to the narrator's child. However, in the absence of a reference to the paternal metaphor, it is impossible for him to find a place in the chain of transmission, and he flees, terrified. Being thus exposed to the fury of the *voice*, the narrator nonetheless finds a means to attenuate the latter's devastating effects:

> I began playing with the cries, a little in the same way as I had played with the song, on, back, on, back, if that may be called playing. As long as I kept walking I didn't hear them, because of the footsteps. But as soon as I halted I heard them again, a little fainter each time, admittedly, but what does it matter, faint or loud, cry is cry, all that matters is that it should cease. (*FL*, 45)

In order to free himself from the voice, the character finds the means to 'play' with it, to find the 'right distance': one that will act as a *littoral*, in the absence of a frontier. Such a 'game' recalls Freud's description of the *fort-da*, whereby the child makes a spool appear and disappear, in an alternation that Lacan situates just before the moment when one raises the symbolic question of the presence or absence of the Other (2013, 490). Indeed, the recourse to playing is indispensible insofar as silence remains the voice that 'continues by other means', so to speak: the character must therefore reassure himself that the cries exist, while attenuating the torment they cause him. To this end, he makes the sound of his footsteps heard, to cover up that of the baby's cries; then he stops, in order to feel their reality anew. By contrast with a nomination, this *inscription* does not halt the cries definitively, it does not create a breach: it only covers up the tumult, stifling it, localising the voice in the form of the sound produced. With these footsteps that remain foreign to any discursive construction, the character asserts his existence with regards to his Other, in the way a child sings to find courage in the dark of night. A parallel to these footsteps can be noted in the following observation Steven Connor makes about Beckett's and Bruce Nauman's work

> There is in both an impulse to walk through or walk out space, as though space would fade unless repeatedly made to start forth by the tread of the foot. Rather than the ground merely preceding and permitting the application of the foot, it comes to depend upon it. (Connor, 2000)

Michel Bousseyroux also emphasises the importance of the footfalls of *Quad*, showing that they alone create a boundary against the 'silence as a *void*' (2000, 189). The footsteps *create* space because they operate an inscription that provides the subject with a concrete support to his existence.

The Inscription of Footsteps: 'Footfalls'

The *dramaticule Footfalls* (written in 1975) offers a striking example of the function of *inscription*, as a means of facing up to the unceasing *voice*: this play allows us to evaluate the structural importance of May's movements, and discern the link between the latter and the text composed of dialogues and monologues. In this work, the *voice* appears as a consequence of May's 'unborn' status. In what Beckett called his 'pacing play' (in Knowlson, 1997, 614), and, contrary to what may be suggested by the preponderant presence of written speeches of great lyrical beauty, May's footsteps are a crucial element. Thus Walter Asmus reports: 'Beckett emphasizes the importance of the footsteps. The walking up and down is the central image, he says. This was his basic conception of the play. The text, the words were only built up around this picture.' Beckett asserts that the 'life-long stretches of walking' are 'the centre of the play, everything else is secondary' (in Asmus). He expresses the subsidiary nature of the words by means of a metaphor, in a letter to Billie Whitelaw: 'The pacing is the essence of the matter. […] The text: what pharmacists call excipient' (19 February 1976, in Whitelaw, 1996, 139).

The relation between pacing and the spoken text is problematic. Lois Oppenheim (2001, 772) stresses the crucial visual aspect of plays such as *Footfalls*, while Stephen Thomson correctly points out the indispensible nature of the written text which composes the image of a concrete, prosaic world: 'Crucially, the two are not merely discrete forces but are inextricably linked' (77). Indeed it is not surprising that Beckett should state the problematics of his works in terms marked by *équivoque*. Regarding his well-known refusal to explain his work—'If people want to have headaches among the overtones, let them' (Beckett, 1998, 24)—Catherine Laws points out that musical affect and the perception of form and structure 'are in part constituted in resonance, timbre, and texture, and the nuances of overtone structures are what a musician is learning to control' (2013, 9). The 'excipient' can be read as a means by which Beckett seeks to 'do the image', placing his structural priorities within a habitable envelope. Indeed, as in all of Beckett's work, the material combines with the evanescent dimension, revealing two irreconcilable facets that allow for no synthesis. If the spoken text envelops May's repetitive action, the images serve as signifying resonators—conveying meaning and spatial extension—to what takes place monotonously and insistently on the level of the bodily movements. Indeed, the assaults of the *voice* demand an efficient action; and if May's narrative unfolds a story, the latter will remain 'spectral' with regards to the torment caused by the unstillable voice. Basically, there is no verifiable relationship between the story recounted and what May (*mais*—'but'—is that really her name…?) achieves, and shows, on stage. What the character accomplishes—her unceasing writing—constitutes the play's structuring element. May exists by virtue of the sound of her footsteps; the latter giving the play its grounding in pure inscription, stripped of the substance suggested by the imaginary. The footsteps abut on the void, on silence.

Like those of the narrator in *First Love*, May's footsteps are destined to stifle the *voice*, as they doubtless were for May Beckett.[39]

39 Deirdre Bair reports: 'She did have difficulty sleeping through the night, and there were often periods when she paced the floor of her room or

The stage directions emphasise: '[...] *clearly audible rhythmic tread*' (*Ff*, 399). It is for this reason that May asks her mother to remove the carpet (401): to hear the sound of the feet is to ensure the possibility of locating the body and limiting the *voice*. The bodily contact with the ground thus being ensured, she can grasp something of her own existence; she can situate herself within space, even if the latter remains plunged in darkness. It is following this same logic that May leans her head against the wall: '[...] bows her poor head against the wall and snatches a little sleep.' Steven Connor (2000) observes that, in the work of both Beckett and Nauman, 'there is the possibility of coming to rest against a surface that holds as well as obstructs, defines shape in denying movement'. This halt and the presence of a solid substance contrast with the insatiable torment, which May experiences in the invasion of the voice, that only the counting of footsteps enables her to break up into discrete portions. The wall appears as a substitute maternal presence that does not assume a human face. By contrast, to not hear the movement of her feet would be to run the risk of finding herself lost in the innumerable crowd of the ceaseless *footsteps* described by the narrator of *The Unnamable*: '[...] all sounds, there's only one, continuous, day and night, what is it, it's steps coming and going, it's voices speaking for a moment [...]' (*U*, 380). The French title of the play, *Pas* marks the effect of May's steps: the adverbial particle *pas* also signifies the negation (*cf.* Connor, 2007, 178), expressing the effort to impose silence on the Other, like the child who protests 'Je ne veux *pas*!' ('I don't want to!'). Shane Weller points out (2006, 73) that lexical repetition links the narrator's footsteps, described at the end of *Premier amour*, to the negation: 'Tant que je marchais je ne les entendais pas, grâce au bruit de mes pas' (*PA*, 55). The English version simply reads: 'As long as I kept walking I didn't hear them, because of the footsteps' (*FL*, 45).

---

wandered through the darkened house as silently as one of the ghosts which she swore haunted it' (10).

The Infinite 'Unborn' Voice of 'Footfalls'

However, while representing an effort to withdraw from the torment, the inscribing footsteps paradoxically remain an expression of the latter, for want of being able to operate a veritable separation, contrary to what Lacan evokes in his invention of an apocryphal episode of *Robinson Crusoe*, where the hero sees a footprint on the sand. Lacan explains[40] that the trace of the footstep (the mark left by real contact) is effaced and forgotten, to become a *signifier* that only has any relationship with other signifiers. In an inversion of this logic of negation, the motif of the footsteps, in Beckett's work signifies '*pas de*' (no) symbolisation, as well as the tireless efforts undertaken to achieve the latter.

The voice thus attains an infinite dimension, suggested by the symbol ∞ May inscribes on stage, where she 'wheels' at the end of each stretch of pacing (Brater, 1987, 61). Steven Connor emphasises that May's pacing also 'carries her inevitably away from herself' (2007, 178). Indeed, the counting of footsteps—as well as that of units of time—is a preoccupation shared by a number of Beckett's characters (Bailey, 151–4), and expresses the action of the unlimited in the sometimes exorbitant figures attained, in the same way as Dom Juan boasts his *mille e tre*, that he can nonetheless only ever approach *one by one* (Lacan, 1975b, 15).

Thus, in the end, May is absorbed by absence, when the spectator finds: '*No trace of* MAY' (*Ff*, 403). Her disappearance reveals her existence as pure inscription, devoid of content, and incapable of attaining an ending. From the start, as Beckett said to Billie Whitelaw: 'Well, let's just say *you're not quite there*' (in Whitelaw, 1996, 143). This reduced physical—meaning: what can be ascertained within 'reality'—presence is what imposes the irreducible presence of the voice as an *a* object, and which traverses May's body, causing her perpetual pacing. If Ruby Cohn explains that the play is both 'wrested from the void'

40 Jacques Lacan, *Le Séminaire*, Livre IX: *L'Identification* (unpublished), lesson of 24 January 1962 (in Rey-Flaud, 122).

(1980, 57) and 'uncovers a void' (95), it is because May's absence is, nonetheless, a particular form of *presence*, as regards the *voice*.

While the 'reading voice', adopted to narrate the 'Sequel', would seem to situate May in the realm of meaningful representations, the description of her movements reveals the interruptions we have observed, animated by *caprice*, rather than in the regular alternation seen on stage. As a consequence, May's existence becomes even more immaterial. She is seen at a complete halt: '[…] stand stark still till she could move again' (*Ff*, 402); then in ceaseless movement: '[…] paced without pause […].'; finally, May disappears: '[…] before vanishing the way she came.' This succession of partly incompatible positions recalls the character of Belacqua, in *Dream of Fair to middling Women*: 'At his simplest he was trine. […] Centripetal, centrifugal and… not' (*DF*, 120). Their underlying unity can however be understood in terms of a Möbian topology, where apparently opposed qualities are situated on the same edge. At the same time, in the middle of the strip, can be found a non-negotiable hole: radical absence, expressive of the fact that May has never had any definitive or concrete existence in discourse.

Indeed, if the voice has such an incidence on May, it is because she is 'unborn', a status conveyed by the impossibility for the mother's voice to confirm her daughter's birth. Beckett explains that the mother was about to say '…the same where she was *born*', that May was not born, as Walter Asmus reports, 'she just began, and he quotes Beckett: 'It began. There is a difference. She was never born'. Indeed, she can only say: 'Where it began. [*Pause*.] It all began' (*Ff*, 401). These sentences perhaps point to the paronyms *began*/*begat*: May *began*, but was not *begat*, in that she was not inscribed in a symbolic transmission. Indeed, the expression 'It all began' designates a breachless whole—experienced as absolute solitude—that does not make up a 'world'.

Beckett asserts: 'The daughter only knows the voice of the mother […]' (in Asmus, 82). Because May is 'unborn', her mother is not simply a member inscribed in a family history but is a voice that pervades her daughter's existence profoundly, and which she is powerless to detach herself from: the mother is incommensurably intimate.

Indeed, in contradiction with any realism, the mother's voice declares: 'She has not been out since girlhood [...]' (*Ff*, 401), thus abolishing all temporality. At the same time, the mother gives a visage to the dimension of the abyss as *real*, declaring to her daughter: 'There is no sleep so deep I would not hear you there' (*Ff*, 399). The mother's presence is this voice emanating from her 'deep sleep'. In this abyss, there is still the possibility of hearing a voice, instead of the daughter being confronted with the torment of the unnameable.

On the structural level however, mother and daughter both participate in the same Möbian topology. Indeed, the mother's voice is situated in her daughter's head, as Beckett confirms, according to Stanley Gontarski: 'My voice is in her head... She hears it in her poor mind' (in Gontarski, 1990, 154). The latter expression suggests that everything takes place in May's head. Consequently, the play seen on stage is situated in this same space: what appears outside, 'in reality' takes place inside. And yet, the spectator is confronted with the exteriority of both the stage and this maternal voice, heard through a loud speaker. This inextricably paradoxical structure makes it impossible to contain the whole within a realistic perspective, where the voice would be situated exclusively within May.

The same indeterminacy characterises the mother/daughter relationship. Beckett unites these two figures so that the concern they express one for the other appears as being reciprocal. In this couple, each one watches over the other, so that it is impossible to separate them, to see them as two totally distinct characters. Thus, the *daughter's* name—*May*—is that of the author's mother: the mother appears here as a daughter. In the same way, the daughter adopts a *maternal* posture, following Beckett's indication to 'clasp her hands across her body in a gesture that seemed to encapsulate her whole being' and that resembled the posture of the *Virgin of the Annunciation* of Antonello da Messina (Knowlson, 1997, 256–7). As Marie-Claude Hubert notes:

> In this image, he unites awaiting for death and awaiting for birth. As the mother before awaited the birth of her daughter, the latter

> now awaits her death, these two deliverances that mark the limits of life. (Hubert ed., 771)

To consider death as a birth is also to assert the impossibility of entering existence.

The inversion of the mother/daughter roles is also suggested in an earlier version of the text, as Stanley Gontarski points out: 'Originally, the Voice expressed an ancient fear, that the daughter might die before her. A terrifying prospect' (1990, 154). In this fear, a death wish can be discerned, on the part of the mother with regards to her daughter; but also the hope that the latter may watch over her mother's death. This reversal reveals something of the latter's powerlessness to give 'birth' to her daughter, as a result of her own anxiety regarding death. Éric Wessler points out that the monologues that follow the initial dialogue echo each other, to form a process of involution: 'May thus recites what she has heard, and the text folds up, not in a simple loop, by a return to the commencement, but within itself […]' (2009, 354). As in *Rockaby*, 'the content of the text ends up enveloping the context in which it is uttered' (393). This can be seen as an example of what Angelo Moorjani calls 'encrypting' (1990, 21), which points to an intermediate zone of 'simultaneous deathlessness and lifelessness' excluded from the reparation provided both by the work of art and mourning. This may be true, provided this dimension is placed in the perspective of melancholy and the 'pure pain of existence' (Lacan, 1966, 777), articulating the motif of encrypting—situated on the imaginary level—in relation to its anchoring in the *structural* fixity Beckett achieves in his later work.[41] Indeed, *How It Is* shows how enveloping involves a risk of mortification, for want of confirmation by an Other (Brown, 2016). However, such enveloping—as seen, for example, in the arms of the rocker in *Rockaby*—represents a means by which the subject lodges his unspeakable, or 'unborn', being in relation to an Other, for want of having been instituted in the symbolic register, in

41 We situate this fixity in relation to 'discursive structures' (see *infra*, p. 320 *sqq*.).

relation to the Name-of-the-Father. Thus, in *Happy Days*, the mound that slowly absorbs Winnie is both an image exposed to the blinding light—correlated with the clichés the character desperately latches on to (Brown, 2011a)—and what covers the invisible abyss that fills her with terror. In the plays, this reverse side acquires existence by virtue of such luminous elevation. The Möbian topology of the infinity motif finds another application here, insofar as it reveals what may appear to be opposing sides as being, in fact, a single surface: the visible manifestation takes on form, expands, then dissolves into invisibility. From a subjective point of view, this complex 'encrypting' movement can be seen as the attempt to become one's own other (*TFN* I, 103; *R*, 441).

In the same way as Belacqua's triple nature, in *Dream of Fair to middling Women*, rested on its third term—expressing his nonexistence—the unity formed by May and her mother circumscribes the former's radical nonexistence. May—who combines her own figure on stage and her mother's voice—has never been 'there'. It is this absence that constitutes the union of death and the failure of birth. The fourth part of the play emphasises May's disappearance: '*No trace of* MAY' (*Ff*, 403). The expression *no trace* signifies the abolition, by the voice, of everything belonging to the discursive register. By way of contrast however, the play itself produces a 'trace', insofar as it gives an amplified form to May's incessant comings and goings. The play also shows the refusal to simply ascribe a positive and univocal value to silence, understood as the unnameable void into which May disappears. Indeed any disappearance will turn into a new appearance, according to the following paradoxical formulation: 'A little later, when as though she had never been, it never been, she began to walk' (402). Beckett marks the alternation between the absolute effacing and the resumption of the footsteps: thus, the latter give form to the unceasing voice.

4. Image and Reading

'Do the Image'

Confronted with the unstillable voice, some characters—such as the narrator of *The Unnamable*—evoke the absence of a word, expressing the idea that there may be somewhere a vocable they could utter, for their torment to come to an end. By virtue of this word, they could have access to a phrastic structuring 'with a beginning, a middle and an end as in the well-built phrase' (*Mo*, 27) that would definitively expel the unbearable *jouissance*. It is in this sense that the Voice of *Cascando* seeks to recount the story of Woburn:

> —story… if you could finish it… you could rest… sleep… not before… oh I know… the ones I've finished… thousands and one… all I ever did… in my life… saying to myself… finish this one… it's the right one… then rest… sleep… no more stories… no more words… (*Cas*, 297)

This string of words expresses the desperate effort to construct a fiction that, were it to be confirmed by a hypothetical Other, would relieve the subject of a burden that it is beyond his means to bear. Indeed, the torment this character endures is such that he can only imagine this achievement as an extinction, as dreamless sleep.

Thus, for want of a paternal metaphor, many characters strive to 'do the image', as expressed in the narrative entitled *L'Image* (first published in 1959), and which ends thus: 'I stay like this no more thirst the tongue goes in the mouth closes it must be a straight line now it's done I've done the image' (*Im*, 168). Bruno Clément notes the difference between this version and the one included in *How It Is* (written as *Comment c'est*, 1958–1960), and where the verb changes: 'I've done the image' becomes 'I have had the image' (*HI*, 31). Beyond the distinction between the imagination as fabrication or passivity, Clément observes that 'it is in this pre-eminence of illusion, in its aptitude to disappear, that the distinctive nature of the Beckettian imaginary resides' (1988, 170).

What seems important to notice, however, is the function of the image for the character. The narrator represents himself as situated outside of a luminous space, lodged in the mud that fills his mouth and impedes speech. This is a situation Beckett's characters can be found in from *Texts for Nothing* onwards. He occupies the realm of the 'unborn' characters: those who do not have at their disposal speech they consider as their own, who are excluded from any community. Progressively, he perceives an image that represents the contrary of his condition: 'I look to me about sixteen and to top it all glorious weather egg blue sky and scamper of little clouds' (*Im*, 166). The pure, unflawed appearance of this image confirms its stereotyped nature (Brown, 2008, 103–6), seeming to indicate its association with an impassive and faultless Other, like the mother in *Company* (*Co*, 5). Faced with the spotless and idealised aspect of these images, the narrator can only situate himself in the position of *refuse*. However, by constructing an image, he succeeds in lodging himself in relation to his other, somewhat in the way that the vanishing point in perspective painting (Nominé) articulates the subject with the representation as a whole, according to the principle formulated by Lacan concerning the *a* object: '[…] the field of reality […] is only supported by the extraction of the *a* object which however gives it its frame' (1966, 554). By constituting the image as a *whole*, the subject succeeds in providing himself with a place with regards to his Other who will henceforth watch over him. Thus, in *Nacht und Träume*, Beckett shows A envisioning 'a replica of himself (B) receiving the succour he longs for' (Herren, 2000, 186). As Graley Herren explains, this composes a *mise en abyme* of what Beckett himself does in inventing such a character in this setup. Catherine Laws (2013, 196) in turn associates this construction with the 'Devised deviser devising it all for company' (*Co*, 30). The image can thus be situated in relation to speech, and its function of *invocation*, as Jean-Michel Vives describes it using the image of the lone singer: 'He invokes, by deploying his voice, an Other, who is of course absent, but that the subject's voice has the power to summon for him, but also for those who hear him' (2012, 44). Addressing the Other represents a means to silence the tormenting voice: by making his own voice heard, the subject diverts the Other's attention. In the same way, the visual image—the icon, in the field of religion, for example—is destined to impede the devouring gaze of the divinity: it serves as a '*gaze-tamer*' (Lacan, 1973, 100). Catherine Laws is quite right to emphasise that in both *Ghost Trio* and *Nacht und Träume*, the use of music 'to summon the virtual company of an absent other [...] is nothing so substantial as an assertion of transcendence, redemption or the suspension of suffering. Rather, it suggests the endlessly replayed echo of the refusal to abandon that possibility' (2013, 198).

Insofar as it is not heterogeneous to language but is determined by the structuring the latter imposes, the image is related to the *voice*, as Michel Bousseyroux demonstrates in connection with *Nacht und Träume*, when he states that what Beckett makes visible is 'this unspeakable object' that acts as 'a call for the sign emanating from the other. A dream of a sign of the Other of desire' (2000, 193). Thus paradoxically, the voice may be mute, just as the presence of the gaze can sometimes be announced by an audible manifestation. The Other mentioned here—situated at the point of an ideal—bears various names, such as 'the inviolable zenith where for amateurs of myth lies hidden a way out to earth and sky' (*LO*, 207) or 'the Wains' (*FL*, 45), the constellation that his father showed to the narrator of *First Love*, and that the latter is unable to locate alone. However, if the Other, for Beckett, is irremediably absent, or 'the absolute absence of the Absolute' (*Dsj*, 33), the imaginary register can designate the place it has abandoned, and which offers a barrier to the *real*. Michel Bousseyroux (2000, 193–4) thus notes that the dream in this play is comparable to the Name-of-the-Father which, for the neurotic subject, is the guardian of the unbearable *jouissance*: it palliates the unceasing and *unlimited* sound of the outside that inflicts endless torment.

What is at stake in the creation of the image appears at the end of *Murphy*: 'When he was naked he lay down in a tuft of soaking tuffets and tried to get a picture of Celia. In vain. Of his mother. In vain. Of his father (for he was not illegitimate). In vain.' (*Mu*, 157).

Here, Murphy attempts to obtain an image of those who surround him, particularly his parents: those whose gaze (according to Berkeley's principle *esse est percipi*) would be capable of returning a unified image of himself.[42] Murphy is thus situated at the opposite pole from Speaker in *A Piece of Monologue*, or the character of *Film*, who both tear up images imposing a stereotyped representation of the stages of their existence. In the end, Murphy's failure to 'do the image' causes his suicide, which is appropriately preceded by a description of fragmentation:

> He could not get a picture in his mind of any creature he had met, animal or human. Scraps of bodies, of landscapes, hands, eyes, lines and colours evoking nothing, rose and climbed out of sight before him, as though reeled upward off a spool level with his throat. (*Mu*, 157)

The Image in 'Rough for Radio II'

Rough for Radio II, written in the early sixties, illustrates the place of the image, precisely in a context where the auditor is in the presence of the voice alone, in the absence of any visual staging. This play includes Animator, accompanied by Stenographer. Animator commands Dick, who is mute, and whose function consists of applying a 'bull's pizzle' to Fox's body. Animator and Stenographer have the task of making the latter produce the word they are seeking—without, however, knowing in advance what it might be—in order to be free.

If Fox has not yet spoken the word that '*may be it*' (*RR II*, 276), he produces a verbal image that unsettles Animator and Stenographer:

42 The specification concerning the reality of the father is ironically necessary, in view of the latter's problematic presence. Indeed, Bruno Geneste (2015) points out the difference between the son's love for his father (manifest in Beckett) and the dimension of respect, which is excluded as a result of the father's evanescence.

> —fatigue, what fatigue, my brother inside me, my old twin, ah to be he and he—but no, no no. [*Pause.*] No no. [*Silence. Ruler.*] Me get up, me go on, what a hope, it was he, for hunger. Have yourself opened, Maud would say, opened up, it's nothing, I'll give him suck if he's still alive, ah but no, no no. (*RR II*, 279)

The irrational nature of this image shocks Stenographer's sense of realism: 'S: [*Scandalized.*] But it's simply impossible! Inside him! *Him!*' (*RR II*, 280). This image arises as a complete whole, without any link to anything of any kind, as Animator remarks: 'And of a sudden, in the same sentence, a woman, with Christian name to boot, and a brother.' Its strangeness results from the fact that this image is not prepared by other utterances. Rather than being the consequence of a preceding construction, it appears without any relationship to an identifiable reality. The other characters cannot refer this motif back to any known family configuration: 'A: Kith and kin? / S: Never a word, sir. I have been struck by it. Mine play such a part, in my life!' The 'brother' is no part of any filial or family link: he is simply a *double*. As a true subjective creation, this image is situated outside of any family chain: 'A father, a mother, a friend, a… Beatrice—no, that is asking too much' (282). In enumerating these identities—persons who, having seen Fox, could testify to his existence—Animator passes from the family[43] (the first conventional idea) to the literary, bookish reference, in order to reduce the strangeness of the image evoked.

Thus situated outside of any metonymical chain, this image is rooted in the impossible, in the manner of a subject's fundamental fantasy that represents its window onto the real (Miller, 2010–11; Wajcman, 2004). Stenographer emphasises this fact when she expresses her indignation at the idea that Fox might have a brother inside

---

43 The term *family* denotes, both in *Proust* and *How It Is* (*HI*, 17, 33), familiar concepts associated with habit: 'But when the object is perceived as particular and unique and not merely the member of a family […] then and then only may it be a source of enchantment' (*Pr*, 22–3). We can also note Beckett's remark: 'The artist who stakes his being is from nowhere, has no kith' (*Dsj*, 149).

him: 'But it's quite simply impossible! Inside him! *Him!*' (*RR II*, 280). By its singular nature, this image reveals its status as an exception: as such, it *founds* a reality, rather than belonging to one. For this reason, it has the function of an 'anchoring point'—Lacan's 'point de capiton' (1998, 196)—that creates a halt in the flow of speech. Thus, Animator observes: '[…] this is the first time […] that he has actually… *named* anyone' (*RR II*, 280). This image appears in the place of the word whose absence hinders the creation of a reality. Since Fox is incapable of uttering the word that '*may be it*' (276), the image occupies this place: '[…] what counts is not so much the *thing*, in itself, that would astonish me too. No, it's the word, the notion' (280). Thus, it is not a matter of confirming the actual believable existence of a brother inside Fox, but of grasping the *function* of naming: the manner in which the image offers a *frame* that circumscribes his *jouissance*. This context sheds light on Monique Liart's qualifying the 'unborn' being as a *delirious metaphor* (1993, 30) for Beckett: one that veils the hole inherent in language. This image—that is offered up to the Other: Stenographer, Animator, and the auditor—can in no way be verified or rationalised, since it imposes a new reality.

The appearance of this image represents a form of *crescendo* in the composition of the play, whose entire final part crystallises around it. Confronted with Fox, Animator exults over the image in turn: with phallic symbols at his disposal (his assistant Stenographer, on one side, Dick's 'bull's pizzle', on the other), he is a caricature of his tormented double. He believes he has seized something concrete: '[…] here… possibly… we have something at last' (*RR II*, 283). The verb used in French (*tenir*) suggests the idea of mastery, as if Animator were grasping an object in his hand. However, he is far from controlling himself. Seeking to set the image within a credible whole, he demands—paradoxically—that Fox produce just anything: '[…] try, at least, what do you stand to lose? [*Beside himself.*] Even though it is not true!' (282). He is most excited and '*Delighted*' (284) at the image produced: '*Warming to his point*'; '*Beside himself*' (282).

In the same way as Fox's image is situated outside of any objective reality, and is unverifiable, Animator is troubled by the absence of the right word, so he demands something that excites him. That is also what causes him to accuse Stenographer—wrongly—of omitting a crucial passage:

> A: Don't skip, miss, the text in its entirety if you please. S: I skip nothing, sir. [*Pause.*] What have I skipped, sir? A: [*Emphatically.*] '...between two kisses...' [*Sarcastic.*] That mere trifle! [*Angry.*] How can we ever hope to get anywhere if you suppress gems of that magnitude?' (*RR II*, 284)

Here—and, apparently, without noticing, or without wanting to know—it is Animator who inserts the 'missing' words. When Stenographer objects that Fox never pronounced them, he calls into doubt her hearing, her memory and her 'good faith'. However, the passage he finds is apocryphal, replacing what Fox does not say: this phrase—that comes, like a verbal 'fantasy', and covers up Fox's silence—does not suffice to free them.

The *équivoque* of the French verb *sauter* ('Ne sautez pas, mademoiselle [...]' [*PR*, 84])—meaning 'skip', 'jump', but also, in its obscene usage 'fuck', like the other verb used in the text: *baiser*, 'to kiss'—associates Animator with the phallic caricature, by contrast with the gaps (or *sauts*) in Fox's text. In this proxy fantasy, Animator aims to enjoy the image created by Fox. However, the effect produced is a form of *hypotyposis*, an almost hallucinatory vision: 'The breast! One can almost see it!' (283). His excitement is such that Animator imagines he heard Fox speak of two kisses. These two kisses are also the ones that Animator—whose place is limited to the level of a verbal exchange—desires to receive from Stenographer, in his dream of forming a couple with her. Such a fantasy is intended to fill in the irremediable scission between these two characters on the one hand, and Fox on the other.

If Animator is excited by the image that he himself invents, the one produced by Fox reveals its function for the victim. The subject—like a mother expecting a child—lodges his double inside himself. Here, an echo can be discerned of the young 'unborn' girl evoked by Jung during his third Tavistock lecture, that Beckett heard in 1935. In Fox's image, it is the double—this 'twin'—that has failed to be born. The role ascribed to Maud, by Fox, corresponds to the aspiration to revive this double, in accordance with what Beckett confided to Charles Juliet: 'J'ai toujours eu la sensation qu'il y avait en moi un être assassiné. Assassiné avant ma naissance. Il me fallait retrouver cet être assassiné. Tenter de lui redonner vie…' ('I have always had the feeling that there was in me an assassinated being. Assassinated before my birth. I had to find this assassinated being. Try to give it life again…', in Juliet, 15). According to the series of *mises en abyme* created by this text, Fox is Animator's double, an idea confirmed by the phonic echo in the final words of these phrases: 'Yes, sir, a life all his own'; 'I might have known' (*RR II*, 278). On a supplementary level, the unborn brother is the double of Fox, who faints at the idea of a brother who may be dead: '[…] if he's still alive […]' (279).

The series of women—*Maud*[44] (*RR II*, 279), *angel* (180), *nanny*—evokes the idea of a comforting, maternal presence, capable of saving the subject from his suffering: their function is thus comparable to that of the image that palliates the void, or the pair of hands that appears in *Nacht und Träume*. If Maud is to try to revive the part of the subject that is mortified, rejected from nomination—'[…] I'll give him suck if he's still alive, ah but no, no no' (279)—the undertaking is desperate, impossible. Of course, the women evoked represent the exact opposite of the torment inflicted by Animator and Dick's bull's pizzle, insofar as their presence makes it possible to deal with something of the unspeakable. However, Stenographer—as Maud's double—offers a contrast with the latter. Animator has the idea of making her kiss Fox, in order to provoke the revelation of the missing word. A confusion can then be observed between the act of kissing and the reaction caused: 'Kiss him, miss, perhaps that will stir some fibre. / Where, sir? / In his heart, in his entrails—or some other part. / No, I mean kiss him where, sir?' (282). If kissing usually represents an expression of

44 'Maud' is the title of a poem (1855) by Tennyson.

affection, it becomes obscene, and capable of unveiling the flesh, devoid of any protective veil provided by the image: 'Why on his stinker of a mouth, What do you suppose? [STENOGRAPHER *kisses* FOX. *Howl from* FOX.] Till it bleeds! Kiss it white! [*Howl from* FOX.] Suck his gullet!' As a result of its violence, the kiss becomes equivalent to the whip blows dispensed by Dick.

The Reading Voice: 'being oneself one's own other'

To 'do the image' is thus a means to create a form of what Beckett calls 'company', in the absence of a symbolic Other. As a form of *invocation*, it is addressed to the Other, causing sufficient presence to temporarily still the tormenting *voice*. However the 'company' that the character seeks often does not succeed in completely palliating his fundamental solitude: indeed, the eponymous text concludes with the word-paragraph 'Alone' (*Co*, 42).

The Beckettian subject is constantly obliged to elaborate his constructions from this condition of radical solitude. If, for the neurotic subject, the Other functions as a guardian of *jouissance*, the psychotic has no such guarantee. As Lacan declares:

> Free men, truly free ones, are precisely the madmen. There is no demand for the little *a* [object], his little *a*, he has it, it is what he calls his voices, for example. […] He does not hold onto the place of the Other, of the great Other, by means of the *a* object, he has the *a* at his disposal. […] Let us say that he has his cause [*a* object] in his pocket […]. (Lacan, 1967)

In the absence of a symbolic Other, the character often finds himself in a position to command the voice, to play the role of both himself and his other. The narrator of the first *Text for Nothing* experiences this situation as a tiresome repetition, as the inability to produce anything new: '[…] always murmuring, the same old mutterings, the same old stories, the same old questions and answers […]' (*TFN* I, 103). Instead of a dialectic based on two signifiers (S_1–S_2), the character is condemned to occupy both complementary places, and to rehash the same utterances. Thus it is that he tells himself stories:

> Yes, I was my father and I was my son, I asked myself questions and answered as best I could, I had it told to me evening after evening, the same old story I knew by heart and couldn't believe, or we walked together, hand in hand, silent, sunk in our worlds, each in his worlds, the hands forgotten in each other. That's how I've held out till now. (*TFN* I, 103)

This passage eloquently expresses the absence of any transmission made possible by the inscription of a lack: the nonexistence of a structure reposing on *limited wholes*. The fact that the narrator evokes the father here indicates that the latter, supposedly representative of symbolic transmission, was unable to assume this function, particularly with regards to the mother. He will, of course, be important for the Beckettian narrator—that of *First Love*, for example, to whom he pointed out the constellation of 'the Wains' (*FL*, 45)—but this love will be accompanied by the recognition of an absence of consistency: the Beckettian father remains radically wanting.[45] *To be one's own other* means that questions and answers are situated on the same level, as the narrator of *How It Is* confirms: 'in the familiar form of questions I am said to ask myself and answers I am said to give myself however unlikely that may appear' (*HI*, 144). As Daniel Sibony points out concerning the footsteps at the end of *First Love*: 'The *voice* of the Other can act as a Third but if one starts it *oneself*, to measure, in relation to its intensity, one's own small movements, there is no Other, and the dual vertigo concludes in coming and going' (Sibony, 171).

Thus, the Beckettian character is obliged be himself his own other, like the figure in *Rockaby*: 'going to and fro / all eyes / all sides / high and low / for another / another like herself / another creature

45 On Beckett's love for his father, see Weller (2009, 42–3). On the salutary function of the father in relation to his son, see Geneste (2008, 153).

like herself' (*R*, 435). This quest ends up in a failure and, when the absence of another is confirmed, she must recognise that she will only ever have herself: 'was her own other' (441). Henceforth, she must talk to herself: 'saying to herself / whom else'. The Beckettian character must create for himself his 'pseudo-others'.

This is possible, however, because language is 'itself alone company' (Lacan 2006a, 179). Structurally, it is the 'discourse of the Other': it can never be a simple emanation of the subject since it is what founds a speaking being (*parlêtre*). Thus, *to be one's own other* means to occupy the place of an other in order to construct the simulacrum of a verbal exchange. In *Company*, the narrator formulates as follows the function of poetic invention: 'Deviser of the voice and of its hearer and of himself. Deviser of himself for company' (*Co*, 16). Hamm imagines his end in the manner of a child, seized by fear of the dark: 'Then babble, babble, words, like the solitary child who turns himself into children, two, three, so as to be together, and whisper together, in the dark' (*Eg*, 126). Recounting a story—a children's story—is a means for the subject to face up to the terror caused by this darkness that represents the gaping hole of his existence. Thus it is that the narrator of 'The Calmative' expects his father to read him a story:

> He might have simply told me the story, he knew it by heart, so did I, but that wouldn't have calmed me, he had to read it to me, evening after evening, or pretend to read it, turning the pages and explaining the pictures that were of me already, evening after evening the same pictures till I dozed off on his shoulder. (*CSPr*, 64)

Here, in order to have a calming effect, the story must be a children's story, one that is repeated and not an invention, not something new: it functions in the manner of a bedtime story, rather than having the status of a literary 'creation'. The repeated story is one that has endured the passing of time: it causes no surprise, since any unforeseen utterance could give rise to the anxiety caused by the *unlimited* voice. This repetition of the same is intended to create a substitute of the father who, fundamentally, is wanting. Indeed, the weakness of the paternal function seems precisely to manifest its effects in the terror experienced by the child, who can only sleep when he feels secure. Since the father's speech alone cannot provide this reassurance, the mediation of the written text is necessary, acting as a third party, so that the child may feel protected: the story's consistency requires to be guaranteed by its written support.

Insofar as it 'rocks' or 'cradles' the child, the story also has a maternal function: instead of being felt as a source of anxiety, this voice is embodied by the presence of another that conveys it. Such is the function of the story, according to the definition offered by Voice B in *That Time*: 'making up to keep the void out just another of those old tales to keep the void from pouring in on top of you the shroud' (*TT*, 390). The story is intended to palliate the terrifying void, the *voice* that manifests itself as *unlimited*. Once it is humanised, the voice becomes soothing music. Speech 'lulls' the subject (*U*, 341) because it calms the torment of the persecuting voice, as the narrator of *L'Innommable* states: 'Ça les endormira […]' ('That will lull them', *I*, 66).

These elements could perhaps nuance the opinion Bruno Clément formulates in an analysis based on a conception of genres, seen in the perspective of innovation and modernity. Noting that Hamm's 'novel'—called a 'roman' in the French version (*FP*, 80)—is 'written' (2009, 160), Clément remarks that 'it is not an existing story but one that is progressively invented in the course of sessions of improvisation' (161). However, this tale is presented as belonging to an obsolete æsthetic, as does the story of the trousers told by Nagg (160). By contrast, Clément points out the qualities of Clov's monologue, which shows that 'literature will henceforth be interior' (165). It seems nonetheless important to note that Hamm's story partially escapes such an evolution: like the 'stories' that many other characters tell themselves, this one is inscribed in reference to the Other—in this case, a known literary genre—and ensures a paternal function.

The act of speaking to oneself, of telling stories, can be found in many of Beckett's works. Winnie reassures herself that she can fill up her day: 'There is my story of course, when all else fails' (*HD*, 163). The status of story-telling is often signalled by the specific tone adopted. Concerning the reader in *Ohio Impromptu*, James Knowlson notes 'Beckett advising him to make his delivery "calm, steady, designed to soothe. Bedtime story"' (1997, 666). In *All That Fall*, Mr Rooney recounts his perception of the accident that occurred while he was in the train and, to do so, he adopts a: '*Narrative tone*' (*AF*, 192, 193, 194). In an effort to ensure the continuity of his story, he asks: 'Where was I in my composition?' (194). Behind his artificial narrative tone, can be heard the suggestion that Mr Rooney might have been linked to the death of the child (Pountney, 105). In this case, his narrative tone may betray a form of over-compensation intended to palliate a feeling of horror.

In *That Time*, the character tells himself stories: 'talking to yourself who else out loud imaginary conversations [...] making it up now one voice now another till you were hoarse and they all sounded the same' (*TT*, 390). The text insists on the absence of any Other, that the character is obliged to palliate as best he can: 'muttering to yourself who else'; 'with your arms round you whose else' (389). In *Embers*, Henry tells himself stories in order to feel a presence, to procure a vital substitute for the 'company' that he lacks:

> Stories, stories, years of stories, years and years of stories, till the need came on me, for someone, to be with me, anyone, a stranger, to talk to, imagine he hears me, years of that, and then now, for someone who... knew me in the old days, anyone, to be with me, imagine he hears me, what I am, now. (*E*, 255)

The slipping operated in this sentence emphasises the function of these stories: it is a matter of endowing oneself with a presence and, more profoundly, someone who could reassure him about his former existence; that is to say, logically, someone resembling a parental figure. However, Henry never manages to finish his stories: 'I usen't to need anyone, just to myself, stories, there was one about an old fellow called Bolton, I never finished it, I never finished any of them, I never finished anything, everything always went on for ever' (*E*, 254). The absence of a conclusion to these stories is consistent with the lack of any ending in general for Beckett's narrators, who evoke the fundamental absence of a symbolic Other capable of offering an 'anchoring point'. Confronted with the *unlimited*, the subject relates stories, talking to oneself, in order to achieve the simulacrum of a *limitation*, but which never fails to collapse, showing up the unstillable *voice* that underlies it.

Thus it is also possible to grasp the status of what Lacan calls 'lucubration',[46] and which can be seen in the spoken text of the *dramaticules*, that is to say their absence of any hold on a referent. The stories in these plays present no factual 'truth' about the lives of the figures who listen to them, but fulfil a *function* for them. This orientation is prefigured in the use of the third person personal pronoun instead of the first, in *Malone Dies*: 'While waiting I shall tell myself stories, if I can. […] they will be almost lifeless, like the teller' (*MD*, 174). The link between the teller and his characters resides in this absence of any vivifying quality. As he is himself devoid of life, Malone gives himself a form of existence through his characters:

> After the fiasco, the solace, the repose, I began again, to try and live, cause to live, be another, in myself, in another. […] My concern is not with me, but with another, far beneath me and whom I try to envy, of whose crass adventures I can now tell at last, I don't know how. (189)

It is when he is faced with death that he endows himself with this new borrowed identity: 'And on the threshold of being no more I succeed in being another' (188). The story he recounts concerns another—named Sapo—with whom he shares no trait of resemblance: 'Nothing is less like me than this patient, reasonable child […]' (31). However, this borrowed identity knows no durable existence, and suddenly turns into Macmann (222). Here, the nominal identity of the character is

46 Lacan uses the term *lucubration* to emphasise the fact that signifying language is powerless to make a breach in *jouissance* that is situated on the level of the real (*lalangue*): 'Language is doubtless made of *lalangue*. It is a *lucubration* of knowledge on *lalangue*' (1975b, 127; our italics).

secondary, since it enters into a metonymical series where no name has more importance than another. However, the invented character does represent the story-teller in an oblique way: the latter finds himself both in his character Sapo—'[…] struggling all alone for years to shed a little light upon himself […]' (187)—and in the identity he attributes to himself: the one who knows 'the joys of darkness'. Basically, this construction testifies to a scission between the plethora of metonymical representations and the subject as inert, impenetrable and real.

This function is expressed in May's story, which starts with the indication 'Sequel' (*Ff*, 402), a term that explicitly belongs to the domain of writing, as Elizabeth Barry notes (2006, 157). Walter Asmus reports Beckett's explanations:

> The Voice in the third part could be a bit more alive than in the first. 'One can suppose that she has written down everything which she has invented up to this, that she will one day find a reader for her story—therefore the address to the reader ('Mrs Winter, whom the reader will remember…'). 'Words are as food for this poor girl.' Beckett says. 'They are her best friends.' (Asmus)

May seeks to constitute, in the guise of a reader, an Other capable of replacing the one who remains radically absent. Finally, writing is intended to provide her with 'company' (an idea reflected in the expression 'best friends') and to be 'food'; that is to say that May seeks to take sustenance from her creations, to endow herself with some consistency, and combat the feeling of dissolution. It is in this sense that, making a distinction that detaches desire from need, Lacan specifies: 'From the start, the child is nourished by words as much as by bread, and he perishes by words' (1994, 189). If the child is not animated by the desire communicated by the words of his others, he will not be physically sustained by food.[47] Thus Beckett shows that creating a *voice*

47 This principle acquires particular force in 'Le Portrait de A.', by Henri Michaux, offering this startling formulation, where the desire to know

object by means of storytelling, and inscribing space by pacing, involve not some evanescent abstraction but point to an eminently material and vital function accomplished by language, that gives the subject consistency and founds an inhabitable reality. This function, as seen previously, remained volatile for Mouth, in *Not I*.

To conclude: in the place of linguistic linking or dialectical articulation—which is usually productive of representation as a coherent whole—the voice can be seen as assuming specific topological forms, being continuous, and simultaneously engendering brutal interruptions in discourse. Beckett's characters experience the voice as determined by the *unlimited*: as fragmentation and an endless murmur that leaves no place for the subject, no possibility for him to find his place in a world of reassuring semblances. This denial or abolition of the subject is also manifest in the intrusions of the tyrannical superego, which appears as a persecuting force.

Confronted with what is impossible to assume and to bear, the subject finds responses in *inscription*, whereby he produces an effective anchoring point to bring the incessant voices to a halt, and in the use of a 'reading voice', both of which restore the tentative presence of an Other, and provide access to a calming framework for existence. In this way, the subject succeeds in assuming the two complementary roles in the simulacrum of a dialogue but, as a construction, this setup is also addressed to an Other who, although radically absent, comes to occupy a structuring place in creation. However, Beckettian creation also gives an apparently more material status to the voice, situating the latter as an exteriority to which machines and apparatuses give a strange consistency. It is this aspect of the voice that will be dealt with in the following chapter.

---

and the appetite for food are perfectly correlated: 'À l'âge de sept ans, il apprit l'alphabet et mangea' ('At the age of seven years, he learnt the alphabet and ate', Michaux, 1998, 609).

IV — Exteriority and Artifice

In the course of the preceding chapters, we saw the voice as an intrusive phenomenon produced by language, which comes to the subject as an external force. In spite of this insistence on exteriority and the voice as real, this development risks being seen as limiting the notion of the voice to the verbal or literary realm: the voice as represented in a written creation. While our study of the staging of *A Piece of Monologue* did highlight the physical distinction between the scene enacted by a *he*, supposed to represent the motionless actor before the spectators, it remains to be shown how the voice exemplifies the proximity of the symbolic to the real, in relation to Beckett's use of technology. Indeed, technology has had an undeniable effect on the extension and impact of the voice in our contemporary age—reinforcing the voice's otherness, perhaps—and Beckett made extremely original use of it in his creation. We shall therefore see that technology heightens or intensifies the strangeness of the voice that comes from without, starting with *Krapp's Last Tape*, where the character treats his recorded voice as a contemptible object.

To further explore the consequences of technology, the latter will be considered as a result of the universalising implications of science. The voice therefore involves the abolition of the imaginary unity whereby speech is ascribed to a physical enunciator, or action imagined as unfolding within the bounds of stable geometrical space: this aspect is particularly true of the radio voice.

However, the effect of the voice is not purely negative, and it will be seen that the Beckettian subject is intimately dependent on it in order to procure a grounding for his existence: it is a vital *jouissance* that palliates the incessant or unlimited voice. At this point too, the subject intervenes as a form of 'sound editor'. Confronted with fragments of discourse—such as the utterances in *Play*, or the split between 'words' and 'music'—the subject cannot rely on a superior agent capable of unifying these elements within an overall dialectic. In order therefore to create for himself a singular place, the subject 'edits', passing from one voice to another. Indeed, such a position does not suppose a detached 'point of view' or access to an overriding meaning, since the 'sound editor' remains vitally attached to the voices, and aims to be affected by them, not just to determine the order of their utterances. That is to say that technology also reveals the voice as situated over a gaping hole in language. We shall examine the variations on this problematic provided by the plays for radio and television.

1. The Voice of the Machine

a. The Recorded Voice

The Otherness of the Recorded Voice

One of the distinctive traits of Beckett's work is the recourse to technological supports to display the recorded voice, thus manifesting the latter's exteriority. This practice is evoked in the prose work *How It Is* (begun in the early 1960s, as *Comment c'est*): 'quaqua meaning on all sides megaphones possibly technique something wrong there' (*HI*, 107); 'unless recordings on ebonite or suchlike'. In fact, Beckett's actual work with technological means goes back to his creations for the radio (*All That Fall* dates from 1956), followed by *Krapp's Last Tape*, with the use of the tape recorder. Finally, the staging of the *dramaticules* makes intensive usage of the recorded voice.

This mode of creativity is not the result of chance but represents a veritable encounter involving the structure of creation, which leads us to find the origins of Beckett's æsthetic innovations in a relationship to language. Indeed, the study of Beckett's voices reveals to what point language is not experienced as something natural: it does not always allow a subject 'to have being and habitat' (*TFN* VIII, 133), to move in a stable and humanised world.

Fundamentally, language engenders an effect of dissonance, in its structuring of the speaking being (*parlêtre*), since the Other is already an integral part of the structure of speech. Thus first of all, the subject always addresses his Other, situated beyond the empirical interlocutor, and his enunciation is modelled in advance by the punctuation the latter provides. In this way, the subject 'cannot listen to himself without being divided' (Lacan, 1966, 533), since in this case, he evaluates his own utterances as they are interpreted by his Other.

A subject who is founded in relation to a symbolic Other—capable of attenuating any confrontation with the unbearable by means of a dialectic—is free to consider language as a simple tool destined to serve communication or self-expression. However, if such an Other is lacking, the subject will find himself exposed to the torment of the *unlimited*: what is then experienced is the incidence of the signifier on the body, which no naming can adequately circumscribe. Thus it is that Lacan, in his later works, described speech as imposing itself as a foreign body, inflicting suffering comparable to an illness: 'The question is rather to know why the normal man, who is said to be normal, does not notice that speech is a parasite, that speech is a veneer, that speech is a form of cancer that human beings are afflicted with' (2005a, 95). Because of its antinatural nature as irreducible to questions of need or instinct, speech produces the effects of a pathological imbalance that it is impossible to absorb or naturalise.

It is because of this exteriority of speech that Mrs Rooney, in *All That Fall*, hears herself speak. She says to Christy: 'Do you find anything... bizarre about my way of speaking? [...] I use none but the simplest words, I hope, and yet I sometimes find my way of speaking very... bizarre' (*AF*, 173). When she hears herself speak, it is not with the reassuring feeling that she is pronouncing words she intended to say: she does not receive a reflection that confirms the conformity of her will to express and the message her interlocutor receives. Because of this absence of naturalness, words do not appear to convey life. Mr Rooney remarks: 'Do you know, Maddy, sometimes one would think you were struggling with a dead language' (194). This character shares the same experience as his wife: 'I confess I have it sometimes myself, when I happen to overhear what I am saying.' Contrary to the voice of reading, which gives the illusion of a reassuring presence, the effect produced here is that of a strangeness that the characters do not master, one that creates a gap between themselves and their own speech.

This experience of strangeness is reinforced by technology which, as Freud pointed out in *Civilisation and Its Discontents* (1930), has made modern man 'a sort of prosthetic god' (Freud, 2010, 109). Ulrika Maude points out that the possibility of recording sound existed as of 1898, but only reached popular consumption in the late 1950s (2009, 63). In particular, it had the effect of distancing sound 'from the conceit of interiority' (62), an essential notion which will be examined later. Recording devices also reduce the relationship to language to what can be subjected to combinations: to its impersonal and reproducible character. Such is the case of music, as François Nicolas notes:

> [...] the musical phenomenon is born with the feeling of mechanical causalities associated with perceived sounds [...]. Whence this double characteristic: *sound is a trace* (of a body), and *as a trace it is entirely reproducible.* Such is the human voice: it is the trace of the human body that emits it, at the same time as it can be perfectly reproduced in the absence of this body. [...] *It is of the essence of sound matter that it cannot be stocked and that we rather have to stock its causes.* (Nicolas, 5)

The voice thus manifests a paradox, since it appears to be expressive of human singularity, at the same time as it betrays a particular affinity with the mechanical and the non-human. Catherine Laws points out, in relation to the radio play *All That Fall*, that 'the recorded voice will always have subtle differences in quality to one emanating from a body in our local acoustic environment' (2013, 169). The recorded voice is thus an artefact. The presence of the recording machine as 'Other' is also sufficient to produce a constraining retroactive effect on speech, leading Steven Connor to note that unlike Vladimir and Estragon's 'free speech', Krapp's 'recorded words are destined to enter into the condition of iterability, marked in advance with the sign of writing' (2007, 145). This principle echoes the practice of combinatory games

(Sardin, 2011, 537–9) in Beckett's work, and which may be found diversely in the logical variations explored in *Watt*, in the episode of Molloy's 'sucking-stones' (*Mo*, 63–9), and in the repetitive movements of the figures in *Quad*. It is also this principle that Lacan developed in his structuralist period—in his famous text on Edgar Poe's 'Purloined Letter', for example—and that rests on a conception of the pre-eminence of the symbolic register that, in this early stage, was deemed capable of covering reality in its entirety. In this perspective, the symbolic is a matter of the permutation of signifiers. The great Other—the 'treasury of the signifier' (Lacan, 1966, 806)—is situated on the level of language understood as an autonomous and complete *whole* (Miller, 1985). As such, this register excludes any subjectivity, any human appearance, any unforeseeable dimension: each movement will be regulated by an impassive Other, within a circumscribed arena, drawn out in advance.

Regarding the use of technology, Yoshiki Tajiri explores what he calls 'the prosthetic voice', which he defines as 'the voice that is mediated by machines or technology—the voice coming from the tape recorder, telephone or radio, for example' (138). He sees this as already present in the voice of *The Unnamable*, where any distinction between sender and addressee 'cannot but be ephemeral because the other can also be the self' (146). He particularly points out the fact that in this novel, 'the distance within the subject is literalised and imagined as an actual physical distance to be traversed' (147). He calls on what Derrida calls 'telephonic interiority', which refers to the way in which the subject is submitted to *différance* and inhabited by the other as a 'telephonic *technè*' (150). Like Steven Connor (2007), Tajiri refers to Derrida's notion of the voice as embodying the imaginary presence of the locutor: the within/without distinction is present as *différance* in the voice (144). However, when Tajiri intends to distinguish between Echo, who 'repeats other people's words' (153), and the narrator of *The Unnamable*, who 'repeats his own words, which he feels are coming from the other' (153), it can be noted that a conceptual framework is lacking. Indeed, the alterity as such is inseparable from the subject, a fact which inspires Beckett to make the following remark: 'S.: "Si on se rend compte de l'écho, on est fichu'" ('If we notice the echo, we are done for', in Atik, 115). This is why Tajiri rightly feels that associating Beckett with Derrida risks subordinating the former to a general theory, where *différance* is simply a matter of verbal metonymy. By contrast, the alterity of language points to a *real*, which allows us to note the specific torsion introduced by technology which is itself a product of the structure of language. Indeed, if is added, to the linguistic code, the function of the *a* object as radically excluded from the *whole*—thus *founding* the latter—one can start to perceive the voice as a dimension that cannot be assimilated. Beckett makes a specific, creative use of this alterity, to which technology gives a singularly new dimension. This problematic of the exclusion of subjectivity is dealt with in an exemplary manner in *Krapp's Last Tape.*

Voice and Gaze: 'Krapp's Last Tape'

Krapp's Last Tape enables us to grasp how the sound recording shows up a problematic relationship to language and the dimension of the voice. This play was written in English in 1958, then translated as *La Dernière bande*, at a time when Beckett was experimenting with radio production (*All That Fall* bears the inscription 'Ussy, September 1956', Ackerley and Gontarski, 11). Graley Herren stresses that 'Beckett's breakthrough in *Krapp* derives directly from his experiments in radio' (2007, 33).

The action of this play unfolds at the time of Krapp's sixty-ninth birthday. As he has done each year since his thirty-first birthday, the character recounts the year that has just gone by on his tape recorder, thus 'externalizing his autobiography' (Esposito, 382). It has already been noticed that Beckett situates the play in a vague future, so that the utilisation of the appliance does not appear to be anachronistic (Ackerley and Gontarski, 302). The process of recording is a chance, for the character, to rail against himself as he was during the preceding years.

This play thus combines the presence of a character on stage and the electrical appliance, which is a support for the *voice.* Insofar as the voice results from the artificial and exterior nature of language, the practice of recording renders Krapp foreign to himself. If the fact that the subject 'cannot speak without hearing himself' (Lacan, 1966, 533) is a structuring element of language, the intervention of the electro-mechanical device makes this strange otherness a constant part of the character's experience. Leslie Hill notes that in this play, 'there is no dominant central presence or unity (save the character of Krapp himself, who is neither fully present nor unified)' (129). It can be observed that this is not just a consequence of Krapp's annual memorial ceremonies but a specific result of the recording process. Graley Herren points out: 'The convention of tape-recording disembodies Krapp's voice, rending his psyche into multiple selves, turning his voice into an objective artefact to be manipulated, and estranging Krapp from himself and from the audience' (2007, 33). Steven Connor emphasises that the words Krapp records are not at all spontaneous, but 'suggest speech under the particular stress that the awareness of a recording brings with it, speech darkened by the threatening shadow of repeatability' (2007, 144). Rosette C. Lamont notes the crucial influence of Proust in Beckett's work, seeing this play as a caricature of *À la recherche du temps perdu*: 'Everything that, for the narrator of *À la recherche* is ascension, and finally triumph, remains here a tangling in the linear, the abasement of the mind that is prisoner of matter' (346–7).

It is necessary, however, to push these remarks further in order to discern, in this recourse to the tape-recorder, a structuring dimension which is revelatory of the degree to which Krapp has always been estranged from himself. Lacan observes, speaking of the recording of a child's voice, 'we only have it in the state of a remainder' (2004, 316). The voice, conventionally considered as belonging to the subject, thus appears as this fallen *remainder*—exteriorised, and an object of misapprehension—that the subject cannot easily accept as his own. Once it is objectivised, the voice becomes *that* (*ça*): a *thing*, stripped of its personalised envelope. It is no longer the element that gives the subject a centre of gravity, a comforting or flattering vision of oneself.

Irit Degani-Raz compares Krapp's tape-recorder to the ambivalent motif of the spear of Telephus, noting a crucial difference:

'Whereas in the original myth the wound precedes its healing, that is "He that wounded shall heal," the modern one develops in the opposite direction, that is, "it that healed shall wound."' (190). Thus, if the tape-recorder has 'the ability to capture moments of Krapp's past and embodies the promise of healing his longing for a lost paradise' (193), it also separates him from 'his previous experience and old egos, turning them into detached objects'.

It could be added that it is a machine that recreates both the past and oneself as objects, as a consequence of the 'utilitarian reason' and universality that deny singularity. Therefore if, usually, the voice remains hidden in speech, it no longer does so here: in this process of objectivisation, the intimate is projected outside. Structurally, the voice represents an element of instability, since it threatens to operate this reversal in an unexpected manner, as Jacques-Alain Miller points out: '[…] we do not use the voice; it inhabits language, it haunts it. It suffices to speak, to see emerge, arise, the threat that what cannot be said may be revealed' (1994a, 29). That which, in the fundamental fantasy, remains hidden, ignored—while nonetheless orienting the subject's existence—is henceforth exposed to the gaze of the Other. With his tape-recorder, Krapp finds himself continually at grips with this exteriorisation.

Krapp undertakes his recordings on his birthdays, that is to say, these dates when one celebrates one's coming into the world. This practice cannot fail to remind us of the problematic nature of birth which, in Beckett's work, is always correlated with death. As Pozzo declares: '[…] one day we are born, one day we shall die, the same day, the same second […]' (*G*, 83). These words do not express the trivial awareness that life leads to death, but rather the fact that the Beckettian subject remains 'unborn'. For Krapp, it is as if he had to reassure himself of the reality of his physical birth, in an effort to come to life for another year. Thus it is that he exclaims, upon seeing the 'dark young beauty': '[…] a big black hooded perambulator, most funereal thing' (*K*, 219). He sees himself as dead from birth, but under the maternal gaze: it is this aspiration that drives him to identify with the child. Beckett describes as follows Krapp's regular excursions, on stage, into the darkness: 'Escape from unutterable self [...]' (Beckett, 1992, 23). It is this unnameable *self* that has haunted Krapp from his very birth. He notes the ambivalent nature of these birthdays: 'Celebrated the awful occasion [...]' (*K*, 217). The equivocal nature of the word *awful* suggests the meanings of 'horrible' or 'inspiring awe'. In this context, his birthday continues to remind Krapp of his status as 'unborn'. This is why he calls his annual ceremonies *post-mortems* (218). It is also for this reason that he feels, most acutely, to what point each iteration marks his birth, but also his progress towards death.

Krapp's birthdays are not an occasion to reassure himself as to the continuity of his existence, but rather to emphasise the latter's discontinuity, and the gaping hole that has always inhabited him. It is this hole that causes the absence of a dialectical link between his successive identities, so that his recordings compose a form of 'palimpsest' (Ackerley and Gontarski, 303), manifesting a 'layering of character'. Each moment evoked appears to be frozen. Beckett already explained something of this phenomenon in *Proust*, regarding the oscillation between *suffering* and *boredom*: '[...] this endless series of renovations leaves us as indifferent as the heterogeneity of any one of its terms, and the inconsequence of any given me disturbs us as little as the comedy of substitution' (*Pr*, 28–9). What operates here is a sort of temporal telescoping, where the successive *selves* all end up occupying the same place with regards to the present Krapp. Indeed, to organise the play around birthdays and repetition is to indicate that Krapp's whole life is a repetition of the same, thus annulling the passing of an entire year: the latter appears as a hole, not as an interval situated within a continuous overall movement.

The recourse to recordings is not indifferent to this state of being 'unborn'. Beckett observes, speaking to Rick Cluchey: 'His whole life has been interruption' (in Lawley, 2007, 90). These interruptions—which Paul Lawley calls a form of 'editing' (2007, 90)—thus testify to his powerlessness to construct a duration that has never been inscribed for him. Indeed, a scission is produced by these recordings of the voice. Like all writing, the tape-recorder supposes the inscription of a full discourse: it cannot include actions that take place in the empty spaces, like this one, indicated by the stage directions: '*Broods, realizes he is recording silence* [...]' (*K*, 222). At other moment: 'KRAPP *switches off, broods, switches on again*' (220). The vision of his dreams is thus situated outside of discourse. Indeed, Krapp remains attached to the idyllic memory of the girl in the punt, but can do nothing at present: the dreams take hold of him, in spite of himself. This dissociation shows that he is powerless to reconcile dream and speech: he is unable to anchor his reveries in an effective discourse. On the contrary, he denigrates the latter: 'Be again, be again. [*Pause.*] All that old misery' (223). It is precisely the rejection of his dreams that inspires his use of the tape-recorder: Krapp can entertain no dialectic link to the past, but must rely on the recording device to make this past—that he violently rejects—exist.

This scission and these ruptures echo the question of asceticism that preoccupies Krapp, and that is expressed through the network of gnostic images. Krapp describes himself as 'separating the grain from the husks' (*K*, 217). This action is conceived as an attempt to attain a state of purity, in the prospect of achieving the *opus magnum* (218): '[...] those things worth having when all the dust has—when all *my* dust has settled' (217). The separation also concerns an eminently Beckettian notion: the opposition between light and darkness. It is Krapp's ideal that drives him to reject love and carnal existence, as Beckett points out: 'Ascetic ethics, particularly abstinence/ from sensual enjoyment. Sexual / desire, marriage, forbidden / (signaculum sinus)' (Beckett, 1992, 45). Krapp confides to his tape-recorder: 'Plans for a less... [*hesitates*]... engrossing sexual life' (*K*, 218). This concern results in the fate that this 'editor' reserves for all things: 'Cut'em out!' (217).

However, Beckett maintains a fundamental indeterminacy between light and dark, summed up in the image of the *equinox* (*K*, 217), which can be associated with the Beckettian vocable *perhaps*.[1] Indeed, this tension between opposed poles is diametrically opposed to the 'mingling' (Beckett, 1992, 31) that characterises the decline of a Krapp

---

1 See *supra*, p. 84–5.

who manifests his failure to achieve his ideal. In spite of his overt will to eliminate the body and impurity, he finds himself fundamentally attached to the latter, as summed up in the motifs of *bananas*, *alcohol*, and *sex*. Krapp expresses an attitude of denial and, instead of attaining the sublime *opus magnum*—that he could at last offer up to his great Other—he only reveals its caricature: grime instead of purity. Indeed, Krapp appears on stage as '*a wearish old man*' (*K*, 215). His trousers and his waistcoat are '*Rusty black*'—the French says '*pisseux*' (piss-coloured, *DB*, 7); his white shirt is '*Grimy*'; his boots are '*dirty white*'. Krapp has failed to achieve the 'memorable equinox' (217) that symbolised his vocation. Instead of reaching the sublime, Krapp only arrives at inertia, the stagnation of his repeated rejections. Dominique Marin points out that having relinquished Bianca to relegate his relationship to the other sex in memory alone,[2] Krapp experiences the 'implacable repetition of the failure of the eradication of *jouissance* by means of the signifier'.

Krapp's decline can be considered in this light, since this ideal determines the character's attitude with regards to his former *selves*, whose image has been consigned to the magnetic tapes. Krapp's asceticism is a result of the injunction originating in his ideal and imperative Other, who orders him to raise himself to an impossible purity. For this reason, it is not astonishing that Krapp fails to realise his ambition. The mingling and the degradation are a result of this very quest: they are the product of his scorn for his former *selves*, in the name of his ascetic ambition. It is under this pressure that he pursues a continual and renewed process of rejection, as Beckett sums up: 'He is treading on his life' (Beckett, 1992, xvii). This rejection drives him to rail against the inadequacy or the failure of his undertaking, his own powerlessness. Krapp's ideal reveals his entire existence as taking place within a notorious and chronic inadequacy: in the eyes of his Other,

2 His relationship with Fanny, an 'old ghost of a whore' (*K*, 222) is no exception, since it too expresses the complete mortification of the phallic function.

Krapp will never be anything other than a miserable failure, a lump of impurity, unworthy of the *opus magnum*.

This perspective raises the question of what *causes* Krapp's speech. Indeed, the voice of the character speaking in the present—on stage and on the tapes—is nothing other than the echo of the voice of his Other. Through the voice, it is the lost Krapp that he hears speaking. He calls the latter '*crap*' and, in doing so, he designates himself as the 'scrap' (an echo present throughout *How It Is*) that he—by the retroactive effect of his enunciation—has now become. That is to say that by continually denigrating his own *selves*, he is denouncing his current state, not only his past ones. The following statement, about darkness, emphasises this identity in a striking manner: 'I love to get up and move about in it, then back here to… [*hesitates*]… me. [*Pause.*] Krapp' (*K*, 217). When he questions his past avatars, Krapp does not ask what desire led him to express himself thus, to make these choices. Were he to address this question of desire, he would recognise himself as having always been the same subject; he would question the link leading from one *self* to another: in this evolution, he would discern the thread that had guided him throughout his life. However, this possibility is non-existent, in the absence of the dialectic authorised by the closure of *limited wholes* and the paternal metaphor. Krapp thus cannot grasp the fact that in the recorded voices, it is himself that he hears, and that he labels thus. In the words of *Company*: '[…] He speaks of himself as of another' (*Co*, 16). Accepting to be a vehicle for the voice of the Other, Krapp rejects life as a value, and expects nothing other than death.

In this insurmountable misconception, the tape-recorder is crucial since, by consigning his successive and objectivised states, Krapp participates in the production of this other imbecile *self* that is incapable of attaining his ideal. He also contributes to perpetuating this same ideal in whose name he speaks. Finally, and conversely, he shows his being as a 'scrap' that is equally impossible to eliminate.

The use of the tape-recorder testifies to the character's morbid attachment to the past, paradoxically, in spite of—or because of—his rejection: 'These old P.M.s are gruesome, but I often find them

[...] a help before embarking on a new... [*hesitates*] ...retrospect' (*K*, 218). It is impossible for Krapp to move ahead: he constantly returns to the past—that of the recorded tape, and of the past year—in order to reject it and mark his powerlessness to operate or assume a break. The voice emanating from the tape-recorder confirms his inability to separate himself from his past, an attitude that Krapp shows in his childish character. His back and forth movements in time create no dialectical binding, and his gestures of rejection are only a means for him to hasten to his end: 'Sneers at what he calls his youth and thanks to God that it's over' (218); 'Thank God that's all done with anyway' (222). In practising these 'P.M.s', he also inhumes himself. For this reason, Krapp is incapable of having a relationship with a woman (he experiences happiness only once the separation with the girl in the punt has been announced), or achieving his vocation of asceticism. He systematically rejects his past in the hope of pleasing his Other; the latter being nothing else but the death that awaits him.

In this endless series of rejections, the recordings appear as a form of defence against death: the voice of the recorded tape is intended to provide Krapp with a protection against this terrifying unknown. It is therefore not a voice that comes from the place of the Other but a reflection, subjected to the scornful gaze of the subject himself, that takes form while he is watched by the Other. The voice involves a relationship to the gaze, driving Krapp to turn around towards the darkness, as Beckett confided: 'Old Nick's there. Death is standing behind him and unconsciously he's looking for it' (in Held). It is with this terrifying presence that Krapp is struggling, giving consistency to the voice that, paradoxically, only announces his imminent death and the failure of his whole undertaking. James Knowlson notes: 'Beckett regularly referred to this look as a "Hain", following the eighteenth-century German writer, Matthias Claudius' (in Beckett, 1992, 21), and for whom 'Freund Hain' (or 'Hein') was an allegorical death figure. This is the gaze that appears at the end of the play, in some of the author's stagings, in the form of the tape-recorder glowing like a 'magic eye' (Beckett, 1992, xvii). This gaze makes of Krapp a spectral entity: his past avatars are phantoms announcing the phantom he is soon to be, once the recording of this 'last tape' comes to an end.

Beckett's notes concerning the phallic[3] function of the microphone can be read in the light of this defensive position. Beckett indicates: 'magnétophone compagne de sa solitude. / agent masturbateur' ('tape-recorder company of his solitude. / masturbatory agent', Beckett, 1992, 67). To listen, for Krapp, is to *jouir.* In his notes, Beckett inserts the indication 'mechanical with gabble' (Beckett, 1992, 32) at each forward wind during the vision. It is associated with the comment: 'Three winds forward mechanical [...] corresponding to this crescendo of ejaculation'. The tape-recorder thus appears as a support used by Krapp for want of being able to maintain human relationships. The character commands this derisory fetishistic adjuvant that is insufficient to repulse the terrifying darkness. He listens to himself, to entertain the illusion of a presence and the feeling of being supported by his ideal Other. Dominique Marin emphasises that as well as attempting to eradicate any impurity, 'Krapp aspires to a last *bande*,[4] that is to say a last, mythical, erection, that will definitively calm him' (Marin, 182).

Krapp reveals his petrification when confronted with the threat against which the voices of the tapes ring out; that is to say, the death that Clov describes thus: 'Something is taking its course' (*Eg*, 98, 107). Its presence can also be heard in the expression 'all moved and moved us' (*K*, 223), which echoes an image Beckett borrowed from the philosopher Geulincx, whose works he read closely during the thirties (Knowlson, 1997, 219; Beckett, 2012). Beckett evokes thus, in *Molloy*, the image of the very relative freedom this philosopher ascribes to man, and in which an individual is confined on the deck of his boat, while the vast current carries him away:

---

3 For a definition of the term *phallus*, see *supra*, p. 60.

4 The French *bander* means to have an erection. Whence the translation of *More Pricks than Kicks* as *Bande et sarabande.*

> I who had loved the image of old Geulincx, dead young, who left me free, on the black boat of Ulysses, to crawl toward the East, along the deck. That is a great measure of freedom, for him who has not the pioneering spirit. (*Mo*, 46)

Thus no solution, no choice could have transformed Krapp's fate.[5] As a result, he anxiously latches on to the things that give him consistency, that allow him to feel his bodily existence. The tape-recorder is one of these objects, as are the bananas and alcohol. The character remains fixed to the past, inert, so that he cannot see death approaching, even if he wishes life were over. So, in the series where Krapp deriding permutes with Krapp denigrated, looms, at the end of the line, the great Other who will judge him: 'You are "crap"'. It is this ultimate reversal that causes his anxiety.

This Other who watches over Krapp's mortified existence can be associated with a maternal figure. It is in the name of this mother—for whom he has remained in perpetual mourning—that Krapp rejects himself, and refuses to engage a relationship with another woman. Paul Lawley notes: 'For the broken Krapp his machine [...] has become a maternal-erotic substitute [...]' (2007, 93). Krapp's various renunciations can be situated in this light. He regrets having given the black ball to the dog. Instead of accomplishing a form of mediation, this object expresses Krapp's obsession with his lost mother. After having been pushed aside by the young maid, Krapp gives in to the dog's begging, and it is a perpetual regret for him: 'I shall feel it, in my hand, until my dying day' (*K*, 220). It is following the injunction of his ideal—represented by his mother—that Krapp renounces the object that could have confirmed a certain acceptance of his carnal side (a place now occupied by alcohol and the tape-recorder). His mother's death does not constitute a liberation but irremediably fixes him at this moment, confirming his status as a scrap.

---

5 'His predicament is finally more ironic than tragic; he could not have made a "correct" decision' (Ackerley and Gontarski, 304).

The thrice-evoked (*K*, 217, 221, 223) story of the girl in the punt is also crucial. This is the girl Krapp attempts to imagine at the play's opening: the one who represents an image of happiness, capable of confirming his liberation from his mother. However, she is pushed aside to give place to his ascetic ambition: '[…] there was a chance of happiness. But I wouldn't want them back. Not with the fire in me now' (223). Relegated to the status of a simple image, she no longer belongs to the continuity of a life that Beckett defined, in *Proust*, as 'a succession of Paradises successively denied' (*Pr*, 26).

Krapp's relationships are thus doomed to fail. It is following the injunction of the maternal ideal that he rejects his sensual side, as in this exclamation describing the frightened refusal of the 'dark young beauty' (*K*, 219) to enter into a conversation with him: 'As if I had designs on her virtue!' (220). It is the asexual dimension that triumphs here: Krapp becomes comparable to 'The vidua-bird!' (219). His identification with his mother is indicated by his hesitation regarding the grammatical gender when he reads the definition of this term: 'State—or condition—of being—or remaining—a widow—or widower.' Mother and son are both struck by a 'viduity' that leads them to death. This mortification drives Krapp to describe himself as 'burning to be gone' (222), having evoked, as follows, his attitude with regards to his dying mother: '[…] wishing she were gone' (219). The intensity of his feeling can be heard in the modification made to the latter expression, which subsequently became: 'brûlant qu'elle en finisse' ('burning for her to have done', Beckett, 1992, xviii).

Thus, Krapp's relationship to his own recorded voice expresses an inertia that keeps him riveted to the disappearance of this mother, and also leaves him confronted with the gaping hole of his own death. The sound recording is what he offers to his Other: it is his 'company', destined to palliate the anguish he experiences when confronted with what is, nonetheless, soon about to devour him.

b. Voice and the Radio

Abolition of the Imaginary

Krapp's Last Tape is a mixed creation, insofar as it combines the presence of a character on stage to whom a certain 'biographical' reality can be ascribed, and the intensive use of the recorded voice. It reveals how the effect of strangeness is produced by the voice, in relation to the representation of a 'person'. With the radio plays, however, the instrument comes to the fore, revealing the principle 'the medium is the message'—according to Marshall McLuhan's dictum[6]—or, in the terms of Lacan: 'there is no metalanguage' (2012, 112), producing a profound mutation in the status of the voice. That is to say that, transformed and transmitted by electrical and mechanical means, the voice acquires a fundamentally structuring dimension: it no longer accompanies the representation of a character and his story, but is the very object of these plays that cover the period from *All That Fall* (1956) to *Cascando* (1963).

For this reason, Beckett's discovery of the radio can be seen as a decisive *encounter* with a medium that brings to light another facet of the voice. Indeed, Matthew Feldman states that working with the BBC's Third Programme may have 'inspired Beckett to write radiogenically—even for works not originally written for radio, like *How It Is*—in the remaining three decades of his creative output' (2014, 42–3). Steven Connor's history of ventriloquism (2009) shows how, over the centuries, the voice has appeared as a detached object, which does not belong to us. Ventriloquism reposes on the idea that '*ça parle*' ('it [a thing] speaks') somewhere outside of us, but it also perhaps reassures us with the idea that someone also commands such a voice. Technology pushes this logic further. Indeed, far from being a neutral factor, it not only enhances certain bodily functions but also subtracts from them (Maude, 2009, 114). In speaking of Theodor Adorno and Max Horkheimer's critique of Enlightenment rationalism, Irit Degani-Raz states that 'what started as humankind's mastery of nature has

6 This question is studied by Linda Ben-Zvi.

been paid for by humans' progressive alienation from nature, eventuating in a radical disjuncture between human beings qua subjects and nature as object that is subordinated to their will' (Degani-Raz, 191). This notion of alienation requires to be pushed much further since, more profoundly, as an extension of language itself, it accentuates the structural imbalance that determines a subject's existence. Indeed radio is a product of science and capitalism,[7] revealing the voice as an effect of the universalising function of the signifier. Both these 'discourses' (as Lacan defines them) are the product of a logical *One* (Miller, 2010–11), founding laws that are universally applicable (*for all x…*) and whose function, therefore, consists of abolishing singularity. This is the effect Walter Benjamin diagnosed in 1935 with relation to the disappearance of 'aura' (75). Indeed, at the dawn of the modern era, Galileo claimed to reduce nature to mathematical laws, which are independent of the senses. Ulrika Maude emphasises the way new visual technologies, such as the X-ray, 'opened up a gap between subjective, human, ultimately fallible vision, and the so-called objective vision of technology' (2009, 117). As a result of these inventions, the body no longer belongs to a subject; it cannot remain ignored, unconscious or preserved as the domain of intimacy, closed off from any intrusion by others: its entire functioning is potentially thrown out into the open. The body is henceforth exposed to the unceasing gaze[8] of communication technology which sees the unseen, and abolishes an individual's status as speaking being, observing him as an inert corpse.[9] Yoshiki Tajiri also notes the consequences of what he calls technological *prostheses*:

7 Steven Connor (1907) has dealt with certain aspects of the development of sound technology in the 19th Century.

8 On the exponential extension of such technology and its impact, see Wajcman (2010, *passim*).

9 This consequence is exemplified by the television series *Crime Scene Investigation*, as studied by Gérard Wajcman (2012). The title of his book is eloquent: 'The Experts: The Police of the Dead'.

> The clear-cut distinction between the body (considered internal and organic) and technology (considered external and inorganic) is being rendered obsolete by advanced medical technologies including genetic engineering. (Tajiri, 2007, 2)

Thus, the prosthetic body 'is the locus for dynamic interactions between the body and material objects (including machines and technological devices), inside and outside, self and other, and for the concomitant problematisation and blurring of these distinctions' (6). These interactions also suggest that the body can be subjected to modifications, while dissimulating the fact that the singular is simultaneously opened up to the unlimited, and is subjected to an obscure will that no tangible or accountable entity controls. This is even more important since the postmodern dematerialisation of technology, which leaves an individual without any physical control over what becomes of his words or images, and exposes him to potentially limitless manipulations.

In this context, Yoshiki Tajiri criticises Derrida's notion that the 'telephonic' structure—whereby the voice reveals a subject separated from himself—constitutes a prior reality, to which technology simply gives an unheard-of extension or amplification:

> In this framework, the actuality of teletechnology inevitably has only a secondary status as a sort of surplus, an engagement which the internal logic of his theory does not necessitate. Herein lies the difficulty Derrida faces in elucidating the specificity of contemporary teletechnology. (Tajiri, 2007, 157)

Tajiri's criticism is also directed at other thinkers such as Heidegger, Freud, Lacan, Deleuze and Guattari, whom he considers reduce technology to its purely subjective function, while ignoring its very *real* impact. It would seem however that both views are correct and necessary. Derrida is perfectly justified in situating the 'telephonic' structure as pre-existing science, and the aim of psychoanalysis is to reveal both the link between subjective reality and such human creations, as well as the latters' subjective impact on each one. This is why Lacanian psychoanalysis points to the extension of the universal through science and capitalism as conditioning our real, and why it is possible, concurrently, to raise the question of the symbolic as having a *real* dimension. Tajiri is thus perfectly justified when he notes the importance of studying Beckett's specific use of technology, going beyond the simply metaphorical evocation of electric devices.

As a result of the radio, the voice appears as an *a* object, detached from the body by an appliance that brings into play the *unlimited*, serial dimension of technology, radically denying the symbolisation produced by addressed speech. To account for this phenomenon, Pierre Schaeffer introduced the term of the *acousmatic* voice: one that could be heard, but whose source remained hidden.[10] Michel Chion (21), followed by Mladen Dolar (2006, 63), emphasises the affinity of these modern media with the specifically acousmatic nature of the voice. Steven Connor also points out that broadcasting sends out a signal 'with no clear idea of where it will be received' (2014a, 65). Beckett confirms this perception when he speaks of his script of *All That Fall*, as being 'for broadcast to the 4 winds' (*L2*, 670). Connor adds that the reception of a broadcast 'always has the sense of an overhearing of an address that is not specifically directed at oneself'. This strange sensation of 'overhearing' situates the point where the exteriority of the voice meets the intimate.

One particularity of the radio voice is that it touches us all the more since its source is not enveloped—relativised, rationalised—by an image that situates it among other components of our world. The voice gives rise to this otherness since it does not allow itself to be absorbed within the soothing unity that the image imposes as a deceptive lure. Such is the force of the radio plays, on which Beckett insisted, asserting, for example, when speaking to Paul-Louis Mignon: '[...] il

---

10 The term originated in the practice whereby Pythagoras' disciples listened to their master through a curtain that excluded any visual contact (Chion, 19). See also Connor (2009, 20).

ne peut être question de les porter au théâtre, car l'expression radiophonique exige une écriture particulière. On écrit autrement pour elle: la parole sort du noir' ('[…] there can be no question of staging them for the theatre, since radio expression demands a special form of writing. You write differently for it: the speech comes out of the dark', in Hubert ed., 2011, 1076). No equivalence can be discerned between the two forms of theatre. More specifically, one cannot consider the stage as having more expressive means at its disposal. Speaking of his radio plays, Beckett notes the limits of stage productions: 'La réalisation scénique détruirait l'ambiguïté' ('The staging would destroy the ambiguity', in Zilliacus, 83).

To grasp the importance of these remarks, it is possible to examine the function of the visible stage space in the light of Lacan's apologue 'the mirror stage' (1966, 93–100), according to which the mirror image is placed in perspective when the child turns around, to receive his Other's acknowledgement that the reflection he sees is actually his own. Thus it is that the symbolic dimension marks its structural pre-eminence over the representation of visual unity, which is in itself alienating. The symbolic allows the subject to identify with his own image, and to *misapprehend the structure* on which the latter rests. In the same way, the stage space tends to comfort a certain idea of mastery: it presents itself as a *whole* organised by the laws of perspective (Wajcman, 2004), which the spectator dominates and can scrutinise at will. This is all the more true as the action of the play is limited to this lit space, delivered up to the gaze.

The recourse to the radio radically removes the calm fascination exerted by the image, leaving the subject alone to grapple with the symbolic register and its implications as *voice*. The radio voice strips off the imaginary exterior—which allows us to identify a 'character' (with his history and personal density) with his proffering of speech—opening up a dimension of absence. Leslie Hill sees Beckett's radio drama as proof of his 'rejection of stage presence as a potential source of recuperative stability' (128). Steven Connor points out that while 'the stage provided a kind of relief, with its palpability, its three-dimensionality', in the case of radio, 'absence and presence enter each other's condition' (2014a, 73). Radio makes it impossible for the auditor to embrace the entire representation—the stage space—at a glance, to persuade himself that he is contemplating the objective environment in which words and actions find their place. The auditor remains dependent on words and sounds, and unable to reassure himself by leaning on a unifying representation. More fundamentally, he finds himself in a position comparable to that of the subject who is inhabited by his *voices*. In these circumstances, speech imposes itself in its anticipatory logic, without one being able, *a priori*, to take advantage of a single privileged view point; the latter being represented by the final punctuation that retroactively confers its meaning on the utterance as a whole. Speech is thus heard as *enunciation*, and the voice is correlated with silence and darkness, by contrast with the overall static quality of the lit stage. This is doubtless what leads Martin Esslin to assert: 'Because they are totally immaterial, aural art forms are in danger of becoming amorphous and demand great clarity of structure and pattern' (366). The voice resonates as the voice of the Other, in its strangeness that cannot be assimilated. If it eliminates the body as a specular whole, it imposes itself in its very concrete reality: as Peter Fifield points out, 'abstraction here seems to mean the condensation of physicality' (2009b, 69–70).

The importance Beckett accords to the *voice* gives rise to a paradoxical reversal whereby it is not the visual dimension which gives the impression one is contemplating living characters but, on the contrary, the prospect of thrusting a visual appearance on the unfolding of the sound that threatens to 'kill' the soul of *All That Fall* as a radio play (in Perloff, 1999, 251): the body must 'die' as a captivating visual image, so that the *voice* may live.

This reversal of the conventional hierarchy produces a feeling of strangeness which can also be understood as an effect of truth, as Beckett describes it in *Proust*, when evoking Marcel's experience of his grandmother's voice:

> It is a grievous voice, its fragility unmitigated and undisguised by the carefully arranged mask of her features, and this strange real

> voice is the measure of its owner's suffering. He hears it also as the symbol of her isolation, of their separation, as impalpable as a voice from the dead. The voice stops. His grandmother seems as irretrievably lost as Eurydice among the shades. Alone before the mouthpiece he calls her name in vain. (*Pr*, 27)

Julie Campbell comments: 'Marcel, Proust's protagonist, is not used to hearing his grandmother's voice in this "real" sense, as his hearing has always been habitually obscured by his seeing' (149). Here, the visual does not provide a supplement of exactness but, on the contrary, it falsifies the dimension of the voice. According to the logic of language, the chattering nature of the networks of meaning make us deaf to this 'nothing' that does not constitute a 'less' but determines a certain relationship to the real. Yoshiki Tajiri underlines the relation of the 'prosthetic voice' and the theme of death and ghosts: 'The mechanical and death both stand in contrast to the live, animate presence of the subject or its intention. It is cut off from its "live" origin' (151). This is a result both of the exteriority of language and the use of technology, which deny the coincidence of a subject with himself: 'The distance inscribed in the structure of telecommunication opens up this ghostly space where no one is present' (152). However, rather than putting forward a purely negative definition, it is crucial to point out the positive presence of *jouissance* that constitutes the voice, and the specific impact of its *unlimited* quality, in Beckett, which justifies the notion of 'dead voices', the subject's mortification, experienced with or without technology, but to which the latter gives a specific extension.

Through the intervention of the technological device, the subject experiences his fundamental absence of interiority. Indeed, the existence of a visual register results from a process of distancing where, following a second extraction of *jouissance*—or a *separation*,[11] instituting the Name-of-the-Father—the subject is capable of perceiving his reflection as such: he distinguishes right and left-hand sides, and

11 See definitions given *supra*, p. 28–30, 64.

intellectualises his perception as being ordered according to the laws of geometrical space (Nominé). Indeed, the presence of the lost *a* object, produced by this separation, drives the subject to scrutinise a picture, to follow its lines of composition, in an attempt to discern what may be hidden 'behind' it: this is why any visible phenomenon appears as an enigma that one seeks to order and interpret. As a consequence also, the experience of interiority is correlated with the subject who is sheltered from the gaze of the Other (Wajcman, 2004). This establishing of the visual field attenuates the voices' strangeness, since the latter are assigned to places that have already been designated. That is to say also that the signifier disappears to the benefit of the signified—the field of reality—which the subject wrongly supposes to be stable, guaranteed by the Other.

However, in the absence of this veiling, the voice imposes itself in its radical exteriority, coming directly from the place of the Other. Lacan defines this difference between the visual dimension and the voice:

> We can see ourselves being seen, that is why we avoid it. But [...] we do not hear from the place where we are heard, that is to say in our head, or more exactly, some do indeed hear themselves being heard, and they are madmen, hallucinating people. [...] They can only hear themselves being heard from the place of the Other, where one hears the Other return your own message, in its reversed form. (Lacan 1991a, 360)

In the hallucinatory structure, the subject hears himself from outside: the voices he perceives are his own, but they appear as belonging to the Other. While assuming the form of an object, they in no way belong to a generality—an 'objective' reality confirmed by others—but intimately concern the subject alone. The voices that the radio plays and the *dramaticules* give substance to thus constitute a subject devoid of any interiority: the latter is, so to speak, completely in the open.

The Space of the Indescribable

The *voice* reveals the efficiency of the symbolic, its coherence, without enveloping it within any reassuring visual dimension; and the radio makes this radical reduction of the imaginary possible. In this respect, the works for radio should not be considered from the point of view of a 'deficit', as Rudolf Arnheim rightly asserts (Hartel, 223), preferring to envisage the art of the radio as a whole, complete in itself, supported by its internal coherency (Hartel, 223). To consider the theatre for the radio as a form somehow destined for blind people would be to suppose that it is a secondary, impoverished art form, in comparison with the wealth of the 'real' world. It would be to ignore the specificity of this form of creation that assuredly displays the structurally fundamental place of the symbolic, which is revealed in the dissociation between the eye and the ear. While the aural dimension can lead us to 'see' scenes via the imagination, the *voice* possesses a specific dimension that escapes its enclosure within imaginary unity, with the confusions (voice/person/world) that the latter entails.

An echo of these questions can be found in the radio plays. The *voice* destroys the imaginary envelope, as is specified in *Rough for Radio I*, when the woman questions the man: 'May one see them? / No, madam. / I may not go and see them? / No, madam' (*RR I*, 267); 'One cannot describe them, madam' (269). The works for radio demonstrate the existence of a domain that radically escapes the conceivable and the descriptive, as the idea is expressed in *Waiting for Godot*, when Vladimir, speaking to Pozzo, asserts the impossibility of depicting the place where they find themselves: 'It's indescribable. It's like nothing' (*G*, 81). Far from being negligible, what escapes the conceivable borders on the real, insofar as it does not comfort our desire for conceptual mastery.

The severe reduction inflicted on the imaginary leads to an ironic treatment of realistic effects, and to a levelling of phenomena that are usually considered distinct. Such is the case of supposedly natural sounds. In *All That Fall*, Mrs Rooney speaks:

> All is still. No living soul in sight. There is no one to ask. The world is feeding. The wind— [*Brief wind.*] —scarcely stirs the leaves and the birds— [*Brief chirp.*] —are tired singing. The cows— [*Brief moo.*] —and the sheep— [*Brief baa.*] —ruminate in silence. The dogs— [*Brief bark.*] —are hushed and the hens— [*Brief cackle.*] —sprawl torpid in the dust. We are alone. There is no one to ask. (*AF*, 192)

These sounds are reproduced because of their referential, realistic nature: the ones often used to create the impression of an environment that the characters move about in. As Steven Connor has pointed out, the ventriloquist's voice gives the illusion of being ubiquitous, of being able to conjure up vast and numerous spaces (2009, 233, 296). It is somewhat, on the aural side, the equivalent of the cinema, in the visual domain. However, their use here engenders the opposite effect. Mrs Rooney expresses her solitude, and the reduction of sounds to these caricatured interventions only serves to emphasise her divorce from the world. In using such artificial sounds, Beckett followed what was originally a suggestion made by Donald McWhinnie, of the BBC (Pountney, 176) and, as Jonathan Kalb points out, they were 'radio drama clichés even in 1956—but are also continually used in ways that remind us of their radiophonic origin' (2007, 127). In this passage, the character appears capable of controlling these sounds—much in the way others command the reading voice—which, for this very reason, can in no way give her the impression of inhabiting the world. Éric Wessler points out that these sounds 'appear solely to illustrate the utterances of the old woman, by virtue of a non-dissimulated *deus ex machina*' (2009, 302). Consequently the animal cries 'constitute no more and no less than a commentary of the occurrences of their *names*, of their designation' (302). This is all the more true as Mrs Rooney's discourse confirms the silence that these sounds render even more opaque: these interventions serve only to designate the silence, and to make it audible, instead of bringing into existence a consistent living universe.

In *Embers*, Henry orders: 'Close your eyes and listen to it, what would you think it was? [*Pause. Vehement.*] A drip! A drip! [*Sound of drip, rapidly amplified, suddenly cut off.*] Again! [*Drip again. Amplification begins.*] No!' (*E*, 255). At these moments, the auditor does not discern the presence of a person capable of producing these sounds: the latter are therefore situated on the same level as the character who speaks, they are part of his subjective reality. However, their specificity also resides in the fact that they are distinct from his speech; they make us hear the *voice* that belongs to the latter's totally separate otherness. These sounds—that obey Henry's commands—are actually *things* that do not enter into the discursive realm. Such is the experience of the auditor, who finds himself constrained to accept the reality of these sounds as *voice*, since he is not free to relegate them to the status of a décor, nor to that of purely cerebral phenomena.

The same principle also applies to the changes of place: nothing—apart from a will to engender a realistic illusion—indicates the passage from one place to another. The reality of the voice causes the abolition of geometrical space, since everything resounds on a background of the absent Other. Because of this fundamental uncertainty, in *All That Fall*, nothing can confirm the reality of the journey accomplished by Mrs Rooney: such an idea can only be a product of the auditor's suppositions. As Jonathan Kalb indicates: '[…] Beckett also clearly intends to suggest that the entire action may take place in Maddy's mind' (2007, 127). That being the case, everything unfolds in the radio set, and only the sounds are real. The characters do not traverse any given space, as Mrs Rooney emphasises: 'Oh, Mr Tyler, you startled the life out of me stealing up behind me like that like a deerstalker!' (*AF*, 174). For Mrs Rooney, as for the auditor, the voices arise out of the dark, instead of lodging themselves within a pre-ordained space.

The abolition of geometrical space—belonging to the visual order—and the flattening out of the different types of sound can be observed in *Embers*. Ulrika Maude remarks that the different spaces 'permeate one another throughout the sonorous overlap' (2009, 58). In this play, Ada arrives from nowhere: simply because Henry called her (*E*, 256–7). Ada asks then, about their daughter Addie: 'What do you suppose is keeping her?' (258). Next, Henry remarks: 'It was not enough to drag her into the world, now she must play the piano' (259). The evocation of her lesson with the *Music Master* is unexpectedly interrupted, as it were by the intervention of a 'sound editor', and the auditor is carried on to Addie's lesson with the *Riding Master*: '*Galloping hooves, "Now Miss!" and* ADDIE*'s wail amplified to paroxysm, then suddenly cut off. Pause.*' These interventions occur, in fact, following Henry's reflections, and not after some movement in space: it is when Ada mentions riding that the corresponding sounds are heard. The latter thus reflect Henry's thoughts, or *voices*. This fact is made palpable by Ada's observation: 'You are silent today.' Thus, the voices that supposedly belong to another space intervene on the same plane as those of the couple; they impose themselves however with a flexibility comparable to that of editing in cinema. In the same way, only the written indication—accessible to the reader, but not to the auditor—enables us to distinguish the space in which Henry imitates Ada, and where the latter cries out, during a scene of intimacy situated in the past: 'HENRY: Don't, don't… / [*Sea suddenly rough.*] / ADA: [*Twenty years earlier, imploring.*] Don't! Don't!' (260). If the cinema imposes the reality of the gaze as a force that manipulates the spectator, the radio imposes that of the *voice*. It produces a reality comparable to that of a dream, where the signifiers that are usually banished during waking, return in all their force, obeying the logic of free association.

The radio gives force to the principle according to which the suggestive power of the voice is inevitably addressed to the subject, whether deictic pronouns be present or not. Clas Zilliacus quotes W. H. Auden:

> In a stage play the audience 'overhear', so to speak the remarks which the actors they see address to each other; in a radio play each remark is heard as addressed directly to the listener, and its effect upon the invisible characters is secondary. (in Zilliacus, 56)

A similar effect is described in *Company*, where the subject—'the hearer' (*Co*, 20), the 'one' (3) who lies in the dark—hears a voice, without being able to determine whether he is the true addressee of the messages. He is *affected* by the voice, but nothing guarantees that he is effectively the receiver intentionally aimed at by another. The 'reasoning' voice of this text[12] voice seeks to determine why, and in what conditions he may be the intended receiver of the utterances he hears: 'If the voice is not speaking to him it must be speaking to another. [...] To another of that other. Or of him. Or of another still' (6). This succession of attempts at reasoning serve the precise purpose of maintaining uncertainty on this point: the voice comes to the hearer and affects him, without him being able to determine if the voice is really addressing him. If such were the case, the hearer would also know the identity of the emitter, who would occupy a position symmetrical to his own.

Such a blurring of the enunciative framework is manifest in *Embers*. From the *incipit*, Henry speaks to himself: 'On. [*Sea. Voice louder.*] On! [*He moves on. Boots on shingle. As he goes.*] Stop. [*Boots on shingle. As he goes, louder.*] Stop! [*He halts. Sea a little louder.*] Down. [*Sea. Voice louder.*] Down!' (*E*, 253). The imperative 'On' does not indicate the identity of the *you* who may be the object of this utterance. Only the written directions (for the reader) or the ensuing sound (for the listener) indicate a cause/effect relationship, suggesting that the character is addressing himself. However it is still necessary to raise the question of what causes such an imperative: who is this Other that drives the character to speak thus? This question is crucial, because by saying *you* to oneself, one clearly echoes the discourse of the Other. Then, when Henry changes his form of enunciation, the identity of the receiver remains uncertain: 'Who is beside me now?'; 'That sound you hear is the sea, we are sitting on the strand' (38). Of course, it may be supposed that the *you* designates the auditor. However, the latter is unable to respond, and Henry—like the actor playing his role—can in no way know if anyone is listening. Thus, nothing contradicts the idea that Henry is talking to himself. The question becomes even more problematic when he orders: 'Hooves!' Once again, the evocation of a metatheatrical dimension can be reassuring: the actor is talking to a

12 The voice characterised by ratiocination; see *supra*, p. 146.

technician. But this hypothesis is ruined straight away: 'Train it to mark time! […] A ten-ton mammoth back from the dead, shoe it with steel and have it tramp the world down!' (253).

The effect thus remains of an extreme strangeness that cannot be absorbed within a reassuring imaginary vision. The fact of addressing someone whose true identity—as an imaginary other—can in no way be discerned causes this blurring of the enunciation that is specific to the *voice*. The auditor is obliged to accept the presence of a *continual sliding* that erodes any hierarchy. Indeed, the *you* changes, becoming, as may be supposed, the phantom of the father: 'My father, back from the dead, to be with me' (*E*, 253); 'Listen to the light now, you always loved light […]. You would never live on this side of the bay […].' Éric Wessler points out that by means of the fiction and the dialogue of his two characters, Henry tries to 'play over a scene that he does not understand: that of the death of his father, as if his vocation to tell stories arose from that' (2009, 310). The fact that his father's body was never found presents us here a situation reminiscent of that of Hamlet: the absence of phallic semblances—embodied by the father—capable of veiling the 'crime of existing'[13] (Lacan, 2013, 293). The fact that Henry restitutes the episode of his father denouncing him as a 'washout' (*E*, 256) points to the difficulty he encounters in existence: the father clearly serves up the insult that is more suited to himself. The latter is inspired by Henry's refusal to go 'for a dip', and returns in the form of the incessant voice of the sea that he constantly attempts to silence. Wessler notes that Henry recounts the scene as a 'theatrical staging, with replies and stage directions' (2009, 312). Indeed, this way of proceeding appears as a substitute for a symbolic subjective inscription: Henry desperately attempts to silence the terrible pain he endures, creating a protective and structuring 'window-frame' (*CSPr*, 156) capable of inscribing him as a subject,[14] and freeing him from the

13 Here, of course, we recognise Lacan's formulation as echoing that of Calderón, quoted by Schopenhauer (254), and later by Beckett.

14 We shall return to the way Gérard Wajcman develops the motif of the window as structuring a subject's fantasy (see *infra*, p. 377). We can also

invading *voice*. By contrast, this sliding between the different voices reflects the absence of an Other capable of founding a stable reality; a structure that the radio sets into place in a particularly convincing manner. It also echoes the gaping hole that causes Henry's suffering: his absence of a subjective identity, his spectral existence; a state that, for the auditor, has the full reality of the *voice*. This use of the voice testifies to Henry's efforts—that are doomed to a certain failure—to make an Other exist, by peopling his solitude. Indeed, to speak is necessarily to *address an Other*; but Henry's speech continues to ring out in deep silence.

The Auditor and the Jouissance of the Voice

As has been noted, the recourse to the radio medium represents a fundamental transformation in the use of the voice, compared to the practice of the theatre. In the latter case, the auditory is relayed by the support the spectator finds in the visual, which mobilises an entire network of meanings. On the stage, the spectator sees the characters represented: the presence of the body favours a conception of psychological unity and the consistency of a surrounding space. In the same way, on the level of the representation, spectator and actor are united by the unique occasion of the performance and by the prohibition of infringing the fourth wall.

By contrast, a rupture occurs when dealing with the radio, annulling any idea of communion between two parties: the voices are heard from a space that remains totally inaccessible to the auditor. Graley Herren observes that the television spectator 'shares neither space nor time with the performers. […] we see mere traces of past performances—absences masquerading as presence' (2007, 65). Like Opener, in *Cascando*, the auditor can turn the appliance on and off, but this operation will not cause the voices to actually stop speaking. This

note that Lacan rejected the effacing of quotation marks, as promoted by Gottlob Frege and Willard Van Orman Quine (Pellion, 101 *sqq.*): quotation marks provide the 'frame' by means of which a subject takes position with regards to the Other, whose words he appropriates.

perception is expressed in the exchange between the man and the woman in *Rough for Radio I*: 'Is it true the music goes on all the time? / Yes. / Without cease? / Without cease' (*RR I*, 267). On a realistic level, everyone knows that the radio broadcasts continually: to turn the set on or off in no way affects the emission of the programmes. However, on another level, these statements express the structure of the voice as *unlimited*: *all the time* (the *voice* is of the order of the continuous) and *without cease* (the *voice* knows no interruption). Thus Steven Connor points out one specificity of radio: 'Offness signifies a certain kind of readiness, an imminently actualizable possibility, rather than a simple negative' (2014a, 72–3). In the same way, in Beckett's work *Film*, the soundtrack is not off, 'but rather full of silence, or offness' (73).

The radio listener finds himself in the position of the Beckettian character who recounts or hears a discourse that does not speak directly to him. Whereas a recording remains at one's disposal, so that it can be heard again, or 'edited', as in the example of Krapp, the radio escapes the listener's control. The latter can only *make himself available* to what takes place without him but which, as a *voice*, possesses a power of suggestion: the voice *concerns* the listener. This dimension is also pointed out in *Esquisse radiophonique*, the original French version of *Rough for Radio I*: 'Je vous demande si c'est en direct. […] / Mais bien entendu, madame' (*ER*, 90). The English version contains the question—'I ask you is it live?' (*RR I*, 268)—but not the man's reply. The principle of a 'live' broadcast—with people speaking or playing music at the same time as the auditor hears them—also demonstrates a structural reality of the voice. Indeed, the latter affects the listener directly, without any mediation, a fact that is pointed out by the *équivoque* contained in the French expression *bien entendu* (meaning 'of course'): the listener *hears well* (*entend bien*), since he is directly, and necessarily, the receiver of the radio's broadcasting.

At the same time, the listener finds himself in a position of powerlessness, reduced to a state of immobility—like the 'unborn' subject—since he cannot intervene or express himself in turn, or enter into a dialogue with those he hears. Beckett thus succeeds in exploiting the radio medium, so as to communicate to the listener something of the reality of the *voice*. Graley Herren emphasises the 'close affinity between the author's creative invasion by mysterious voices and the radio listener's invasion by broadcast voices' (2007, 31). Indeed, the listener resembles the creator who extracts himself from the 'traversable space' (*TFN* III, 111) of reality, to devote himself to listening to the voices that are only indexed on the symbolic register. Thus, the radio subjects the listener to the same experience as the characters: he feels the reality of the voices, and that of their regular effacing from his field of perception. Like the critics alluded to in *Cascando*, it would be supposed that the author's experience is purely a matter of literary convention, a 'manner of speaking' or an invention and that, for this reason, the voices are situated 'in his head', a judgement that radio shows to be simplistic. Thus, the invisible comes into play, as Opener points out: 'They don't see me, they don't see what my life is, they don't see what I live on, and they say, That is not his life, he does not live on that' (*Cas*, 300). Through listening, the radio represents one modality of Beckett's approach to 'getting down below the surface [towards] the authentic weakness of being' (in Knowlson, 1997, 492).

In this sense, the radio does not aim to flatter the public, but rather to set to work the *jouissance* of the *voice*, as evoked in *Rough for Radio I*. The woman asks: '—*you* like that? / It is a need' (*RR I*, 269). Indeed, it is not a *pleasure*, a term that suggests the possibility of escaping displeasure, of eluding the obstacles that might disrupt the reassurance of meanings. On the contrary, the *need* is something the character cannot detach himself from; this fact entails the use of the pronoun *that* (in French: *ça*) which, designating something that does not belong to any category, has a pejorative connotation: 'A need? *That* a need?' ('Besoin? De ça?' *ER*, 92). One has to suppose that the listener finds himself vitally dependent on this sound that enables him to silence the tormenting *voice*. Indeed, the term *need* designates particularly the relationship to an object (in this case, the *jouissance* of the voice) in its unspeakable dimension, its intimate nature which is unacceptable for the community. The *voice* is thus related to refuse, scraps (Lacan's *a* object) and, as a consequence, it assigns the man to a position of immobility: 'So you are here all the time? / Without cease' (*RR I*, 167). Riveted to the *voice* object—and in response to the latter's continuous flow—the man's immobility is unceasing.[15]

The radio set thus appears as an *organ*. Pierre Chabert points out that Krapp has 'an intense physical and visceral relationship with this object, this other "body" that is the tape recorder' (Chabert). In *Embers*, Henry too—who speaks to himself—proves to be strongly attached to the appliance that accompanies him on his walks: 'Now I walk about with the gramophone' (*E*, 261). As an 'organ', the radio permits the subject to frame, to limit the tormenting voice. In the same way as a physical organ expresses a unified perception of the body instead of its fragmentation, the *voice* as a circumscribed object gives the subject a grounding, localising his *jouissance*.[16] The voice as an organ takes on substance by means of a technological device—tape-recorder, radio, television—that situates the voice as coming from the Other, as exterior.

Insofar as it allows the subject to deal with the *voice*, the appliance-organ supposes a topology: constituting a closed space, it creates a separation from the *unlimited*. Thus it is that, in *Embers*, the interior of Bolton's house reflects the motif of the 'refuge' or the 'skull': the sheltered place where the subject finds a haven from the unbearable. In *Le Monde et le pantalon*, Beckett defines the topology of this space as follows: 'Espace et corps, achevés, inaltérables, arrachés au temps par le faiseur de temps, à l'abri du temps dans l'usine à temps (qui passait sa journée dans le Sacré-Cœur pour ne plus avoir à le voir) [...]' ('Space and body, completed, inalterable, torn away from time by the maker of time, sheltered from time in a time factory [who spent his day in the Sacré-Cœur so he would no longer have to see it?] [...]', *MP*, 28).

15 Beckett writes thus to Robert Pinget: 'Ne vous désespérez pas, branchez-vous bien sur le désespoir et chantez-nous ça' ('Do not despair, plug yourself soundly in on despair, and sing that for us', *L2*, 604).

16 We could associate it with Schopenhauer's 'dream-organ', in his 'Essay on Spirit Seeing and everything connected therewith' (in Herren, 2007, 9).

Following a Möbian structuring, the only shelter is situated in the very heart of the danger. Thus, the subject lodges himself in the construction that produces the voice—the radio set—in order to find shelter from the tormenting *voice*. *How It Is* formulates this conception when the narrator torments Pim: 'that's not all he stops nails in armpit he resumes cheers done it armpit song and this music as sure as if I pressed a button I can indulge in it any time henceforward' (*HI*, 64). The torment the narrator inflicts on his double Pim is transformed for him into soothing music. The motifs of the 'skull' and the radio represent places where the subject finds himself reduced to silence—cut off from others, identified with inert substance—where he comes to existence as 'unborn', but where he can also listen to the *voices*. The radio is the 'skull' or the *wombtomb*[17] where the subject is constituted, in the company of his voices.

The Other: A Spectral Voice

According to the paradox formulated by François Nicolas concerning music, the recorded voice, by finding a support in a technological device, also appears to restore human presence. Proust noticed as much, with regards to the telephone, in the episode where Marcel hears the voice of his grandmother:

> A real presence, this voice so close—in an effective separation! But also anticipation of an eternal separation! Quite often, listening in this way, without seeing the one who is speaking to me from so far, it has seemed to me that this voice was clamouring from the depths whence no one returns, and I have known the anxiety that was to take hold of me one day, when a voice would come back thus (alone and no longer deriving from a body that I was never to

---

17 *Cf.* 'The many metaphoric displacements of the crypt, the head and hell, asylums and dungeons […] can be seen as so many attempts to project into a *here* and *not here*. The strange status of these places of containment, from which Beckettian time's abysmal structure is derived, emphasises simultaneously an afterlife and a pre-life […]' (Moorjani, 1990, 26).

> see again) murmur in my ear words that I would have wished to embrace, in passing, on lips forever dust. (Proust, 125)

The voice transmitted by the telephone is, to a certain degree, comparable to the recorded one.[18] Beckett comments this passage:

> [...] he hears his grandmother's voice, or what he assumes to be her voice, because he hears it now for the first time, in all its purity and reality, so different from the voice that he had been accustomed to follow on the open score of her face that he does not recognise it as hers. (*Pr*, 26–7)

It would be difficult to better express the effect of strangeness engendered by the voice, when it is freed from the body, ceasing to be an auxiliary phenomenon of the *persona* to become, effectively, a *voice*. The voice is a sign of the radically inaccessible nature of the other: that by virtue of which the latter will always escape us. At the same time, the reproduction of this voice makes the singularity of the other person present again, as Proust emphasises:

> As soon as our call has resounded, in the night full of apparitions to which our ears alone open up, a light sound—an abstract sound—that of the distance suppressed—and the voice of the dear one addresses itself to us. (Proust, 125)

The one who hears the voice is subjected to its effects of suggestion, since what resonates in him is the way in which he is marked by the signifier; and also the way the latter conveys an intimacy beyond the meaning of the words pronounced.

---

18 Anne Atik notes that Beckett was interested in the use Jean Cocteau made of the telephone in his 1930 text *La Voix humaine* (Atik, 45), and which he mentions (*Pr*, 26).

This encounter with insurmountable distance and extreme proximity highlights the spectral dimension of the voice. Kevin Branigan notes the progressive importance of this quality in the radio plays: 'With each new radio play, the representation of a phenomenal world is rejected in favour of more and more ethereal worlds which are ideally conveyed through the radio medium' (140). This quality is inherent in the intervention of technology, and also affects the creation for television which, as Graley Herren points out, 'is an illusion of light and sound; there is no there there' (2007, 4).

According to Gaby Hartel, Rudolf Arnheim stresses that in radio, 'all action "grows piecemeal from nothingness"' (223). The reality of the characters—or, rather, of the Beckettian *figures*—is thus rooted in this nothingness. This abolition of space entails freeing the voice from the constraints of distance: the voice can be reproduced anywhere, independently of its emitter. Thus it is that Majorie Perloff associates this ubiquitous quality with death:

> If radio (or the phonograph) has the capacity to bring voice into someone else's public or private space, the disembodiment of that voice, Beckett was quite aware, is a sign that its owner is, whether literally or figuratively, 'dead.' Radio, to put it another way, does not allow us to distinguish the living from the dead; their recorded voices, after all, occupy the same soundscape. (Perloff, 1999, 249)

This status of the 'dead' voices remains problematic, as can be shown with regards to silence. If, concerning Krapp, the tape-recorder supposes that what is recorded is reduced to the words pronounced, the radio voice gives an important place to silence. Indeed, from a realistic point of view, the one who does not speak, on the radio, disappears. As Arnheim asserts: 'Whoever has nothing to play vanishes completely out of the picture, simply does not exist' (in Hartel, 224). The ontological guarantee that the stage seems to offer is deliberately overthrown, in Beckett's work for radio. In *All That Fall*, Mrs Rooney declares to Tommy and Mrs Slocum: 'Don't mind me. Don't take any notice of me. I do not exist. The fact is well known' (*AF*, 179). However, she also insists, referring to her silence: 'Do not imagine, because I am silent, that I am not present, and alive, to all that is going on' (185). The metatheatrical nature of this remark reminds the auditor that silence is nothing other than the voice continuing in another form. Of course, sound—testifying to the efficiency of the signifier—is presence, but it also points to a gaping hole: silence, and the subject's disappearance, which also confirms the continuation of the unstillable voice.

Mladen Dolar points out that 'the voice stands at a paradoxical and ambiguous topological spot, at the intersection of language and the body, but this intersection belongs to neither. *What language and the body have in common is the voice, but the voice is part neither of language nor of the body*' (2006, 73). Thus in the context of radio, if the body is evacuated in the sense of an imaginary existence, it persists in its enigmatic connection to the voice. Speaking of the conception of *All That Fall*, Beckett explains in a letter to Nancy Cunard: 'Never thought about Radio play technique but in the dead of t'other night got a nice gruesome idea full of cartwheels and dragging feet and puffing and panting which may or may not lead to something'[19] (5 July 1956, *L2*, 631). It is not without interest to note the circumstances of this conception: the expression *dead of night*—echoing *A Piece of Monologue* (425)—situates the voice in relation both to the effacing of the visible and to death. It is therefore necessary to understand these words in reviving the origin of their metaphorical meaning. Beckett pursues the idea of death, evoking the image of the living dead. That is to say that the mortification, here, does not produce a calming effect but, on the contrary, it places the subject in contact with the unlimited. It is at this

19 This proximity with the body can be associated with what Michel Chion calls the 'I-voice' in cinema, and which results from two techniques: 'close-miking', that 'creates a feeling of intimacy with the voice', and the absence of reverb, so that the voice cannot 'be inscribed in a concrete identifiable space' (51). Steven Connor also points out the way the invention of the telephone reinforced the impression of intimacy, leading to its use as an erotic tool (2009, 381).

place that the subject, deprived of his corporeal envelope, finds himself stripped bare, exposed to the torment of the unstillable *voice*. The radio voice would thus seem to bring into play the part where a subject is caught in the 'eternalisation of his desire' (Lacan, 1966, 319): where he is eternal in spite of himself, since his existence is pinned down by the signifier and absorbed within the signifying chain whence he is unable to escape. The radio renders palpable the state of 'nightmare thingness' (*CSPr*, 69) experienced by a ghost such as that of old Hamlet, powerless to find a final resting place. Here, the relationship to the body does not concern its image, but rather a *contingent* encounter, that escapes the regularity of any law. It is in this sense that Beckett's remark about *All That Fall* can be understood: '[…] to "act" is to kill it' (in Perloff, 1999, 251). To impose an image on a work intended to show the effect of the voice is to stifle it, since only the voice can give substance to these 'unborn' beings: it is in the radio plays that they find their native place, where they feel as if they have never been 'there'.

Aspects of the 'Sound Editor'

If the radio plays are based on the subjection to the voice, Beckett also constructs the figure of a character who acts as 'sound editor'. Numerous figures occupy this function already observed in the role played by Krapp: the man, in *Rough for Radio I* (1961); Croak, in *Words and Music* (1961); the spotlight, in *Play* (1962–1963); Opener, in *Cascando* (in French, 1963); the voice of Bam, in *What Where* (1983); Listener, in *Ohio Impromptu* (1981). This final example shows that the presence of the 'sound editor' covers a substantial period in Beckett's work.

The function of 'sound editor' does not assume identical forms, from one work to another. Notably, variations can be discerned in the degree of its identification with its status as a character. Thus, the spotlight, in *Play*, is a 'sound editor', but remains completely impersonal—as a material element of the staging—and intervenes from outside the space of the figures on stage. However, this function acquires a human identity in the works for radio *Cascando* and *Words and Music*, where it appears as a character—successively Opener and Croak—hesitating between words and music. In *What Where*, the voice that controls the movements on stage from '*a small megaphone at head level*' (*WW*, 469) is, according to the stage directions, the 'VOICE OF BAM'. This voice is the latter's double, situated at a distance from his visible figure. The idea of the double assumes a visual form in *Ohio Impromptu*, where Listener and Reader are: '*As alike in appearance as possible*' (*OI*, 445).

The function of sound editor results from the fact that the subject encounters difficulties in considering himself as the bearer of the speech that 'parasites' him. Indeed, the sound editor is cut off from the action or the stories related. This dissociation is not new: it already existed with the subject who, in several works, invented stories for himself, so they would keep him 'company'. In earlier prose texts, the narrator often described himself as being separated from the discourse he develops: such are the narrators of *The Unnamable* and *Texts for Nothing*. In the following sentence in French, the *équivoque* is thus heard, according to which *je suis* (I am) can be understood either as a form of the verb *être* (to be) or the verb *suivre* (to follow): '[…] je les suis bien, toutes ces voix, toutes les parties […]' (*TPR* I, 119) ('[…] I can follow them well, all the voices, all the parts […], *TFN* I, 102). In *The Unnamable*: 'Is there a single word of mine in all I say? No, I have no voice, in this matter I have none' (*U*, 341). In spite of having no voice, this narrator remains the vehicle for the words that traverse him: he seeks to avoid being 'trapped' by this discourse that, paradoxically, imposes itself on him and that he passes on to the reader.

In contrast with these prose works, the specificity of the sound editor's function resides in the use of an electric support for recording or transmission. The beginnings of this can be seen in the character of Krapp; this function is later developed in the radio plays and in certain *dramaticules*. However, it would seem simplistic to only observe the anecdotal dimension: to adopt a constructivist perspective and seek to interpret this approach as a way of making the listener (for the radio) and the spectator (of plays) more 'active', placing them alongside the creator. This was the idea of Rudolf Arnheim, who imagined the listeners creating 'their own, personal programme' (Hartel, 225). On the contrary, when listening to a work of Beckett, the auditor does not receive the work in 'kit' form, he does not create his own broadcast: he hears the effect of an original creation, with a cause and with constraints that remain to be defined.

The function of sound editor fundamentally brings to the fore the discriminating nature of the signifier, exposing the irreducible cleavage inherent in language. Such is, for example, the oscillation between *words* and *music*, in *Words and Music* and *Cascando*, where reconciliation proves to be impossible. In the light of this insurmountable distance, it is necessary to identify the structural heart of these plays as being situated in the *function* of sound editor, rather than in the fable that gives the text its substance. Indeed, one thing that singularises the sound editor is his absence of interiority or subjectivity, in the ordinary sense of those terms. His relationship to creation is of a performative nature: he turns on, and off, he starts, he stops. However, in spite of this impersonal dimension which appears dominant, it is possible to discern the manner in which he seeks to be affected by these voices he has us hear. This leads us to see the sound editor as the expression of a subjective function. Indeed, Éric Wessler shows how Krapp, like Hamm in *Endgame* and Henry in *Embers*, appears as a 'failed writer' (2009, 308), and that the dimension of reflexivity—the character acting as stage director, for example—intervenes as a way of compensating for this lack of achievement. This ultimately means that the function of sound editor is a way of dealing with the failure to become a subject. While his characters are thus impelled to resort to these technological devices to palliate their radical insufficiency, and establish 'a pseudo-unconscious' (2009, 303), Beckett uses writing, creation, to bring into play his status as a subject in relation to language.

The Inhuman Sound Editor: 'Play'

Although *Play* (1962–1963) is not a work for the radio, its use of the function of 'sound editor' requires to be examined alongside the other texts that resort to such a setup. Here, the 'sound editor' appears as a tormentor: situated above the space of the stage, he assumes the form of a spotlight that points itself at the faces of the three 'characters'—two women separated by one male figure—imprisoned in urns, causing them to pronounce fragments relating a triangular love relationship they were once involved in.

This setup can be understood as an expression of the persecuting aspect of the signifier: the construction here is developed from the characteristics of the discourse imposed on Mouth in *Not I*, or on the narrator of *The Unnamable*. Both *Not I* and *Play* (*cf.* Germoni) share this specificity that consists of their texts being delivered at an inhuman pace. Words here assume a material form, insofar as their meaning is evacuated: the *voice*, as such, becomes primordial. Thus, speaking of Beckett's directing of *Play*, Michaël Lonsdale notes: 'Il voulait qu'on parle à une vitesse de mitrailleuse' ('He wanted us to speak at the speed of a machine-gun', in Ackerley and Gontarski, 444). Indeed, Beckett himself saw words as 'dramatic ammunition' (in Ackerley and Gontarski, 446). This traumatising effect is a result of the action of the spotlight, which Billie Whitelaw describes as 'an instrument of torture' (in Ackerley and Gontarski, 445).

It is therefore important to discern the dimension of the *voice* in this combination of a text delivered at an extremely high speed and the intrusive action of the spotlight, both of which contribute to the destruction of meaning. It can be noted that if psychology is largely present in the story of adultery related by the figures in the urns, it is eliminated by the rapid delivery that cancels the slightest 'effect of *effort to speak*' (Beckett, 1998, 145). The movements of the spotlight—goading the figures to pronounce their phrases—also render impossible any interaction between them. According to Deidre Bair (549), Beckett wrote each voice separately, before cutting the text up and interweaving the fragments obtained. In this way, as Marie-Claude Hubert emphasises, Beckett 'introduced a true revolution in theatrical dialogue which, until then, functioned as a question and answer game', adding that no dialogue is generated (Hubert ed., 246), even though the three discourses form a weaving pattern, and compose a single story.

The separation between the figures is crucial. Steven Connor observes:

> We are to assume that none of the three knows of the presence of the other two, despite the fact that their urns are touching and that they are all contributing to the unfolding of their shared story. Theirs is a condition of non-coincident participation. (Connor, 2014a, 77)

Erik Tonning emphasises the effect of the breaks in confirming the characters' isolation: 'Each has only an extremely confined repertoire of clichés at his or her disposal, and the words of the others are not acknowledged as communicative acts, but simply transposed into another closed system of responses' (70). The characters' 'purgatorial' condition deprives them of anything that might comfort the realistic perception of their story, such as the circumstances or their psychological motivations. Their speech is deprived of its grounding: their monologues unfold in a void. In a stark contrast to the depiction of their former lives, no interaction is possible; the characters no longer have any means to compare their respective fates, to situate themselves in relation to the others. They can no longer pursue a debate or a combat: each one faces the spotlight alone. Thus the play does not create a 'world': the latter is definitively abolished. When H exclaims: 'To think we were never together' (*Pl.*, 316), it can be understood that this choice has now taken on its most acute reality.

What unity that may be ascribed to the figures is situated exclusively on the side of the spotlight, which functions as a 'sound editor'. Stanley Gontarski reports, concerning the drafts: 'Dialogue disappeared. The figures never speak to one another but respond to a mechanical stimulus, an inquisitorial light like a fourth character […]'

(in Beckett, 1999, xviii). The central role given over to the spotlight is emphasised by the latter's personification. The stage directions indicate a preference for only one spotlight, to produce the effect of 'a unique inquisitor' (*Pl.*, 318), who dominates his 'victims'. This exclusive and persecuting relationship is pointed out in the stage directions of the French version, *Comédie*: '*La parole leur est extorquée par un projecteur se braquant sur les visages seuls*' ('Speech is extorted from them by a spotlight that is aimed at their faces alone', *Com.*, 10). An anecdote confirms this orientation, since Alan Schneider (78) recounts how, with the actors, he had identified the spotlight with the author. As a 'character', the spotlight is comparable to the author/sound editor who imposes his whims on the actors, at the risk of breaking their willpower and emptying them of all humanity. Billie Whitelaw explains the necessity of a human support in rehearsing: 'We used to rehearse it with the stage manager playing the light, pointing a finger at us, giving us a cue. And before each performance, we sat down, the three of us and he, pointing his finger' (in Beckett, 1999, xviii).

This tyrannical aspect of the spotlight is not unrelated to the characters' dehumanised appearance, which can be compared with *Quad*, where anonymous and asexual figures wearing djellebas circulate according to the laws of mathematical permutation. This particular play exemplifies Beckett's remark about Leibniz: 'Above all reality hovers fate prescribed by logic'.[20] Erik Tonning comments that each re-emergence of these figures 'appears as rigidly bound to the overall outworking of the serial pattern' (Tonning, 2007, 243). In other words, character is totally effaced, to the benefit of the signifier's combinatory logic. Consequently, what is manifest in *Quad*, in an impersonal movement regulated on the level of the whole, is inseparable from its effects of depersonalisation, apparent in the physical aspect of the actors. A similar effect can be found in *Play*: '[...] *three identical grey urns* [...]. *Faces so lost to age and aspect as to seem almost part of urns*' (*Pl.*, 307). The manuscripts confirm this quest for anonymity, as in this remark made by George Devine, that Erik Tonning assumes was communicated by

20 TCD 10967/212 (in Tonning, 2007, 213).

Beckett: 'Abstract—effaced faces like old writing on stone—opposite of underlined'.[21] The actors' voices should manifest the same anonymity, being devoid of personality or psychology, and marked by 'what Beckett described as a "recto-tono", the tone used by monks 'as they read from sacred texts at mealtimes' (Knowlson, 1997, 515). In a letter to Alan Schneider, Beckett also established an explicit link between the tone of the voices and the characters' visual aspect: 'Voices grey and abstract as the faces, grey as cinders—that is what seems to me right' (26 November 1963, Beckett, 1998, 145).

In spite of appearances to the contrary, the play does not evidence a unilateral relationship, according to which the spotlight would content itself with imposing its will on the powerless figures in the urns. It is thus necessary to study more closely how the interaction between the two parties is constructed. Firstly, it can be noted that, like the actors, the characters experience the spotlight's intrusion as a form of torture or harassment, and want to be free of the persecution: '[…] all dark, all still, all over, wiped out…' (*Pl.*, 307). The characters have an antagonistic relationship with the spotlight, as expressed in the 'meditation' section: 'Get off me! Get off me!' (313).

This persecution is echoed in the story, as if the dimension of meaning were intended to occult what unfolds on the side of the Other-spotlight. On this plane where all the entangled relationships between the characters unfold, the vocabulary reproduces the expression of physical harassment: 'Give me up as a bad job. Go away and start poking and pecking at someone else' (*Pl.*, 312). The change of love partner reflects the idea that the spotlight may finally abandon his 'victim', and relieve the latter of his intrusive presence: 'Weary of playing with me' (317). The idea both of levity (the possibility of changing partners) and of caprice (insincerity) is suggested by the verb *to play*. In the use of the verb *to go out*, the idea of extinguishing the spotlight enters into an equivocal relationship with that of *exiting*: 'When you go out—and I go out. Some day you will tire of me and go out… for

21 RUL 1581/15 (in Tonning, 2007, 58).

good' (312). Picking up a topological metaphor used by H. Porter Abbott, Erik Tonning comments: 'Such moments may create a kind of "Möbius-strip effect", where the words seem to refer to the present of performance—to *our* recognition of stifled voices—as much as to the torturing light within the fictional world' (Tonning, 2007, 69). To this remark it can be added that, in these references, it is rather a form of *équivoque*, where the words *simultaneously* echo the characters' love triangle, their situation under the spotlight, and their presence before the spectators in the theatre.

While Paul Lawley has interpreted the clichéd nature of the adultery story as reflective of 'the "relation" of the light to its victims' (Lawley, 1984), it could be added that this may be understood as a result of having a spotlight play the role of 'sound editor', contrary to the human characters found in the radio plays. As it appears in the 'Killcool' manuscript that preceded the writing of *Not I*, both the light and the 'assumed voice'—coming from without, and enjoining the 'normal voice' to live—are associated with the imperative dimension (Pountney, 96). In *Happy Days* in particular, the blazing light is a factor of persecution by the superego, and results precisely in a language composed of rigid stereotypes (Brown, 2011a, 106–8), where meaning is inflexibly determined, to the detriment of the nuances ordinarily afforded by enunciation. On the other hand, as Paul Lawley shows, the characters speak in order to free themselves from this tyranny, seeking a refuge in 'the shade of words' (Lawley, 1984).

To the intrusion that they endure from the spotlight, the characters ascribe intentionality, in accordance with their personalised vision of the latter: 'Have I lost… the thing you want? Why go out?' (*Pl.*, 315); 'And you perhaps pitying me, thinking, Poor thing, she needs a rest.' They imagine that this oppressive presence is animated by an intention that remains inaccessible to them. Their dismay engenders all the questions that they raise, in the hope of knowing what they should do to enjoy relief: 'Is it something I should do with my face, other than utter? Weep?' (314).

However, on the side of the spotlight, the existence of such intentionality remains doubtful. The characters wonder: 'Is anyone listening to me? Is anyone looking at me? Is anyone bothering about me at all?' (*Pl.*, 314); 'Am I as much as… being seen?' (317). Sometimes, they formulate the conclusion: 'Looking for something. In my face. Some truth. In my eyes. Not even.' Basically, the supposed intentionality is devoid of the slightest content: 'Mere eye. No mind. Opening and shutting on me.' Behind the persecution inflicted by the spotlight, can be noticed the anguished intuition that perhaps the spotlight seeks nothing: 'And that all is falling, all fallen, from the beginning, on empty air. Nothing being asked at all. No one asking me for anything at all' (314). Turning to Berkeley's axiom *esse est percipi*—quoted in Beckett's presentation of *Film* (*F*, 323)—one understands that it is the absence of being perceived (*percipi*) that is problematic. The spotlight's silence—since it is exclusively confined within the realm of the visible—is thus crucial: the characters appear to consent to the functioning of a system that is pre-ordained, but whose rules remain unspoken. The Other never formulates what he is seeking: he never engages himself in discourse but contents himself with triggering speech in the immobilised figures. It is impossible to discern what might cause this Other to desire: to know what could satisfy him, arouse his curiosity, in order for him to enter into a dialogue relationship. On the side of the spotlight, there is no personal being to 'acknowledge receipt' (Lacan, 1981, 213), to signal some form of inscription of what is being said. Thus, in the combining of the fragments of discourse, everything unfolds between the characters and the spotlight and, more profoundly, with regards to the gaping hole of an Other that remains forever absent. This rupture in the discursive register makes the story insignificant, and poses an obstacle to the weaving of a coherent fiction between the characters. In *Play*, there is no Other to satisfy; no mutilation offers the possibility of *giving meaning* to what the characters endure: 'Bite off my tongue and swallow it? Spit it out? Would that placate you?' (*Pl.*, 314). The will to accomplish a form of sacrifice appears to be dictated by the fantasy: an expedient intended to give meaning to that which, radically, proves to be devoid of any. This absence of any discernable intentionality condemns the characters to eternal repetition, as noted in the final stage directions: '*Repeat play*' (317).

The installation this play composes manifests a strong element of constraint. Although the spotlight dominates the stage and the characters, it has its limits, since it is powerless to create or compose. Paul Lawley (1984) observes that the 'light obliges them to speak but it does not necessarily determine what they speak'. In this sense, it appears to be just as constrained as the figures in the urns: it has at its disposal a luminous beam to point, to trigger speech, but is itself condemned to remain *mute*. Its options consist either of soliciting the three characters simultaneously (producing a cacophony, as in the 'chorus' parts), or of passing from one to the other, as if selecting successive radio stations. The spotlight must split itself among the three voices, being incapable of constructing a unified discourse with the material offered by its victims.

To describe the stage installation of this play, we can adapt[22] the 'L Diagram' (*Schéma L*) developed by Lacan in his early teachings (1966, 53). This diagram, which follows the form of an *X*, shows the *symbolic* axis—indicating a relationship to truth—stretching between two poles: Subject/Other. This axis is crossed by that of the *imaginary*—which occults the symbolic relationship—where the two figures *a*/*a'* mirror each other. In this layout, it is possible to identify the spotlight (the Other) facing the subject which lies outside of any representation and, finally, the characters visible on stage, along the axis of the imaginary. M—caught between W1 and W2—appears on stage as a visible representative of the subject. This principle seems to be valid insofar as the division experienced by the spotlight between the three

22 This comparison remains a simple analogy, and not a strict application: since the symbolic Other is far from offering a guarantee, in Beckett's work (whence the pre-eminence of the *unlimited*), there is no truth to be attained. What remains is the incommensurable *rift* between the constitutive elements. For a visual transposition of this diagram, see *supra*, p. 85.

voices is reflected in M's division between two women. This horizontal distribution of the functions allows us to show that the characters' story serves to occult their fundamental relationship to the spotlight.

The 'vertical' axis would thus seem to determine the play's perspective, making the spotlight, as Katherine Weiss observes, 'the prosthetic eyes and ears of the audience' (188). Extending this principle further, it could be said that the spectator-*subject* sees himself represented, in the persecuted figures, as an *object* manipulated by the light. Indeed, unifying the play's layout within a single dynamic allows us to understand that the subject is not simply the victim of an external torturer, but is the one who is applying the torture to himself. Thus can be found expressed the principle formulated by Schopenhauer, whom Beckett read assiduously in the late 1920s: 'Tormentor and tormented are one. The former is mistaken in thinking he does not share the torment, the latter in thinking he does not share the guilt' (IV, § 63, 354). Indeed, Schopenhauer states that 'the difference between the inflicter of suffering and he who must endure it is only phenomenon, and does not concern the thing-in-itself which is the will that lives in both'. Beckett follows this principle specifically, in *Play*: 'The inquirer (light) begins to emerge as no less a victim of his inquiry than they and as needing to be free, within narrow limits, literally to act the part, i.e., to vary if only slightly his speeds and intensities' (Beckett, 1999, xxii). Paul Lawley usefully extends this principle to *Words and Music*, *Cascando*, and *Rough for Radio II*, where 'the Master is seen to be subject to the obligation to create no less than his Slave(s), and to be therefore slavishly dependent upon the slave—for only the slave can create' (1984). If Beckett does not necessarily espouse the metaphysical implications of this theory—and which suppose the purely ephemeral status of the '*principium individuationis*'—he does utilise this inescapable looping that implacably binds the two agents within the same construction.

Indeed, and by contrast, if spotlight and tormented figures are united within the same structure, they are also separated by an insuperable *gap*, which can be associated with the following remark Beckett made to Charles Juliet regarding creation: 'Il faut être là—index pointé sur la table – et aussi – index levé vers le haut – à des millions d'années-lumière. En même temps…' ('One must be there—index pointed at the table—and also—index raised—millions of light-years away. At the same time…', in Juliet, 66–7). It is from the point of view of an unfathomable, and totally opaque Other—situated at the 'zenith'—that the spectator observes the paltry drama in which the characters are entangled, and which is their only existence: the *hic et nunc* in which they are entrapped. What is at stake is not only the love triangle (what M calls 'all that'), but a form of competition aiming to attain an absolute perspective, beyond the insignificant content of existence: 'I know now, all that was just… play. And all this? When will all this— […] / All this, when will all this have been… just play?' (*Pl.*, 313). However, it is precisely this absolute point of view that the characters cannot achieve: the possibility of maintaining the double perspective is the prerogative of the creator only. The characters remain eternally attached to a reality from which they are henceforth excluded; to a world that words constantly recall and place before their eyes.

If this vertical perspective seems the most immediately convincing way to conceive of the play's setup, it would also appear useful to rotate the 'L Diagram' slightly, and to situate spotlight and figures in the urns closer to the specular *a/a'* axis. Indeed, the role played by the light belongs typically to the imaginary plane; and, in the work of Beckett, it is inappropriate to postulate a 'subject' related to symbolic 'truth' which, as such, belongs to the realm of *limited wholes*. This modification therefore shows the Other/subject axis in relation to the *unlimited*, centred on a void, while the duality *spotlight/figures* manifests an unstable and persecutory relationship. Having no point of reference outside of itself (other than language as unlimited), the spotlight is split between the three figures, with nothing to guide it in its quest. The three figures also know not what they are expected to reveal, and possess no truth they might hide. They respond only to the physical aggression inflicted on them with fragments of speech that, in their clichéd nature, are the only responses possible, when faced with a speechless and hostile light. That is to say, no fiction or dialogue is conceivable, where there is no Other capable of instituting addressed speech. The specular structure thus reveals a complete absence of any *relation*, which Beckett described, for example—when speaking of paintings by Jack Yeats—as '2 entities that will never mingle' (*L1*, 540).

Thus, the figure of the spotlight appears as an inscrutable 'sound editor': the one that composes the play as a whole, but who is incapable of providing its meaning. Far from being all-powerful, the spotlight is animated by a force that it is incapable of grasping: it can only rely on the characters' stereotyped representations to gather minimal fragments that may—however indirectly—shed a glimmer of light on its existence.

The Sound Editor as the Character's Double: 'What Where'

In *What Where*, the role of sound editor is played by the voice projected by means of an electric device, the latter being explicitly named 'VOICE OF BAM' (*WW*, 469). The text revised after the television production in Stuttgart in 1979 also adds this detail: 'V: [This is BAM.]' (Beckett, 1999, 409). In the text, the device is described thus: 'V *in the shape of a small megaphone at head level*' (*WW*, 469). The indication of the height invites the spectator to associate the megaphone with the figure of Bam; in the same way as the lamp in *A Piece of Monologue* is, by virtue of its being calibrated on the human body, associated with the Speaker (*PM*, 425). The text of *What Where* suggests that the other figures appearing on stage are all doubles of the subject: '*Players as alike as possible. / Same long grey gown. / Same long grey hair*' (*WW*, 469). Thus a hierarchy is established, where the Voice is dissociated from Bam who, in turn, is included in a series of doubles, from whom he is distinguished only by his place in the permutations.

This voice appears as a reflection of the subject Bam, whose function is to organise the action of the play. Using the pronoun *I*, his utterances accompany the action: 'First without words. / I switch on' (*WW*, 470, 471). The judgements that the voice pronounces determine the repetition of the same movements, or the progression to the following stage: 'Not good' (470); 'Good' (461); 'Good. / I switch off. / [*Light off.* P.] / I start again' (471). The voice informs the spectator of the temporal scansion of the performance and the fiction: 'Time passes' (470). However there is no 'situation of communication' since the voice does not directly give orders: the figures enter and exit the stage, as if they know what to do; in other words, as if they shared Voice's evaluations.

As it is detached from Bam, Voice is notable for its particular quality. Pierre Chabert indicates that it is necessary to distinguish '2 voix souvenir & Bam' ('two voices memory and Bam', in Beckett, 1999, 451). Martha Fehsenfeld notes that in the television production: 'There was a slightly higher frequency in [the voice] of the younger Bam, and a lower, deeper effect in the older Bam' (in Beckett, 1999, 451). In the *Stuttgart Notebook*, Beckett remarks, about the voice (*Stimme*, in German): 'S's voice prerecorded. / Bam's, but changed / (enfernt [removed, distant])' (in Herren, 2007, 186). He adds: 'Bam's voice in dialogue with some colour. S [Stimme] colourless' (Beckett, 1999, 451). Contrary to the plane where the action unfolds, Voice appears as the part of the subject that, drawing his authority from the Other, orders, observes, evaluates, judges: it manifests the nature of a *superego*. For this reason, it appears to be devoid of any subjectivity: it dominates the stage, but is incapable of moving physically, contrary to the series of B–M.

The mechanical voice assumes the appearance of a mortified entity. This quality is emphasised in the revised text by a mirror effect, where the two identities resemble each other, while giving Voice a spectral status: 'V = *mirror reflection of* BAM*'s face, slightly distorted, faintly lit* [...]. *Four-five times the size of* P [*playing area*] *faces. Eyes closed throughout*' (Beckett, 1999, 409). Stanley Gontarski points out that Bam's face has become 'an enlarged and distorted death mask' (in Beckett, 1999, 415). This replacement emphasises precisely the strict *equivalence* between the use of the sound device as a 'dead voice', and this new iconic element.

This invention, however, is rigorously faithful to the very structure of the *voice*, as it is manifested in *What Where*. Walter Asmus reports: 'Abruptly he begins: The problem of the voice. One could imagine it coming from the grave, trying to reconstruct how it was.

And what it was. And where the way out is. Beckett points to *The Lost Ones*' (in Tonning, 255). Coming back from the dead, the voice is radically cut off from the world of the living. If the voice, by virtue of its function—that of a symbolic order—'dominates' the stage, it is because it is a representation of the vantage point of the latter: a reflection of the subject as he is inhabited by the Other, and who observes himself from this point. Voice is thus comparable to the spotlight in *Play*, being able to order the action, but powerless to participate in it. However, far from acting as a persecutor, Voice here manifests a certain powerlessness, since the reconstruction it achieves of 'how it was' does not necessarily reflect any referential reality. The voice emphasises: 'In the present as were we still' (*WW*, 470). Everything is recounted in the present—the moment of the performance—but this enunciation *hic et nunc* is only a pale reflection of what remains radically out of reach. The voice states 'It is spring', but this indication has no link to a present reality, outside of the enunciation itself. Voice cannot make time past present again, nor extract any truth from it. Thus, its symbolic efficiency—its capacity to organise a scene—is correlated with an entirely spectral existence, that is to say the shadows that trace the outlines of an impossible.

If Voice belongs to the *symbolic*, the 'characters' or figures—the series of B–Ms—compose an *imaginary* plane, in the manner of the three characters of *Play*: this register composes the fictional level of the 'dramatic' action. Here, the voice of Bam is not toneless: 'Bam's voice in dialogue with some colour' (Beckett, 1999, 451). The figures that move around on this plane are supposed to relive the past, or to make it live again. The voice can thus be identified with a 'Bam 1' superimposed on the 'Bam 2' visible on stage. In this fiction—where Bam speaks to Bom, etc.—the voice is finally identified with a corporeal existence.

In order to circumscribe the status of Voice more closely, it is necessary to study the permutations it presides over, and which Ulrika Maude associates with looping structures in computer programmes (2009, 131–2). On the stage, Bam receives each one of the other figures—torturers in turn—asks them if their victim 'said' the answer to the questions asked of them. When the torturer responds negatively, he himself becomes a victim. The progression of the combinations can be represented in a series where the torturer is placed above the bar, and his victim below, as follows:

$$\frac{\text{Bom}}{x} \searrow\!\!\rightarrow \frac{\text{Bim}}{\text{Bom}} \searrow\!\!\rightarrow \frac{\text{Bem}}{\text{Bim}} \searrow\!\!\rightarrow \frac{\text{Bam}}{\text{Bem}} \searrow\!\!\rightarrow \left[\frac{\text{Bom}}{\text{Bam?}}\right]$$

It can firstly be noted that according to the self-correction made by the Voice, Bom's entry is not a new action: 'In the end Bom appears. / Reappears' (*WW*, 471). Then, what reinforces the mystery of this absence of a commencement is the fact that at first, Bom enters, without us knowing *whom* he may have tortured: 'He didn't say anything?' (472). The pronoun *he* has no identifiable antecedent (it is therefore indicated by the symbol x). At the end of the chain, Bam exits, followed by Bem, who will be his victim. However, what is missing, to complete the chain, is the combination in which Bam would occupy the place of victim, undergoing an interrogation at the hands of Bom (this eventuality is indicated between square brackets). Susan Brienza finds the same logic at work in *How It Is*, where the absent fourth part can be interpreted as reflecting the unbearable present: 'But if the whole book consists of part 4, then the present tense (for how it is to *be* tortured) is the valid one for the entire monologue, but too painful to be sustained' (111). In the succession thus formed, the represented victim must give the possibility of saying something about one who is forever absent, and who is situated on the hither-side of the chain:

$$\frac{\text{Torturer}}{\text{Silent victim}} \qquad \frac{>}{//} \qquad \frac{\text{Bam}}{x \text{ (absent victim)}}$$

In this diagram, the torturer transmits to Bam the absence of a response that he receives from his silent victim. In the final analysis, this mechanism must be reported back to Voice (which is that of Bam):

Torturer	>	Voice
Victim	//	*x* (absent victim)

Indeed, a strange notation appears concerning the number of agents in this play: 'We are the last five' (*WW*, 470). The B–Ms—being ordered by means of the series of vowels *a, e, i, o*—number four. On this point, Stanley Gontarski notes two hypotheses:

> 'We are the last five.' With only four characters listed, the fifth may be the separate, remembering consciousness, the 'Voice of Bam', the voice, as it were, 'from beyond the grave', according to Beckett. [...] the fifth character might be the already dispatched figure whose name might contain the missing fifth vowel. Bom does not appear, we may recall, but 'Reappears'; having already failed to elicit the required information from another (Bum?), he enters 'head bowed'. (in Beckett, 1999, 415 and 449).

Indeed, it would be appropriate to situate the fifth character both on the side of Voice and on that of the missing character. Regarding the latter, André Bernold questions Beckett: '– Lorsque, lors du premier interrogatoire, Bam interroge Bom (*Il n'a rien dit?*), qui est-ce, *il*? /– C'est celui qui n'apparaît pas. Il est mort, *erledigt.* C'est la cinquième voyelle, Bum. C'est une sinistre histoire…' ('When, during the first interrogation, Bam questions Bom [*He didn't say anything?*], who is *he*?' / 'He is the one who does not appear. He is dead, *erledigt.* He is the fifth vowel, Bum. It is a sinister story…', Bernold, 37–8). The unnamed *Bum* is curious, and he can be associated—in a very vivid way—both with the idea of a 'vagabond' (like his predecessors: Mercier and Camier, Molloy, Vladimir and Estragon…), or with the scatalogical preoccupations of earlier works. It nonetheless remains that he is excluded, relegated to the domain of the unsaid.

The other B–Ms compose a spectral domain: the space where the action takes place, in an accelerated temporality, punctuated by the seasons, but where everything falls back into fundamental solitude. That is to say that the *imaginary* register here conserves this function of veiling the void, without dissimulating it, without offering the illusion of a liveable life, without instituting the register of meaning.

That is also to say that the B–Ms come down to being emanations of the subject alone, represented firstly by the Voice—that remains present throughout the play—then by Bam, who disappears towards the end. The subject of this play experiences radical solitude, in spite of the ephemeral peopling enabled by the phrase 'In the present as were we still.' (*WW*, 470). The play is structured by an unfolding movement followed by the final enfolding or closure. This folding is discretely outlined in French by the organisation of the stage according to the three directions: *ouest*, *nord* and *est* (*West*, *North*, *East*), whose initials spell: *one*.

The play is thus structured according to a distribution between, on the one hand, the paradigmatic axis Voice/Bam/*I*, and, on the other hand, the zero, the gaping hole. It is particularly in the darkness offstage that the torture takes place. From this hole, no knowledge can be drawn: 'BOM: He didn't say anything? / BAM: No' (*WW*, 472). As for vivid words such as *torture*—that we, as critics, so readily resort to—they are totally absent from the text, which uses far more equivocal expressions: 'You gave him the works?' As Matthieu Protin points out (2014, 284) when emphasising the contrast with Artaud, Beckett's theatrical works attenuate violence, by stylising it. In other words, *What Where* does not tell a story or evoke dramatic actions: it deals rather with the subject mortified by language and incapable of attaining knowledge. The latter would consist in the possibility of including, by virtue of a dialectic, something of the *pastout* or the *unlimited* that torments the Beckettian subject, and of subjecting him to a form of exclusion under the aegis of the paternal metaphor. This dimension that can never be absorbed is marked both by the initial hole—the unnamed victim—and by the conclusion: 'That is all. / Make sense who may. / I switch off' (476). The subject—represented by the Voice—remains absolutely singular, *devoid of equals*. Such a subject could be summed up as follows:

<u>Voice</u>
0

The Beckettian death/birth conjunction—devoid of any dialectic—reappears here: '[…] one day we are born, one day we shall die, the same day, the same second, is that not enough for you?' (*G*, 83). That is what can be heard, in the theatrical tradition, announced by the adjective *last*: 'We are the last five. / In the present as were we still' (*WW*, 470). The adverb *still* is equivocal, as it signifies both the persistence in time, and immobility. Whereas in tragedies, the inaugural *At last* announces that the hero is about to find himself grappling with his destiny—the moment when his desire will take form, with its terrifying consequences…—this conjunction acquires a singular acuity in the case where the subject is directly in contact with the invisible, *real* Thing, as is the case in Beckett's work.[23]

That is also to say that there is a hole—comparable to 'E supposed a danger zone' (*Q*, 453) in *Quad*—that is linked to the subject's existence as *real*. The Voice arises at the place of this absence of representation that it will never be able to tell of. That is the reason why this *0* appears as the real of the subject that the work of creation has the mission to bring to being: '[…] enfer d'irraison d'où s'élève le cri à blanc, la série de questions pures, l'œuvre' ('[…] hell of irrationality whence arises the blank cry, the series of pure questions, the work', *Dsj*, 56). *What Where* gives voice to these 'questions pures', devoid of any content in the realm of meaning. It is also precisely faced with the 'cri à blanc', caused by the torment endured, that the victims offer, in return, their 'no reply'. Far from the imaginary having served to dissimulate this dimension, it has, on the contrary, contributed to its designation as a radical absence. Voice is mortified, because it is understood as the subject who experiences this solitude that consists of never being able to derive knowledge in response to the questions he

23 Beckett's 'in the end' thus contrasts with the structuring opposition signifier/repression, that operates in classical tragedy (*cf.* Mehta, 384).

asks of others, who are only simulacra: there will never be any dialogue, nothing new will ever spring up as a revelation.

The Sound Editor Affected in Return: 'Cascando', 'Rough for Radio I'

If Beckett's remark emphasising the status that the spotlight-sound editor in *Play* shares with his victims has been taken into account, it remains to be seen how this common condition manifests itself. Insofar as the sound editor represents a subjective function and not some sort of agent situated in a realistic 'world', he cannot be considered as the initiator of a univocal action, addressing creatures that he remains detached from. He has a structural relationship with them, and therefore needs to be understood as seeking something that concerns him intimately. Indeed, by inaugurating action on the stage, he is pursuing knowledge that ceaselessly escapes him. In *What Where*, this reciprocity does not only materialise when Voice of Bam expresses its reticence or approval of the dialogue: 'Not good. / I start again' (*WW*, 473); 'Good.' His presence can also be identified in the exclamation: 'Ah!' (474): at this moment—when Bim returns to Bam the question 'Where?'—Voice shows that its expectancy has attained its maximal intensity. It is also necessary to understand this exclamation as being symmetrical to the cries—which remain virtual—of the victims. The latter can be identified with the 'cri à blanc' ('blank cry', *Dsj*, 56) that resonates in the silence of the Other; that is to say, in the impossibility of any response that causes the Beckettian subject's torment. The play's repeated actions serve to prepare the ground, so that this cry will produce absolute silence.

The sound editor's quest to be affected by the play he organises is particularly illustrated in two works for radio: *Cascando* and *Rough for Radio I*.

Cascando—written in December 1961 (Knowlson, 1997, 497) and published in French in 1963—presents 'Opener' who seems to be an impersonal presence, but who also expresses an intimate need to listen to the voices emanating from the radio. It is useful to mention that Beckett here inscribes his creation in the field of modernity[24], not postmodernity. Steve Connor points out that Beckett's radio work 'activates this archaic sense, very literally, of the work *of* radio, the strenuous ardors of audition' (2014a, 69). It is thus not a question of the pervasive presence of radio apparatuses grafted onto the body, but of listening as a very physical and intentional act, limited in time and space, rather than being dispersed or melting into background noise. Listening here involves a bodily relationship to an external device which occupies an essential function for the subject. In this play, Opener indicates that he 'opens' and 'closes' the appliance, first having Voice and Music (the latter being composed by Marcel Mihalovici) heard in alternation, then simultaneously. Graley Herren notes that both Opener and Voice of Bam 'are aural entities who preside from a detached position outside the action proper. Both are clearly invested in the action and yet remain removed' (2007, 183). Indeed, as in *What Where*, Opener manifests no personality. He is split, insofar as he enunciates and comments his own utterances: 'OPENER: [*Cold.*] It is the month of May… for me. / [*Pause.*] / Correct' (*Cas*, 297). He is thus his own 'sound editor'. As in *What Where* also, the opening sentence contains the first person pronoun, and is uttered in an impersonal tone, as if it were indispensible to graft himself onto the symbolic agent in order to found a beginning. That is to say that in the absence of any pre-existing reality, for want of a solid foundation enabling him to keep the *real* at a distance, the subject has to find a starting point in an imperative, as in the inaugural 'On' (*E*, 253) of *Embers*. By means of this command, he gives voice to his mortifying Other who is, however, the only one capable of providing him with an inscription in existence. Only then can the subject consent to this utterance, and recognise it as being its own. Opener then intervenes in the manner of the narrator of *How It Is*, with his interpolated clauses *I quote*, testifying both to the setting at a distance (or a questioning of the utterance's veracity) and an acceptance that the phrase may belong to him.

---

24 This term is defined *supra*, p. 34. This notion will be studied more precisely at the end of this chapter. See *infra*: p. 370.

Opener's action consists entirely of opening and closing two sound sources, and in the minimal commentary he offers. However this action constitutes the play's structuring element, like May's footsteps in *Footfalls*, and which Beckett called 'the essence of the matter', as opposed to the text, 'what pharmacists call excipient' (in Whitelaw, 1996, 139). Steven Connor points out the central role of the switch in listening to the play:

> The knobs are the only audible and executive parts of whatever apparatus is being used to convey and listen to the sounds. In a sense, they control the whole play, which then becomes an apparatus for tuning into the agon of listening to radio. (2014a, 75–6)

As Clas Zilliacus remarks, 'instead of focussing on a story', *Cascando* 'focusses on the storytelling condition' (143). What Beckett situates at the heart of his plays' structure is thus this symbolic dimension.

Indeed, Opener undertakes no act of 'creation': instead of elaborating a story—his own, or that of another—he accomplishes a purely mechanical action: he is not the producer of what he hears and shares with the listener. He receives, in a passive manner, voice and music that come to him as external phenomena. Insofar as they concern the *voice*, Opener is incapable of assuming them: he can only regulate the delivery of these manifestations that appear to be mutually incompatible, in an effort to reconcile them. In spite of this aim, opening and closing appear as *arbitrary* movements, devoid of any explicit justification.

However, the action Opener accomplishes is vital to him: 'It's my life, I live on that' (*Cas*, 299). It is worth noticing the chiasm that structures this expression: whereas *my life* seems to denote extension, *I live* expresses the way his life is dependent on this activity. No less remarkable is the insistence on *that*. This pronoun appears in Beckett's famous response to the question '*Pourquoi écrivez-vous?*': '*Bon qu'à ça*' ('Why do you write?' 'Only good for that', *cf.* Hubert ed., 2011, 157). This contracted pronoun—*ça* instead of *cela*—expresses a pejorative evaluation, similar to the titles designating his work as refuse or 'scraps' (Brown, 2013b). To describe his work in such terms is to adopt the perspective of an ideal Other, who accepts nothing less than perfection. The Beckettian subject sees himself as a scrap in comparison with such an extreme exigency, and yet this dimension refuses to be eliminated. One is therefore led to conclude that *ça/that* is related to the *a* object, that is to say, '*that jouissance*', that is not sanctioned by the Other but remains vital for the subject. As the Voice says in the French version: 'ça ma vie…' ('that [is] my life…', *Cas*, 47). The subject's entire life is at stake in this activity: something that the others—who, by definition, are the auditors of this radio play—are incapable of seeing.

The vital status of this activity distinguishes it from any conception of 'pleasure'. Opener does not seek to procure enjoyable sensations: his activity concerns a dimension situated 'beyond the pleasure principle', as Freud would say. Opener describes his activity thus: 'I'm afraid to open. / But I must open. / So I open' (*Cas*, 302). A certain form of courage and duty drives him to open. We find a similar concern in *Embers*, where the sound of the sea is omnipresent, constituting the enveloping space of the play as a whole. Clas Zilliacus (89) remarks: 'More than two hundred pauses are called for in the text of *Embers*. Thus the sea, which goads Henry on by surfacing in every one of them, achieves the dignity of dramatis persona.' Ada does not understand how Henry can remain near the sea, since he cannot bear it:[25] 'And if you hate it why don't you keep away from it? Why are you always coming here? [*Pause.*] There's something wrong with your brain […]' (*E*, 260). Moved by simplistic thiking, servile to 'concrete' conceptions, Ada is incapable of comprehending the topology of the 'organ' that enables Henry to deal with the voice: the way creation frames and circumscribes that which torments the subject and will not allow him to forget.

25 Everett Frost (258), alluding to one of Beckett's letters to Georges Duthuit (*L2*, 134), describes the sucking sound of the sea as 'a painful analogue to a Geulincxian self-examination of his life and memories'.

In *Cascando*, the 'mixing' that Opener carries out must have an effect on him, a fact which leads him to express his reaction to what he hears: 'OPENER: [*With* VOICE *and* MUSIC, *fervently*.] Good!' (*Cas*, 304). In this judgement, an echo can be heard of the stages of the Creation story, in the book of Genesis: 'Good'—in French: 'C'est bien!' (*Cas*, 60)—expresses the capacity of the radio voice to 'do the image', to create an object capable of palliating the void. Thus, and in spite of appearances, this activity is a form of artistic creation, with its vital dimension: 'It's my life, I live on that' (299).

The voice's exteriority is a crucial element in the construction of this play. Voice and music are independent of one another—Opener can have them heard together, without them merging—but they are also independent of Opener, in the same way as, on a structural level, the subject ascribes the *voice* to the Other. Here, Opener connects himself to this *jouissance*—from which he can extract no knowledge—in order to regulate it, and to live. He does so in the same way, more or less, as a subject finds support in his ability to have nocturnal dreams. However, as a mortified subject—like the other 'sound editors'—Opener has no 'fantasy': he cannot take refuge behind a personal 'world view', in reference to an imaginary identification. Consequently, the radio's real presence is indispensable to pacify his voices.

For this reason, one cannot conclude that there is any identification of Opener with the character Woburn, in the story recounted by Voice.[26] Opener is no more Woburn than the speaker is the character whose story is recounted by the *dramaticules*, such as Speaker in *A Piece of Monologue*. Of course, it is possible to say:

> As a figure of the writer, like Krapp or Molloy, Opener splits into a Voice that dialogues with Music to elaborate an endless fiction

26 Clas Zilliacus (129) states: '[…] Voix is not regarded by its author as one indivisible story but a compound of two, made up of an *élément soi* and an *élément histoire*; […].'

> whose character, Maunu [in the French version], may also reflect the image of the first narrator [...]. (Alexandre-Bergues, 195)

Indeed, Woburn's utterance—'in my life...' (*Cas*, 297) ('ça ma vie...', *Cas*, 47)—and that of Opener—'It's my life, I live on that' (299) ('C'est ma vie, je vis de ça', 52)—echo each other, which explains why Woburn's story arouses intense interest in Opener. However, one cannot erase this dissociation, this effect of strangeness that Opener points out when he reports the opinions expressed about him: 'They said, It's his own, it's his voice, it's in his head' (302); 'No resemblance. / I answered, And that...' Behind the pronoun *they*—the indefinite *on*, in French (56)—can be discerned the voice of literary critics intent on establishing a relationship between the voice and the personality of Opener. However there is no similarity, as Opener demonstrates by switching on the music: 'I answered, And that... [...] / ...is that mine too?' Thus, Music and Voice unfold on the same plane, since both voices are situated outside Opener, rather than being emanations of his personality which, as can be seen, is almost nonexistent.

A degree of similarity can be established between Opener's activity and that of Beckett himself, listening to his own voices. And yet, what a work like *Cascando* demonstrates is that these voices cannot be relativised: their specificity should not be devaluated by reducing them to some 'psychological' reality. Thus, Opener subjects the auditor of the radio play to an experience that is analogous to his own: the listener experiences the opening and closing of the other voices (voice and music) as movements he does not control, and that keep him in a state of uncertainty. Opener also experiences this arbitrary dimension, which drives him to undertake a succession of operations. As a medium, radio offers precisely the possibility of demonstrating the reality of this invisible object which is the *voice*: 'They don't see me, they don't see what my life is, they don't see what I live on, and they say, That is not his life, he does not live on that' (*Cas*, 300).

In *Rough for Radio I* (originally written in French, in 1961, under the title *Esquisse radiophonique*), the sound editor—designated by the simple pronoun *He*—also seeks to obtain an effect on himself, his final distress becomes apparent when he is powerless to control the voices' fading. The movement of the play leads us from empty chattering to its reversal: to the absence of any Other capable of providing a symbolic response.

The play is divided into two parts. The first part sheds light on the function of sound editor, by creating an opposition between two characters. Firstly, the man introduces the subject of the play, composing a sort of exposition: the woman asks questions, having come, apparently, to *see* what a radio is. This expositional function also extends to the man, insofar as the two characters allow the constitution of an imaginary plane, providing information of a visual nature, by contrast with the voices' invisibility.

In the first part, the man endures the woman's intrusion. He emphasises the reality of his solitude: 'When one is alone one is all alone' (*RR I*, 268). She in turn notes that he does not seek her company: 'You suffered me to come' (267). The *équivoque* of the verb *suffer* suggests that the man tolerates her, but also that her visit is somehow unpleasant. In this part of the play, the man remains passive, contenting himself with responding to his visitor's questions by *yes* or *no*. The woman's presence seems intrusive, in her desire to institute an imaginary dimension: she insists on having access to a visible representation that would complement the audible. Like one who listens to the radio, so to say (she also switches the set on), she is willing to listen, but she also wants to see, a prospect the man refuses.

The woman thus offers a reflection of the listener: her presence constructs a *mise en abyme* where she represents the trivial attitude of the latter. Indeed, she appears as superficial, repeatedly seeking to see what cannot be seen, that is to say, the *voice*: 'May one see them? / No, madam. / I may not go and see them? / No, madam' (*RR I*, 267). This search for a grounding in the visible inspires her question when she is about to leave: 'Is that a Turkoman?' (269).

The contrast between the two characters is also reflected in the separation between words and music. The woman questions: 'They are not together? / No. / They cannot see each other? / No' (*RR I*, 268). Indeed, these same utterances can be applied to the two characters who appear to be engaged in a conversation, but who do not communicate. In particular, the man reveals nothing of what really poses a problem for him, that is to say, the fading of the voices, which causes his suffering in the second part of the play.

Not only does the woman belong to the realm of the visible but, insofar as the use of words often supposes the dimension of meaning, she is situated on the side of speech, whereas the man belongs to silence, his words being limited to monosyllables. Not only does he play the role of sound editor, in relation to the radio set, but he also gives directions to his visitor in a neutral, informative tone. Basically, the woman can be considered as the subject 'divided' by speech, insofar as she asks questions, seeks to discover, to interest her interlocutor, to obtain knowledge about what she does not know. She also asks questions about the man's condition, in an effort to understand him. She thus seeks to engage an intersubjective relationship, while her interlocutor feels the irreducible nature of his own solitude. In this way, the two characters together give form to a fundamental absence of any relation: to the abyss that characterises the *voice*.

This play stresses the limits of the sound director's power: the latter cannot create, but remains dependent on the manifestations of the voice. Whereas, in the first part, the man endures a form of intrusion in his personal space, in the guise of the visit paid by the woman, in the second part (*RR I*, 269), the movement is reversed, since he seeks contact with the outside, calling the doctor on the telephone. He is worried, and his tone is vehement: '…most urgent!' (270). By mobilising two supplementary appliances—radio and telephone—this part of the play introduces an apparatus 'to the power of 2', in a *mise en abyme*.

The fading of the voices drives the man seeks help from doctor *Macgillycuddy* (*RR I*, 270). The latter has a comical name—particularly when it springs up in the French version—somewhat comparable to the name *Godot*. Ruby Cohn (271) puts forward the idea that 'it blends gills and cud to suggest a monstrous animal'. Such an entity is not unlike Caliban, in Shakespeare's *The Tempest*, and who is called a 'moon-calf' (Act II, sc. 2), and of whom Trinculo wonders if he is 'a man or a fish? dead or alive?' Contrary to the visitor who enters the man's home, this character is situated 'off stage', since he can only be contacted by telephone. Indeed, it could be said that he embodies a sham character, who serves to point out the absence of the Other: *in fine*, the absence of a word capable of putting an end to the protagonist's torment. This absence is manifest in the incomprehension of the doctor, who obliges his interlocutor to insist: 'what?… no!… no question!… ENDING I tell you… nothing what?… to be done?… I know there's nothing to be done…' (*RR I*, 270). The man is obliged to repeat because the doctor understands nothing about his problem. His title as 'doctor' suggests that he should be able to provide a response to suffering. Only at the end of the play is an explanation provided for the disquiet that the woman noticed at the beginning: the malaise, whose origin the man had not revealed, was caused by the disappearance of the voices, that had already begun. That is to say that the radio no longer provides the response to the man's *need*.

Whereas the voice provides a form of 'company', the man's final cry for help confirms his fundamental solitude. On the level of language, this solitude is stressed by the impossibility of achieving a signifying 'loop' resulting from the effective presence of a symbolic Other: the man fails to receive an adequate response. Of course, he did assert: 'I ask no one to come here' (*RR I*, 267). However, he requests the doctor's presence, but instead of the reassurance of a visit, his demand only serves to introduce the theme of waiting, in the *clausula*: 'Tomorrow… noon…' (271). These words prolong the waiting, after the doctor's first announcement: 'in an hour?… not before?…' The imposed waiting testifies to an enunciation turned towards the future, but which can never attain a final punctuation capable of conferring meaning. The very idea of such an anchoring point is indicated by the verb *to reach*, used by the doctor's secretary: '[…] can't reach him… no idea… […] the moment he gets back…' (270). The one who could provide a response to the character's suffering remains absent—physically (necessitating the use of the telephone) and symbolically (he cannot be contacted)—while another answers in his stead. The promise 'Tomorrow… noon…' (271) echoes the derisory signifier *Godot*, the name that engenders interminable waiting.

The auditor of this radio play experiences the same absence as the character. During the first telephone call, the man does not name the problem that motivates his call, so that the listener too does not immediately understand what is at stake. In the same way, the doctor's absence, conjugated with the motif of the telephone, produces an interrupted, partial, dialogue. The listener is led to *hear absence*: he is deprived of half of the telephone conversation, so that he feels the absence of response that causes the character's suffering. The interruptions thus indicate the place of an absent other. In the second part of the play, the auditor encounters the torment of an *enunciation* that is stripped bare, that fails to achieve the status of a closed *utterance*, and the man finds himself definitively alone: 'but she's left me… ah for God's sake… haven't they all left me?…' (*RR I*, 270). The character only has the telephone at his disposal to establish contact with others.

This solitude sheds light on the function of the insult that comes after the man's supplications, engendering a form of musical alternation. The end of the conversation with the doctor's secretary reads as follows: 'I told you so!… most urgent!… most urgent!… [*Pause. Low.*] Slut!' (*RR I*, 270). The end of the conversation with the doctor is symmetrical to the preceding one: 'wait… don't go yet… wait! [*Pause. Sound of receiver put down violently. Low.*] Swine!' (271). These insults can be understood as a response to the absence of the Other, as can be observed in *Endgame*, where Hamm concludes his prayer by denouncing the nonexistence of God: 'The bastard! He doesn't exist!' (*Eg*, 119). Far from being a provocation, the insult provides the only form of punctuation and 'signifying looping' the characters have at their disposal: a bitter statement of failure. As Lacan notes, the insult is 'of dialogue, the first word as it is the last' (2001, 487): it contains the same mortifying injunctive force as the *you*, rendered equivocal in the French *tu es/tuer*[27] (you are/to kill). It also offers an anchoring

27 See *supra*, p. 104.

point, whereby the subject frees himself from an invasive Other, in order for an eventual dialogue to take place. Jean-Claude Milner emphasises the dehumanising mechanism of the insult: 'Far from [the subject's] singularity as such being aimed at, it is only seized at the point where it is absorbed into a multiplicity that effaces it' (2007, 100). For the character of *Rough for Radio I*, the insult serves as the only possible way to palliate the void, by the violent rejection of the other, reduced to a mute object. His insults seem to enter into resonance with the sound of the telephone; the auditor actually hears, by contrast with the dying sound of the radio: '*Sound of receiver put down violently. Pause. Click*' (RR *I*, 270). Like the click of the receiver, the insult marks the point of an impossible: the absence of a reply, the radical divide that nothing can attenuate for the character. The final absence is that of sound ending, of a gaping hole, wherein the character risks falling and becoming inexistent, as Marjorie Perloff (1999) seems to suggest, in relation to *Embers*: '[…] if there is really no sound, the listener must assume that the receiver isn't working, that there is either failure in the particular channel of transmission or a mechanical failure that has somehow turned off the set.' That is to say, an impossibility of silencing the incessant and *inaudible voice*.

Between Words and Music

If Words and Music represent two sides of the *voice*, it is necessary to look more closely at the relationship between these two aspects in the three radio plays—*Rough for Radio I*, *Cascando* and *Words and Music*—that make use of these two elements.

Words and Music—written in November–December 1961 (Knowlson, 1997, 497), just before *Cascando*—represents two sides of the voice in the form of characters. Pascale Alexandre-Bergues (765) sees this personification as a technical challenge resembling that of Jean Tardieu, 'who had staged a Monsieur Mot [Mr Word] and a Madame Parole [Mrs Speech] in *L'ABC de notre vie*, a performance poem first produced in May 1959'. This choice does have drawbacks. For example, it imposes the necessity for the text to activate the register of meaning, without being able to guarantee a comprehensible execution. The same applies to the stage directions referring to the music: '*Discreet suggestion for following.* [...] *More confident suggestion for following*' (*WM*, 293). And yet it seems that the triangle composed by Croak, Joe and Bob can appear less convincing than the radio set in *Rough for Radio I* and *Cascando*. Indeed, the personification of Words and Music suggests that the characters are united within a homogenous space, whereas the intermediary of the radio set, in the other plays, allows the voice to be understood directly as emanating from another space, as a heterogeneous element: the listener discovers a subject confronted with the enigma of these voices that come to him, and that he attempts to regulate.

In *Words and Music*, Words is presented as loquacious, characterised by his use of hollow formulæ devoid of any subjective impact, somewhat in the manner of Winnie, in her monologue. According to Words, the subject of his discourse is indifferent. Whether he speaks of *sloth* or *love*, he reproduces the same speech: '[...] sloth is the LOVE is the most urgent [...]' (*WM*, 288). Words appears as pure verbosity, containing only a slight part of meaning, but without any expressivity: he conveys the discourse of the Other, as consigned in the repertoires of rhetoric.

Words also represents the trap of meaning, showing that words can deceive, since their meaning is multiple and uncertain; a fact which gives rise to the interrogations: 'Is love the word? [*Pause. Do.*] Is soul the word? [*Pause. Do.*] Do we mean love, when we say love? [*Pause. Pause. Do.*] Soul, when we say soul?' (*WM*, 289). Of course, these questions are also stereotyped, serving to show the inanity of Words' discourse. The terms he uses 's'alignent de façon à s'annuler mutuellement' ('line up so as to mutually annul each other', *MP*, 28), as can be particularly noticed in the repetition of the vocable *love*. These rhetorical questions reveal above all a hollow discourse.

If Words rejects Music, it is because he demands the 'light' of the discursive realm. He immediately objects to Music's presence: 'How much longer cooped up here in the dark? [*With loathing.*] With you!' (*WM*, 287). He cannot bear the idea that something might escape the register of meaning, the mastery—which is only apparent—of speech. However, Music obliges him to let go, and to accept the melodic line: '*Trying to sing this*' (290). At this moment, he resorts to the versified form, manifesting his lyrical capacity. He nonetheless also falls back into the discursive register, as can be heard in this contrast between the two characters: 'MUSIC: *Warm suggestion from above for above.* / WORDS: [*Disregarding, cold.*]' (291). What follows is discursive, explicative, rather than lyrical: 'WORDS [*Gently expostulatory.*]' (292). Finally, Words ends up by espousing the register of music: 'All dark no begging / No giving no words / No sense no need' (294). Here, Words adopts the register of the *voice*, as a state situated beyond truth. Such is also the effect produced in the end. Words, feeling alone, turns to Music and begs: '[*Imploring.*] [...] Again. [*Pause. Imploring.*] Again!' Like the 'sound director' Croak before him, he seeks to feel the effect of the music, and the last sound he produces is no longer of a discursive order: '*Deep sigh.*'

In reality, the darkness—'dark' (*WM*, 287)—is also that of the radio: however unwillingly, Words is also voice, firstly because of the absence of meaning he makes manifest, but also because the auditor hears him through the radio medium.

As the arrangement of *Words and Music* suggests, Words and Music form a 'pseudocouple' composed of two 'characters' who, being radically heterogeneous, cannot merge into one. Rosemary Pountney (62) notes that the appearance of the woman's face 'is the catalyst that unites Croak's two themes and brings about the union of Words and Music'. However, Croak remains powerless to recover the lost opportunity: he cannot return to the 'woman lost' and, as Marjorie Perloff points out, he is 'prey to the torment inflicted by his own "words" and "music"' (2007, 171), which he is unable to control. She adds, regarding the tone of the play, that 'Yeats's epic image—a "woman Homer sung"—has become, in the Beckettian universe of the late twentieth-century, a figure of mock-heroic proportions, no more than the subject of a contest between Words and Music, which the latter wins' (172). Words and Music can only, through the incommensurable distance that separates them, achieve an agreement, in order to let the auditor hear 'the music of the spheres', as evoked in *Cascando*: 'From one world to another, it's as though they drew together' (*Cas*, 301) ('D'un astre à l'autre, on dirait qu'ils tombent d'accord', *Cas*, 55). The French word *accord* can mean both 'agreement' or a 'chord' in music. In this play, Opener succeeds—if only temporarily—in achieving a certain unity: 'As though they had linked their arms' (*Cas*, 303). In this sentence, Voice and Music create a new image, that of the *outing*. It is perhaps possible to see a link with the two walkers, evoked in *Le Monde et le pantalon* (*MP*, 25), who leave together from porte de Chatillon, and whose paths never cease to part. This association would appear consistent with Beckett's refusal to envisage a union that might abolish the separation inherent in his experience of language. Catherine Laws points out, regarding *Words and Music*:

> The words are not 'transformed' *into* music; the most that can be said is that Words seems to need Music's help, and that Beckett implies that the expressive power of language increases when Words follows the lead of Music and the two are heard together. (Laws, 2013, 325)

She also indicates that the music Morton Feldman wrote for the play 'suggests the impossibility of stable roles of leader and follower, or of the words and music ever truly coming together' (339).

It is well known that in the artistic field, the question concerning the relative superiority of words and music has been debated for centuries (*cf.* Ackerley, 2011, 67–8). In *Cascando*, Voice—who represents the musicality of *words*—manifests a very different character from that of Words, in *Words and Music*. Ruby Cohn notes that he 'has two strands—self and story' (272). That is to say that Voice attempts to elaborate a narrative. It is borne by *enunciation*, by the anticipatory movement and the fragmentation engendered by the signifier in its differential dimension: '—story… if you could finish it… you could rest… sleep… not before…' (*Cas*, 297). The text's fragmentation expresses urgency, the impossibility of attaining a final punctuation that would allow Voice to compose an utterance bearing a clear meaning: like narrators in earlier works (*The Unnamable*, for example), Voice seeks to find—or to 'hit[] on' (*TFN* VIII, 133)—the right word. It thus suffers the torment of language that supposes the vital necessity of following the metonymical chain of signifiers, in the hope of arriving at a final punctuation. What Voice represents is therefore the opposite of the Beckettian 'reading voice' or bedtime story:

> —story… if you could finish it… you could rest… sleep… not before… oh I know… the ones I've finished… thousands and one… all I ever did… in this life… with my life… saying to myself… finish this one… it's the right one… then rest… sleep… no more stories… no more words… (*Cas*, 297)

This result is inaccessible to Voice, because the anticipatory movement leads, with each fragmentary utterance, to a gaping hole whereby language never ceases to escape him: no word, no name, can ever endow the signifying chain with enclosure.

The importance of this voice for Opener can be understood: the French name *Maunu* can be declined as *mot-nu* (naked word) or *maux-nus*, which Ruby Cohn translates as 'naked miseries' (272). The name *Woburn*, in the English version, evokes *woe*, and also the idea *burn*,[28] which may express the urgency that inhabits the character. Rosemary Pountney points out that in the drafts, he was designated as 'the guilty one' (122). The following remark may be read in the same perspective:

---

28 However, a dictionary furnishes the following explanation for the patronymic: 'This ancient name is of Anglo-Saxon origin, and is one of the earliest topographical surnames existing today. The derivation is from the Old English pre 7th Century "burna, burne", spring, stream, which was originally used as a topographic name for someone who lived beside a stream.' (<http://www.surnamedb.com/Surname/Burn>).

> Like *Embers*, *Cascando* contains Beckett's first rethinking for performance of formal techniques originally cultivated in his stories and novels. Voice's relationship to his subject (read: surrogate self), for instance, is the same as Jacques Moran's in *Molloy*, E's in *Film*, and the spotlight's in *Play*, one of pursuit; Worburn is as much chased as described. (Kalb, 2007, 133)

In each of these examples, the character contemplates his *alter ego*, who experiences the torment of endless speech.

In *Words and Music*, Music evokes a completely different dimension, thus justifying the contrast between these two agents. It fully testifies to the destruction of meaning as expressed, for example, in *Murphy*, where Celia reflects about the eponymous hero: '[…] each word obliterated, before it had time to make sense, by the word that came next so that in the end she did not know what had been said. It was like difficult music heard for the first time' (*Mu*, 28). Beckett asserts that *Words and Music* 'ends unequivocally with the victory of music' (in Ackerley and Gontarski, 561), thus following Schopenhauer's judgement in this field (Frost, 259). Not all critics share this opinion. Of course, Pascale Alexandre-Bergues asserts, about the idea of harmony: 'The latter appears in the play as a utopian ideal, if not an illusion. Words has great difficulty following Music in the two songs he composes and, in the combat that opposes them, it is he who finally seems vanquished […]' (765). But Chris Ackerley objects: 'The challenge facing the composer is to construct a score capable of transcending the erotic libretto. This seems not to have been achieved; […] the music cannot sublimate the eroticism of the poetry' (2011, 72). Everett Frost states that '*both* words and music […] are "catalytic" in the presence of each other. They achieve something that neither could have achieved on their own' (262). The opposition between the two is insoluble for structural reasons, and it is this unresolvable quality that Beckett's work as a whole explores and puts to the test. As regards music, Beckett did indeed see music as an ideal form of art, as Catherine Laws points out in relation to his reading of Schopenhauer and Proust:

> Beckett's negative bias results in part from the elevation of music to a position of metaphysical otherness; his pessimistic presentation of themes arises from his doubting the validity of a literary art that takes worldly experience as its material but aspires towards a state of music. (Laws, 2013, 59)

And yet, it is patent that Beckett chose to work primarily with language, not with music as a composer. Instead of settling this question, it is necessary to take into account the perspective that will situate both aspects in their relationship to language.

According to one perception, speech tends to draw the voice within the enclosure of nomination and meaning, thus reducing the impact of *jouissance*: such is the function that Lacan ascribed, in his early teachings, to the symbolic register. Thus, the *voice* properly speaking remains dissimulated behind the discursive. However, there is also a register where this *jouissance* continues to penetrate speech, that is encountered, for example, in the autistic subject's experience of what Lacan called *lalangue*:[29]

> [...] his relationship to signifying 'moteriality' hinders him from moving towards meaning. Since, to find the effect of meaning in language, it is necessary for the value of *jouissance* of the 'sound' object to have fallen. In autism, we have a coalescence of sound and words that maintains, without any loss, the wordy *jouissance* included in language. (Borie, 79–80)

Music reveals the presence of the *a* object, the part that remains refractory to meaning. Contrary to speech, which maintains the differential nature of the *signifier*, and the latter's retroactive mechanism, music is an object. Belonging to the register of the *letter*, it is identical to itself and devoid of interruption: indeed, even the silences are music that 'continues by other means'. However, if music can, occasionally, have a soothing effect, it is because it presents itself as a rampart

29 *Cf. supra*, p. 99 *sqq.*

against the torment of the *unlimited*. Therefore, in the words/music dichotomy, the contrasted reactions of Opener, in *Cascando*, can be observed. On the one hand, confronted with speech, he exclaims: 'OPENER: [*With* VOICE.] Come on! Come on!' (*Cas*, 302). On the other hand, confronted with music, he sighs: 'OPENER: [*With* MUSIC.] God' (303). The same alternation appears in *Rough for Radio I*: 'HE: [*With* MUSIC.] Good God!' (*RR I*, 270); 'HE: [*With* VOICE. *Shrill.*] Come on! Come on!' Thus, in *Cascando*, Opener's exhortation expresses the wish that Woburn may arrive at his destination; however, his sigh is associated with the idea of the divinity, as designated in many of Beckett's texts. Precisely, the existence of God is both evoked—like Hamm as a child, who cried in the dark for his parents to come (*Eg*, 119)—and constantly called into doubt, in accordance with Beckett's æsthetics of indeterminacy, and according to which the nonexistence of the Other is posited simultaneously with the idea of his existence.

One aspect of the writing of *Rough for Radio I* and *Cascando* requires attention: the transcription of music in the form of written symbols. This polarity of words and musical signs can be traced back to *Dream of Fair to middling Women*—albeit in quite a different perspective—where Beckett quotes an extract from the score of Beethoven's Seventh Symphony (Laws, 2013, 93–6). Admittedly, in *Words and Music*, in the absence of speech, the role of Music is indicated by annotations concerning his action and attitude: '*Suggestion for following*' (*WM*, 290); '*Interrupts with improvement of this and brief suggestion.*' These indications are important insofar as they support Music's personification. Nonetheless, Music cannot be associated with speech, or spoken words, a fact that reduces his presence in the written text. In *Rough for Radio I*, the music appears as the notation of a dotted line (......), not as a musical score. In the French version of *Cascando*, Music's interventions are indicated by series of discontinuous dashes (—). These symbols indicate the part that belongs to the voice: the sounds the character listens to. It is significant that Beckett indicates, prior to any form of content (musical work, a text to deliver), the fact that what is in question here is the *voice* as *writing*.

Michel Protin (2013) has pointed out that, when it comes to stage directions in particular, certain theatrical texts (*Quad*, notably) present Beckett's notation as pure writing. That is to say, they give indications for the execution or, in the case of the radio plays, they only inscribe the *place of execution*, instead of 'being' this artistic form itself.[30] The text thus gives us writing, a trace devoid of content: it offers another way of designating the voice as invisible, indescribable. François Nicolas stresses this relationship between music and writing:

> It appears that the primordial letter in music is that of the *duration of silence* [...]. The scar in the note—because of the fact that musical thought exists—is thus the letter of silence; which leads us to say that the scar of the note is a crochet rest [...] rather than a *pause* [...]. (Nicolas, 5)

Thus, writing is considered as *ex nihilo* musical structuring, 'working from the void of the score and not from the infinite of sound material' (6). In this sense:

> *Writing* thus names what institutes music as a thought, insofar as writing names the fact that music works from the void (of silence) and not from sound. [...] Or: *writing* is what holds-together-as-one an unbridgeable gap between void and infinity, between silence and sound. (Nicolas, 6)

As Beckett writes, in *Worstward Ho*: 'Blanks for when words gone. When nohow on' (*WH*, 99); or elsewhere, regarding Rimbaud and Beethoven: 'The terms of whose statements serve merely to delimit the reality of insane areas of silence, whose audibilities are no more

30 This may be one reason why, as Catherine Laws indicates, 'the play seems to proceed as if its [Music's] role is clear and understood. [...] music in this play seems to be treated as if it will sound and mean the same in any realisation; as if it exists as a pure idea [...]' (2013, 328; originally: 2001, 279).

than punctuation in a statement of silences' (*DF*, 102). The blanks are *inscribed*, they mark the presence of the voice. This recalls Beckett's idea of devoting a play to Beethoven deaf, and in which it would simply be a matter of 'making heard the absence of a voice' (Bernold, 53), a dialogue where only the part of one of the interlocutors would be legible. That is to say that the voice would have been presented as an absence. Thus, the voice is related to writing, to the *letter*, which is identical to itself. In the same way as music emerges from silence, *the voice is, above all, silence*, not an aural phenomenon. In the same way as the dotted line escapes meaning, the voice manifests itself where the signifier goes beyond the latter. The written sign—dot or dash—remains what marks silence, the emergence of the *voice*.

It is for this reason that voice, radio and silence all belong to what escapes any resemblance. Thus, in *Cascando*, Opener declares: 'They say, It's his own, it's his voice, it's in his head.' (*Cas*, 302); 'No resemblance. / I answered, And that…' Voice and silence escape any form of resemblance, since they abolish the imaginary. It is for this reason that Beckett could assert 'Music always wins' (in Worth, 137). It should be added, however, that Beckett never ceased to leave such a triumph unresolved: voice and silence maintain a tension devoid of any resolution. The complexity of the relationship between language, music and written signs is underscored by Morton Feldman when he explains the task of composing the score for *Words and Music*. He notes that Beckett 'is thinking of music all the time' (in Laws, 2013, 341). What however is revealed is that without authoring the score, Beckett was indeed working in relation to what he wished to be heard: 'He was actually writing the music.' According to Feldman's testimony, Beckett's written text thus aimed at circumscribing the place to be occupied by music: the site of the latter is marked by the dots and dashes.

In *Rough for Radio I*, voice and music emanate from the same appliance. The visitor asks: 'Are they… subject to the same… conditions?' (*RR I*, 269). However, they remain heterogeneous, being like two parallel lines that never join up: 'They are not together? / No' (268). Voice and music can only come together in a simultaneity devoid of any resolution. This absence of a synthesis is both the result of an absolute and non-dialectical rupture, and a structural opposition, as can be understood by means of the *équivoque* in the French version, and absent in the English: 'Ils ne peuvent pas s'entendre? / Non' (*ER*, 91). In its reciprocal interpretation, the pronominal verb *s'entendre* has two meanings: 'to hear each other' or 'to get on together'. It thus expresses both the way in which the voice approaches the inaudible, and the absence of any address that might allow the two forms of the voice to enter into a dialectic.

In *Rough for Radio I*, the voices only meet up in silence, in death: 'they're together... [...] like... [...] ...one...' (*RR I*, 271); '*Together, failing.*'; 'meet?... how could they meet?... what?... what are all alike?... last what? ... gasps?' (271); 'the breathing... I don't know...' The image of respiration—or what engenders this impression—serves to express their proximity one to another.

The two facets of the voice also unite in the division between death and birth. The voice's 'death' occurs at the same time as the birth. The doctor was to come 'in an hour' (*RR I*, 271), but his secretary calls to say there are 'two confinements', so he has to put off his visit until tomorrow. This idea sheds another light on the utterance: 'what are alike?... last what?... gasps?...': not only are last gasps all alike, but they can also resemble the cries of a new-born baby.

Instead of being inscribed in a reassuring cycle, this encounter between death and birth dramatically reinforces the character's solitude: he has to get by without the doctor's presence; he is excluded from the succession of generations. He no longer has the possibility of passing—as in a weaving movement—between Voice and Music, to situate himself in reference to one and the other. The man finds himself abandoned: the voices die together. Indeed, birth implies paternity, confronting the character with the absence of a paternal metaphor (as described in the *explicit* of *First Love*). Birth also leaves the character in the presence of the *unlimited*, deprived of any means to face up to it. Precisely, the announcement of the birth inscribes the absence of a doctor, of a metaphorical Other. All that is left is a promise: 'Tomorrow... noon...' (*RR I*, 271). At this moment, the man finds himself truly alone. Then, the voice also dies: the word *whisper* (just before the man's final words) follows the passage: '[*Low.*]... there's more... they're together... TOGETHER...' The character speaks loudly when he attempts to provoke the Other, but he whispers when he moves closer to the voices. Thus, the latter fade into silence and solitude. When the radio falls silent, the insatiable *voice* reaches extinction: it attains the silent movement of writing.

The use of technology in Beckett's works for the radio and the television is particularly revealing of the voice's relation to the real, allowing it to escape fictional evocation, and its reliance on the written word. The reader of Beckett's fiction could content himself with considering the voice as an attractive or vivid metaphor for language, or relegate it to the realm of style (writing marked by 'interruptions', for example). It is true that the theatre imposes the constraints of performance which may give the voice more impact, since the musicality of the text requires to be tested in live situations that show up unforeseen aspects of what may have originally appeared conclusive on the written page. Indeed, this reality led Beckett to revise and modify his texts according to the theatrical space and the actors involved. Technology goes beyond such effects of framing by the act of performance, however decisive they may be. It introduces a far more radical estrangement of the voice object: it demonstrates and makes palpable the fact that the voice does not belong to a subject—as a tool or as an attribute of his psychology or body—but is experienced as a foreign body that intrudes on him, that infiltrates his intimacy. As a product of science, technology places the subject in the presence of an *unlimited* dimension that can never be tamed or assimilated. It is however in this dispossession that the Beckettian subject most firmly recognises his existence. The use of the sound appliance thus becomes a key device to approach and deal with his voices.

Some of the plays we have just studied—such as *Play* and *What Where*—rely on apparently geometrical arrangements that cannot be limited to the specific function of the 'sound editor', who alternates between sound sources. These figures—which we have occasionally represented in the form of diagrams—appear to be ascribed the role of structuring discourse, thus offering another way of dealing with the voice. This aspect requires particular attention.

2. Discursive Apparatus

The recorded voice, emanating from a mechanical or electrical device, belongs intrinsically to the place Beckett ascribes to the discourse of the Other, which it is impossible for the subject to assimilate. However the recourse to a device destined to give form to the voice is not limited to the use of technology. In this chapter, we shall study the use Beckett makes of geometrical setups, which we compare to what Lacan defined—in what he calls 'four discourses'—as the material conditions for social bonds. The artificial nature of what appears, in Beckett's work, as specifically subjective structures, rests on the coordination of four functions or roles—including, for example, that of 'witness' and 'scribe'—and aims at engendering a discourse. The voice here does not appear as the incessant and invasive one encountered in *The Unnamable* or *Not I*, for example, neither is it the completely disembodied one produced by the radio. The structures studied here take the form of a 'system' destined to circumscribe the voice and contain it. If the linguistic organisation of pronouns, examined earlier, manifested an absence of cohesion, the recourse to 'apparatuses' seems to be presented as a response, as an effort to create a substitute form capable of functioning.

After defining these structures, and seeing their presence in Beckett's work, it will be necessary to return to the notion of *inscription*, considered as a material operation, but this time in relation to the effect of language as 'torture': as the action whereby words anchor themselves in the flesh. If the voice is often a source of torment, this suffering is irremediably a part of language.

Here, the notion of the *unary trait* (Freud's *Einziger Zug*) will prove important. Lacan defines it as the subject, insofar as the latter 'is constituted secondarily in relation to the signifier' (1973, 129). He illustrates this point as follows:

> The first signifier is the notch, which marks, for example, that the subject has killed *one* beast [meaning: an extraction of *jouissance*], thanks to which, he will not get mixed up in his memory when he has killed ten others. He will not have to remember which is which, and it is proceeding from this unary mark that he will count them. (Lacan, 1973, 129)

As indicated earlier, a signifier 'only signifies insofar as it is different from any other signifier, including itself' (Bruno, 96). Thus the *unary trait*, as evidenced by Mouth's exemplification of the *drive*[31], has no complementary signifier to situate it within any sequence (S_1–S_2). Comparable to what Hélène Cixous calls Beckett's *zero* (18), this '*one* one' (Lacan, 1973, 129) lays the conditions for the actual number *one* to open the series of numbers.

By achieving an inscription, through apparently behaviourist methods, the subject succeeds in physically circumscribing and locating the voice, instead of succumbing to the abolition of all subjectivity. This construction also rests on the supposed existence of an absent 'Master', who appears to be motivated by the will to grasp some form of knowledge regarding his own unknown.

While such action seems brutal, it occupies a marginal position, since it reveals, on its reverse side, the way the subject escapes all efforts to succumb to complete abolition. The apparatus thus appears as destined to highlight its own point of failure.

Discursive Structures

A number of Beckett's works evoke a veritable sort of apparatus, whose components are articulated in a form of structuring comparable to the one Lacan elaborated in his Seminar *L'Envers de la psychanalyse* (1969–1970), in the 'four discourses'—that of the 'master', the 'university', the 'hysteric', and 'psychoanalysis'—working from Freud's 1925 classification of three impossible tasks: to educate, to

31 See our analysis *supra*, p. 120 *sqq*, and the account of Lacan's reference to Japanese calligraphy, p. 137.

govern and to psychoanalyse.[32] To these can be added the 'discourse of capitalism', which marks the *unlimited* dimension of our postmodern world—its absence of any breach or outside (any 'anti-capitalism' simply promotes another form of capitalism)—and where new objects of consumption are perpetually produced in order to fill in any lack, thus hindering the subject from questioning himself as to his own singularity. Analysing the universal misunderstanding surrounding Marx's famous sentence 'Religion is the opium of the people', Jean-Claude Milner (2014, 83–105) shows one comparable effect on language, when the fourfold structure composing the figure of proportional analogy ('2 is to 4 what 3 is to 6') collapses, so that each of the four terms communicate indifferently. This produces the facile—but disastrously efficient—rhetoric of modern political discourse. Suzanne Dow (15) speculates that 'had Lacan pushed his reading of Beckett further back in 1968, he might perhaps have come to theorise the discourse of the analyst a little sooner than he actually does'. In accordance with Lacan's principle that a 'quadripartite structure is always a requisite in the construction of a subjective organisation [*ordonnance*]' (Lacan, 1966, 774), these discourses represent logical constructions composed of four positions, among which four terms permute, thus defining the particular discourse in question. Insofar as they determine the four possible types of social bonds and the conditions productive of speech, these discourses function according to the model of the fundamental fantasy, designating and integrating the lack, via the *a* object. If these structures are thus unmasked in Lacan's teaching, it is a consequence of the decline of the paternal metaphor: the fact that the symbolic register has proven to be no longer adequate to deal with the *pastout* or the *unlimited.* Henceforth, the Name-of-the-Father and the symbolic register can only be considered as *semblances,* situated within a context of generalised relativity. In Beckett's work therefore, bringing such a framework into the open and the necessity

32 In his preface to August Aichhorn's work *Verwahrloste Jugend* ('Wayward Youth'). Instead of *psychoanalyse*, the word originally used was *to heal.* Lacan takes up this question in 1970, in 'Radiophonie' (2001, p. 443–6).

of conceiving such an apparatus, results directly from the *unlimited* nature of the voice, and of the signifier that imposes itself in relation to the real. It is therefore a form of *substitute* (*suppléance*), in the absence of an agent that, in the manner of the paternal metaphor, could shelter the subject from the unbearable.

In an earlier study, we situated (2008, 141–4) the figures of 'scribe' and the 'witness', in *How It Is*, within such a discursive framework. Russell Smith associates this model with the figure of Dante who, as a scribe, notes down the words of Virgil, the latter speaking in the place of the damned who are devoid of articulated speech (2008, 353–4). In this respect, Smith observes that Virgil serves as guarantor of 'a unitary truth' (354) that disappears in *How It Is*. Indeed, in this text, two failures are apparent: the indistinction of the *I*, and the constantly fragmented speech (356).

The presence of these constructions in Beckett's work manifestly originates in the radical split between the subject and his voices, which Iain Bailey (148–9) associates with the function of scribe presented by the Biblical image in *The Unnamable*: 'I am Matthew and I am the angel' (*U*, 295). He sees the origin of this structure in the abandoned text 'On le tortura bien', contained in the second *Textes pour rien* notebook, and traces its presence through various divided figures or 'pseudocouples'. He observes that 'the "scribe" of later works is abstracted and repeated, like the Marxian capitalist or wage-labourer: generic identities that correspond to a function' (149). Stéphanie Ravez sees a form of masochism in the repeated scenes where the passive ego is assailed by a tormentor (2011, 625), a perception that stands in a marked contrast with Alain Badiou's notion of *How It Is* as offering, in its sadistic encounters, wonderful discoveries of the 'Other', and the evocation of 'alterity' (2003, 16). Éric Wessler's analyses (2009) open up this field in a singularly coherent manner within the perspective of Beckett's particularly complex practice of 'self-reflexivity'[33]

33 '[...] self-reflexivity, that is to say the immanent commentary of the work's form, allows to establish with certainty irony as consubstantial to

whereby—through emblematic figures of the writer, the use of specular structures and irony—literature reflects the conditions of its coming to being and, by the same token, the way subjectivity is structured. This notion will be studied more precisely in order to situate the general importance of discursive structures. Michel Bousseyroux establishes a contrast between Lacan's 'discourse of psychoanalysis', and the geometrical figure—a square with two diagonal lines—traced by the circulating figures in *Quad*. By excluding one of the two diagonals, Lacan's diagram marks the 'suspension of that which, of the real, remains *in abeyance of being written*' (Bousseyroux, 2000, 188). Beckett's square diagram, on the other hand, reveals the *impossible* through exhaustion of the *possible*, as a result of the 'discourse of the master'.

The System of the MMM

One of the first expressions of Beckett's prosthetic device can be found in *Murphy*, written in English in 1935–1936. In the psychiatric institution called the Magdalen Mental Mercyseat ('MMM'), a nurse does rounds to check on the patients confined in their cells. In passing, he switches on the light and, having looked through the judas, he presses the 'indicator' (*Mu*, 148), in order to inform Bom, the supervisor. The latter device functions as follows: 'The indicator recorded the visit, together with the hours, minutes and seconds at which it was paid, on a switchboard in Bom's apartment.'

Of course, this system can be replaced in its historical context: Chris Ackerley indicates that Beckett mentioned this procedure in his *Whoroscope* Notebook; but he also adds that 'there was such a system at the Bethlehem Royal Hospital, in effect a model of a neurological stimulus-response system' (Ackerley, 2010, 189).

On this point, it is worth remarking the suffering inflicted on the patients by the light, a motif also present in *Play*. Thus: 'The nurse had merely to depress a switch before each door, flooding the cell with light of such ferocity that the eyes of the sleeping and waking opened

the concept of literature and, in a general manner, of representation' (Wessler, 2009, 231).

and closed respectively [...]' (*Mu*, 148). This light is the same as the 'blaze of hellish light' (*HD*, 140) that torments Winnie. In the part of the novel dealing with the psychiatric hospital, Beckett undertakes a scathing criticism of the manner in which such institutions deal with mental suffering. However, the origin of such a system—in the psychological theory oriented by a conception of conditioning (resulting from what Lacan calls the 'discourse of the master')—also suggests the necessity to address the question of language and the voice.

The system used at the MMM depends upon a prosthetic setup composed of four terms: the patient, the nurse, the indicator and, finally, Bom. Each of these elements has a precise function in a discursive structure that can be described as follows:

nurse (light)	>	indicator (inscription)
patient (in his cell)	//	Bom (switchboard in his apartment)

The members situated outside the manifest chain, or who appear to be inactive, are inscribed under the bar: the patient—who suffers the intrusion—and Bom, who observes the result. The inscription that confirms the reality of the visit is achieved by means of the nurse who, firstly, floods the cell with light and observes the patient, then presses the indicator. That is to say that on the upper level, besides the fact of physical movement, also appears a discursive chain that obeys a metonymical cause/effect mechanism. On the lower level, however, appear two terms that remain static, and fundamentally separated. Indeed, this whole mechanism is intended to provide Bom with the information he seeks about the patient (and which is reduced to its simplest expression, since it is a matter of ascertaining that the latter is not causing any problems), who represents the unknown factor in this equation. That is to say, what is important to grasp is what is at stake on the side of the question Bom asks (without really inquiring, since he remains inactive and at a distance, sheltered in his apartment, behind his switchboard) about the patient. However, an incommensurable gap can be noticed between these two terms: the result of the inscription will never reveal the slightest 'truth' about the patient.

Structurally, the latter designates an *impossible*, the importance of which comes to the fore as a result of a systematic malfunctioning. The narrator notes, ironically, the idea that the efficiency of this system could have been improved by a more economical mechanism:

> The indicator would have been still more ingenious if it had been activated by the light switch, or even by the judas shutter. For many and many were the visits recorded for Bom's inspection, and never paid, by nurses who were tired or indolent or sensitive or fed up or malicious or behind time or unwilling to shatter a patient's repose. (*Mu*, 148)

In this system that appears to be regulated like a machine, the intervention of a human element impedes any perfectly adequate inscription. The recourse to such a mechanism thus indicates the absence of a pacifying structuring, a fact highlighted by the element of chance or caprice that remains incalculable, escaping any recording. The excessively mechanistic nature of this system of surveillance appears to be a woefully inadequate response intended to deal with the voice as *pas-tout* or *unlimited.*

Circumscribing the Subject's Unknown: 'Molloy'

In *Murphy*, the discursive apparatus appears in the context of the protagonist's search to cut himself off from the 'big world' (*Mu*, 112), and to confine himself within the 'little world' of the asylum: absolute constraint supposedly giving him access to absolute liberty. By contrast, *Molloy* would seem to open up 'traversable space' (*TFN* III, 111) by its use of the quest structure, based on the idea of an autonomous hero. However, this construction is undercut both by the circularity of the protagonists' movement, and by their nature as doubles (Brown, 2015). Molloy is apparently now (in the first pages of the novel) in his mother's room, but his journey leaves him lying in a ditch.

Moran leaves the comfort of his home and ends up in a state similar to that of Molloy. Ruby Cohn observes: 'The second quest shades the first, and each tale loops back to its beginning' (2001, 161–2). If these characters' many points of resemblance are well established (Moorjani, 1976; Ackerley and Gontarski; Connor, 2007), their status as doubles is not univocal, since they compose a chain: Moran has been sent to compose a report on the eponymous hero who, in turn, hopes to settle the question of his mother, who remains absent.

Thus, behind the *fable* of this novel lies the subjective question of writing, which appears as the result of a *voice*: it is this aspect that sets the story into perspective, and causes its ruin. Molloy and Moran both experience the capricious nature of the voice, which causes words to come and go without warning. Molloy observes: 'Yes, these imperatives were quite explicit and even detailed until, having set me in motion at last, they began to falter, then went silent, leaving me there like a fool who neither knows where he is going nor why he is going there' (*Mo*, 81). Moran encounters the same problem: 'And when it ceases, leaving me in doubt and darkness, I shall wait for it to come back, and do nothing [...]' (126).

The necessity of writing intervenes as an imperative, as an order emanating from without and that imposes itself on the characters. Thus, Molloy evokes the visits of a man: 'He gives me money and takes away the pages. [...] When he comes for the fresh pages he brings back the previous week's. They're marked with signs I don't understand. Anyway I don't read them' (*Mo*, 3). The visitor represents the agent of a superego, informing the subject that his production does not fit in with what is required by the master. This demand, however, remains undecipherable: 'It was he told me I'd begun all wrong, that I should have begun differently' (4). What makes these exigencies opaque and disquieting is that the subject has no definable interlocutor: none he could question to obtain further details.

Throughout his part of the novel, Moran has the task of writing. He explicitly states the function of the voice, towards the end:

> And if I submit to this paltry scrivening which is not of my province, it is for reasons very different from those that might be supposed. I am still obeying orders, if you like, but no longer out of fear. […] For it [the voice] is within me and exhorts me to continue to the end the faithful servant I have always been of a cause that is not mine, and patiently fulfil in all its bitterness my calamitous part […]. (*Mo*, 126)

Moran describes himself as a simple executor, not as one who writes from his own invention: he obeys a voice, because he possesses no means to transform it into a subjective function, in order to formulate his own utterances. The dimension of exteriority expresses the fact that the subject feels powerless to determine the part he could take in this writing, that he nonetheless feels to be necessary.

The apparently indeterminate appearance of the narration—its seemingly disorderly and metonymical unfolding—finds its structuring aspect in the discursive apparatus that confirms the unity between the novel's two parts. Contradicting the notion of an autonomous hero, the discursive structure reveals what one is *subjected to*, in relation to the Other, a fact that causes the involution of the two quests. Indeed, in his 'inquiry' about Molloy, Moran's writing is part of a structure similar to the one encountered in *Murphy*. Firstly, the events of the novel have an entirely subjective status and, as Elizabeth Barry notes, the characters 'themselves become simply outward manifestations of inner needs or desires' (2006, 174). Such is, in fact, the nature of the voice, which only addresses the subject. As Moran recognises: 'For who could have spoken to me of Molloy if not myself and to whom if not to myself could I have spoken of him?' (*Mo*, 107). In this sentence, the two characters appear as a 'pseudocouple' whose existence covers up a dimension radically excluded from representation. Indeed, Moran appears to be the part of Molloy that observes himself from the point of view of an ideal determined by the superego. This character who is obsessed by order appears affected, from the outset, by a degradation that influences his entire existence: 'My life was running out, I knew not through what breach' (97); 'And what I saw was more like a crumbling, a frenzied collapsing of all that had always protected me from all I was always condemned to be' (143). It is in these circumstances that he receives 'the order' (87) to undertake his quest for Molloy.

The bond that unites these doubles is instituted by a torsion, whereby the two identities can never meet up and which are therefore rooted in the dimension of the real. This structure can be defined as follows. From the beginning of the novel, Molloy identifies himself with his mother (*Mo*, 3), whose place he occupies in her room. Moran, on the other hand, undertakes his quest to learn something about Molloy, as if the latter required some external agent to study his case. Moran declares: 'I knew then about Molloy, without however knowing much about him' (108). Molloy preserves an inaccessible quality, remaining a subjective construction, from Moran's point of view: 'Between the Molloy I stalked within me thus and the true Molloy, after whom I was so soon to be in full cry, over hill and dale, the resemblance cannot have been great' (110). The English translation adds the adverbial qualification 'within me', which is absent from the French: Molloy is thus related to the 'unborn' twin evoked by Fox (*RR II*, 279; *cf.* Moorjani, 2004a, 178). Consequently, Moran's quest appears to be determined by its structure: it can be understood as the mask of an inaccessible dimension. The inquirer cannot know how he knew Molloy, not simply because the latter is part of himself, but because he represents a part that is fundamentally excluded from any linguistic articulation. This construct can be represented thus:

Molloy	<	Moran
Mother	//	*x*

In this way, a loop is established: something—the *x* that remains excluded from any representation—drives Moran to inquire about Molloy, who is extremely close to his mother. This representation—where Molloy appears as a fallen being and, consequently, partially capable of being apprehended—is all that Moran can grasp with regards to the voice that torments him. It is because of this impossibility of naming the fundamental gaping hole, that the two sides—Molloy/Moran—cannot meet: the two characters' paths never cross each other, and Moran acquires no knowledge about his other.

Faced with this gaping hole, the subject multiplies the agents that intervene in the act of inscription:

> The fact was there were three, no, four Molloys. He that inhabited me, my caricature of same, Gaber's and the man of flesh and blood somewhere awaiting me. To these I would add Youdi's were it not for Gaber's corpse fidelity to the letter of his messages. Bad reasoning. For could it seriously be supposed that Youdi had confided to Gaber all he knew, or thought he knew (all one to Youdi) about his protégé? Assuredly not. (*Mo*, 110)

These 'four Molloys' are nothing but attempts to palliate the impossibility of saying anything about the 'true' Molloy: that is to say, beyond the wandering and degenerate character presented in the first part of the novel, and who remains fundamentally nameless.

If Moran suffers a process of degradation comparable to that of Molloy, it is because he is himself subjected to a superego that declares him to be as degenerate as any of his 'patients' (*Mo*, 132). Indeed, in this prosthetic structuring, the orders come from Youdi: originally called 'le directeur' (Ackerley and Gontarski, 660), and whom Moran refers to as 'the chief' (103). The latter never appears, whence his status as *cause*: the one who gives the impulse to write. As such, Youdi is the name[34] given to this *voice* that persecutes Moran. He can be seen as an avatar of Mr Knott, in *Watt*, of Mr Endon, in *Murphy*, of Godot,

34 While Simon Critchley quotes Martha Nussbaum's interesting interpretation of *Youdi* with *you die*, the association with *Yahveh* (Critchley, 167) is groundless, as its Hebrew consonantal root (YHD) has not the slightest philological or paronymical connection with the tetragram YHVH. However, the link between *Gaber* and the angel ('messenger') *Gabriel* is perfectly coherent (GBR).

or of the 'master' (*U*, 361) in *The Unnamable*, who commands Worm's persecutors. Indeed, if these multiple tormentors belong to language in its *metonymical* dimension, the narrator of *The Unnamable* evokes the place of a 'master' whose function, ideally, should be to bind the whole together; that is to say, who should render possible the second extraction of *jouissance*—or *separation*—leading to the constitution of a *limited whole*, under the aegis of the Name-of-the-Father. Such a function continues to be missing, a fact that the narrator of *L'Innommable* emphasises in mathematical terms: 'Ils seraient x qu'on aurait besoin d'un x-et-unième' ('If they were x, we would need a x plus one', *I*, 132). By its extraction, this *x* would at last found a coherent and *limited whole*.

For want of this operation, the narrator of *The Unnamable* formulates the hypothesis of a 'master' who ordains this action. However, the fact that the latter has no palpable existence makes this supposition risible: '[…] he'd turn out to be a mere high official, we'd end up needing God […]' (*U*, 368). The 'master' embodies the obscure will that is symmetrical to the subject who must come to being. Whereas he is perfectly inaccessible, unknowable, he seems nonetheless convinced of the subject's existence: 'He is there, says the master, somewhere, do as I tell you, bring him before me, he's lacking to my glory' (361). This symmetry of the subject and the 'master' gives rise to the analogy of the former with God: '[…] I alone am immortal, what can you expect, I can't get born […]' (376); '[…] I am alone here, the first and the last […]' (374). Like God, the subject is 'the alpha and the omega'—being situated outside of finite human existence—insofar as only one who is subjected to the 'paternal metaphor' and 'castration' can know death. Éric Wessler notes that in Beckett's work, 'God is always invoked as the ultimate guarantee capable of a stability that could stop the paradoxical self-referential tangling of textual levels' (2009, 361). The solitude evoked by the Unnamable demonstrates that the subject constitutes an *absolute singularity*, situated outside of any series: '[…] I too have the right to be shown impossible' (369). There is nothing other than oneself. Finally, the image of the master also collapses, appearing as an 'everlasting third party' and as a simple fiction, which has no consistency when confronted with the incessant *voice*. This enables Elizabeth Barry to note that although 'Molloy and Moran seem to have antithetical experiences of authority, one submitting to and one administering it' (Barry, 180), even Moran is subjected to an unknown authority, and his quest for power 'is undone not by his failure to adopt the position of the powerful, but by the doubt cast on the whole edifice of power itself'.

In *Molloy*, Gaber is the bearer of a message from Youdi ordering Moran to leave, and then to write. Through his intermediary, the voice addresses the subject exclusively: 'He wants it to be you, God knows why, said Gaber. [...] He said, replied Gaber, that no one could do it but you' (*Mo*, 89–90). That is to say that the voice's powerful injunction is not inscribed within any articulation, nor in the composition of any overall reality. It conveys the imperative force of the pronoun *you*:[35] 'And it must have appeared natural, to me that each agent had his own particular messenger, and to Gaber that each messenger had his own particular agent.'[36] (102). This absence of articulation results in the fragmented annotations brought by this messenger: it is impossible for the subject to assimilate the voice. Granted, Gaber possesses a notebook with inscriptions, but what he consigns to writing has no equivalent in his memory. In the same way as the voice is addressed to a single subject, writing is related to the latter alone; it is thus illegible for others:

> To be undecipherable to all but oneself, dead without knowing it to the meaning of one's instructions and incapable of remembering them for more than a few seconds, these are capacities rarely united

35 *Cf. supra*, p. 145.

36 The fact that the subject finds himself confronted with a single representative of the 'master' confirms his exclusion from the register of language (instituted by the paternal metaphor) by virtue of which he apprehends himself as 'one among others'. The oppressive nature of this structuring is described by Henri Michaux in 'Mon Roi': ' [...] il est bien évident que c'est lui le Roi, et moi son sujet, son unique sujet' ('[...] It is quite obvious that he is the King, and I am his subject, his only subject', 1998, 423).

> in the same individual. No less however was demanded of our messengers. (*Mo*, 102).

The articulation of these different agents can be represented by situating them within the following discursive structure:

Moran	<	Gaber
Molloy	//	Youdi

Youdi, who is the source of the messages, represents the unknown, the voice from which emanates the imperative conveyed to Moran through Gaber, the messenger or scribe. Situated at the end of the chain, Molloy is the one about whom Youdi seeks to obtain knowledge. The whole construction is reversed when Moran has to act as scribe (*Mo*, 126), following the injunctions of the voice: Moran hypothetically addresses to Youdi his story about Molloy: 'A letter from Youdi, in the third person, asking for a report. He will get his report' (169).

However, the entire system ends up by being absorbed once again into the realm of the subject, who remains irremediably alone:

> And, to keep nothing from you, this lucidity was so acute at times that I came even to doubt the existence of Gaber himself. And if I had not hastily sunk back into my darkness I might have gone to the extreme of conjuring away the chief too and regarding myself as solely responsible for my wretched existence. (*Mo*, 102-3)

This solitude is of an absolute nature: the state of the subject without any Other, and to whom the prosthetic structure gives a visage, by means of the writing undertaken by Molloy and Moran.

Inscription as Torture

If *Molloy* evokes, behind the screen of the manifest narration, a discursive setup driven by a threatening injunction, other texts of the same period deal with this voice by describing its impact as a form of physical torture. The latter's inclusion in the prosthetic structuring represents a means to palliate the subject's difficulty finding a representation in language; to ensure a degree of consistency when he is confronted with the *unlimited* that brings the threat of *aphanisis* or fading:[37] when the subject is reduced to the *cut* inscribed by the signifier that represents him. The risk of subjective abolition is, as has already been noted, particularly present both in *The Unnamable* and in *Not I* (Knowlson and Pilling, 197), where the 'character' is reduced to the status of a mouth. The aspiration to consistency is centred on the body, marked by the impact of the signifier.

According to common experience, the body is something an individual *possesses*: this verb emphasises the aspect of exteriority, according to which the subject experiences himself as being distinct from his corporeal representation. Lacan's apologue of the 'mirror stage' demonstrates that the notion of the body conceived of as a whole is anchored in the symbolic Other, and is thus the result of an evacuation of a part of *jouissance* which, otherwise, would submerge the subject. However, if the latter finds himself confronted with the *unlimited*, this possession is radically called into question, since the imaginary then proves to be fragile. The subject finds himself constantly faced with the insatiable *drive*.

The voice has a problematic status here. In the early years of his Seminar, Lacan defined its specificity by contrasting it with the visual register. He emphasised that the ears 'are in the field of the unconscious, the only orifice that cannot be closed' (1973, 178), which means that the signifier imposes itself totally on the subject, to the point of leaving him with no other choice than to express his consent: 'The refusal to hear is a force that no subject, unless he has a special

37 Regarding the subject, Lacan asserts: '[…] if he appears on one side as meaning, produced by the signifier, on the other, he appears as *aphanisis*' (1973, 191). The term *aphanisis* is derived from the works of Ernest Jones. On this question, and the terms *alienation/separation* used in what follows, see *supra*, p. 64.

gymnastic preparation, really has at his disposal. It is precisely in this register that the specific force of discourse is manifested' (1981, 340). It is by invocation or enunciation—'*making oneself heard*' (1973, 178)—that the subject seeks to silence the other.

By contrast with the voice, the advent of the visual register involves '*having oneself seen*' (Lacan, 1973, 178), which 'is indicated by an arrow that really returns back to the subject', allowing the latter to feel his consistency—and his independence—in the gaze of the Other.[38] As Jean-Claude Maleval explains, this calming effect results from a second extraction of *jouissance*—an operation of *separation*—whereby signifiers can support meanings established by convention (192). It is at this stage that the voice can 'cease making itself heard'.

The Unnamable describes the dematerialising effect of the voice. Whereas the body takes on consistency by the localisation of objects, the Unnamable is powerless to situate himself: 'No, I can't move, not yet. One minute in a skull and the next in a belly, strange, and the next nowhere at all' (*U*, 346). It is thus the acephalous *drive* that prevails, reducing the subject to the minimal *cut* line (*trait*) produced by the signifier.[39] In *The Unnamable*, metaphorical equivalents of this *unary trait* can be found in the motifs of the 'partition' or the 'tympanum':

> [...] perhaps that's what I am, the thing that divides the world in two, on the one side the outside, on the other, I'm in the middle, I'm the partition, I've two surfaces and no thickness, perhaps that's what I feel, myself vibrating, I'm the tympanum [...]. (*U*, 376)

The Unnamable experiences himself as being reduced to the representation—imaginary, in this passage—of pure difference: the opposition between one signifier and another.

---

38 The visual as a '*dompte-regard*' ('gaze-tamer'), with regards to the Other, is dealt with in *Seminar XI* (Lacan, 1973, 100), and by Gérard Wajcman (2004).

39 *Cf. supra*, p. 129–30.

As Mladen Dolar points out, the voice is situated at the paradoxical intersection of language and the body (2006, 73): it is both separated from the body, and intimately attached to it, notably through the imperative *superego*[40] which, as Lacan emphasises, marks the subject's relationship to the signifier (1994, 212). Of course, the superego is usually associated with the supremacy of the law, the enforcement of the rules of civilised society. However, such constraints find their foundation—following Freud's *Totem and Taboo*—in the sacrifice of the mythical father of the primitive horde who, as he enjoys all the women, represents an absolute and impossible *jouissance* (Lacan, 2007, 106). Since the pre-eminence of the law is founded precisely on this exception (or repression), it can never be free of it, and the more the law extends its universality, the more it activates the unlimited *jouissance* of the *drive* that demands the abolition of all law and all subjectivity. In *Civilisation and Its Discontents* (1930), Freud shows how the subject interiorises the aggressive drives he would naturally turn towards others. If culture—life in society—demands that the individual renounce his aggressive impulses, this authority is internalised, with the result that 'nothing can be hidden from the superego, not even one's thoughts' (Freud, 2010, 150). Indeed, the more one is virtuous, the more it exerts its severity (151). Freud then makes an extremely powerful statement when he concludes: 'What started with the father [the mythical father, then the superego] finishes with the mass' (160). The effects of the latter have been manifest in 20th Century totalitarian régimes. Thus, in the words of Mladen Dolar, the superego presents itself as 'the Other of the Other' (2006, 100). Far from having a pacifying effect, it appears as an absolute, and commands the subject to *jouir* (enjoy, Lacan, 1975b, 10), that is to say, it orders the subject to submit himself to the displeasure that underlies all pleasure. In the subject's fantasy, it may appear—after a logical reconstruction—in the image of the father who beats the child (Freud 1968), revealing the latter's dependency on this violence in order to exist.

40 For our initial definition of this term, see *supra*, p. 157–8.

Henri Rey-Flaud refers to the example of Dom Louis, in Molière's *Dom Juan*, to illustrate the transformation entailed by the superego with regards to the *unary trait*, pointing out that the subject is originally founded 'at the place of enunciation, the site of the *mute* signifier of *das Ding*, that it is impossible to articulate' (215). However, the superego transforms this signifier, giving it form and substance. The proper noun is then deprived 'of its function as signifier of the disappearance of the subject' (214) to become 'the insignia of the "person", an emblem of the ideal that is embodied in a spotless and faultless lineage and which, for this reason, asserts its mastery on the subject, thus revealing, under the waxen mask of the noble father, the sneering of the superego'. Whereas the subject's absolute singularity is the living refutation of any postulate of continuity, linguistic articulation and social bonds belong to the realm of the *imaginary*, reinforcing the superego that 'presides, like a Commander [*i.e.* the fateful figure that appears at the end of *Dom Juan*], over everything that, between speaking beings, ensures a form of relationship' (Milner, 2007, 12). This continuity can be seen as an absolute—as in Kant's *categorical imperative*—that admits of no exception.[41]

As a result of the superego's intervention, an insatiable violence will be unleashed, as expressed by the narrator of *The Unnamable*:

> They are too hard to please, they ask too much. [...] Let them scourge me without ceasing and evermore, more and more lustily (in view of the habituation factor), in the end I might begin to look as if I had grasped the meaning of life. (*U*, 347)

Throughout this novel, the persecutors seek to force the subject to accept the restrictive character of words and names, with the mortification that they entail. As in *Murphy* and *Molloy*, *The Unnamable* reproduces a combination of the roles of master, tormentor and victim,

41 Throughout *Civilisation and Its Discontents*, Freud thus situates the superego in relation to demands, formulated by culture, that the individual sacrifice his drives in order to live in community.

aiming to cause Worm to 'be born'. However, the tormentors are not all-powerful, and the use of force does not produce convincing results: '[…] they are doing the best they can, with the miserable means at their disposal, a voice, a little light […]' (361). They are reduced to supposing that a subject exists, and that he possesses knowledge that they—insofar as they represent pure language, devoid of any corporeal existence—are incapable of possessing. Indeed, they seek to derive knowledge from the body in order to absorb the Unnamable within language: 'But how can they know he suffers? […] He makes no noise. A little with his whinging perhaps' (360). The unspeakable subject possesses a knowledge that escapes words, and which the tormentors/signifiers strive to catch, in order to enclose him within the network of language.

In order to free himself from this continual torment, the subject may find himself driven to reiterate the mark of the original inscription that situates him in relation to the Other, as is undertaken in the traditional practice of tattooing (Lacan, 1973, 129). Thus, it is in order to continue inscribing this trait that Lemuel, at the end of *Malone Dies*, inflicts suffering on himself. The narrator describes him as being assailed by his voices:

> For when not rooted to the spot in a daze he was to be seen, with heavy, furious reeling tread, stamping up and down for hours on end, gesticulating and ejaculating unintelligible words. Flayed alive by memory, his mind crawling with cobras, not daring to dream or think and powerless not to, his cries were of two kinds, those having no other cause than moral anguish and those, similar in every respect, by means of which he hoped to forestall same. (*MD*, 260)

Lemuel shows himself to be tormented by his voices, whose assaults know no end. They alternately transfix him or drive him to permanent agitation. If his cries are 'unintelligible', it is precisely because the invasion by the voice destroys the consistency of any meaning and articulation. However they are not exclusively the effect of these voices, but are also intended to silence them, to expel the unbearable 'moral anguish'.

The actions inflicted on Lemuel's body have the same function as his cries:

> Physical pain, on the contrary, seemed to help him greatly. And one day rolling up the leg of his trousers, he showed Macmann his shin covered with bruises, scars and abrasions. Then producing smartly a hammer from an inner pocket he dealt himself, right in the middle of his ancient wounds, so violent a blow that he fell down backwards, or perhaps I should say forwards. But the part he struck most readily, with his hammer, was the head, and that is understandable, for it too is a bony part, and sensitive, and difficult to miss, and the seat of all the shit and misery, so you rain blows upon it, with more pleasure than on the leg for example, which never did you any harm, it's only human. (*MD*, 260-1)

To inflict blows on the body does not cause pain—as it would for anyone free of such torments—but, on the contrary, it calms suffering. By beating his body—thus adopting the position of his Other, with regards to his body henceforth reduced to the status of an object—Lemuel succeeds in imposing a limit on the insatiable voices so that, instead of traversing him, they are localised in one part of the body. To reinscribe the *unary trait* thus allows him—but only temporarily—to evacuate *jouissance*. The preference for the head, in this operation, appears as the consequence of the fact that the persecuting voice resounds in the skull, evacuating the subject, who no longer finds any place of refuge capable of placing the voice at a distance. It is as a result of the voice's assaults that the head becomes a 'hell', as the voice tells Joe: 'You know that penny farthing hell you call your mind…' (*EJ*, 362).

The metonymical context in which the torture intervenes is described in *How It Is*. In this text, it is no longer language—represented by evanescent figures—that traverses the subject and makes him suffer, but the narrator and his doubles—forming 'pseudocouples'—who inflict the torture on each other.

One approach used by the narrator is based on speech, and consists in seeking to make Pim play the role of a 'mirror': sketching the evanescent outline of an *I/you* relationship, the possibility of speech addressed to another in order to silence the voice. For the narrator crawling in the mud, the function of his double consists of reporting elements of language and meaning emanating from the world above, in order to obtain an inscription in relation to them: 'that life then said to have been his invented remembered [...] that thing above he gave it to me I made it mine' (*HI*, 72). The idea of what life may be is passed on from one to the other: 'dear Pim come back from the living he got it from another that dog's life [...] I'll give it to another' (72–3). In this manner, the narrator hopes to acquire an identity: 'Bem come to cleave to me where I lay abandoned to give me a name his name to give me a life make me talk of a life said to have been mine above in the light before I fell' (109). The imaginary *other* is intended—as in the identification with the mirror image—to procure a form of signifying retroaction[42] and dialogue: to give the subject a life 'above'—in relation to his symbolic Other—that is to say, an existence that will at last be believable, a fiction that is confirmed by his others. This enterprise is thus diametrically opposed to the Unnamable's violent refusal to be trapped and imprisoned in linguistic identifications.

The narrator hopes that with the aid of Pim, he will succeed in circumscribing the *voice* as a rigorously external phenomenon. This attempt fails, however: 'if he heard a voice if only that if he had ever heard a voice voices [...] the voices no knowing surely not' (*HI*, 74). This failure is followed by relapse into confusion: 'I talk like him Bom will talk like me only one kind of talk here one after another the voice said so it talks like us the voice of us all quaqua on all sides then in us when the panting stops bits and scraps that's where we get it our old talk' (76).

---

42 See *supra*, p. 61–2.

Thus, the creation of an imaginary *other* does not suffice to found the retroaction that could situate the subject in the symbolic register; silence and turmoil once again prevail: 'silence more and more longer and longer vast tracts of time we at a loss more and more he for answers I for questions [...] YOUR LIFE HERE BEFORE ME utter confusion' (*HI*, 73–4); 'he has stopped I have made him stop suffered him to stop it's one or the other not specified the thing stops and more or less long silence not specified' (84). Although the voice temporarily assumes the identity of a fellow being 'Pim', no dialogue can develop between the narrator and his double. The verbal association of *Pim* and 'the thing'—both appear to be names of the voice that has stopped talking—testifies to the absence of any real difference be tween them, so that the subject cannot end up disposing of his own voice: the loop of speech goes from *me* to *Bom* and back, but the terms of the exchange envisaged mutually cancel themselves out.[43]

While Shane Weller sees a negation of the other in Beckett's early work—a 'process of *saming*' (2006, 25)—reflected in the violence that breaks out in novels like *Mercier and Camier*, *Molloy* and *Malone Dies*, he does not see 'ethics' in the terms of Lévinas, for whom 'it is precisely the ethical relation with the Other that constitutes an escape from the horror of the *il y a*' (29), the incessant voice associated earlier with a 'fundamental noise' (Žižek, 1995, 84). He considers that 'in Beckett the *il y a* certainly appears to be irreducible and inescapable in a way that it is not for Levinas, blocking the path to the ethical' (Weller, 2006, 29). For this reason, he advances the category of the 'anethical' based on the imperative *il faut*. The latter is not a value, but 'simply a blank at the very heart of Beckett's *œuvre*, a very specific nothing around which that *œuvre* is painstakingly constructed' (Weller, 2006,

43 Our reading thus fits into the division Russell Smith sees in readings of *How It Is*: on the one hand, those who adhere to Badiou's notion of the encounter with the Other, and the reading whereby the witnesses are simply 'figments created and discarded by a solitary imagination' (Smith, 2008, 352). We shall pursue this analysis and respond to Smith at the end of this chapter (*infra*, p. 369).

193). Weller considers the *il faut* as not being 'characterized by an affirmation that precedes all negation or all value' (194): it is beyond any axiology, or Badiolian affirmation.

However, what is lacking, in Weller's analysis, is the notion of *jouissance* as material positivity. Consequently, it is unclear what this 'blank' is, or what Beckett does with this confrontation: Weller brings us to the verge of the absence of the Other, without following it up. As described, this blank appears as a 'nothing' that ignores the presence of a gaping hole or *jouissance* to be dealt with and constantly hemmed in by writing. And yet, Beckett evokes the idea with extreme precision: 'La négation n'est pas possible. Pas plus que l'affirmation. [...] Il faut se tenir là où il n'y a ni pronom, ni solution, ni réaction, ni prise de position possibles... C'est ce qui rend le travail si diaboliquement difficile' ('Negation is not possible. No more than affirmation. [...] One has to stand where there is no possible pronoun, solution, reaction, taking of position... That is what makes the work so devilishly difficult', in Juliet, 68). That is to say, the 'blank' represents an untenable position where the subject finds himself devoid of any 'means' or 'desire' (*contra* Badiou): nothing but his existence and the imperative to go 'on'. This corresponds to the 'between' of *The Unnamable*: '[...] where you suffer, rejoice, at being bereft of speech, bereft of thought [...]' (*U*, 367), but which also includes the unconditional obligation to speak.

This is where torture provides the means to find an anchoring. The use of torture—which Anthony Cordingley studies in terms of 'pedagogical' tyranny—represents a different approach, since it supposes a physical efficiency. It is not a question here of following meanings, with their propensity to fade into the unbearable cacophony of the *voice*. The narrator becomes the instrument of language, seeking to observe on Pim's body what the effect of an inscription might be and, by doing so, to endow his double with a concrete existence: 'for ever in the mud but I'll quicken him you wait and see' (*HI*, 52). Pim's suffering offers evidence of life: 'the voice extorted a few words life because of cry that's the proof good and deep no more is needed a little cry all is not dead one drinks one gives to drink goodbye' (122).

By virtue of this operation, the narrator is no longer exposed to the void—deprived of any bodily consistency—rather, he is at last the receptor of the tangible proof of his own existence. The narrator makes the aim of this torture explicit: 'the paltry need of a life a voice of one who has neither'.

By acting on the body of his double, the narrator undertakes a form of domestication or training that resembles behaviourist methods, since his will to achieve an inscription in the body does not succeed in *instituting a subject.* The action appears as stereotyped, since it amounts to applying a system: 'conceive a system then apply I can't get over it make it work' (*HI*, 94). The actions accomplished consist in driving the fingernails or an opener into different parts of the partner's body, and inflicting blows on his skull. The failure of this approach is already patent in the tools used, since the narrator does not use articulated language but a code intended to produce univocal effects: 'he cries I withdraw it thump on skull the cries cease it's mechanical' (67). This code is intended to have a performative effect: 'the thump on the skull signifying stop at all times and that come to think of it almost mechanically' (64). In spite of its rigidly stereotyped nature, the process can end up in confusion: 'when stabbed in the arse instead of crying he sings his song what a cunt this Pim damn it all confuse arse and armpit horn and steel the thump he gets then I give you my word' (67).

Instead of instituting an exchange, the narrator acts on his partner to consolidate himself: he imagines he can evacuate a part of his own torment, by localising it in his double. He creates an external voice that functions in the manner of a calming sublimation: 'claw dig deep furrows drink the screams' (*HI*, 53). The cries are comparable to nourishment, a voice that the narrator can enjoy, like the one produced by a radio set: 'that's not all he stops nails in armpit he resumes cheers done it armpit song and this music as sure as if I pressed a button I can indulge in it any time henceforward' (65). The cries that ring out are thus intended to silence the tormenting voice of the Other.

Insofar as it is a product of the *superego*, torture supposes an intention that remains obscure, since the tormentor *utters nothing.* Like the spotlight in *Play*, the one who inflicts this suffering cannot enunciate what he expects of his double: he intervenes through mute torment. As a result, the impulse and the elaboration of hypotheses constitute the driving force behind this training: 'what else can I do could I do if I were put to the pin of my collar / think perhaps at a pinch it's possible what else am I doing at this moment' (68). The torture thus becomes the *cause* of speech: 'what sun I have said no matter I've said something that's what was needed seen something called it above [...] to have a moment's peace I have it I had it opener arse following scene and words' (86). The breaks in the sentences indicate the torture, since this speech that is supposedly ascribed to Pim is also the narrator's; the torture continues behind the utterances: 'the tormentors being mute' (119).

The failure of this approach is dictated by its very definition. The characters permute among themselves in order to achieve these inscriptions, but in doing so, they propagate the unceasing voice: 'rumour transmissible ad infinitum in either direction' (*HI*, 120). The *unlimited* remains devoid of any breach, as in the previously quoted expression: 'infinitum alone commensurate with us'. No knowledge can result from this system, since it is impossible to distinguish the 'interlocutors'. As the text hypothesises concerning the encounter between victim and tormentor: 'he is merely in fact describing himself to two lifelong acquaintances'. These hypotheses and ratiocinations about the possibilities of permutations simply represent the extension—on a much vaster scale—of the initial problematic, such as the absence of knowledge. The necessity to resort to bodily inscription only confirms the absence of the symbolic structuring that, were it to exist, would have instituted the subject once and for all.

In *The Unnamable*, the narrator finds himself a victim of torture emanating from words conveyed by the voice, and which he identifies in the form of his evanescent tormentors. By contrast, in *How It Is* the subject appears as a tormentor who finds relief in the cries he produces in others. And yet, the establishment of this relationship serves to explore the subject's relationship to himself: to himself as other. By imagining the two reciprocal positions, he endows himself with a representation of these places that remain refractory to any dialectical binding or articulation. As seen in relation to the spotlight in *Play*, tormentor and victim are one, but they are united in the absence of any symbolic Other, in the presence of the *unlimited* dimension that leaves the subject plunged in his profound solitude: 'it's no I'm sorry no one here knows anyone either personally or otherwise it's the no that turns up I murmur it' (*HI*, 123).

'Rough for Radio II': from Torture to an Ephemeral Birth

Quoting Leo Bersani and Ulysse Dutoit, Tyrus Miller (255) emphasises that in his later plays, Beckett moved from the representation of a tormented narrator to the question of the coercion he endures at the hands of external agents to make him speak. However, the unity of the various agents involved needs to be examined, as it appears for example in *Rough for Radio II*, a play originally written in French as *Pochade radiophonique*, possibly in the 1960s (Ackerley and Gontarski, 489). In this text, the roles of tormentor and tormented compose a veritable discursive structure, where each of the positions occupied, each of the functions represented, expresses the manner whereby the subject deals with himself and with his own strangeness.

This text illustrates the manner in which the apparatus is utilised in an effort to extract speech from the victim, with the aim of humanising him or bringing him into existence. Angela Moorjani sees a form of enfolding of different levels at work, where ghostly figures move 'within an enwombed and entombed theater of the mind', doubled by their tormentors (Moorjani, 2004, 179). Rather than this notion of enveloping—which remains on an imaginary level[44]—it would

44 The same critique is made by Dominique Chauvin concerning Didier Anzieu's oft-cited theory of the '*moi-peau*' (ego-skin). She states: 'The theme of the container is assuredly encountered in Beckett, but it is, as it seems to me, presented for what it is, that is to say a narcissistic and mortifying prison' (Chauvin, 13). The sack in *How It is* not only contains objects, it also imprisons the character; a fact that becomes clear when

seem preferable to read the various elements as part of a Möbian structure, where all the components of a theatrical production (via the radio, in this case) are situated on the same plane (Regnault, 1989, 115). This is particularly important since the 'within' is radically 'without', in both senses of the term, and cannot be reduced to a place situated among various mutually reinforcing layers.

The discursive apparatus formed by the characters appears as a consequence and a manifestation of the impossibility of being 'born', a motif that is situated at the centre of the play. The 'characters' here are clearly endowed with precise functions. Hélène Laplace-Claverie sees in them 'the diffracted projection of an *ego* that is torn between contradictory drives', the representation of the artist 'exerting on himself a violence that is both creative and destructive, a source of suffering and of enjoyment' (in Hubert ed., 805). Rather than simply 'contradictory drives' however, it would seem that Beckett presents here a construction that lays out—in lieu of a structuring dialectic within language—the way the writer functions. Thus can be found represented the suffering flesh (the victim Fox), the tormentor (Dick), the director displaying his literary knowledge (Animator), the scribe (Stenographer) and the invisible Other (who remains unnamed). Martin Esslin (379) compares these characters realistically, at first, to the members of a team of radio employees, then (381) defines them as an allegory of components situated inside the artist's creative mind: subconscious source, critical faculty (Animator), torturing determination, erotic fantasies (Stenographer). This interpretation is most appropriate but, as this work presents a persistent construction in Beckett's creation, it would seem important to view it in terms of its subjective consequences. Once again, these characters are arranged somewhat in the manner of Lacan's 'four discourses':

---

contrasted with the dimension of the *voice* in the same work, and which ends up dominating in the *explicit* (Brown, 2016). See also *supra*, p. 109.

A / S	>	Dick (mute)
(*absent Master*)	//	Fox

As the examples of *Murphy* and *Molloy* suggest, it is necessary to add, to the characters enumerated at the beginning of the text, the absent and invisible Master. He appears as the one who *causes* the action and the dialogues. Finally, the action bears on Fox who, in return, is required to shed light on what the absent Master is incapable of knowing about himself.

The respective roles can be further detailed as follows. Regarding the 'Master', Steven Connor observes:

> The absent Godot, in Beckett's first performed play, who is saviour and tyrant at once, seems the origin and reference point of all power in the play, even though that power is never visible in itself. (2007, 196)

Like Youdi, the Master of this play—who apparently assumes the collective form of a committee—is the one for whom the others prepare reports. Devoid of any personalised presence, he is manifestly the author of the initial series of recommendations. Expressing no clear motivation, it is nonetheless he who, acting as *cause*, seeks to extract knowledge regarding the subject. In his status as *superego*, he expresses himself in a stiff, official, and repetitive manner: '…instantly renew our standing exhortations […]' (*RR II*, 276). His demands concern a report on the 'results', and are accompanied by 'exhortations' that, in the French version, are described by the Stenographer as being anything but lenient: '[…] recommandations [qui] ne sont pas tendres pour nous […]' (*PR*, 68). For the listener, these remarks do not emanate directly from the obscure Master but are relayed by his agents, Animator and Stenographer.

This Master thus situates himself on the purely institutional or symbolic register, demanding that his agents report only articulate speech: 'Kindly to refrain from recording mere animal cries, they serve only to indispose us' (*RR II*, 276). This exhortation can be associated with Nagg's description of Hamm's childhood: 'We let you cry. Then we moved you out of earshot, so that we might sleep in peace' (*Eg*, 119). The parental *other* appears as one who does not suffer the child's cries, and who, consequently, leaves no breach to accommodate the latter's suffering. The master is also particularly concerned by quantified language, seeking to catch 'the meanest syllable' (*RR II*, 276). As he is impermeable to nuanced formulations, he cannot know exactly what he himself expects, nor how to orient his quest. Consequently, he demands an exhaustive compilation of Fox's words. Like the sound directors Opener (*Cascando*) or Bam's Voice (*What Where*), he embodies an attitude of neutrality; but he also wishes the results obtained to be totally objective: 'Kindly to ensure full neutralisation of the subject when not in session, especially with regard to the gag, its permanence and good repair' (276). This arrangement supposes an alternation between a faultless presence (allowing to gather information) and absence, where Fox is required to remain incapable of uttering a word.

Animator and Stenographer are the Master's agents. Their function is to be the recipients of Fox's speech: they collate his words, in order to inscribe them and raise them to the status of acceptable utterances. In this respect, Angela Moorjani (2004, 178) sees the play as displaying a parody of the psychoanalyst seen as a Kleinian combined parent. This perception is doubtless enlightening, as Stenographer and Animator appear to encounter the difficulty of making Fox's case fit into the mould of conventional discourse and pre-conceived notions.

As director, Animator represents the Master's will: he is comparable to Pozzo who, as a tormentor, appears in Godot's absence. Indeed, the similarity of the two figures can be noted, since Beckett 'toyed with identifying Pozzo as Godot, unaware that those waiting are Vladimir and Estragon: "But the messenger"' (Ackerley and Gontarski, 453). As the receiver of Fox's speech, he attempts to make the latter's words fit into a grid. For example, Stenographer raises the question of acceptable expressions: 'He is weeping, sir, shall I note it?' (*RR II*, 279); '[...] can one say it in English? / I have never come across it, miss, but no doubt.' Animator tries to find a link between past utterances and the ensuing production. He seeks to establish what has already been written down and what remains to be said—'Has he used that turn before, miss?' (277)—with the aim of constructing a discourse and composing a coherent form.

Being situated on the level of established discourse, Animator uses bookish language, by contrast with Fox. He makes an æsthetic comment (*RR II*, 279), then reproaches himself with his use of literary references: 'Ah these old spectres from the days of book reviewing, they lie in wait for one at every turn' (280). His attitude leads him to address Fox as if the latter were a '*backward pupil*' (281): 'But since you have failed so far to let it escape you, it is not by harking on the same old themes that you are likely to succeed, that would astonish me' (282). Animator is determined to format Fox's speech: 'Don't ramble! Treat the subject, whatever it is!' (281). This notion recalls that of the 'pensum' (*U*, 304), in *The Unnamable*. Animator thus represents the Other insofar as he imposes an implacable norm.

As for Stenographer's role, it is complementary to Animator's: she gives herself over to personal and affective allusions, describing Fox's tears as being a 'human trait' (279), thinking of her 'nanny' (280); or her 'kith and kin': 'Mine play such a part, in my life!'

As an agent or 'appendage', both of the Master and the couple Animator/Stenographer, Dick appears as an ironic figure: the phallic allusion contained in his name is accompanied by the utilisation of the bull's pizzle (in French: '*nerf de bœuf*', the *bœuf* being an ox, and therefore… castrated). By contrast with the couple Animator and Stenographer, he is 'mute' (*RR II*, 274), and his action bears directly on the body, testifying to the manner in which the signifier imprints itself into the flesh: he is thus situated outside any articulation or meaning. His role is exclusively expressive of the vociferation of the superego, whose action Lacan sums up in the equivocal injunction *Jouis!* (enjoy)/*J'ouïs* ('I hear'… and obey, 1966, 821). Such is the function of the bull's pizzle, which uses to full advantage the resources of the radio. Dick's silence is thus associated with pure sound—perceived by the listener—aiming to cause Fox's speech. Dick also shows a link with the function of sound editor, since Steven Connor reminds us that 'the principal reference for the word "switch," until the nineteenth century, was a whip or lash, usually made of a flexible twig or branch' (2014a, 77), a connotation absent from the French *commutateur*, used by Beckett.[45]

At the heart of this setup, Fox's body is the mute object—*Vox* (Esslin, 381)—from which the others seek to tear speech that remains anchored in his flesh. In return, however, the others are a *voice* for Fox, filtering and ordering his words according to the criteria of established discourse. Paul Lawley notes this reciprocal relationship: 'Fox is obviously *contained* by Animator and Stenographer, but his discourse, which is itself about containment and issuing forth, seems in turn to contain (by representing) the ontological position of all three figures' (1988, 5). If Fox resembles Lucky, in *Waiting for Godot*—in that he speaks at the orders of the Other—his role seems more complex that that of his predecessor, as he embodies a paradox: being exposed to his tormentors, he appears as a supposed source of knowledge. In return, he needs the others in order to speak: incapable of possessing knowledge for himself, he is obliged to rely on his tormentors to give his utterances some form of reality.

Indeed, the recourse to a discursive apparatus is intended to bring about a production: it determines the action of the play, whose 'goal' (*RR II*, 281) is to produce the word that will overthrow the necessity of its existence, and thus set the characters free.[46] However, while the discursive device holds the various elements together, it is constitutionally flawed, since the roles show irremediable breaks between their respective functions. Firstly, the Master is a split entity, as he remains absent and thus incapable of intervening in the action that

---

45 The *Littré* dictionary defines the *commutateur* as a device 'that serves to change the direction of an electric current'. This definition therefore does not suggest the latter's cessation.

46 Such a notion of freedom is systematically rejected by Beckett, for example, in his refusal of oriental mysticism (in Juliet, 20), or his remark concerning Murphy tied to his rocker: 'In the end it is better to perish than be freed' (in Knowlson, 1997, 247).

he delegates to his subordinates. Moreover, not only do his sole utterances appear exclusively in written form, but they are not addressed to any *you*. The imperative he uses is expressed in the infinitive, not by verbs conjugated in a personal mode: 'Kindly to refrain [...]' (*RR II*, 276). If Animator and Stenographer appear to be united in their action on Fox, they are both complementary and separated: not only does Stenographer resist Animator's amorous advances, but they are separated by the barrier of age, as Stenographer is much older than her, and laments his lost youth.

Fox also manifests a scission: he emits cries when whipped, but is incapable of commenting on his situation or the blows he receives. His speech is in no way addressed to his tormentors: he is thus incapable of ascribing meaning to his own words. As he is unable to be animated by his own intentionality, he depends on the tormenting apparatus.

This constraining setup has prosthetic value, in that it compensates for the fact that the characters have not the slightest idea of what they are aiming at. They possess no means to guide Fox: they can only goad him on and exhort him. When Stenographer asks if she should note 'the play of feature too' (*RR II*, 275), Animator replies: 'I don't know, miss. Depending perhaps.' To Fox, he admits: 'Of course we do not know, any more than you, what exactly it is we are after, what sign or set of words' (282). Animator and Stenographer are subject to hesitation, to failure, so that Stenographer also risks noting Fox's cries as well: 'Drat it! Where's that eraser?' (277); 'Careful, miss. / Have no fear, sir' (278). Animator also has a failing memory, which is one reason why he is dependent on the written reports: 'But, my dear child, I don't remember yesterday [...]' (283). In fact, if no one knows what the Master is seeking, it is precisely because he himself knows nothing in this respect: he is obliged to rely on his agents to extort knowledge from Fox who, in turn, is equally as ignorant, while supposedly possessing the knowledge being sought.

The breaks inherent in the mechanism's construction are also apparent in Animator, who proves to be capricious, alternating between contrary positions. He declares they have time—'[...] the house is not on fire' (*RR II*, 278)—then immediately expresses urgency: '[…] can't you see that old time is aflying?' In the same way, his self-conscious speech (like Pozzo's) on the use of 'caress' (278) to make the patient speak is immediately followed by the order to use the whip. He alternates erratically, passing from Fox to Stenographer, and is himself unable to keep on the same topic. Despite his effort to link Fox's utterances together, the fragmented result appears as a form of weaving devoid of any structuring articulation: 'A: [*Sigh.*] Good. Where were we? / […] S: "…live I did, no denying, all stones all sides"—inaudible—"walls—" / A: [*Ruler.*] On! [*Silence.*] Dick!' (278).

The splitting is also echoed in the diverse registers of language used by the characters: Fox, on the one hand, Stenographer and Animator, on the other. Fox's language—broken up into 'vignettes'—is lyrical, while that of Stenographer and Animator is satirical. Whereas Fox's words are borne along by the movement of pure *enunciation*, his tormentors aim to come up with a result capable of forming a whole. Moreover, Fox's descriptions are devoid of any sexual allusion: he evokes giving birth to his twin, and a miraculous *Maud* giving suck, but nothing concerning what may have led them both to such a condition. He can only latch on to an unreal image: one that gives consistency to his impossible being.[47] Fox is cut off from the others by his metaphorical language: speech that is aimless (with regards to the institution), and that does not necessarily interest his handlers (*RR II*, 281–2). By contrast with Fox's absence of sexuality, an excessive multiplication of phallic motifs can be seen on the side of his tormentors. If only the '*bull's pizzle*' (275) actually touches Fox's flesh, Animator brandishes his '*cylindrical ruler*'. Stenographer taps with her pencil—'*She strikes with her pencil on her desk*' (277)—an instrument that imitates Animator's ruler, while she reads the text: 'F: […] —but no, no no. [*Pause.*] No no. [*Silence. Ruler.*]' (279). Ordinarily, the 'phallus' unifies representation—it is 'the signifier intended to designate as a whole the effects of the signified' (Lacan, 1966, 69)—by designating a lack, on its reverse

---

47 *Cf. supra*, p. 228–33.

side (710). To operate this function, it remains 'veiled'[48] (692). Here however, the overt and repeated usage of the phallic motif—in its caricatured substitutes—precisely reveals its absence as a structuring element: the insistent *absence* of a word.

Compared to the static or synchronic nature of the discursive setup, the play as a whole maintains a dynamic movement. Paul Lawley (1988) has pointed out the numerous images of movement and blocked birth. Indeed, the series of breaks in the structure contrast with the play's metaphors of movement: passing through tunnels, the 'vermin in the lingerie' (*RR II*, 275), motifs of coupling. These images create a simulation of continuity that unfolds on the background of impossible saying. The play as a whole moves from the opening evocation of the actors in the discursive apparatus, the rules to be applied, the procedure to be followed, towards the final situation where Fox has passed out, and the couple Stenographer and Animator are united in their excitement over the image of Maud and the unborn twin. The notion of separation remains, since the characters' union only exists in the image, which in turn, is centred on the word *between*: '...between two kisses...' (284). This motif can be compared to *Words and Music*—'the lips part and the eyes [...] open' (*WM*, 293)—or to *Eh Joe*: 'Say "Joe" it parts the *lips*...' (366), and the association with parturition suggested by *A Piece of Monologue*: 'Birth. Parts lips and thrusts tongue between them.'[49] (*PM*, 428). That is to say, the separation points to the possibility of the subject's coming into existence. Finally, Stenographer and Animator are powerless to account for the image Fox produces, they can only *en jouir* (enjoy it); that is to say identify with it and use it to support their own togetherness, at Animator's initiative: *jouir* meaning the way the real can be repressed and thus serve the establishment of a discursive structure.

Fox's collapse seems crucial to the structure of the play: he is reduced to formless flesh by two symmetrical means: firstly by the institutional setup—the 'tube-feed' (*RR II*, 276) 'per buccam' or 'per

48 *Cf. supra*, p. 60.

49 As suggested *supra*, p. 179–80.

rectum'—and secondly by the maternal image, when Animator orders Stenographer to kiss Fox. In this passage, Animator's words create confusion: it is unclear whether it is the kiss or its effects that should be located in 'his heart, in his entrails—or some other part' (282). Animator specifies the mouth: 'Till it bleeds! Kiss it white! [*Howl from* FOX.] Suck his gullet.' This action can be seen as a caricature, not only of Tennyson's Maud (Lawley, 1988), but also of the motif of the comforting but invisible feminine visage present in *Nacht und Träume*, one that Rosemary Pountney (28–9) finds in Yeats' *The Only Jealousy of Emer*, where the Goddess Fand offers to free Cuchulain from future incarnations by kissing her; or the one in *Krapp's Last Tape*, or again in *Words and Music*. All these plays present evocations of lost opportunities, as pointed out by Marjorie Perloff (2007). Stenographer's violent intrusion causes Fox to faint. He is thus evacuated from the scene, and the auditor is left with the mutual excitement of the couple around the newly discovered image, which enables them to forget the conditions presiding over its appearance. In the end, Fox is forgotten, as are the imperative masters. However, this is the only union Stenographer and Animator will know: they attain here a form of—temporary—freedom. This image—a new creation—is the lyrical product of the play's constraining discursive structure. Such a result is nonetheless fragile, as it remains impossible to determine what 'the' word sought may be. The auditor ends up with the suggested possibility of 'being born', while Fox himself remains inert.

The effect of the discursive apparatus is experienced within the context of the radio medium. In the course of the play, the auditor finds himself in the position of Stenographer and Animator, since he also questions Fox' utterances. But he is also blind, and remains in the dark like the 'victim', who is incapable of ascribing meaning to his words. The radio represents a 'wombtomb' (*DF*, 121)—an external organ—where the characters, as pure voices, remain in a spectral state. Thus the radio cannot bring about any 'birth' other than that of the voices produced in the play itself.

'What Where': the Irremediable Abyss

The construction of *What Where* also depends on a discursive montage centred on the physical sufferings inflicted on a victim. This play shows that which escapes the tormentor's power, and the way in which the subject remains refractory to the influence of discourses: in spite of the signifier's imperative dimension, the influence exerted on the body fails to extort knowledge. This play thus shows the impossible avowal of truth. Both a form of continuity and an evolution can be noticed since *Krapp's Last Tape*. Indeed, the places of tormentor and victim were already present in Krapp himself: he is successively 'tormentor'—disparaging his former identity—and 'victim', insofar as, relegated to the status of a recorded voice, he is railed against by his new avatar. What remains constant in *Krapp's Last Tape* and *What Where*, is the role of the superego: the character embodies this voice, in his systematically pejorative appraisals (Krapp) and in the imperative emanating from Voice of Bam. However, in *What Where*, the expression of physical and moral degradation disappears.

This *dramaticule* picks up the motif of the torments inflicted in *How It Is*: the echo is particularly apparent in the use of the variations on the name *Bam*.[50] A realistic origin has been suggested for the torture theme: Beckett is said to have been moved by the suffering of political prisoners in Turkey.[51] However, the play's construction reveals a will

---

50 It has been noted that the names follow a variation that echoes Rimbaud's sonnet on the vowels. In accordance with Beckett's practice that consists of creating a fault, an error—in his mathematical calculations (for example, see Stevens, 166)—the last vowel is missing: the one that would read, ironically, **Bum*. We can also add the allusions to Russian clowns Bim and Bom that traverse several of Beckett's works (Cohn, 1962, 203).

51 Gontarski notes: 'The echo of politics sounded in *Catastrophe* is resounded in the interrogatory *What Where* with its plot suggestive of repetitive, mindless torture. In Stuttgart, moreover, Beckett thought for a while to make the political level of the piece more overt by having each

to detach this notion from its historical and political context, so that suffering appears both as purified and more universal. That is to say that instead of basing his creation on an event whose reality is supported by a generalised discourse (in the media, in history books), Beckett raises the question of what such a situation may mean for himself, as a subject. In other words, any readily accessible references would make the play more understandable, but would also make it of more circumscribed interest. Reducing it to its structural components brings the work closer to any intimate meaning it may have for its author, but simultaneously opens it up to dimensions shared by every subject.

Whereas Bam engages an exchange with the series of his doubles, the *Voice of Bam* intervenes as a 'director', only capable of commanding the play's unfolding. This voice appears as devoid of any *knowledge*, which is reserved for the level of the representation and the victims. Whereas it governs the movements as a whole, the Voice cannot dictate the characters' actions directly (by means of the pronoun *you*, for example): indeed, the characters already know what is expected of them. The structuring of this device thus excludes any dialogue between Voice and the figures. As previously seen,[52] instead of verbal exchange, the play institutes a series of permutations that unfold following Voice of Bam's dictates, which constitute the centre of the play.

The repetitive nature of the permutations—testifying to the absence of a dialectic—contributes to the enigmatic force of this text. The presence of two opposed aspects can be discerned here: on the one hand, the permutations indicate their predictable nature and, on the other hand, the dimension they seem to hide—the scenes of torture—is in complete contrast with this monotony. This antithesis is similar to the one between boredom and suffering, described in

---

character wear a Tarboosh, fez-like headgear often associated with Armenians. As Beckett suggested, "If you think of the political situation in Turkey'" (1987, 121).

52 *Supra*, p. 293–4.

Proust,[53] and where boredom is correlated with habit: 'The fundamental duty of Habit, about which it describes the futile and stupefying arabesques of its supererogations, consists in a perpetual adjustment to the conditions of its worlds' (*Pr*, 28). However, suffering represents the suspension of this natural adaptation:

> The pendulum oscillates between these two terms: Suffering—that opens a window on the real and is the main condition of the artistic experience, and Boredom—with its host of top-hatted and hygienic ministers, Boredom that must be considered as the most tolerable because the most durable of human evils. (*Pr*, 28)

These descriptions allow us to detach *What Where* from its anecdotal associations—the evocation of physical torture—and to situate it in relation to a structural question. What is striking here is that there is no articulation between these two opposed aspects—boredom and suffering—but rather an *oscillation*, a movement from one extreme to the other. In this sense, either the signifier mortifies the subject and excludes any elaboration of knowledge on his part, or it inflicts unbearable suffering that alone is 'real'. However, in *Proust*, Beckett uses the word *window*, a term that reveals the fact that there is never any direct access to the real; only an aspect of it can be perceived, by means of a certain framing:[54] in the same way, in *What Where*, the only access

53 This antinomy originates in Schopenhauer: 'Hence its life swings like a pendulum to and fro between pain and boredom, and these two are in fact its ultimate constituents' (312). We can however note that it is already present at the end of Voltaire's *Candide* (1759), associated with a Manichean: 'Martin surtout conclut que l'homme était né pour vivre dans les convulsions de l'inquiétude, ou dans la léthargie de l'ennui' ('Martin in particular concluded that man was born to live in the convulsions of disquiet, or in the lethargy of boredom', 150). We know that Beckett read *Candide* on 7 February 1935 (Nixon, 2011, 24)

54 The window is thus that of the 'fundamental fantasy', that circumscribes and localises the real (Wajcman, 2004, *passim*).

to the subject's real is through partial saying; what Lacan called '*mi-dire*'.[55]

The minimalist æsthetics of this play are a result of the fact that it is centred on a question of language, where the signifier inflicts suffering. This idea is already hinted at in French, in the *équivoque* of the verb that underlies the action of the play: *donner la question* (to torture). The questions *what?* and *where?* are the very object—the substance—of the encounters between victim and tormentor.

According to the combinatory rule governing the movement of the play, the spectator sees the exchange between tormentor and victim, but the fragments of dialogue he hears between Bam and the tormentor are followed by the departure of the new couple towards an area off stage, where the torture sessions are supposed to take place. Thus, there is a distribution of space: the calm tone of the dialogue is followed by what can be imagined as the torment inflicted. However, it is in this sense that one can understand the refusal to make explicit the action that unfolds at these moments. Bam questions the tormentor: 'You gave him the works?' (*WW*, 472). These attenuated evocations reveal the dimension of *mi-dire*, demonstrating that the domain outside of speech cannot be understood, since it is radically excluded from any representation, it is beyond anything conceivable.

Something of the status of the torment can be grasped here. Indeed, it can be supposed that the *real* dimension of the torment inflicted surpasses anything that words are capable of expressing. It can be conjectured that the victims are submerged by an *unlimited* suffering that abolishes any subjectivity, as seen with Mouth or the Unnamble, who lose all perception of their bodies. Consequently, there is no way to convert this suffering into an 'experience' that might belong to the subject. Thus it is that the evocation of each session of torment first makes mention of cries: 'He wept? / Yes. / Screamed? / Yes. /

55 'I always tell the truth: not all, because to say it all, we are unable to. To say it all is impossible, materially: the words are lacking. It is even via this impossible that the truth is attached to the real' (Lacan, 2001, 509). On the idea of *mi-dire* (Lacan, 1991b, 118-9).

Begged for mercy? / Yes' (*WW*, 473). It concludes however by the victim's passing out: 'Then why stop? / He passed out. / And you didn't revive him? / I tried. / Well? / I couldn't.' The use of the modal auxiliary *could* highlights the absence of *means* that guides Beckett's experience as a writer, as he expresses it, for example, in *Proust*: 'The artistic tendency is not expansive, but a contraction. And art is the apotheosis of solitude. There is no communication because there are no vehicles of communication' (*Pr*, 64). If the sessions cause real suffering—diametrically opposed to Proustian *boredom*—the latter is not endowed with any meaning, and domination reaches its limits when the victim passes out as a result of unspeakable torment. This experience is situated beyond the domain where Lemuel's cries resound: the subject is effaced, escaping the ascendancy of his tormenter and becoming inaccessible to himself.

If the action of the play points toward this offstage area, what the spectator sees is centred on the measured exchanges between Bam and the successive tormentors, bringing to the fore the dimension of speech. Here, the construction of the play—the device it creates—manifests a series of disjunctions resulting from the linguistic question it deals with. The Voice of Bam, which arises independently of the body—'V in the shape of a small megaphone at head level' (*WW*, 469)—is expressive of an imperative agent, whose action on the body is intended to be unilateral: the Voice commands and the figures obey. In turn, the tormentors torture and the victims confess. However, this univocal dimension is fragmented. Initially the visible figures—the imaginary bodies, or the *spectres*, we may say—do not line up correctly: upon Bam and Bom's first appearance, the Voice declares: 'Not good' (470). That is because the Voice notices that Bam must be alone; the actors do not automatically adapt to the utterances: an unforeseeable element needs to be taken into account. Then, Bam appears as a relay to the Voice; but by the very fact of addressing his questions to an interlocutor, he ascribes knowledge to another. These tormentor-interlocutors are relays or phantoms of Bam, who entrusts them with a mission and questions them within the visible space onstage. We can recognise the manner in which the Beckettian subject continually seeks—for want of a symbolic Other—to institute the two poles of a dialogue: 'Yes, I was my father and I was my son, I asked myself questions and answered as best I could [...]' (*TFN* I, 103). However, it can also be noted that the tormentors display a certain resistance, since they refuse to confess, with the result that Bam accuses them of lying. Finally, the victims refuse to declare anything to their tormentors: they too are radically refractory.

The fragmentation can also be observed in the exchanges, in the complement that the interrogations are supposed to elicit. These questions systematically evoke a certain idea of totality. When Bam gives the mission for the following session, his interlocutor replies: 'Is that all? [...] Then stop?' (*WW*, 473). If, when faced with the *équivoque* at work in this reply from the next tormentor, Bam never ceases to demand a precise item of information by means of an indefinite pronoun, it is because no real dialogue is possible. This *all* is thus reminiscent of the expression 'revolving it all' (*Ff*, 400) in *Footfalls*: an *all* that remains intact, escaping any form of characterisation.

Indeed, the questions Bam formulates immediately point to a referent that is supposedly known, in a questioning that has, however, always been under way, and that will never cease: 'He didn't say anything?' (*WW*, 472); 'He didn't say it?' The indefinite pronoun *anything* echoes the axiom '*Nothing is more real than nothing*' (*MD*, 186); that is to say, it brings into play the real: that which surpasses the nameable and meaning. In the same way, the questions in the title appear to be exorbitant: *What?* and *Where?* imply the totality of existence. Instead of being circumstantiated—articulated in relation to a verb—they are pronounced as a whole, in the form of adverbial phrases.

The questioning assumes this form because the subject must confess what his obscure Other—the 'master' (*U*, 361), according to the Unnamable—is himself unable to formulate: the subject must respond precisely from the place where he has not been instituted. His Other can only ask him to provide the response to an exorbitant question. Consequently, *What?* can only express the demand to identify the subject's object of *jouissance*, that which constitutes his very existence. From a grammatical point of view, this object is *indefinite: an* object among others. The question *where?* aims to locate this *jouissance*, in order to situate it within specific coordinates. Here could be found an object accompanied by the definite article (*the* object), testifying to the accomplishment of a selection among a series of possibilities. In sum, through his questions, the Voice aims to grasp the Thing that is at the heart of the victim's unnameable.

This *unlimited* exigency causes the disjunctions that appear in the course of the dialogues. According to the title, the exorbitant nature of the imperative emanating from the Voice of Bam is split between *what* and *where*. Firstly, Bam asks Bim to pose two questions: 'What must he confess? / That he said it to him. […] And what' (*WW*, 273). These questions are divided into *confess that*: it is a question that is articulated (by means of a completive subordinate clause linked to the introductive question); and *confess what*: whose articulation is weaker, since it is only attached to what precedes it by the conjunction *and*. For this reason, the sentence 'And what' is equivocal, and can be understood in two ways; either: 1. as a direct object, where the victim confesses *what*. 2. as a question addressed to the victim or to the tormentor (for the latter: *'Well, what?').

Then the question is split into *that* and *where*: 'What must he confess? / That he said where to him. / Is that all? / And where' (*WW*, 475). Once again, the utterances seek to define the *jouissance* in an absolute manner, but they can only do so by accepting a scission into two separate utterances. The phrase 'he said it to you' (473) is addressed to the tormentor who refuses to confess, while the utterance 'And where' concerns the victim, who has still not confessed. Thus a division appears in the meaning: **where the victim did it*/ **where he said it*.[56] This same question can also be addressed to the tormentor, who should reveal what he knows about the victim. Faced with his interlocutor's powerlessness to produce the truth, Bam is obliged to object: 'It's a lie' (473, 476). Here he expresses his suspicion of a refusal, on the tormentor's behalf, to give up the truth. Thus, having been constrained to delegate this role to an interlocutor—a fact that, by itself,

56 This last interpretation is confirmed (Beckett, 1999, 419).

produces a division—he finds it is impossible to have confidence in the very one he has entrusted with the functions of tormentor.

All Voice of Bam's efforts are aimed at grasping the combined response of tormentor and victim, and which would constitute the Truth. However, whether it be the *boredom* side or the *suffering* side, it is impossible to extract any such truth: torment is *doing*, not the elaboration of knowledge which, as such, is dependent on a symbolic inscription. The pursuit of the chain of successive couples confirms this fundamental absence of knowledge: having sought to extort a response from the victim, it is then the tormenter who is questioned. However, the exchange of places does not allow the subject to attain what remains out of reach. The chain is thus potentially infinite, whereas the power Bam exerts is limited in nature. Indeed, the torture started long before the play opens (hence the immediate use of the verb *reappear*), and it can be supposed that it is destined to be continued after the play ends. The characters disappear from the stage, and do not come back; but everything is ready to start all over: these spectres do not die but reappear in turn. They cannot all enter on stage at the same time, testifying to the elusive *ferret*[57] that never ceases to run behind all the successive combinations.

In this alternation devoid of any dialectic, it appears impossible to achieve a total whole. It is certainly worth remarking the absence of a question mark in the title, which suggests that the questions *where?* and *what?* remain bereft of any response, signifiers devoid of a complement. *What* and *where* appear as bare assertions, bordering on the dimension beyond meaning: on the place of the subject as real.

This helps situate the conclusion to this play, where Voice recalls the journeys of the earlier works, in order to negate them: 'In the present as were I still. / It is winter. / Without journey. / Time passes.

57 Lacan describes the ungraspable aspect of desire and its metonymy with reference to the game where an object is passed around a circle from one person to another, behind their backs. It is accompanied by the song '*Il court, il court le furet…*' ('the ferret is running'). The lyrics compose a bawdy spoonerism that can be read as: 'the priest is screwing…'

/ That is all. / Make sense who may. / I switch off' (*WW*, 476). This abrupt conclusion appears enigmatic. It is worth referring here to Éric Wessler's remarks concerning the difficulty of inscribing an ending to 'From an Abandoned Work', where the progression of the text—which cannot be endless—results in its dissolution 'and a veering out of the itinerary marked out by direct and conscious self-reflexivity' (2009, 304). In this work, the latter device proves to be incapable of symbolising or integrating within subjectivity the unspeakable 'latent text', resulting in an arbitrary ending or cutting off. This problematic ending finds an answer in the conclusion of *Come and Go*, where the subjective dimension is contained within silence: 'The text is silent about the subject, it exists in its silencing' (330). This leads us to interpret the ending of *What Where* as showing the identity of Beckett's *M* characters reversed into the interrogative *W*. Such questioning remains open, and is thus, in turn, forced back onto the spectator, in a self-reflexive gesture.[58] At this moment—and as in *Come and Go* (Wessler 2009, 323)—the spectator finds himself abandoned to his own unanswered questions, while the subject that the play brings into being assumes existence through his voluntary silencing: this act is no longer arbitrary but signifies the ultimate confrontation with a dimension devoid of any answer. Here, the subject exists in his accepted nonexistence, in his exclusion from signifying language and, ultimately, in his total rejection from representation: it is he who is excluded.

Thus, the action of the superego is intimately linked to the ineffable. It is worth noticing that the title *What Where* is foreshadowed in *Embers*, in the dismay expressed by Addie in her successive questions: 'What?' (*E*, 258); 'Where?' (259), whereas the music master commands her to strike a precise key: 'Eff! Eff!' Here the superego's imperative demands that the subject name the impossible, a prospect that was already rejected in *Watt*: '[…] the unutterable or ineffable, so that any attempt to utter or eff it is doomed to fail, doomed, doomed to fail' (*W*, 62).

58 This cutting off recalls the pencil that runs out at the end of *Malone Dies*.

Defining the superego,[59] Michel Silvestre (267) identifies it as follows: 'It is from the Other that the object is subtracted so that the subject can found his [fundamental] fantasy on it.' This subtraction makes the Other incomplete, so that it cannot know in the subject's stead. That is to say that the Other is characterised by a breach by virtue of which the subject can come to existence. However, the superego reinforces the guilt that prompts the subject to respond to the limitless exigency to complete his Other. Thus, in the equivocation *jouis!/j'ouis!* (enjoy/I hear), where the force of the voice resounds, the superego commands: 'Jouis! [enjoy] Only, remember that it is from me that you received it. And bear in mind that I will not allow you to do just anything, bear in mind that now, I am watching you.' In the absence of the Name-of-the-Father that limits the impact of the superego, the Beckettian subject of the earlier works feels guilty for his very existence, and hears the injunction to repent for being born (*G*, 13). In these circumstances, it is impossible for him to determine what his fault may be, as the narrator of *The Unnamable* declares: 'Perhaps one day I'll know, say, what I'm guilty of' (*U*, 362).

In these later works however, if the injunction to give up the unknown of his existence remains, the latter appears as an impossible. As Elizabeth Barry points out about *Play*, the figures on stage will never say what is required of them, contrary to what can be observed in the encounter between Molloy and the policeman: 'Beckett's characters at last seem to relinquish the need to find "imperatives" that might give purpose and meaning to their existence' (2006, 204). She adds: 'Their here-and-now may feel punitive, but it cannot be connected with the interpretation—the judicial process of recreating the past by seeking the "right" or incriminating words—is thwarted' (205).

What Where is particularly instructive in this respect. At the same time as the play shows the omnipresence of this superego, it also reveals the point where the latter fails. In speaking to André Bernold, Beckett mused about the importance of the word *where*: 'C'est une vieille histoire que je ne comprends pas. Je me suis demandé ce que

59 See *supra*, p. 157–8, 336.

signifie *où*. Peut-être où est l'issue? La vieille histoire de l'issue…' ('It is an old story that I do not understand. I wondered what *where* meant. Perhaps where is the way out? The old story of the way out…', in Bernold, 35). Michel Bousseyroux confirms this perception, pointing to the dimension where language borders on a structural silence: '"Where" is the place of the final silence that words cannot reach, the one we encounter before having found our words […]' (2000, 201). He emphasises the fact that the confession—were it to be accomplished—would mean the radical abolition of the subject:

> *Was wo* is the impossible confession of the where without which *jouissance* would not take place. Impossible for the subject to give his confession to satisfy the desire of the Other, unless he succumbs to that which has made of himself a hole: the voice-object, the instrument of the Question. The worst would be for, through this confession, truth and *jouissance*, to become Siamese. (Bousseyroux, 2000, 201)

In other words, *where* is the place where the subject is fixed, located in his materiality, incapable of letting himself be born away by the endless chain of signifiers—'scattered by the everlasting words' (*TFN* XI, 144)—a position which would suppose that the 'speaking being' is weighed down by no substantiality. In this respect, David Addyman usefully points out how Beckett's written exchanges with Georges Duthuit on painting relate identity to a *where* (186), a dimension that remains highly problematic in *The Unnamable*. He quotes Beckett: 'One may just as well dare to be plain and say that not knowing is not only not knowing what one is, but also where one is, and what change to wait for, and how to get out of wherever one is […]' (*L2*, 98). While, as Jacques-Alain Miller points out with regards to the perpetual metonymy of the signifier, the subject can be perceived as a 'logical inconsistency' (1994b, 13), the *where* of *jouissance* marks a point of consistency that is 'always true': it is a constant. Thus, by localising *jouissance* through torture, Bam designates the gaping hole that cannot be circumscribed: the fundamental absence of an answer that the Beckettian subject is called upon to complete. In the same way, *The Unnamable* shows that in the impersonal dimension of language—that inflicts a behaviourist manipulation on its victim (*U*, 361), in the aim of capturing Worm within the light of meaning—the victim refuses to dissolve himself in his great Other. The subject's very specificity is to constantly resist such a fate, remaining on this impossible border between his alienation to the signifier, and the *unlimited* that threatens to annul him. Finally, if the interrogations in *What Where* progress towards the *where?*, this final question remains unanswered, since all that will ever be known about it are the words actually exchanged, not those situated in some mythical 'beyond': 'The *where* of "it enjoys" is nowhere else than there where "it" speaks […]' (Bousseyroux, 202), that is to say, supported by the speaking being (*parlêtre*).

Containing the 'unlimited'

Thus, by means of these various devices or setups, the apparatus aims to provide a border for the voice, instituting an obscure Master who emits orders and whose demands expect to be satisfied. A chain is formed, with a 'witness' and a 'scribe', entertaining the prospect of achieving an inscription that will set the voice at a distance, that will produce limits. However, the narrator constantly finds himself confronted with the malfunctioning of this system, as a consequence of the *unlimited*: he risks *aphanisis* or fading. Confusion and the impossible persist as the reverse side of the apparatus. What is being sought is a form of symbolisation—the institution of a paternal metaphor—allowing the extraction of this *jouissance*. That is what is expressed in *Rough for Radio II*, where the Master knows nothing, and the characters seek a word that, once it is pronounced, will at last free them from their endless mission. By contrast, *What Where* shows how the articulation persists, by virtue of the subject's resistance: for want of a word to symbolise his *jouissance*, he will never let go of that which constitutes him, in spite of the battering inflicted by the superego.

The discursive structure—or 'apparatus'—thus makes its appearance in *Murphy*, and is present in the '*Trilogy*' and in *How It Is*. It is perhaps not fortuitous that it should initially take form in the context of the asylum, where the imposition of constraint is centred on the alienated subject under surveillance, and who is the object of behaviourist conditioning, as indicated by the reference to Skinner (*Mu*, 147). The possible implication of the situation experienced in psychoanalysis can be noted,[60] to the extent that the latter also involves a particular awareness of the discursive structure of language. In spite of its radical difference to the asylum, psychoanalysis is also an artificial structure in which the analysand, brought to consider the foundations of his own symptoms, and to call into question his personal as sumptions—the categories that govern his existence—can encounter a degree of persecution associated, for example, with Bion's notion of 'attacks on linking'.[61] Indeed, Lacan's discourses are structured by a 'master signifier', a single anchoring point which commands the *whole*. The presence of this signifier can be felt in the fact that the discursive structure supposes a *cause* (situated outside the chain of speech), the retroactive mechanism of speech (whereby the words the subject addresses to the Other return to him, so he becomes aware of the way his identification is retroactively founded by the latter), finally, a *product*, which will never coincide with the cause.

Beckett remains in relation to this master signifier—as Suzanne Dow has demonstrated in her remarkable study of one of Lacan's rare allusions to Beckett—as well as experiencing the need to break it up in order to bring into play the *unlimited*. In *Murphy*, this signifier is at work in the will to control and condition the suffering internees, in order to curb their folly. *The Unnamable*, by contrast, mobilises a potentially endless—*unlimited*—flow of words, revealing the

60 Miller and Souter thus see the figure of Basil, in *The Unnamable*, as a version of the analyst (Miller and Souter, 69). However, little is put forward to substantiate this claim.

61 See *supra*, p. 102–4.

narrator's attempts to detach himself from any linguistic or discursive determination or framework.

Discursive structures thus show, firstly, the condition of the production of speech and creation, based on the 'master signifier' (S_1); secondly, how the *unlimited* is partly circumscribed by means of this binding: the subject arrives at no subjective abolition, no existence as 'will-lessness, a mote in its absolute freedom' (*Mu*, 72), such as Murphy dreamt of. Discursive structures also bring to light the limits of production in the effort to circumscribe the voice. This is one example of Beckett's *form* that 'accommodates the mess' (in Driver, 23), where the literary construction remains distinct from the formlessness it hems in, as Beckett says: 'Paradoxalement, c'est par la forme que l'artiste peut trouver une sorte d'issue. En donnant forme à l'informe. Ce n'est peut-être qu'à ce niveau qu'il y aurait une affirmation sous-jacente' ('Paradoxically, it is through form that the artist can find a sort of way out. By giving form to the formless. It is perhaps only on this level that there could be a subjacent affirmation', in Juliet, 36).

Daniel Katz suggests that the singularity of *Watt* lies in 'its interrogation of group or communal structures, and the mechanism by which the sense of belonging or estrangement is built' (66). He works here from Freud's *Civilisation, Society and Religion*, which shows the elements necessary to compose a group, and points out:

> Watt's fixations are less on the other servants or even Mr Knott than on the customs and rituals that constitute the household. [...] Like the Cartesian God, Knott becomes a necessary hypothesis for the functioning of a series of repeated rituals that create subjective identifications. (Katz, 64)

Watt would thus forshadow the discursive structures analysed in this chapter. However, what Katz calls this 'necessary hypothesis' does not found belief in Beckett's work: contrary to Descartes' vision, the master signifier is not 'God', precisely because the whole setup is presented as a *construct.* What Katz's analysis does reveal is how the discursive apparatus allows the subject to find a calming structure that attenuates the force of his unbearable singularity, protecting the subject from unlimited *jouissance*. Indeed, in linking *Watt* to 'Les Deux besoins' (*cf.* Brown, 2011d, 107), Katz situates the mysterious entities Knott and Youdi in relation to a form of absolute *jouissance*, pointing out that they are beyond 'need'—as is Mr Endon in *Murphy*—and drawing a parallel with William Burroughs' work *Junky* (194, n. 16). He points out that such an absolute requires to be refused: '[…] the artist needs to need, rather than not to need […].' Molloy asserts this idea: 'No, there were no words for the want of need in which I was perishing' (*Mo*, 30).

This perception of a vital need indicates that these discursive structures do not produce a homogeneous situation, but allow for the inscription of a form of alterity, which is a question Russell Smith raises with regards to the structures of *How It Is*. He quotes Shane Weller in this respect, who discounts the attainment of 'speaking the truth of being' at the end of this novel (in Smith, 2008, 357). The agents called 'witness' and 'scribe' disappear at the end of the text, and the narrating voice is involved in a dialogue with an unseen other. Smith observes:

> Significantly, there is no mention of the 'means to note,' which leads to the conclusion that there must be a scribe to produce the text, and thus the narrator's attempt to deny the existence of the witness is belied by the existence of the text itself. (Smith, 2008, 358)

Contrary to Weller, he sees proof here of otherness, stating that 'alterity is written back even into the structure of the narrator's claim to solitary autonomous creation'. However what needs to be added to this analysis is the status of allocution, since the narrator speaks to the voice in the same way as the Unnamable does to his 'delegates' (*cf.* Katz, 104). In doing so, he asks his unseen other to confirm what he says. The enunciation involved in creation thus entails a struggle with the invasive *voice*, in order to proffer an *invocation*, or bring the phatic function into play (Lacan, 2004, 318); it is a way of *inscribing* the subject's voice, of creating a void in the Other. The latter can in no way be seen as an authority, since it remains on the level of *perhaps*, the sign of a breach created in the *unlimited* voice. This allows us to show something of the actual functioning of speech, rather than leaning on the vague notion of 'alterity' in its binary opposition to 'identity'.

It is possible here to trace the common ground uniting our initial definition of the Beckettian voice as *unlimited*, and the discursive structures Beckett brings to the fore in certain works. It is here also that Beckett can be situated within the context of modernity—in the terms used to define it earlier[62]—as distinct from postmodernity. Jean-Claude Milner develops the idea of the fourfold structure—which he names 'quadruplicity', following translations of Heidegger—summing it up in the pairs of terms masculine/feminine, parents/child[63] (2003, 119). This recalls Lacan's assertion, quoted earlier, that a 'quadripartite structure is always a requisite in the construction of a subjective layout' (1966, 774). The first of the two oppositions points to the encounter with the radically other (*limited wholes*, in contact with the *unlimited*), with its complex dialectics that admit of no simple resolution. The second involves the question of transmission, 'from generation to generation': the dialectical movement (S_1–S_2) that necessitates continually taking up the past and reinventing it in the incalculable present, for the unknown but necessary future.

This structuring principle combines both Lacan's 'four discourses' and his formulæ of sexuation[64] which maintain a radical dissymmetry between masculine and feminine, the latter being productive of a dialectical logic. Thus, as shown by Serge André (295), the

---

62 See *supra*, p. 34.

63 The notion of quadruplicity is reflected in Paul Stewart's consideration of 'misopedia', which reinstates the dimension of reproduction in relation to the 'Cartesian paradigms of mind/body, male/female dichotomy' (2011, 122).

64 Developed *supra*, p. 68–9.

response to Freud's question 'What does a woman want?'[65] is that she wants a *supplément d'inconscient* (an unconscious supplement), meaning a dimension that, being repressed, becomes part of her subjective structure, instead of abandoning her to an untameable *jouissance*. The work of art also articulates the *limited whole* as a discursive structure—including the master signifier (S_1)—to the dimension of singularity, since it makes 'representations serve to appropriate what tears them apart' (Milner, 2007, 59), revealing the unceasing voice that underlies them. Thus the presence of the formulæ of sexuation also means that the universal *limited wholes* do not suffice, but that the *unlimited* supposes countless Names-of-the-Father whereby each one invents his own singular responses to the absence of the Other. On the other hand, that also means that the function of the norm and *limited wholes* are not abolished.

In this context, Milner evokes the 'Jewish name' (*le nom juif*), that is to say the specific function of the signifier or the name *Jew*. He asserts that it is the only one that 'has been able to rest *solely* on quadruplicity' (2003, 119). As such, it creates *division* within the subject, and is the object of intense and universal hatred[66], because it refuses to be assimilated within the contemporary postmodern *unlimited*,[67] which demands that all the components of reality be transformable, with the ambition of abolishing all differences and annihilating any obstacle to its extension.

The combination of sexual difference and the succession of generations is recognised by Éric Wessler, when he notes the structuring whereby certain Beckettian characters—masculine and feminine—are situated in relation to the 'unborn' subject. For example, Hackett

65 Freud's formulation actually used the definite article: 'Was will das Weib?' (André, 19). The adaptation is intended to reinstate the indispensible dimension of singularity.

66 This status is overtly ascribed, on an international level, to Israel. The title of Milner's 2003 book—'The Criminal Penchants of Democratic Europe'—points out the paradoxical nature of this anti-Semitism.

67 This *unlimited* is therefore a result of the universal extension of science and capitalism, as we noticed *supra*, p. 258.

and the Nixons seek to understand Watt and to impose a meaning on him, in a passage that implicitly alludes to the birth of the subject (2009, 258). Winnie, in turn, is faced with the Shower or Cooker couple. The example of Animator and Stenographer striving to make Fox speak, in *Rough for Radio II* could also be added. The place of the subject can be associated with the 'être assassiné' ('assassinated being', in Juliet, 15) whose existence Beckett felt within him, as represented in *All That Fall*, when Dan Rooney attempts to hide from Maddy the death of the baby that causes the delay of the train (Wessler, 2009, 305-6). Indeed, Wessler emphases that the 'effort to give, precisely, a "meaning" to an embryo of fiction [...] always takes place within a dramatic structure where the relationships between the sexes are marked by conflict, and where the protagonists form a trio' (257). Such a prosthetic structuring is necessary for characters who 'do not understand how to assume their situation or their function in a sexual logic, nor moreover in the mechanism of reproduction; as if they proved to be incapable of being subjects of their sexuality' (342).

To situate more precisely the origin and the impact of such structures—both in Beckett and in Lacan—it is useful to go further back, and to take into account the evolution of discourse in Western civilisation. In his study of Beckett's self-reflexive structures, Éric Wessler cites sociologist Niklas Luhmann as demonstrating how art becomes detached from any non-artistic determinant at the beginning of the 18th Century (2009, 163), thus asserting 'at the same time as its contingency, its autonomy and its legitimacy' (370). This status is clearly established at the end of the same century, and specifically becomes the instrument by which knowledge is acquired regarding a subject (188). Philippe Lacoue-Labarthe and Jean-Luc Nancy (13–4) point to the origins of Romanticism in a 'triple crisis': economic, political and Kantian. This change can be ascribed to an effect of the disintegration of collective ideals guaranteed by the divinity, by an over-arching cosmic order that confirms the pre-eminence of the paternal metaphor. Indeed, the latter manifests the destructive effect of signifier's universality, and its rejection of any singularity. As a result of the abolition of an external, transcendent agency, authority will henceforth be internal, located in the pure exteriority of language. This evolution unleashes the violence of the superego, as evidenced in the work of Sade and in Kant's categorical imperative. Following such a mutation, the subject can no longer find a foundation in metaphysical certainties, but only in his inscription in the *symbolic* which, in Beckett's work, will in no way be correlated with an absolute, as it was with the German Romantics.

The event of the post-modern era has pushed this problematic even further. The development of capitalism and information technology imposes the unlimited extension of the crushing and universal logic of the *One* that brooks no exception. In 1955, Lacan stated that the calculating machine—ancestor of the computer—is essentially symbolic, and is much more dangerous for mankind than the atom bomb (Lacan, 1978, 111). This is ostensibly the case of surveillance technology (Wajcman, 2010) and, as has long been known, in capitalism any revolt or contestation is readily absorbed as part of the overall system.

In this respect, Nathalie Charraud points out that the internet perpetuates a state of alienation since here—and contrary to what founds the construction of the subject—the object is not lost. And yet, what distinguishes humanity is the capacity to imagine and create—the subject is not exclusively symbolic—since these activities bring *lack* into play. The subject has to face up to *anxiety* (*angoisse*): the sentiment that does not deceive (Lacan, 2004, 92), and which precedes the loss of the object. At this moment, the subject names the Other, designating what he is, as an *object*, in the desire of his Other. This is precisely what Beckett regularly does, when his narrators and figures situate themselves as objects exposed to the gaze of another.

Discursive structures reveal their necessity for a subject when the latter is faced with the *unlimited*, understood as a situation devoid of any breach, of any exterior, that effaces subjectivity and the singularity of a subject's *jouissance*. The principle that Jean-Claude Milner names 'quadruplicity' maintains that a subject's singularity can never be absorbed within another category, such as gender,[68] race, or '*generic*' humanity.[69] Suzanne Dow's analysis would seem to concur with this approach, when she historicises and politicises Beckett in relation to Joyce. Noting that, contrary to his master, Beckett explicitly situated his writing on the side of 'subtraction' (in Knowlson, 1997, 352), she asserts:

> [...] this practice, following Lacan, works to produce a knowledge that the contemporary shameless subject lacks. This knowledge [...] is a knowledge of the S_1, or master signifier, as determining the singularity of the subject's position within speech, and which causes her [*sic*] fading or division beneath it, as the price of subjecthood as such. (Dow, 15–6)

This 'fading' is particularly tangible in *Not I*, and it would seem clear that Beckett maintains the eminently crucial status of singularity and the subject's radical division—impossible to eliminate—that results from language.

Regarding the structure he pointed out in *Watt*, Daniel Katz states: 'In the works composed during the famous "siege in the room," these questions will have largely disappeared through a sort of phenomenological reduction of all that they presuppose' (66). However, the discursive apparatus is indeed present in *Molloy*, but is pushed to the background, or reduced to episodes in *How It Is*: it is necessarily more tenuous in the fiction, where it is confined to the imaginary register. However, it finds its place again when Beckett chooses to write for and work with the theatre. While the earlier plays retain a degree

---

68 See *supra*, our critique of the notion of 'gender', p. 69–72.

69 The term belongs to Alain Badiou, and Milner's description fits perfectly, showing how 'postmodern' thinking is in harmony with the former's Platonic ideology: 'But when we come to the real, the new man is only full of emptiness. He is neither man nor woman, he has neither father nor mother nor child. His only spouse is a form, of which between the whole and the *pastout*, he ignores the law. He has placed quadruplicity outside of himself' (2003, 125).

of fiction, the use of the tape recorder in *Krapp's Last Tape* inaugurates the process leading to the minimalism of the later plays. In these texts, the discursive structure is not only represented, but it is also grounded in the real presence of spectators, the constraint consisting of creating a performance in a given place and at a given time: elements that are part of the address to an Other. Ludovic Janvier thus points out that Beckett's choice to work with the theatrical medium engendered a structural *separation*: it was 'intended to break the linearity that culminated in the *Texts for Nothing*' (2012, 15), and where 'the vectorial tension [was] unleashed towards a fleeing target, and endless story'. H. Porter Abbott (85) sees the theatre as a way of saving—in the guise of the character embodied on stage—Beckettian humanity that was perpetually threatened with disintegration in the prose works. This concords with the remark Beckett made to André Bernold, after discussing his work with Jim Lewis and the Süddendeutscher Rundfunk: 'Il me faudrait des acteurs-substantifs' ('I would need substantive-actors', in Bernold, 65). Matthieu Protin (2014) convincingly shows how Beckett's work directing his early plays confronted him with the very concrete components of the theatrical discursive set-up: the specificities of different actors, the presence of spectators, the performance as a unique occasion. The play, as staged, becomes a distinct object, while the original text becomes *other*. He also shows that 'where the author decomposes, the stage director recomposes, anchoring the actor's lines in the conditions of enunciation in order to achieve a binding of the different exchanges that abolish any chance' (334). Éric Wessler also observes that in turning to the theatre, Beckett abandons his narrator-characters who represent a 'subject that is too disembodied and too self-conscious, the one who until now held the pen' (2009, 195). He adds that these characters 'cease to consciously confront the absurdity of their human existence, they *live* it, and often in a grotesque manner' (195). Within this discursive structure, Beckett is able to create a breach or an opening (Geneste, 2014), also bringing to light the *unlimited* dimension as the 'mess' that the artwork contains and gives form to.[70] For a subject faced with the impossibility of 'being born', such structures succeed in holding together a discursive *whole*, while revealing unbreachable ruptures: Beckett's concern with what Leslie Hill calls 'disjunctive effects' (75). They reveal what *drives* speech, while marking its strict limits.

Éric Wessler (2015) has situated this major evolution as starting with 'From an Abandoned Work' (1954–1955), where Beckett started using a more brutal and condensed syntax, and where sentences manifest 'an aspiration towards contraction', where 'appositions replace conjugation' and the syntax 'regularly tends to evacuate the subject'. This movement can be illustrated by the motif of the 'abscess', as explored by Évelyne Grossman, when she sums up: 'In its abject or sublime version the writing of the abscess is at the heart of Beckett's first work. Little by little, however, it is effaced, to be replaced by the *dry* asceticism of his late works' (1998, 39). Indeed, the melancholy evidenced by the earlier works pointed to the mechanism—studied by Freud in *Mourning and Melancholia*—whereby the 'the shadow of the object fell upon the ego, which could now be condemned by a particular agency as an object, as the abandoned object' (2006, 292). In these conditions, the ego 'is overwhelmed by the object' (295). This results in the subject's submission to the crushing judgment *You are Krapp/crap!*, and the prevalence of the excremential object, such as the mud in which the creatures of *How It Is* endlessly crawl, or the wealth of Ballyba in *Molloy*, of which the narrator abruptly refuses to speak (Van Hulle, 2010a, 72–5). It is this invading presence which stifles the subject's voice in *Texts for Nothing*: '[…] this unnamable thing that I name and name and never wear out, and I call that words' (*TFN* VI, 125). By contrast, Beckett's ulterior '*dry* asceticism' (Grossman, 1998, 39) points to the evacuation of this object.

70 It would also be important to point out how work on theatre production was indispensible for Beckett's establishing of the final text, as of *Krapp's Last Tape* (Gontarski, 1998). This work provided a retroactive punctuating effect, bringing into play the theatre-object as Other.

The discursive structure also offers Beckett a fixity that was lacking in the metonymical continuity found diversely in the prose works such as the '*Trilogy*' and *Texts for Nothing*. In 'Sans', Éric Wessler points out, 'the rhythm, the sonorities and the distribution of cadences, particularly by the use of monosyllables, confer above all […] the fixity that was lacking in the abandoned works' (2009, 287). He emphasises how the earlier narrators and protagonists were condemned to express their pain 'in the boundless forests and immense, measureless plains, where their being ends up being disseminated, [so that their cry] resounds like an echoless voice, whose gaping hole is a wound' (292). What such a subject aspires to is a structure akin to the 'window-frame' (*CSPr*, 156) that the narrator of 'From an Abandoned Work' desperately attempts to contemplate. The recourse to both the theatre and the 'closed space' writings answer to this need. This is how, for example, in *Happy Days*, Winnie inaugurates the feminine characters who endure their distress, rather than evoking it from an ironical position, contrary to earlier figures (Wessler, 2009, 195).

This motif also brings us back to Leon Battista Alberti as the one who, as early as 1435, first gave the modern subject his theoretical grounding. Assimilating the window (*fenêtre*) to the frame of a painting, he endowed the latter with the separating functions of the signifier: the frame operates both a logical link and a separation. It inscribes and detaches an object (Wajcman, 2004, 312) from its surroundings, rendering it visible and offering it up to the subject's gaze. In the same way as the signifier produces 'repression', the frame not only opens up a vista to the subject, but it also hides the latter in its shadow (371), sheltering him from the 'all-seeing gaze' (387) of an omnipotent Other. Moreover, the inscription of the frame establishes discursive limits in that it not only encloses what it encompasses, but it also frames the unlimited space surrounding it (102).

Beckett's constant and extremely ingenuous use of intertextuality induces us to situate his great Other on the side of literature as universal, in harmony with what Éric Wessler emphasises as the aspiration of the German Romantics, who sought to ground literature in the autonomous subject. He states that for Beckett, 'a subject only exists in the text'[71] (2009, 366). In this perspective, literature legitimises itself, and gives the subject his 'juridical' grounding (265, 348, 366). Wessler observes that self-reflexivity is 'comparable to the devising of the subject in his accession to the symbolic Law through the order of language' (299), an observation that can be extended to the discursive structures. The place of the subject is thus essential here, in that 'self-reflexivity is henceforth assigned a function corresponding less to that of the superego than to the establishing of a pseudo-unconscious' (303). The function of creation is thus to palliate the confrontation with the lack of an unconscious.

However, contrary to Joyce, who aimed to include the totality of learning, Beckett worked in the direction of intension.[72] This choice results in his sometimes depreciatory attitude with regards to the 'loutishness of learning' (*CPo*, 55), revealing the impact of the superego as pushing towards a goal situated at infinity, comparable to the vanishing point in perspective painting (Wajcman, 2004, 342), and which operates as the only hypothetical guarantee possible. That is to say that Beckett was simultaneously steeped in learning, but that he fought against its pretention to cover the whole of reality by virtue of its power to name and its capacity to signify. This perception suggests the association of Beckettian learning with the secondary 'excipient' (in Whitelaw, 1996, 139) he spoke of in relation to the text of *Footfalls*, as opposed to the crucial importance of May's pacing.

Henceforth, the double bar marking the *impossible* in the discursive structures is located within the very structure of language: the combination of the inclusive *perhaps* and the exclusive *neither*; the obligation to go *on*, and the radical impossibility of doing so. One analysis that singularly sheds light on this new perspective is Mariko Hori

71 'Literature: it indeed seems that it is, as a last resort, the only reality [...] that Beckett's characters have succeeded in assimilating [...]' (Wessler, 2009, 371).

72 'The more Joyce knew the more he could. He's tending toward omniscience and omnipotence as an artist. I'm working with impotence, ignorance' (in Shenker, 148). See also Wessler (2009, 162) and Connor (2014a, 152-75).

Tanaka's comparison of Beckett's theatre to Japanese Noh. This critic shows how the Japanese actor, like the Beckettian one,[73] 'must discard his/her self-consciousness and be aware of his/her own body objectively'(107), in order to be completely determined by the signifier. She quotes Anna McMullan who evokes 'maximum concentration and absolute control of one's body and voice' (in Hori Tanaka, 110). This is specifically how the actor works with his body—which, according to Lacan, composes 'the alphabet' (2013, 328) of unconscious discourse—insofar as he 'lends his limbs, his presence, not simply as a marionette, but with his truly real unconscious, that is to say the relationship of his limbs to a certain history that is his own'. In his Seminar *Identification*, Lacan comments Akira Kurosawa's film *Rashomon* (1950), where interludes suspend the fighting, and the combattants, separately, 'turn around three times on the spot, making, to I know not what unknown point in space, a paradoxical bow'.[74] Henri Rey-Flaud (85) states that 'it is not a ritual but a ceremony that aims, beyond representation, at symbolic death'. Contrary to imaginary death—where one reflects back on all one is about to lose—the Japanese warrior confronts 'the instant that suddenly strips him [...] of all the fortuitous accidents of his history, to place himself at the point of Φ [the phallus[75]], the founder of his history, where the signifier that is the possessor of all its virtualities avows that it is also the signifier of his death' (86). Contrary to his earlier work, Beckett's later creation brings

73 For a particularly eloquent example, see *supra*, Billie Whitelaw's experience, p. 127–8.

74 Lesson of 27 June 1962 (unpublished).

75 The phallus can thus be quite different from its usual meaning. Lacan points out that if Hamlet does not strike Claudius, it is because what he is really aiming at, behind the pallid figure of the usurper, is the 'real phallus': '[...] the completely enigmatic manifestation of power as such' (2013, 416). He will only attain this aim unintentionally, and at the cost of his own life (417).

into play the phallus in this form: the assertion of the subject's existence at the very point of his abolition.[76] This phallus is what gives such force to the theatrical works representing spectral figures and situations: it renders present both the concrete impact of the signifier, and the voice's *unlimited* quality.

If therefore, in the late theatre, the actor is subjected to the apparently absolute control of the text and the stage director, his real presence is crucial, since the final effect perceived by the spectator is the *way* the actor 'subjects' himself to the discourse—to the *voice*—of his Other. The latter is, in this case, 'Beckett' as writer and director who, in turn, gives form to the voice of his own Other. What is commonly called Beckett's 'abstraction'[77] is the way he puts to work and represents the subject as absolutely determined by the signifier. When Michel Bousseyroux speaks of the mouvements in *Quad* which aim to exhaust the possible, he notes that the dancers are reduced to silence: 'What operates as the silent saying of the demand "let it function!",[78] without flinching, is all the more stripped bare. That is to say: the saying *par excellence* that is deduced from the discourse of the Master' (2000, 190). This shows the discourse of the Master as an imperative that gives its grounding to the unconscious, insofar as the master signifier (S_1) represses or evacuates the subject. The Master demands that institutions function without hinderance: any obstacle must be abolished. He takes no interest in the unease a subject may experience with regards to the system, and *speech* is perfectly superfluous. The dancers

76 Here, we can refer back to Lacan's reference to the way the singular *trait* in Japanese calligraphy 'crushes the universal' (2001, 16). See *supra*, p. 137.

77 We can recall here Beckett's remark concerning his characters: 'Mais je vous engagerai à y voir moins l'effet d'un effort d'abstraction, ce dont je suis peu capable, que le refus d'atténuer tout ce qu'ils ont à la fois de complexe et d'amorphe' (*L2*, 389) ('But I would urge you to see in them less the result of an attempt at abstraction, something I am almost incapable of, than a refusal to tone down all that is at one and the same time complex and amorphous in them', *L2*, 391).

78 In French, the verb *marcher* means both to walk and to function.

in *Quad* thus efface all manifestation of subjectivity, refusing to put a 'stain on silence and nothingness'.[79]

However, through his creation, Beckett does just that. What remains at this stage is the *subject* as *object* of this discourse, present in Beckett's work with *lalangue*, which reresents the ultimate condensation of discursive structures. Matthew Feldman points to the lasting influence of the radio creations, stating that 'the especially "sonorous" nature of Beckett's later work owes a debt of as-yet inestimable measure to his extensive collaboration with the BBC' (2014, 54). As we have seen, the radio introduces a radical change in discursive structuring, bringing forcibly into play the signifier in its relation to the voice. Éric Wessler notes that starting with 'From an Abandoned Work', in order to deal with 'incomprehensible internal violence', writing 'must opt for repetition and rhyme, that is to say for a language that Beckett will draw palpably nearer to in a few years, that of *Sans*, of *Not I*' (2009, 338). As Lacan succinctly states it: 'Failure [*ratage*] is the object' (1975b, 55). In this perspective, Beckett's 'rhythm and syntax of extreme weakness'[80] belongs to this tight link to the symbolic in its mortifying dimension, and the '*empêchement*' (*MP*) necessarily contained in—or produced by—the symbolic. This is the contrary of exploiting some sort of formula in order to deploy a wealth of expressivity. Neither does it strictly mean to practice 'attacks on linking'[81] but, rather, to see how the subject is radically determined by the signifier, and to find a form of support in the place where the latter breaks down. It is in this respect that Beckett stated to Charles Juliet: 'Le travail antérieur interdit toute poursuite de ce travail. [...] Chaque fois, il faut qu'il y ait un pas en avant.' ('Previous work prohibits any pursuit of this work. [...] Each time, there must be a step forward', in Juliet, 20). This is the point of impossibility that Beckett repeatedly verifies in his later creation. And yet, it is also here that, in creation, something of the *phallic*

79 Interview in *Vogue* (after Beckett's being awarded the Nobel Prize), December 1969.

80 Letter to Barbara Bray, 11 March 1959 (*L3*, 211).

81 See *supra*, p. 102–8.

register returns, as Henri Rey-Flaud's remark concerning the Japanese warrior suggests. Or, as Marie-Hélène Brousse points out about *Endgame*, at the point where everything that gives our world its consistency has disappeared—'There's no more [...]' (*Eg*, 97)—creation provides a form of uplifting: 'The phallus has deserted the stage. But as Beckett is an artist of language, he makes it shimmer [*miroiter*] yet again for us, in laughter.'

Singularity of the Voice: A Conclusion

In a previous book, *Beckett, les fictions brèves: voir et dire*[1] (2008) we explored the scission between two facets of Beckett's work, a dissociation between the dimensions of *seeing* and *saying* that unfold according to the two following propositions. Firstly: of a complete utterance, whose final punctuation confirms its meaning, it can be said that we *see* what it means; but a sentence that does not come to completion, that is pure *saying*, is declared to be obscure, we *do not see* what it means. In Beckett's *saying*, the subject utters without any Other hearing him; however, *seeing* often reveals the image of a world endowed with a frozen meaning, where the enunciator's subjectivity finds no place to inscribe itself, to be represented. In this context, the dimension of *saying* reveals pure subjectivity, the reality of a subject exposed to the *voice*. This same study pointed to the Beckettian voice as unceasing, showing the monologue that unfolds in some texts as rooted in an unbreachable alterity, with no symbolic Other present in order to close off saying, and give form to an utterance.

The aim of the present work has been to examine in some depth, and more systematically, one of these two dimensions: that of *saying*, as a manifestation of the voice. This new study can hardly claim to be exhaustive, since the *voice* manifests itself at every level of Beckett's creation. At most, its aim has been to establish a number of constants defining the *voice*, and to discover the extent of its presence throughout Beckett's work.

The choice was made to approach the voice in its 'subjective' dimension. That is to say that it seemed preferable not to work directly from pre-existing æsthetic categories, since the latter would have limited the voice to its phenomenological dimension: to consider it as a simple given, and to settle for seeing how Beckett innovates in the field of literature. This path would have obliged us to proceed largely

1 A detailed account of this work is given, in English, in a book review by Isabelle Ost.

by imposing various divisions without discerning their unity. Like Bruno Clément,[2] for example, we would have noticed that the voice 'occupies a regularly ambiguous place, both internal (included in discourse and more often an internal voice) and external (it arises as an apparition)' (2007, 24); that the narrator often quotes it; that it has a prescriptive character. We would also have studied the way the voice is affected by the separation or doubling of characters and narrative agents. Following Sarah West, the 'performative voice' would have been investigated, to understand how the written text demands to be rendered vocally, and how it has, in the late theatre, an *acousmatic* nature. All these observations are perfectly pertinent and enlightening. However, were we to limit ourselves to these aspects, it would have been impossible to discern the logic underlying the voice's diverse and paradoxical facets: only the theoretical tools offered by Lacanian psychoanalysis provide this possibility. Above all, these approaches would have excluded any chance of discerning the existential importance of the voice, in a subject's relationship to language.

If literary creation supposes the articulation of its production to the field of existing forms and to literary history—themes, genres and the history of ideas—it also remains that behind a work there is a subject who feels the imperious *need* to create, a question that Beckett precisely highlighted, in relation to creation, in his 1938 text 'Les Deux besoins' (*cf.* Brown, 2011d). Far from being limited to its relationship to the potentially domesticated and remunerative realm of culture, creation is linked to an unbearable dimension of existence. It can then be understood as a subject's *response* to the latter: one that takes form and existence in a work that also circumscribes it and makes bearable. The association with the voice is patent in this striking formulation offered in 'Les Deux besoins': '[…] enfer d'irraison d'où s'élève le cri à blanc, la série de questions pures, l'œuvre' ('[…] hell of unreason whence arises the blank cry, the series of pure questions, the work', *Dsj*, 56). The subject here is not one who, situated on the plane of utterances,

2 Bruno Clément studies these elements both in his book (1994) and, in a more concentrated manner, in his articles (2007; 2008).

apprehends himself as master of his own consciousness and acts, but rather one who remains unknowable to his own self.

To combine an approach anchored in a theoretical framework and recognising the importance of subjectivity leads us to acknowledge the centrality of Beckett's voices. The latter do not boil down to being one aspect among so many others in Beckett's universe, such as the characters or the spaces evoked. That is to say—to use an example that is nonetheless common in his work—the voices are not simply in the characters' 'heads'. In the same way, the voice cannot be understood as a purely literary device, in a dialogue with the limits of genres. On the contrary, it is an integral part of the subject or the 'speaking being'.

In this perspective, the first chapter works from Lacan's conceptualisation of the voice as the part that remains excluded from the signifier's retroactive mechanism: it can be heard at the place where nomination—along with the reassuring stability it promises—fails to exhaustively express the subject's being.

It was then necessary to go one step further, since the Beckettian voice does not remain dissimulated or stifled behind meanings: on the contrary, it remains 'in the open'. That is to say that it does not only found the signifying chain by pointing to the latter's firm anchoring in an exception that inscribes a *limit*—such is the function of the Name-of-the-Father—but it also indicates the possible abolition of this limit, marking the existence of an *unlimited* dimension which cannot be subjected to negation or extraction. This *unceasing* voice is the one that is heard, for example, in the narrator of *The Unnamable*, or in his successor in *Not I*. To give its maximal extension to this voice, Lacan's assertion according to which for the schizophrenic, 'all the symbolic is real' (1966, 392) provided a reference point. Language appears here not as a network of meanings, but as something that 'parasites' (Lacan, 2005a, 95) the subject, confronting him with a dimension that is irreducibly beyond all meaning. The corresponding condition, in Beckett's writing, is that of being 'unborn': this metaphor serving to designate the status of the subject who, not having been instituted in relation to the desire of his Other, finds himself irremediably in contact with the *unlimited* quality of language. As early as 1929, Beckett indicated that this abandonment confirmed 'the absolute absence of the Absolute' (*Dsj*, 33). The Beckettian subject finds himself facing an absence that nothing can palliate, other than the *creation* that endows it with form. Both this absence and the Beckettian unlimited—particularly in the works of the middle period—can be linked to the structure of melancholy, where the subject experiences the impossibility of escaping existence: his eternal confinement within language, untouched by any vivifying desire. With the 'phallic' register proving eminently problematic, the Beckettian subject is both 'born' and 'unborn', being unable to successfully integrate either state.

This definition and initial description of the Beckettian voice opened the way—in the second chapter—for a closer study of the voice's linguistic structure, by examining the role of pronouns. The deictic *I* and *you* prove to be problematic since, by nature, they are anchored in an extralinguistic dimension, which they articulate with social reality, materialised by dialogue. In Beckett's work, the *I* is absolutely alone, rather than being situated symmetrically in relation to an interlocutor; however, this uncoupling of the system of pronouns is not simply negative, since it gives existence to the *voice*, as a positive presence. What comes to the fore in *Not I*, is the ceaseless *drive* that destroys any notion of bodily unity, but whereby Mouth gives expression to this *real* by her insistent rejection of the pronoun *I*. The singularity of *Company*, however, consists of describing an attempt to found the hypothetical subject identified by the *I*, by means of binding the *you* and the *he*: the fictional failure is precisely what renders the *voice* palpable in this text. *A Piece of Monologue* offers a fiction using the pronoun *he*, which nonetheless is expressive of the very real subject who remains excluded from the *I*. However, the staging of the play attains the status of a ritual offered up to an Other capable of recognising the 'unborn' subject, who thus acquires a temporary and substitute 'birth'.

The third chapter looked successively at two topological aspects of the voice as *real*, then two forms of response. In earlier texts—*Waiting for Godot*, the '*Trilogy*'—the voice appears as a continuous *rustling* or a *murmuring* that nothing can silence. This aspect is expressed in the motif of the 'dead voices', which testify to the original absence of an interlocutor capable of instituting the subject within a vivifying exchange: they inhabit a subject that is mortified, incapable of moving in the consistent or plausible reality that Beckett named 'traversable space' (*TPR* III, 111). However, they manifest their potential *superego* nature when they persecute the character of *Eh Joe*, who endeavours to reduce them to silence.

On the reverse side, this force of the *unlimited* voice produces the interruptions that are constant throughout Beckett's work, but particularly in the utterances composing plays such as *Krapp's Last Tape*, *Not I* and *Play*. Any such rupture is absolute, hindering discourse from producing the continuity—associated with the register of plausible reality—of a linguistic articulation. For the Beckettian subject, no third term mediates between two irreducible poles. Some characters make this alternation audible by means of the *knock* (*Ohio Impromptu*), in an effort to mark an end, and inaugurate a new start. In doing so, they also cause the imperative nature of the voice to resound, exhorting themselves to continue, in the face of the impossibility of moving on. This voice of the superego also manifests itself by intrusions in the body: the bell that, for Winnie, is like 'a gouge' (*HD*, 162), or concretely physical attacks in *How It Is* or *Rough for Radio II*. The only 'law' governing the frequency of the interruptions is, precisely, the absence of any regularity or governing principle: the interruptions manifest the incidence of *caprice*, the anomic dimension that is precisely a function of the *unlimited*. In the course of his work however, Beckett puts this fragmenting force to work, showing it as a way of 'accommodating' the uncontrollable 'mess' of existence, engendered by language.

Confronted with this radical absence of any pacification ensured by the symbolic register, the Beckettian subject invents responses. *Inscription* represents one of the possibilities at his disposal: it is a physical response, for want of a nomination capable of repressing the unbearable. To *inscribe*—whether it be by weaving words and sentences or making footsteps heard (*First Love*, *Footfalls*)—is not to inaugurate a symbolic enunciation capable of silencing the voice. It is—for want of achieving an extraction of *jouissance* 'once and for all'—to trace an edge, to produce sounds that remain impregnated with the substance of the ceaseless voice.

Another response to the voice is for the subject to 'do the image', as is expressed in the text entitled 'The Image'. The subject produces a representation, in relation to which he occupies the place of waste or refuse. Such an image offers a degree of protection from the voice. In *Rough for Radio II*, it takes the place of the word (the paternal metaphor) whose absence can 'pollute the whole of speech' (*MD*, 186), for the Beckettian subject. Finally, the adoption of a *reading voice*—playing oneself the role of the absent Other (*Texts for Nothing*, *Rockaby*, *Embers*)—represents a means to face up to the voice: this simulacrum of a dialogue is addressed, as a whole, to the Other, as can be seen in the staging of the 'ritual' in *A Piece of Monologue*. This address offers the possibility of procuring some consistency and reassuring oneself when confronted with the void.

The fourth chapter showed that the conception of the voice is not limited to the purely literary realm, but reveals its relation to the exteriority and otherness materialised by technological devices: particularly by the recourse to the recorded voice in the plays, from *Krapp's Last Tape* to the *dramaticules*, including the plays for radio and television. Technology intervenes as a consequence of the universalising discourse propagated by the extension of science and capitalism, whose effect is to radically deny or exclude the subject, thus extending the impact of the voice. Notably, the intervention of technology reveals strikingly how the voice is an object detached from the body: it is heard as a spectral manifestation of the *unlimited*, instead of it being enclosed within corporeal bounds. Krapp uses his tape-recorder as a means to keep at bay his anxiety of death, while also revealing his frozen and mortified character: his inability to assume his own choices and his evolution from one year to another. Beckett's use of radio allows him to show the voice at work, destroying the *imaginary* dimension that occupies the visual aspect of the stage. On the radio, the voice is what cannot be imagined: even in *All That Fall*, the form of the play removes any idea that the characters are moving about within any concrete space. In these circumstances, the listener is, like Beckett's 'unborn' characters, entirely dependent on the voice's movement: he is deprived of any interiority. The radio is the voice of the Other, or the Other as voice, of which the listener feels himself to be the sole addressee. Such a device is not purely negative, since it also functions as a vital 'organ', offering the subject a means to palliate the unbearable or *unlimited* voice.

In the radio plays, as in some *dramaticules*, the voices conveyed by electrical devices are often manipulated by a 'sound editor' who makes them heard, or who turns them off. Experiencing his exclusion from subjective enunciation, his inability to 'create', this character produces his singular place through this structuring activity: in the absence of a superior or detached view point, he passes back and forth, from one voice to the other. In *Play*, this role is played by the spotlight which orders the discourse of the figures situated in urns. As the light is itself deprived of speech, it can only induce the latter in the figures on stage. For this reason, far from being a simple persecutor, it experiences a torment symmetrical to that endured by its 'victims'. In *What Where*, this role is played by Voice of Bam, emanating from a megaphone, and who organises the movements of the figures on stage. The director thus appears to be situated in relation to the symbolic register, whereas the visible figures belong to the imaginary; the function of these two dimensions being to circumscribe the gaping hole present in language.

It is always a question—as in *Play*—of the sound editor being affected by the play he organises, as can be observed in *Cascando* and *Rough for Radio I*. He actually *needs* the voices, and is overwhelmed by extreme anxiety when they disappear, being unable to bring them back. The opposition between *words* and *music* (*Words and Music*, *Cascando*) offers another treatment of this function: the sound director testifies to the impossibility of achieving a true mediation between the register of meaning, and the voice devoid of meaning. Only the work of creation can deal with this breach on a material level.

Finally, certain works (*Murphy*, *How It Is, Molloy*) show the effort to contain and localise the *voice* by means of a geometrical apparatus or prosthesis, comparable to Lacan's 'four discourses' that found social bonds. Thus four figures arranged and endowed with distinct functions form a discursive whole—subject, witness, scribe, master—and their efficiency consists in achieving an inscription. These structures seem to be, to a certain extent, a response to the dislocation of linguistic binding noted in the use of pronouns. While with Lacan, they determine the nature of social bonds, Beckett's devices serve a specifically subjective function. At the basis of this setup, an absent 'Master' appears to be the agent who seeks to grasp something about his own unknown, that is to say, he is the subject insofar as the latter is real. In this way, the subject who finds himself in the most absolute solitude can imagine he is facing another, within a situation of interlocution. However, the artificial character of these systems rapidly becomes apparent, since they inevitably reveal the point where they fail to found a coherent and autonomous discourse. The torture sessions of *What Where* show how the subject finally escapes any attempt to absorb him within the register of meaning. This setup brings into play the way the categories of sexuation and the succession of generations combine to fundamentally structure language, and are vital for subjectivity as refractory to any categorising: discursive structures create a vital 'window-frame' allowing the subject to exist in his radical singularity. This enables us to define the acute and very concrete relationship to language that marks Beckett's late work, and the movement from mortification by the signifier towards a vivifying use of creation.

One of the aims of this study has been to affirm the centrality of the voice in Beckett's creation. On this point, we heartily agree with Daniel Katz's assertion: 'For Beckett, consciousness starts not with *speaking*, but with *hearing*. […] The Beckettian cogito would be, "I hear, therefore I am"' (86). We have attempted to push this perception further, and to point out the way the voice involves *jouissance* that borders on the real, on an inhuman dimension of language. The recourse to the insights of Lacanian psychoanalysis is crucial here, not to lay claim to any definitive interpretation but, on the contrary, to open up a field that merits further exploration. The extreme musicality of Beckett's writing, the density of his use of the resources of language—be it intertextuality or *équivoque*—could be appreciated more deeply, it would seem, by taking into account the subjective construction required to deal with the opaque dimension of *jouissance* inherent in what has often been called Beckett's 'abstraction'. In other words, the way a creator plays out his existence in his relation to the materiality of words. In particular, it is crucial to see how a work of creation constitutes a response to the unfathomable absence of any Other. Thus, the fragmenting of linguistic structures, the omnipresent interruptions, or the absence of meaning is a domain that can be developed in relation to what is at stake for a subject; this also means dealing with the aspect of Beckett's creation that borders on the non-literary.

In this study of the *unlimited voice*, any idea of pathology has been resolutely excluded. If the question of the *pastout* or the *unlimited* was explored by Lacan in relation to feminine *jouissance*, and to psychosis—with 'Joyce the Symptom' (1975), many years after his first approach in *Seminar III* (1955–1956)—its importance is that it does not simply concern some 'negligible' or 'pathological' cases but, as Beckett put it, 'Everyman' (in Feldman, 2006, 112). 'Everyone is mad, that is to say delirious', as Lacan stated in his later developments.[3] Indeed if, in set theory, a whole is founded by the part that is extracted—and that negates it—then any *limited whole* will in turn be anchored in a part that is *unlimited*, that cannot be defined, to which one cannot ascribe attributes. In return, this dimension is what allows us to put all naming and all discourses into perspective, to ascertain the part that founds and structures them.

Thus if Beckett deals with the voice as *unlimited*, it is certainly not in the postmodern spirit of optimism and exaltation, denouncing or 'challenging' conventional structures. As Suzanne Dow has shown, commenting an allusion by Lacan,[4] Beckett maintains the importance

3 Jacques Lacan, 'Journal d'*Ornicar?*', *Ornicar?*, no. 17–18, 1979, p. 278.

4 'As regards the garbage bin, in this era dominated by the genius of Samuel Beckett, we know a bit about it' (Lacan, 2006a, 11).

of the 'master signifier' that founds discourse, seeing it as a necessary artifice or construct. By this means, his creation circumscribes the dimension of the impossible and makes it operative. Creation is *doing*, not producing a metalanguage destined to communicate or convey meaning which, as Lacan pointed out, is always based on a fundamental incomprehension or misunderstanding. Beckett's creation, like Joyce's, '*is that something itself*' (*Dsj*, 27): his work makes the *voice* present for the reader or spectator, who thus experiences an encounter with this part that touches and disturbs him profoundly, in an intimate way and, paradoxically, as something completely foreign and impossible to tame, as Beckett expressed, according to Tom Driver's account of their conversation:

> What I am saying does not mean that there will henceforth be no form in art. It only means that there will be new form, and that this form will be of such a type that it admits the chaos and does not try to say that the chaos is really something else. The form and the chaos remain separate. The latter is not reduced to the former. That is why the form itself becomes a preoccupation, because it exists as a problem separate from the material it accommodates. (in Driver, 23)

If form and chaos remain separate, it is because the latter—like the *voice*—cannot be *assimilated*: it carries within it its inherent part of otherness.[5]

In relation to *Hamlet*, Lacan stated that 'poetic creations engender, more than they reflect, psychological creations' (2013, 296): they do not duplicate, but produce a completely new, unheard-of reality. Thus Beckett's use of voice technology does not reproduce the given.[6] On the contrary, it represents a *response* to the postmodern

---

5 '[...] in order for it to respond, we need to incorporate the voice as the alterity of what is said' (Lacan, 2004, 318).

6 A work like *What Where* does not give a glimpse of the horrors of 'the Global Village' (Maude, 2009, 134), for example.

world: his creation *reclaims* subjectivity from the disastrous effects of technology and science. Beckett creates a singular voice—a salutary silence—in the midst of the infinite chattering of modern capitalism and technology: the endless verbiage that aims to block out perception of the structure (*jouissance*) that founds such a discourse as an imperious, ferocious voice commanding obedience.

By creating a breach, a rift, in such a voice, Beckett's creation produces a dimension of freedom. If making one's voice heard gives the *real* weight of a subject's being (Lacan, 2013, 458) and silences the Other, it can be asserted that such is the function of Beckett's work. As Mladen Dolar (160) says, the voice 'comes back to us through the loop of the Other' but, it should be added, it is the latter's absence that thus takes on form in Beckett's work. By addressing a public his creation resounds in the 'absolute absence of the Absolute' (*Dsj*). Cutting short any effort to make meaning, his creation makes possible a response on the part of the reader and the spectator.

Bibliography

Abbreviations

JOBS: *Journal of Beckett Studies*. Edinburgh UP.

SBT/A: *Samuel Beckett Today/Aujourd'hui*. Amsterdam/New York, Rodopi.

Other Works by Samuel Beckett

The following references complete the list of abbreviations and editions provided at the beginning of this study.

_______. 1985. *'Happy days': The Production Notebook of Samuel Beckett*. James Knowlson (ed.). London: Faber & Faber.

_______. 1992. *The Theatrical Notebooks of Samuel Beckett*, vol. III: *'Krapp's Last Tape'*. James Knowlson (ed.). London: Faber & Faber.

_______. 1993. Knowlson, James and Dougald McMillan (eds.). *Theatrical Notebooks of Samuel Beckett*, vol. I: *'Waiting for Godot' with a revised text*. James Knowlson and Dougald McMillan (eds.). London: Faber & Faber.

_______. 1998. *No Author Better Served: The Correspondence of Samuel Beckett and Alan Schneider*. Maurice Harmon (ed.). Cambridge [Mass.]: Harvard University Press.

_______. 1999. *The Theatrical Notebooks of Samuel Beckett*, vol. IV: *'The Shorter Plays'*. S. E. Gontarski (ed.). London/New York: Faber & Faber/Grove Press.

_______. 2009. *The Letters of Samuel Beckett*, t. 1, *'1929–1940'*. Martha Dow Fehsenfeld and Lois More Overbeck (eds.). Cambridge: Cambridge University Press.

_______. 2011. *The Letters of Samuel Beckett*, t. 2, *'1941–1956'*. George Craig, Martha Dow Fehsenfeld, Dan Gunn, Lois More Overbeck (eds.). Cambridge: Cambridge University Press.

_______. 2012. *Notes de Beckett sur Geulincx: Arnold Geulincx, Samuel Beckett.* Nicolas Doutey (ed.). Besançon: Les Solitaires Intempestifs, 'Expériences philosophiques'.

Works on Beckett

Abbott, H. Porter. 1990. 'Late Modernism: Samuel Beckett and the Art of the Œuvre'. In Brater and Cohn (eds.): 73–96.

Ackerley, Chris. 2004. 'The Uncertainty of Self: Samuel Beckett and the Location of the Voice'. *SBT/A,* no. 14: *'After Beckett/D'après Beckett'*: 39–51.

_______ and Stanley E. Gontarski (eds.). 2004. *The Grove Companion to Samuel Beckett.* New York: Grove Press.

_______. 2010. *Demented Particulars: The Annotated 'Murphy'.* Edinburgh UP.

_______. 2011. 'Éléments recyclés dans *Words and Music/Paroles et musique*'. In Brown (ed.), 2011c: 57–76.

_______. 2014. 'Samuel Beckett and the Aesthetic Dilemma'. In Gontarski (ed.): 17–24.

Addyman, David. 2014. 'Where Now?: Beckett, Duthuit and *The Unnamable*'. *SBT/A*, no. 26 : '*Revisiting 'Molloy', 'Malone meurt'/'Malone Dies' and 'L'Innommable'/'The Unnamable'*': 179–91.

Alexandre-Bergues, Pascale. 2011. '*Cascando*'. In Hubert (ed.): 194–6.

_______. '*Paroles et Musique.*' In Hubert (ed.): 764–6.

Alphant, Marianne and Nathalie Léger (eds.). 2007. *Objet Beckett.* Paris: Centre Pompidou/IMEC éditeur.

Asmus, Walter. 1977. 'Practical aspects of theatre, radio and television: Rehearsal notes for the German premiere of Beckett's "That Time" and "Footfalls" at the Schiller-Theater Werkstatt, Berlin', Helen Watanabe (trans.). *JOBS*, no. 2, Summer 1977. <http://www.english.fsu.edu/jobs/num02/Num2WalterAsmus.htm> (accessed 24 April 2015).

Atik, Anne. 2006. *Comment c'était: souvenirs sur Samuel Beckett*, Emmanuel Moses (trans.). Paris: Éditions de l'Olivier.

Aubarède, Gabriel d'. 'En attendant Beckett' [interview with Samuel Beckett]. *Les Nouvelles littéraires*, n° 1746 [Paris: Larousse], 16 February 1961: 21.

Badiou, Alain. 2003. *On Beckett*, Alberto Toscano and Nina Power (trans. and eds.). Manchester: Clinamen Press.

Bailey, Iain. 2014. *Samuel Beckett and the Bible*. London: Bloomsbury, 'Historicizing Modernism'.

Bair, Deirdre. 1978. *Samuel Beckett: A Biography*. London: Jonathan Cape.

Baker, Phil. 1997. *Beckett and the Mythology of Psychoanalysis*. Houndmills, Basingstoke, Hampshire: Macmillan Press/New York: St. Martin's Press.

Barfield, Steven, Matthew Feldman and Philip Tew (eds.). 2009. *Beckett and Death*. London: Continuum, 'Continuum Literary Studies'.

Barry, Elizabeth. 2006. *Beckett and Authority: The Uses of Cliché*. Houndmills/Basingstoke/New York: Palgrave-Macmillan.

________. 2009. 'Beckett, Augustine, and the Rhetoric of Dying'. In Barfield, Feldman and Tew (eds.): 72–88.

Ben-Zvi, Linda. 2008. 'Beckett, McLuhan, and Television: The Medium, the Message, and "the Mess"'. In Ben-Zvi and Moorjani (eds.): 271–84.

________ and Angela Moorjani (eds.). 2008. *Beckett at 100: Revolving it All*. Oxford UP.

Bernard, Michel. 1992. 'Structure hystérique et obsessionnelle dans le discours beckettien'. In Rabaté (ed.): 91–110.

________. 1996. *Samuel Beckett et son sujet: une apparition évanouissante*. Paris: L'Harmattan, 'Psychanalyse et civilisations'.

Bernold, André. 2006. *L'Amitié de Beckett: 1979–1989*. Paris: Hermann.

Bishop, Tom and Raymond Federman (eds.). 1985. *Samuel Beckett*. Paris: L'Herne, LGF, 'Le Livre de poche; biblio; essais; no. 4034'.

Blanchot, Maurice. 1986. *Le Livre à venir*. Paris: Gallimard, 'Folio; essais'.

Blau, Herbert. 2008. 'Apnea and True Illusion: Breath(less) in Beckett'. In Ben-Zvi and Moorjani (eds.): 35–53.

Bousseyoux, Michel. 2000. 'Samuel Beckett: la *Quad*-rature du pire'. In *Figures du pire : logique d'un choix, éthique du pari (Dante, Hölderlin, Beckett, Blanchot, etc.)*. Toulouse: PU du Mirail, 'Psychanalyse &': 175–203.

Branigan, Kevin. 2008. *Radio Beckett: Musicality in the Radio Plays of Samuel Beckett.* Bern: Peter Lang.

Brater, Enoch. 1987. *Beyond Minimalism: Beckett's Late Style in the Theater.* New York/Oxford: Oxford University Press.

_______ and Ruby Cohn (eds.). 1990. *Around the Absurd: Essays on Postmodern Drama.* Ann Arbour: University of Michigan Press.

Brienza, Susan. 1987. *Samuel Beckett's New Worlds: Style in Metafiction.* Norman/London: University of Oklahoma Press.

Brousse, Marie-Hélène. 2013. 'Œdipe après Colone: *Fin de partie*'. *Lacan Quotidien*, no. 285, Tuesday 5 February <http://www.lacanquotidien.fr/blog> (accessed 24 April 2015).

Brown, Llewellyn. 2008. *Beckett, les fictions brèves: voir et dire.* Caen: Lettres modernes Minard, 'Bibliothèque des lettres modernes'.

_______ (ed.). 2010. *Samuel Beckett 1: 'L'Ascèse du sujet'.* Caen: Lettres modernes Minard, 'La Revue des Lettres modernes, no. 46'.

_______. 2010. 'Samuel Beckett: du désir au roc de l'existence'. In Brown (ed.): 147–74.

_______. 2011a. 'Cliché and voice in Samuel Beckett's *Happy Days*'. *Limit(e) Beckett*, no. 2, Spring: 1–24. <http://www.limitebeckett.paris-sorbonne.fr> (accessed 24 April 2015).

_______. 2011b. 'Voice and Pronouns in Samuel Beckett's *The Unnamable*'. *JOBS*, vol. 20, no. 2: 172–96.

___________ (ed.). 2011c. *Samuel Beckett 2: 'Parole, regard et corps'.* Caen: Lettres modernes Minard, 'La Revue des Lettres modernes'.

_______. 2011d. 'Visible et regard chez Beckett: "Le Besoin de voir"'. In Brown (ed.): 105–33.

_______. 2011e. Review of Pascale Sardin, *Samuel Beckett et la passion maternelle ou l'hystérie à l'œuvre.* In Brown (ed.): 205–8.

_______ (ed.). 2013a. *Samuel Beckett 3: 'Les "dramaticules"'*. Caen: Lettres modernes Minard, 'La Revue des Lettres modernes'.

_______. 2013b. 'Les '*dramaticules*' de Samuel Beckett: un "genre" et une forme'. In Brown (ed.): 11–45.

_______. 2013c. '*Rockaby/Berceuse* de Samuel Beckett : un "poème à jouer"'. In Brown (ed.): 185–216.

_______. 2013d. Review of Peter Fifield, in Barfield, Feldman and Tew (eds.). In Brown (ed.): 295–6.

_______. 2013e. 'Voix et illimité dans *L'Innommable*'. *SBT/A*, no. 25: *'Beckett in the Cultural Field/Beckett dans le champ culturel'*: 239–52.

_______ (ed.). 2015. *La Violence dans l'œuvre de Samuel Beckett: entre langage et corps*. Paris: Lettres modernes Minard, 'La Revue des Lettres modernes; Série Samuel Beckett, no. 4' (forthcoming 2015).

_______. 2015. 'Doubles imaginaires et violence dans *Molloy* de Samuel Beckett'. In Brown (ed.) (forthcoming 2015).

_______. 2016. 'Topologie de l'objet autoréflexif chez Samuel Beckett: le sac de *Comment c'est*, "une voix une vie"'. In Éric Wessler and Luc Fraisse (eds.). *L'Œuvre en miniature: les objets autoréflexifs dans la littérature européenne*. Paris: Classiques Garnier, 'Rencontres' (forthcoming).

Bryden, Mary. 1997. 'Sounds and Silence: Beckett's Music'. *SBT/A*, no. 6: *'Crossroads and Borderlines/L'Œuvre carrefour/L'Œuvre limite'*: 279–88.

_______. 2010. 'Clowning with Beckett'. In S. E. Gontarski (ed.): 358–71.

Butler, Lance St John and Robin J. Davis (eds.). 1990. *Rethinking Beckett: A Collection of Critical Essays*. London: Macmillan.

Campbell, Julie. 2009. '"A Voice Comes to One in the Dark. Imagine.": Radio, the Listener, and the Dark Comedy of *All That Fall*'. In Barfield, Feldman and Tew (eds.): 147–68.

Casanova, Pascale. 1997. *Beckett l'abstracteur: anatomie d'une révolution littéraire*. Paris: Seuil, 'Fiction & Cie'.

Caselli, Daniela (ed.). 2010. *Beckett and Nothing*. Manchester UP.

Chabert, Pierre. 1982. 'The Body in Beckett's Theatre'. *JOBS*, no. 8, Autumn <http://www.english.fsu.edu/jobs/num08/Num8Chabert.htm> (accessed 24 April 2015).

_______ (ed.). 1990. *Revue d'esthétique*, no. hors série: *'Samuel Beckett'* [Paris, Éditions Jean-Michel Place].

Chauvin, Dominique. 1995. 'Beckett, l'espace et le temps'. *Lettre Mensuelle* [École de la Cause freudienne, Paris], April, no. 138: 12–6.

Chevallier, Geneviève, Delphine Lemonnier-Texier and Brigitte Prost (eds.). 2009. *Lectures de 'Endgame'/'Fin de partie' de Samuel Beckett.* Rennes: Presses Universitaires de Rennes, 'Didact. Anglais'.

Chevigny, Belle Gale (ed.). 1969. *Twentieth Century Interpretations of 'Endgame'.* Englewood Cliffs [N.J.]: Prentice-Hall.

Cioran, Emil. 1985. 'Quelques rencontres'. In Bishop and Federman (eds.): 45–52.

Cixous, Hélène. 2007. *Le Voisin de zéro: Sam Beckett.* Paris: Galilée, 'Lignes fictives'.

Clément, Bruno. 1988. 'Les Yeux fermés (la poétique imaginaire de Samuel Beckett)'. *Les Temps modernes*, no. 509, décembre: 160–71.

_______. 1994. *L'Œuvre sans qualités.* Paris: Seuil, 'Poétique'.

_______. 2007. 'Les Voix de Samuel Beckett'. *Accents* (revue de l'Ensemble intercontemporain), no. 31, 15 January: 22–5.

_______. 2008. 'Mais quelle est cette voix?'. *SBT/A*, no. 19: *'Borderless Beckett/Beckett sans frontières'*: 89–101.

_______. 2009. 'Les Trois récits de *Fin de partie*'. In Chevallier, Lemonnier-Texier, Prost (eds.): 155–69.

Clifton, Glenn. 2011. 'Pain without Incarnation: *The Unnamable*, Derrida, and the Book of Job'. *JOBS*, vol. 20, no. 2: 149–71.

Cohn, Ruby. 1980. *Just Play: Beckett's Theatre.* Princeton: Princeton University Press.

_______. 2001. *A Beckett Canon.* Ann Arbor: University of Michigan Press.

Connor, Steven (see also *infra*: general works)

_______. 2007. *Samuel Beckett: Repetition, Theory and Text* [1988]. Aurora [Colorado]: The Davies Group, 'Critical Studies in the Humanities'.

_______. 2008a. 'The Shakes: Conditions of Tremor'. *The Senses and Society*, 3: 205–20. <http://www.stevenconnor.com/shakes/> (accessed 24 April 2015).

_______. 2008b. '"On Such and Such a Day… In Such a World": Beckett's Radical Finitude'. *SBT/A*, no. 19: '*Borderless Beckett/Beckett sans frontiers*': 35–50.

_______. 2008c. 'Beckett and Bion'. *JOBS*, vol. 17, September: 9–34.

_______. 2014a. *Beckett, Modernism and the Material Imagination.* Cambridge UP.

_______. 2014b. '"Was that a point?": Beckett's Punctuation'. In S. E. Gontarski (ed.): 269–81.

Cordingley, Anthony. 2012. '"Beckett's 'Masters": Pedagogical Sadism, Foreign Language Primers, Self-Translation'. *Modern Philology*, [University of Chicago Press], vol. 109, no. 4, May: 510–43.

Cousineau, Thomas. 2011. 'Deleuze and Beckett: Disguising Repetitions in *Endgame*'. *Limit(e) Beckett*, no. 2, Summer: 25–36 <http://www.limitebeckett.paris-sorbonne.fr/two/cousineau.html> (accessed 24 April 2015).

Davis Robin J. and Lance St. J. Butler (eds.). 1988. *'Make Sense Who May': Essays of Samuel Beckett's Later Works.* Gerrards Cross: Colin Smythe, 'Irish Literary Studies; 30'.

Degani-Raz, Irit. 2008. 'The Spear of Telephus in *Krapp's Last Tape*'. In Ben-Zvi and Moorjani (eds.): 190–201.

Didier-Weill, Alain. 1990. 'Beckett, la deuxième mort'. In Chabert (ed.): 147–8.

Dolar, Mladen. 2010. 'Nothing has changed'. In Caselli (ed.): 48–64.

Dow, Suzanne. 2014. 'Lacan with Beckett' [2010]. *Nottingham French Studies,* Ruth Cruickshank and Adam Watt (eds.). 53.1: '*Writing, Reading, Grieving: Essays in Memory of Suzanne Dow*': 1–18.

Driver, Tom. 1961. 'Beckett by the Madeleine'. *Columbia University Forum* IV, Summer: 21–5.

Elam, Keir. 2007. 'Dead heads: Damnation-Narration in the "Dramaticules"'. In Pilling (ed.): 145–66.

Esposito, Lucia. 2009. 'Mnemosyne Goes Electric: Samuel Beckett and the Soundscapes of Memory'. *Textus*, XXII: 379–394.

Esslin, Martin. 1986. 'Samuel Beckett and the Art of Radio'. In Gontarski (ed.): 360–88.

Fehsenfeld, Martha. 1990. 'De la boîte hermétique au regard implacable: le champ de l'image va se rétrécissant dans l'œuvre théâtrale de Beckett', Édith Fournier (trans.). In Chabert (ed.): 363–70.

Feldman, Matthew. 2006. *Beckett's Books: A Cultural History of Samuel Beckett's 'Interwar Notes'*. London/New York: Continuum, 'Continuum Literary Studies'.

_______. 2014. 'Becketts Trilogy on the Third Programme'. *SBT/A*, no. 26: *'Revisiting 'Molloy', 'Malone meurt'/'Malone Dies' and 'L'Innommable'/'The Unnamable'*: 41–62.

Ferrini, Jean-Pierre. 2013. 'Beckett, lecteur de Dante'. In Brown (ed.): 219–52.

Fifield, Peter. 2008. 'Beckett, Cotard's Syndrome and the Narrative Patient'. *JOBS* vol. 17, September: 169–86.

_______. 2009a. 'Beckett's Amnesiacs, Neuropsychology, and Temporal Moribundity'. In Barfield, Feldman and Tew (eds.): 128–46.

_______. 2009b. 'Gaping Mouths and Bulging Bodies: Beckett and Francis Bacon'. *JOBS*, vol. 18: 57–71.

Frost, Everett C. 2014. 'Beckett's Radio Plays'. In S. E. Gontarski (ed.): 251–65.

Geneste, Bruno. 2008. 'Beckett inusable alangui'. *L'En-je lacanien*, no. 11: *'Le Parlêtre'*, December/2: 137–54.

_______. 2013. 'Lalan/goisse de Samuel Beckett'. *L'En-je lacanien*, 2013/1 no. 20: 33–48.

_______. 2014. 'Le Nom comme corps et le corps comme Autre' (unpublished).

_______. 2015. 'Samuel Beckett, l'"entre" vivifiant de *lalangue* et l'hiatus sinthomatique: contrer ces vérités du surmoi'. In Brown (ed.) (forthcoming).

Germoni, Karine. 2011. '*Play/Comédie* de Beckett: la recherche, toujours recommencée, d'une musique idéale'. In Brown (ed.): 27–56.

Gontarski, S. E. 1985. *The Intent of Undoing in Samuel Beckett's Dramatic Texts.* Bloomington: Indiana University Press.

_______ (ed.). 1986. *On Beckett: Essays and Criticism.* New York: Grove Press.

_______. 1987. '*What Where* II: Revision as Re-creation'. *Review of Contemporary Fiction*, 7/2: 121.

_______. 1990. '"Ressasser tout ça" avec *Pas*'. In Chabert (ed.): 151–6.

_______. 1998. 'Revising Himself: Performance as Text in Samuel Beckett's Theatre'. *Journal of Modern Literature*, Fall, vol. 22, no. 1: 131–45. <http://www.samuel-beckett.net/GontarskiRevising.html> (accessed 24 April 2015).

_______. 2002. 'The Body in the Body of Beckett's Theater'. *SBT/A*, no. 11: '*Samuel Beckett: Endlessness in the Year 2000/Samuel Beckett: fin sans fin en l'an 2000*': 169–77.

_______ (ed.). 2010. *A Companion to Samuel Beckett.* Chichester: Wiley-Blackwell, 'Blackwell Companions to Literature and Culture; 63'.

_______ (ed.). 2014. *The Edinburgh Companion to Samuel Beckett and the Arts*, Edinburgh University Press.

Graver, Lawrence and Raymond Federman (eds.). *Samuel Beckett: The Critical Heritage.* London: Routledge.

Grossman, Évelyne. 1998. *L'Esthétique de Beckett.* Paris: Sedes, 'Esthétique'.

_______. 2000. '"T'occupe pas de mes moignons": le Théâtre de la cruauté de Samuel Beckett'. In Dumoulié (ed.): 186–97.

_______. 2005. '"Il n'y a pas de métalangage" (Lacan et Beckett)'. In Marty (ed.): 147–55.

Hartel, Gaby. 2010. 'Emerging out of a Silent Void: Some Reverberations of Rudolph Arnheim's Radio Theory in Beckett's Pieces'. *JOBS*, no. 19.2: 218–27.

Hayman, Ronald. 1980. 'An Interview with Martin Held', trans. Helen Watanabe. In *Theatre Workbook 1: Samuel Beckett, 'Krapp's Last Tape'*, James Knowlson (ed.). London: Brutus Books: 67–70.

Held, Martin. 'Martin Held talks to Ronald Hayman'. *Times* (Saturday Review), 25 April 1970.

Herren, Graley. 2000. 'Splitting Images: Samuel Beckett's *Nacht und Träume*'. *Modern Drama*, 43 (2): 182–91.

_______. 2007. *Samuel Beckett's Plays on Film and Television*. New York/Basingstoke: Palgrave Macmillan.

_______. 2012. 'Mourning Becomes Electric: Meditating Loss in *Eh Joe*'. In Hori Tanaka, Tajiri and Tsushima (eds.): 43–65.

_______. 2014. 'A Womb with a View: *Film* as Regression Fantasy'. In S. E. Gontarski (ed.): 237–50.

Hill, Leslie. 1990. *Beckett's Fiction in Different Words*. Cambridge UP, 'Cambridge Studies in French'.

Hori Tanaka, Mariko. 2012. 'The Body in Pain and Freedom of the Mind: Performing Beckett and Noh'. In Hori Tanaka, Tajiri and Tsushima (eds.): 93–113.

_______, Yoshiki Tajiri and Michiko Tsushima (eds.). 2012. *Samuel Beckett and Pain*. Amsterdam/New York: Rodopi, 'Faux titre; 372'.

Hubert, Marie-Claude. 1994. 'Corps et voix dans le théâtre de Beckett à partir des années soixante'. *Cahiers de l'Association internationale des études françaises*, vol. 46, no. 1: 203–12.

_____________ (ed.). 2011. *Dictionnaire Beckett*. Paris: Champion, 'Dictionnaires et références; 21'.

Janvier, Ludovic. 1999. 'Beckett était obsédé par la voix', interview with Aliette Armel. *Magazine littéraire*, no. 372, January: 34–7.

_______. 2012. 'Entretien réalisé par Martin Mégevand'. *Littérature*, no. 167: *'Samuel Beckett'*, September: 7–22.

Jejcic, Marie. 2011. 'Samuel Beckett: l'enjeu topologique du sujet'. In Brown (ed.): 161–77.

Jones, David Houston. 2008. 'From Contumacy to Shame: Reading Beckett's Testimonies with Agamben'. In Ben-Zvi and Moorjani (eds.): 54–67.

Juliet, Charles. 2007. *Rencontres avec Samuel Beckett.* Paris: P.O.L.

Kalb, Jonathan. 1989. *Beckett in Performance.* Cambridge UP.

_______. 2007. 'The Mediated Quixote: The Radio and Television Plays, and *Film*'. In Pilling (ed.): 124–44.

Kaltenbeck, Franz. 2005. 'La Psychanalyse depuis Samuel Beckett'. *Savoirs et clinique*, no. 6: *'Transferts littéraires'*, October: 191–200.

_______. 2006. 'Le Symptôme en acte'. *Savoirs et clinique*, no. 7: *'Art et psychanalyse'*, October: 9–21.

_______. 2010. 'Le Monologue de Samuel Beckett sur la mort: "Ne fut jamais d'autres questions"'. In Brown (ed.): 87–104.

Katz, Daniel. 1999. *Saying I no more: Subjectivity and Consciousness in the Prose of Samuel Beckett.* Evanston [Illinois]: Northwestern University Press.

Kenner, Hugh. 1969. 'Life in the Box'. In Chevigny (ed.): 53–60.

Kiely, Robert. 2014. 'On Mediumship and Voices in the Trilogy'. *SBT/A*, no. 26: *'Revisiting 'Molloy', 'Malone meurt'/ 'Malone Dies' and 'L'Innommable'/ 'The Unnamable'*': 41–62.

Kim, Hwa-Soon. 1996. *The Counterpoint of Hope, Obsession, and Desire for Death in Five Plays by Samuel Beckett.* New York: Peter Lang, 'Currents in Comparative Romance Languages and Literatures'.

Knowlson, James.

_______ and John Pilling. 1979. *Frescoes of the Skull: The Later Prose and Drama of Samuel Beckett.* London: Calder.

_______. 1997. *Damned to Fame: The Life of Samuel Beckett.* London/Berlin/NewYork: Bloomsbury.

_______ and Elizabeth Knowlson. 2006. *Beckett Remembering Remembering Beckett: A Centenary Celebration.* New York: Arcade Publishing.

_______. 2010. 'A Writer's Homes—A Writer's Life'. In Gontarski (ed.): 13–22.

Kristeva, Julia. 1985. 'Le Père, l'amour, l'exil [1976]'. In Bishop and Federman (eds.): 256–68.

Lamont, Rosette C. 1985. 'Krapp, un anti-Proust'. In Bishop and Federman (eds.): 341–60.

Laplace-Claverie, Hélène. 2011. '*Pochade radiophonique.*' In Hubert (ed.): 802–5.

Lawley, Paul. 1984. 'Beckett's Dramatic Counterpoint: A Reading of *Play*'. *JOBS*, vol. 9: 25–42. <http://www.english.fsu.edu/jobs/num09/Num9Lawley.htm> (accessed 24 April 2015).

_______. 1988. 'The Difficult Birth: An Image of Utterance in Beckett'. In Davis and Butler (eds.): 1–10.

_______. 2007. 'Stages of Identity: from *Krapp's Last Tape* to *Play*'. In Pilling (ed.): 88–105.

Laws, Catherine. 2001. 'Music in *Words and Music*: Feldman's Response to Beckett's Play'. *SBT/A* no. 11: 279–90.

_______. 2013. *Headaches Among the Overtones: Music in Beckett/ Beckett in Music.* Amsterdam/New York: Rodopi.

Lemonnier-Texier, Delphine. 2013. 'Les Vestiges du monologue tragique dans *A Piece of Monologue/ Solo*: la spectropoétique du je(u)'. In Brown (ed.): 71–85.

_______, Geneviève Chevallier and Brigitte Prost (eds.). *L'Esthétique de la trace chez Samuel Beckett: écriture, représentation et mémoire.* Presses universitaires de Rennes.

Liart, Monique. 1993. 'La Jouissance spécifique du phénomène psychosomatique'. *Quarto* [Bruxelles], no. 51: *'Du sens'*, June: 15–9.

_______. 1999. 'Une Tache sur le silence'. *Quarto* [Bruxelles], no. 67: *'Curable, incurable'*, March: 29–34.

_______. 2012. *Psychanalyse et psychosomatique: le corps et l'écrit.* Paris: L'Harmattan.

Marin, Dominique. 2003. 'Un magnétophone ne suffit pas'. *Clinique de la vie amoureuse*, Actes des Journées nationales de Juillet 2003, Forum du Champ lacanien, Toulouse: 179–86.

Maude, Ulrika. 2008. '"A Stirring Beyond Coming and Going": Beckett and Tourette's'. *JOBS*, vol. 17, September: 153–168.

_______. 2009. *Beckett, Technology and the Body*. Cambridge UP, 2009.

McMillan, Dougald and Martha Fehsenfeld. 1988. *Beckett in the Theatre*. London: Calder.

McMullan, Anna. 2005. *Theatre on Trial: Samuel Beckett's Later Drama* [1993]. London/New York: Routledge.

Mehta, Xerxes. 2010. '"Down, all going down…": The Spiral Structure of Beckett's Theater'. In Gontarski (ed.): 372–88.

Mellamphy, Dan. 2006. 'A Look Anew at Beckett's other Peg'. *Modern Drama*, 49: 4, Winter: 491–500.

Mével, Yann. 2008. *L'Imaginaire mélancolique de Samuel Beckett: de 'Murphy' à 'Comment c'est'*. Amsterdam/New York: Rodopi, 'Faux Titre; 320'.

Miller, Ian, and Kay Souter. 2013. *Beckett and Bion: The (Im)Patient Voice in Psychotherapy and Literature*. London: Karnac Books.

Miller, Tyrus. 2000. 'Beckett's Political Technology: Expression, Confession and Torture in the Later Drama'. *SBT/A*, no. 9: *'Beckett and Religion; Beckett/Aesthetics/Politics'/ 'Beckett et la religion; Beckett/L'Esthétique/La Politique'*: 255–78.

Moorjani, Angela. 1976. 'A Mythic Reading of Molloy'. In Moriot-Sir, Harper and McMillan III (eds.): 225–35.

_______. 1990. 'Beckett's Devious Deictics'. In Butler and Davis (eds.): 20–30.

_______. 2004a. 'Beckett and Psychoanalysis'. In Oppenheim (ed.): 172–193.

_______. 2004b. 'Peau de chagrin: Beckett and Bion on Looking Not to See'. *SBT/A*, no. 14: *'After Beckett/D'après Beckett'*: 25–38.

_______. 2006. 'Œil goulu et œil révolté'. *SBT/A*, no. 17: *'Présence de Samuel Beckett/Presence of Samuel Beckett'*: 265–80.

Moriot-Sir, Édouard, Howard Harper and Dougald McMillan III (eds.). 1976. *Samuel Beckett: The Art of Rhetoric.* Chapell Hill, U.N.C. Dept. of Romance Languages, 'North Carolina studies in the Romance languages and literatures: Symposia'.

Murphy, P. J. 1990. *Reconstructing Beckett: Language for Being in Samuel Beckett's Fiction.* Toronto/Buffalo/London: University of Toronto Press.

Nguyên, Albert. 2010a. 'Les Clefs de lalangue: Beckett, Cixoux, Joyce et… Lacan'. *L'En-je lacanian*, no. 2/15: *'Rencontre et répétition'*: 67–111.

________. 2010b. 'Beckett, le kioukanko-man'. *L'En-je lacanien* [Érès éditions], no. 14: *'Pour quoi la poésie?'*, June: 111–38.

________. 2011. 'L'Épasseur de langue essorée, Beckett'. *L'En-je lacanien*, no. 17: *'Sens, hors-sens et équivoque'*, December: 69–86.

Nixon, Mark. 2011. *Samuel Beckett's Germain Diaries 1936–1937.* London: Continuum,

________. 2012. 'Pleasure and Pain in Early Beckett'. In Hori Tanaka, Tajiri and Tsushima (eds.): 27–42.

Oppenheim, Lois. 2001. 'A Preoccupation with Object-Representation: The Beckett-Bion Case Revisited'. *The International Journal of Psychoanalysis*, vol. 82, part 4, August: 767–84.

________ (ed.). 2004. *Palgrave Advances in Beckett Studies.* Houndmills: Palgrave-Macmillan.

________. 2008. 'A Twenty-First Century Perspective on a Play by Samuel Beckett', *JOBS*, vol. 17, September: 187–198.

Ost, Isabelle. 2013. Review of Brown, 2008. *JOBS*, vol. 22, no. 2: 240–4.

Perloff, Marjorie. 1999. 'The Silence That Is Not Silence: Acoustic Art in Samuel Beckett's *Embers*'. In Lois Oppenheim (ed.). *Samuel Beckett and the Arts: Music, Visual Arts, and Non-Print Media*, New York/London: Garland Publishing: 247–68. <http://marjorieperloff.com/stein-duchamp-picasso/beckett-embers> (accessed 24 April 2015).

________. 2007. '"An Image from a Past Life": Beckett's Yeatsian Turn'. *Fulcrum*, no. 6: 165–76.

Pilling, John (ed.). 2007. *The Cambridge Companion to Beckett.* Cambridge UP.

Pountney, Rosemary. 1988. *Theatre of Shadows: Samuel Beckett's Drama, 1956–1976.* Gerrards Cross: Colin Smythe, 'Irish Literary Studies no. 28'.

Protin, Matthieu. 2013. 'Le Paradoxe des "*dramaticules*" "ambigus": du dramatique au théâtral'. In Brown (ed.): 49–69.

_______. 2014. *Pratique et poétique du drame: Beckett auteur-metteur en scène de son premier théâtre.* Doctoral thesis presented at Université de la Sorbonne Nouvelle—Paris III. (forthcoming: Paris: Presses universitaires de la Sorbonne nouvelle).

Rabaté, Jean-Michel (ed.). 1992. *Samuel Beckett: Intertextualites et Psychanalyse*, Colloque de Dijon (16 Mars 1991). Cahiers du Centre de recherches image texte langage, Département d'anglais, Université de Bourgogne, 'Interfaces. Image Texte Langage'.

_______. 1996a. 'Beckett's Ghosts and Fluxions'. *SBT/A*, no. 5: *'Beckett et la psychanalyse/and Psychoanalysis'*: 23–40.

_______. 2012. 'Bataille, Beckett, Blanchot: from the Impossible to the Unknowing'. *JOBS*, 21.1: 56–64.

_______. 2014. 'Beckett's Masson: From Abstraction to Non-Relation'. In S. E. Gontarski (ed.): 131–45.

Ravez, Stéphanie. 2011. 'Masochisme.' In Hubert (ed.): 622–6.

_______. 2013. 'Quand Beckett fait son cinéma… au théâtre: une lecture de *Solo*'. In Brown (ed.): 87–107.

Regnault, François. 2007. 'Vénus'. In Alphant and Léger (eds.): 41–4.

Rose, Arthur. 2014. '"So little in doubt"?: Revisiting *The Unnamable*'. *SBT/A*, no. 26: *'Revisiting 'Molloy', 'Malone meurt'/'Malone Dies' and 'L'Innommable'/'The Unnamable'*': 211–23.

Ross, Ciaran. 2004. *Aux frontières du vide: Beckett, une écriture sans mémoire ni désir.* Rodopi, 'Faux titre; 249'.

Salisbury, Laura. 2010. '"Something or Nothing": Beckett and the Matter of Language'. In Caselli (ed.): 213–36.

_______. 2012. *Laughing Matters, Comic Timing*, Edinburgh UP.

Sardin, Pascale. 2009. *Samuel Beckett et la passion maternelle ou l'hystérie à l'œuvre*, Bordeaux: Presses universitaires de Bordeaux, 'Couleurs anglaises'.

_______. 2011. 'Jeux combinatoires'. In Hubert (ed.): 537–9.

Schneider, Alan. 1986. "Comme il vous plaira': travailler avec Samuel Beckett'. In Bishop and Federman (eds.): 75–102.

Shenker, Israel. 1979. 'Israel Shenker in "New York Times"' [5 May 1956]. In Graver and Federman (eds.): 160–3.

Sibony, Daniel. 1987. *Le Féminin et la séduction*. Paris, LGF, 'Le Livre de poche; biblio; essais'.

Sinoimeri, Lea. 2011. '"Close your eyes and listen to it": Schizophonia and Ventriloquism in Beckett's Plays'. *Miranda*, no. 4, Nathalie Rivère de Carles and Philippe Birgy (eds.). Université Toulouse-Le Mirail, June. <http://miranda.revues.org/1924> (accessed 24 April 2015).

_______. 2012. 'Théâtre, radio et archives: les voix de la mémoire chez Samuel Beckett'. In Lemonnier-Texier, Chevallier and Prost (eds.): 167–86.

Smith, Russell. 2007. '"The acute and increasing anxiety of the relation itself": Beckett, the Author-Function, and the Ethics of Enunciation'. *SBT/A*, no. 18: *'"All Sturm and no Drang": Beckett and Romanticism; Beckett at Reading 2006'*: 341–54.

_______. 2008. 'Bearing Witness in *How It Is*'. *SBT/A*, no. 19: *'Borderless Beckett/Beckett sans frontières'*: 351–60.

Stevens, Brett. 2010. 'A Purgatorial Calculus: Beckett's Mathematics in *Quad*'. In Gontarski (ed.): 164–81.

Stewart, Paul. 2006. *Zone of Evaporation: Samuel Beckett's Disjunctions*. Amsterdam: Rodopi, 'Faux Titre; 287'.

_______. 2011. *Sex and Aesthetics in Samuel Beckett's Work*. Palgrave/Macmillan, 'New Interpretations of Beckett in 21st C'.

Tajiri, Yoshiki. 2007. Sam*uel Beckett and the Prosthetic Body: the Organs and Senses in Modernism*. Palgrave Macmillan.

_______. 2012. 'Everyday Life and the Pain of Existence in *Happy Days*'. In Hori Tanaka, Tajiri and Tsushima (eds.): 151–69.

Thomson, Stephen. 2010. '"A Tangle of Tatters": Ghosts and the Busy Nothing in *Footfalls*'. In Caselli (ed.): 65–83.

Thurston, Luke. 2009. 'Outselves: Beckett, Bion and Beyond'. *Journal of Modern Literature*, 32 (3): 121-43.

Tonning, Erik. 2007. *Samuel Beckett's Abstract Drama: Works for Stage and Screen 1962–1985*. Oxford: Peter Lang, 'Stage and Screen Studies; no. 10'.

_______. 2010. '"Nor by the Eye of Flesh nor by the Other": Fleshly, Creative and Mystical Vision in Late Beckett'. *SBT/A*, no. 22: *'Debts and Legacies'*: 223–39.

Tucker, David. 2014. '"Oh lovely art": Beckett and Music'. In Gontarski (ed.): 373–385.

Vilar, Pierre. 2011. 'Munch, Edvard'. In Hubert (ed.): 692–3.

Van Hulle, Dirk. 2010a. 'En écrivant *Godot:* Beckett et la peine d'écrire'. In Brown (ed.): 71–83.

_______. 2010b. 'Adorno's Notes on *Endgame*'. *JOBS*, no. 19.2: 196–217.

Vives, Jean-Michel. 2015. 'La Psychanalyse à l'écoute de Beckett'. *Psychologie clinique*, 2015/1, no. 30 : 153–64.

Watson, David. 1991. *Paradox and Desire in Samuel Beckett's Fiction*. New York: St. Martin's Press.

Weiss, Katherine. 2002. 'Perceiving Bodies in Beckett's *Play*'. *SBT/A*, no. 11: *'Endlessness in the Year 2000/Samuel Beckett: fin sans fin en l'an 2000'*: 186–93.

Weller, Shane. 2006. *Beckett, Literature and the Ethics of Alterity*. London: Palgrave Macmillan.

_______. 2009. '"Orgy of False Being Life in Common": Beckett and the Politics of Death'. In Barfield, Feldman and Tew (eds.): 31–49.

_______. 2010. 'Beckett and Ethics'. In Gontarski (ed.): 118–29.

Wessler, Éric. 2009. *La Littérature face à elle-même: l'écriture spéculaire de Samuel Beckett.* Rodopi, 'Faux titre; 339'.

_______. 2015. 'La Violence comme métaphore de l'écriture dans l'œuvre de Beckett'. In Brown (ed.) (forthcoming).

West, Sarah. 2010. *Say It: The Performative Voice in the Dramatic Works of Samuel Beckett.* Amsterdam/New York: Rodopi, 'Faux Titre; 352'.

Whitelaw, Billie. 1978. 'Practical Aspects of Theatre, Radio and Television', interview with James Knowlson. *JOBS*, no. 3, Summer. <http://www.english.fsu.edu/jobs/num03/Num3Practicalaspectsoftheatre.htm> (accessed 24 April 2015).

_______. 1996. *Billie Whitelaw… Who He?* New York: St. Martin's Press.

Worth, Katherine. 1999. *Samuel Beckett's Theatre: Life Journeys.* Oxford: Clarendon Press.

Worton, Michael. '*Waiting for Godot* and *Endgame*: Theatre as Text'. In Pilling (ed.): 67–87.

Wulf, Catharina. 1997. *The Imperative of Narration: Beckett, Bernhard, Schopenhauer, Lacan.* Sussex Academic Press.

Yapaudjian-Labat, Cécile. 2015. '*Worstward Ho* de Samuel Beckett: la violence du *logos*'. In Brown (ed.) (forthcoming).

Zilliacus, Clas. 1976. *Beckett and Broadcasting: A Study of the Works of Samuel Beckett for and in Radio and Television.* Åbo Akademi, Åbo, in *Acta Academiæ Aboensis*, Ser. A Humaniora, vol. 51, no. 2: 1–223.

Žižek, Slavoj. 2009. 'Beckett With Lacan'. *Lacan dot com* <http://www.lacan.com/article/?page_id=78> (accessed 23 December 2009).

General Works

Agamben, Giorgio. 1999. *Remnants of Auschwitz: The Witness and the Archive*, Daniel Heller-Roazen (trans.). New York: Zone Books.

Allaigre-Duny, Annick. 'À propos du sonnet de Lacan "Hiatus irrationalis"'. *L'Unebévue*, no. 17: '*Les Bigarrures de Jacques Lacan*', Spring 2001: 27–48.

André, Serge. 1995. *Que veut une femme?* Paris: Seuil, 'Points; Essais'.

Arasse, Daniel. 2011. *Le Détail: pour une histoire rapprochée de la peinture.* Paris: Flammarion, 'Champs, art'.

Bakhtine, Mikhail. 1970. *La Poétique de Dostoïevski*, Isabelle Kolitcheff (trans.). Paris: Seuil.

Barnet, Marie-Claire. 2003. 'To Lise Deharme's Lighthouse: *Le Phare de Neuilly*, A Forgotten Surrealist Review'. *French Studies* [Oxford], Vol. 57, issue 3, July: 323–34.

Barthes, Roland. 1993. *Essais critiques IV: le Bruissement de la langue*. Paris: Seuil, 'Points'.

Baudelaire, Charles. 1975. *Œuvres complètes*, vol. I, Claude Pichois (ed.). Paris: Gallimard, 'Bibliothèque de la Pléiade'.

Benjamin, Walter. 2000. *Œuvres*, vol. III, Maurice de Gandillac, Rainer Rochlitz and Pierre Rusch (trans.). Paris: Gallimard, 'Folio; essais'.

Borie, Jacques. 2012. *Le Psychotique et le psychanalyste*. Paris: Éditions Michèle, 'Je est un autre'.

Bousseyroux, Michel. 2014. 'Les Trois états de la parole: topologie de la poésie, poésie de la topologie'. *L'En-je lacanien*, no. 22: 49–62.

Breton, André. 1988. *Immaculée Conception, Œuvres Complètes,* vol. 1, M. Bonnet (éd.). Paris: Gallimard, 'Bibliothèque de la Pléiade'.

_______ and Paul Éluard. 1990. *The Immaculate Conception,* Jon Graham (trans.). London: Atlas Press.

Brodsky, Graciela. 2006. *L'Argument: commentaire du 'Séminaire XI' de Lacan*. Jacques-Alain Miller (ed.), Anne Goalabré and Jean-Luc Monnier trans. Paris: ECF, 'rue Huysmans'.

Brown, Llewellyn. 2007. *L'Esthétique du pli dans l'œuvre de Henri Michaux*. Caen: Lettres modernes Minard, 'Bibliothèque des lettres modernes', no. 45.

_______. 2012. *Savoir de l'amour*. Paris: Éditions Michèle.

Bruno, Pierre. 1992. 'Le Dit sur la schizophrénie'. *La Cause freudienne* [CD version], no. 22: *'Psychanalyse et psychothérapie'*, October: 88–98.

Céline, Louis-Ferdinand. 1993. *Romans*, vol. IV, Henri Godard (ed.). Paris: Gallimard, 'La Pléiade'.

Charraud, Nathalie. 2015. 'L'Internet, une nouvelle figure de l'Autre?'. *Lacan quotidien*, no. 486, 7 March: <http://www.lacanquotidien.fr/blog/> (accessed 24 April 2015).

Chatenay, Gilles. 1999. 'Le Champ freudien et le champ lacanien'. *La Cause freudienne* [CD version], no. 41: '*Le Sacrifice de la castration*', April: 77–83.

Chion, Michel. *The Voice in Cinema.* Claudia Gorbman (trans.). New York: Columbia UP, 1999.

Connor, Steven (see also *supra*: works on Beckett)

_______. 1997. 'Voice, Technology and the Victorian Ear': <http://www.stevenconnor.com/phones.htm> (accessed 24 April 2015).

_______. 2000. 'Shifting Ground' [originally: 'Auf schwankendem Boden', in the catalogue of the exhibition *Samuel Beckett, Bruce Nauman* (Vienna: Kunsthalle Wien): 80–7]. <http://www.stevenconnor.com/beckettnauman> (accessed 24 April 2015).

_______. 2005a. 'Ears Have Walls: On Hearing Art'. *FO A RM, 4*, 48–57, <http://stevenconnor.com/earshavewalls.html> (accessed 24 April 2015).

_______ (ed.). 2005b. *The Cambridge Companion to Postmodernism* [2004], Cambridge UP.

_______. 2005b. 'Postmodernism and literature'. In Steve Connor (ed.): 62–81.

_______. 2006. 'Strings in the Earth And Air': <http://stevenconnor.com/strings/strings.pdf> (accessed 24 April 2015).

_______. 2009. *Dumbstruck: A Cultural History of Ventriloquism.* Oxford UP.

_______. 2010. 'Chiasmus': <http://stevenconnor.com/chiasmus.html> (accessed 24 April 2015).

_______. 2011. 'Auscultations'. *SoundEffects*, vol. 1, no. 1: 6–18. <http://stevenconnor.com/ausculations.html> (accessed 24 April 2015).

Critchley, Simon. 2004. *Very Little… Almost Nothing: Death, Philosophy, Literature.* London/New York: Routledge.

Deleuze, Gilles. 1993. *Critique et clinique.* Paris: Minuit.

Deleuze, Gilles and Félix Guattari. 1980. *Capitalisme et schizophrénie: mille plateaux.* Paris: Minuit, 'Critique'.

Depelsenaire, Yves. 1993. 'Du savoir supposé sujet'. *Quarto* [CD version], no. 51: '*Du sens*', June: 33–6.

Descartes, René. 1996. *Discours de la méthode* suivi d'extraits de *La Dioptrique*, des *Météores*, de la *Vie de Descartes* par Baillet, du *Monde*, de *L'Homme* et de *Lettres*, Geneviève Rodis-Lewis (éd.), Paris, Flammarion, 'GF-Flammarion'.

Didier-Weill, Alain. 1990. 'Beckett, la deuxième mort'. In Chabert (ed.): 147–148.

Dolar, Mladen. 2006. *A Voice and Nothing More*. Cambridge [Mass.]/London: MIT Press, 'Short Circuits'.

Donne, John, Meditation no. 17. In *Devotions upon Emergent Occasions* (1624). Web.

Dumoulié, Camille (ed.). *Les Théâtres de la cruauté: hommage à Antonin Artaud*. Paris: Desjonquères.

Finkielkraut, Alain. 1996. L'H*umanité perdu: essai sur le XX*[e] *siècle*. Paris: Seuil, 'Points: essais'.

Freud, Sigmund. 1968. *Métapsychologie*. Paris: Gallimard, 'Idées'.

________. 2002. *Névrose, psychose et perversion*, Jean Laplanche (trans.). Paris: PUF, 'Bibliothèque de psychanalyse'.

________. 2006. *The Penguin Freud Reader*, Selected and introduced by Adam Phillips. Penguin Books (epub format).

________. 2010. *La Malaise dans la culture*, Dorian Astor (trans.). Paris: Flammarion, 'GF Flammarion'.

Grigg, Russell. 2005. 'Lacan and Badiou: Logic of the *Pas-tout*'. *Filozofski vestnik*, Vol. XXVI, no. 2: 53–65.

Jabès, Edmond. 1987. *Le Livre des marges*. Paris: LGF, 'Le Livre de poche; Biblio; Essais'.

Jodeau, Laetitia and Laurent Ottavi (eds.). *Les Fondamentaux de la psychanalyse lacanienne*. Rennes: Presses universitaires de Rennes, 'Didact Psychanalyse'.

Jolibois, Michel and Pierre Stréliski *et alii* (eds.). *Le Conciliabule d'Angers: effets de surprise dans les psychoses*. Paris: Agalma, 'Le Paon'.

Koyré, Alexandre. 1929. *Jacob Bœhme*. Paris: Vrin.

Kurosawa, Akira. 2006. *Le Château de l'araignée* [2 DVD]. Wild Side Films, 'Les Introuvables'.

Lacan, Jacques. 1965. *Le Séminaire*, Livre XII: *Problèmes cruciaux pour la psychanalyse* (unpublished).

_______. 1966. *Écrits*. Paris: Seuil, 'Le Champ freudien'.

_______. 1967. 'La Formation du psychiatre et la psychanalyse', 10 November (unpublished).

_______. 1973. *Le Séminaire,* Livre XI: *Les Quatre concepts fondamentaux de la psychanalyse*. Paris: Seuil, 'Champ freudien'.

_______. 1975a. *Le Séminaire,* Livre I: *Les Écrits techniques de Freud*. Paris: Seuil, 'Champ freudien'.

_______. 1975b. *Le Séminaire,* Livre XX: *Encore*. Paris: Seuil, 'Champ freudien'.

_______. 1978. *Le Séminaire,* Livre II: *Le Moi dans la théorie de Freud et dans la technique de la psychanalyse*. Paris: Seuil, 'Champ freudien'.

_______. 1979. 'Journal d'*Ornicar?*'. *Ornicar ?*, no. 17-18: 278.

_______. 1980. *De la Psychose Paranoïaque dans ses rapports avec la personnalité*. Paris: Seuil, 'Points; essais; 115'.

_______. 1981. *Le Séminaire,* Livre III: *Les Psychoses*. Paris: Seuil, 'Champ freudien'.

_______. 1986. *Le Séminaire,* Livre VII: *L'Éthique de la psychanalyse*. Paris: Seuil, 'Champ freudien'.

_______. 1991a. *Le Séminaire,* Livre VIII: *Le Transfert*. Paris: Seuil, 'Champ freudien'.

_______. 1991b. *Le Séminaire,* Livre XVII: *L'Envers de la psychanalyse*. Paris: Seuil, 'Champ freudien'.

_______. 1994. *Le Séminaire,* Livre IV: *La Relation d'objet*. Paris: Seuil, 'Champ freudien'.

_______. 1998. *Le Séminaire,* Livre V: *Les Formations de l'inconscient*. Paris: Seuil, 'Champ freudien'.

_______. 2001. *Autres écrits.* Paris: Seuil, 'Champ freudien'.

_______. 2004. *Le Séminaire,* Livre X: *L'Angoisse.* Paris: Seuil, 'Champ freudien'.

_______. 2005a. *Le Séminaire,* Livre XXIII : *Le Sinthome.* Paris: Seuil, 'Champ freudien'.

_______. 2005b. *Des Noms-du-Père.* Paris: Seuil, 'Champ freudien'.

_______. 2006a. *Le Séminaire,* Livre XVI: *D'un Autre à l'autre.* Paris: Seuil, 'Champ freudien'.

_______. 2006b. *Écrits,* trans. Bruce Fink. New York: Norton.

_______. 2007. *Le Séminaire,* Livre XVIII: *D'un discours qui ne serait pas du semblant.* Paris: Seuil, 'Champ freudien'.

_______. 2011. *Le Séminaire,* Livre XIX: *...ou pire.* Paris: Seuil, 'Champ freudien'.

_______. 2013. *Le Séminaire,* Livre VI: *Le Désir et son interprétation.* Paris: Seuil, 'Le Champ freudien'.

Lacoue-Labarthe, Philippe and Jean-Luc Nancy. 1978. *L'Absolu littéraire: théorie de la littérature du romantisme allemand.* Paris: Seuil, 'Poétique'.

Lévinas, Emmanuel. 1981. *Otherwise than Being or Beyond Essence,* Alphonso Lingis (trans.). The Hague/Boston/London: Nijhoff.

Lukács, Georg. 1967. *History and Class Consciousness,* vol. III, Rodney Livingstone (trans.). Cambridge [Mass.]: Merlin Press. Also available: <https://archive.org/details/GeorgLukacsRodneyLivingstone-HistoryAndCLassConsciousness> (accessed 4 May 2015).

Lysy, Anne. 1993. 'Raser le sens: le gay sçavoir'. *Quarto* [CD version], no. 51: '*Du sens*', June: 53–8.

Maleval, Jean-Claude. 2010. 'Comment entendre la voix?'. In Jodeau and Ottavi (eds.): 185–97.

Marty, Éric (éd.). 2005. *Lacan et la littérature.* Paris: Éditions Manucius, 'Le Marteau sans maître'.

Michaux, Henri. 1998. *Œuvres complètes,* vol. I, Raymond Bellour (ed.). Paris: Gallimard, 'La Pléiade'.

Miller, Jacques-Alain. 1985. 'C'Struc dure'. *Pas tant* [Toulouse], no. 8-9, November–December: 4–11.

_______. 1993. 'Clinique ironique'. *La Cause freudienne* [CD version], no. 23: '*Énigme et la psychose*', February: 5–10.

_______. 1994a. 'Jacques Lacan et la voix'. *Quarto* [CD version], no. 54: '*De la voix*', June: 30–4.

_______. 1994b. 'Le Vrai, le faux et le reste'. *La Cause freudienne*, no. 28: '*Le Vrai, le faux et le reste*', October: 9–14

_______. 1997a. 'De la surprise à l'énigme'. In Jolibois and Stréliski (eds.): 9–22.

_______. 1997b. 'Vide et certitude'. In Jolibois and Stréliski (eds.): 225–31.

_______. 1999. 'Les Six paradigmes de la jouissance'. *La Cause freudienne*, no. 43: '*Les Paradigmes de la jouissance*', October: 7–29.

_______. 2000. 'Théorie du caprice'. *Quarto* [CD version], no. 71: '*La Force du même*', December: 5–16.

_______. 2010-2011. 'L'Être et l'Un' [unpublished course of his seminar *L'Orientation lacanienne*].

_______. 2012. 'Présentation du thème du IXe congrès de l'AMP'. *Lacan quotidien*, no. 216, 28 May: <http://www.lacanquotidien.fr/blog> (accessed 24 April 2015).

Milner, Jean–Claude. 1978. *L'Amour de la langue.* Paris: Seuil, 'Connexions du champ freudien'.

_______. 2003. *Les Penchants criminels de l'Europe démocratique.* Lagrasse: Verdier.

_______. 2007. *Les Noms indistincts* [1983]. Lagrasse: Verdier, 'Verdier poche'.

_______. 2011. *Clartés de tout: de Lacan à Marx, d'Aristote à Mao*, interviews with Fabian Fajnwacks and Juan Pablo Luccelli. Lagrasse: Verdier.

_______. 2014. *La Puissance du détail: phrases célèbres et fragments en philosophie.* Paris, Grasset, 'Figures'.

Nicolas, François. 1998. 'De l'instance de la lettre dans la musique'. *Quarto* no. 65: '*Les Lettres de la jouissance*', Winter: 3–10.

Nominé, Bernard. 1995. 'Pour une perspective lacanienne'. *La Cause freudienne*, no. 30: *'Images indélébiles'*, May: 92–106.

Pellion, Frédéric. 2000. *Mélancolie et vérité*. Paris: Presses universitaires de France, 'Psychopathologie'.

Proust, Marcel. 1987. *À la recherche du temps perdu*, vol. II. Paris: Robert Laffont, 'Bouquins'.

Rabaté, Jean-Michel. 1996b. *The Ghosts of Modernity*. Gainesville: University of Florida Press.

_______. 2001. *Jacques Lacan: Psychoanalysis and the Subject of Literature*. Houndsmills: Palgrave.

Rey, Alain (ed.). 2005. *Dictionnaire culturel en langue française*. Paris: Le Robert.

Rey-Flaud, Henri. 1996. *L'Éloge du rien: pourquoi l'obsessionnel et le pervers échouent là où l'hystérique réussit*. Paris: Seuil, 'Champ freudien'.

Regnault, François. 1989. *Le Théâtre et la mer*. Paris: Imprimerie nationale éditions.

_______. 1996. *La Doctrine inouïe: dix leçons sur le théâtre classique français*. Paris: Hatier, 'Littérature; brèves'.

_______. 1997. *Conférences d'esthétique lacanienne*. Paris: Agalma.

_______. 2006. *Percé jusques au fond du cœur: choix forcés dans* Le Cid *de Corneille*. Paris: Navarin.

Rimbaud, Arthur. 1986. *Collected Poems*, Oliver Bernard (trans.). London: Penguin.

_______. 1992. *Œuvres complètes, correspondance*, Louis Forestier (ed.). Paris: Robert Laffont.

Schopenhauer, Arthur. *The World as Will and Representation*, vol. I, E. F. J. Payne (trans.). New York: Dover, 1969.

Shakespeare, William. 1980. *Hamlet*, T. J. B. Spencer (ed.). Penguin Books, 'The New Penguin'.

Skriabine, Pierre. 1992. 'L'Encre et le pinceau'. *Quarto* [CD version], no. 36: *'L'Écrit'*, February: 36–39.

Silvestre, Michel. 1987. *Demain la psychanalyse et autres textes*. Paris: Navarin.

Spiegelman, Art. 1991. *Maus II, A Survivor's Tale: And Here My Troubles Began.* New York: Pantheon Books.

Vaissermann, Alain. 1994. 'Les Voix du psychotique'. *Quarto* [CD version], no. 54: '*De la voix*', June: 4–6.

Viennot, Éliane. 2014. *Non, le masculin ne l'emporte pas sur le féminin! petite histoire des résistances de la langue française.* Donnemarie-Dontilly: éditions iXe.

Vives, Jean-Michel. 2012. *La Voix sur le divan: musique sacrée, opéra, techno.* Paris: Aubier, 'Aubier Psychanalyse'.

Voltaire. 2003. *Candide ou l'optimisme*, Frédéric Deloffre (ed.). Paris: Gallimard, 'Folio'.

Wajcman, Gérard. 1998. *L'Objet du siècle.* Lagrasse: Verdier, 'Philia'.

_______. 2004. *Fenêtre: chroniques du regard et de l'intime.* Lagrasse: Verdier, 'Philia'.

_______. 2010. *L'Œil absolu.* Paris: Denoël, 'Médiations'.

_______. 2012. *Les Experts: la police des morts.* Paris: PUF.

Žižek, Slavoj. 1995. 'La Voix dans la différence sexuelle'. *La Cause freudienne*, no. 31: '*Le Dire du sexe*', October: 82–92.

Index

Works by Beckett

Index of Psychoanalytical Concepts

Page numbers in italics indicate passages offering a definition or a conceptual development.

General Index

***ibidem*-Verlag / *ibidem* Press**
Melchiorstr. 15
70439 Stuttgart
Germany

ibidem@ibidem.eu
ibidem.eu